Business **Grammar Builder**

Macmillan Education
Between Towns Road, Oxford OX4 3PP
A division of Macmillan Publishers Limited
Companies and representatives throughout the world

ISBN: 978-0-333-99076-6

First published 2002

Designed by Mike Brain Graphic Design Limited, Oxford
Cover design by Jackie Hill at 320 Design
Cover photo: Getty Images
Illustration on page 186 by Ed McLachlan

The author would like to thank David Riley for his direction and vision, Ceri Jones for her perceptive
and ever-helpful comments, Celia Bingham for her patient and sympathetic editing and
Jill Leatherbarrow for her thorough work on the Index.

The author and publisher would like to thank the following for permission to reproduce their
copyright material:
Adapted extract from 'A Race Against Time' by Rebecca Wright from *EuroBusiness* Magazine,
May 2001, reprinted by permission of EuroBusiness on p219
Extract from 'Through the Wringer' from *Economist.com*, copyright © The Economist Newspaper Ltd,
London 2001, reprinted by permission of The Economist on p145.

Whilst every effort has been made to locate the owners of copyright, in some cases this has been
unsuccessful. The publishers apologise for any infringement or failure to acknowledge the original
sources and will be glad to include any necessary correction in subsequent printings.

The author and publisher would like to thank the following for permission to reproduce their
cartoons:

Cartoonbank.com pp 15 © 2002 Bob Zahn from cartoonbank.com. All Rights Reserved; 18 © The
New Yorker Collection 1995 Ed Fisher from cartoonbank.com. All Rights Reserved; 39 © The New
Yorker Collection 1986 Leo Cullum from cartoonbank.com. All Rights Reserved; 47 © The New
Yorker Collection 1992 Lee Lorenz from cartoonbank.com. All Rights Reserved; 62 © The New Yorker
Collection 1995 Richard Cline from cartoonbank.com. All Rights Reserved; 75 © The New Yorker
Collection 1997 Richard Cline from cartoonbank.com. All Rights Reserved; 91 © The New Yorker
Collection 2000 Leo Cullum from cartoonbank.com. All Rights Reserved; 99 © The New Yorker
Collection 1979 Robert Weber from cartoonbank.com. All Rights Reserved; 102 © 2002 Robert
Mankoff from cartoonbank.com. All Rights Reserved; 115 © The New Yorker Collection 1994 Danny
Shanahan from cartoonbank.com. All Rights Reserved; 119 © The New Yorker Collection 1975 Dana
Fradon from cartoonbank.com. All Rights Reserved; 147 © The New Yorker Collection 1998 Richard
Cline from cartoonbank.com. All Rights Reserved; 163 © The New Yorker Collection 1989 Leo
Cullum from cartoonbank.com. All Rights Reserved; 175 © The New Yorker Collection 1988 Charles
Barsotti from cartoonbank.com. All Rights Reserved; 183 © The New Yorker Collection 1995 Robert
Mankoff from cartoonbank.com. All Rights Reserved; 191 © The New Yorker Collection 1972 J.B.
Handelsman from cartoonbank.com. All Rights Reserved; 194 © The New Yorker Collection 1993
Robert Mankoff from cartoonbank.com. All Rights Reserved.
CartoonStock pp 51, 83, 87, 111, 123, 151, 159, 171

Printed and bound in Hong Kong

2011 2010 2009
15 14 13 12 11

Paul Emmerson

Business
Grammar
Builder

MACMILLAN

4

Contents

Test bank (for diagnosis or review)

Appendices

Answer key

Index

List of grammar terms

Active form
The **active form** of a verb is when the person or thing doing the action is the subject of the verb: *I **wrote** the report*. Compare with 'passive form' on page 9.

Adjective
An **adjective** helps to describe a noun or pronoun: *It's a **small, modern** storage device*.

Adverb
An **adverb** adds information about *when, where* or *how* something happens: *I did it **yesterday**. I did it **quickly***.

Article
Articles are the word *the* (= the definite article) or *a/an* (= the indefinite article).

Auxiliary verb
An **auxiliary verb** (*be, do* and *have*) is used with other verbs to make tenses and passive forms: *He **is** working in Milan. Where **did** you go? Two hundred people **have** been made redundant*.

Clause
A **clause** is a group of words that contains a subject and a verb. It may be a sentence or only part of a sentence.

Conditional
A **conditional** is a sentence that includes *if, unless*, etc, and states something that must be true (the condition) before something else can be true or can happen (the result).

Continuous form
The **continuous** is the form of the verb that suggests that an action is in progress. The continuous form ends in *-ing*.

Determiner
A **determiner** is a word like *the, some* and *every*. It is used before a noun or adjective to show which thing you mean.

Gerund
A **gerund** is an *-ing* form of a verb used like a noun: ***Smoking** is not allowed. My hobby is **sailing***.

Imperative
An **imperative** is when we tell people what to do. We use the base form of the verb: ***Come** here. **Switch** off the light*.

Infinitive
The **infinitive** is the base form of the verb (*work, go*, etc). It is used with or without *to*: *I hope **to see** you next week. I must **go** now*.

The *-ing* form
The ***-ing* form** is the form of the verb that ends in *-ing*. When it is used as a verb or adjective it is sometimes called a 'present participle': *I saw him **leaving**. A **boring** meeting*. When it is used as a noun it is sometimes called a 'gerund' (see above).

Intransitive verb
An **intransitive verb** is a verb that does not take an object. For example, the verb *arrive* is intransitive: *I **arrived** here last week*. In this sentence there is no object. Compare with 'transitive verb' on page 9.

Modal verb
A **modal verb** is a verb like *can, will, might* and *should*. It gives a meaning like ability, obligation, probability, permission, etc.

Noun
A **noun** is a word that is the name of an object, idea, place or person: *a **car**, **democracy, Singapore, Robert***.

Noun phrase
A **noun phrase** is a group of words, including a noun, which can act as a subject or object of a sentence: *people, some people, some people who were here yesterday*.

Object
The **object** is the word that describes the person or thing that is affected by the verb: *I installed **some new software** on my PC*.

Passive form	The **passive form** is used to show how the subject of the verb is affected by the action of the verb: *The report **was written** by me*. Compare with the active form on page 8.
Past participle	A **past participle** is the form used in the perfect tense or passive structures. You can find it in the third column of tense tables. For example: *worked* is the past participle of *work* (this is a regular past participle), *gone* is the past participle of ***go*** (this is an irregular past participle).
Possessive	A **possessive** is a form that shows who or what something belongs to: *my/your* (possessive adjectives), *mine/yours* (possessive pronouns), etc. It is also used to show other types of relationships: ***my father; my hometown; my employer***.
Phrasal verb	A **phrasal verb** is a verb with an adverb or preposition that has a different meaning from the verb used alone: *The plane **took off***.
Preposition	A **preposition** is a word like *at, behind, in, through, to, with* used before a noun or pronoun to show place, time, direction, etc.
Pronoun	A **pronoun** is a word like *it, me, you, him, her*, etc, that takes the place of a noun: *Have you been to Warsaw? **It** has changed a lot over the last few years.*
Question tag	A **question tag** is a short question like *isn't it?* or *don't you?* that you add at the end of a sentence to check information or ask if someone agrees with you: *It's hot, **isn't it?***
Reflexive pronoun	A **reflexive pronoun** is mainly used to show that the person who does the action is also the person affected by it: ***She** introduced **herself** to me at the coffee break.*
Relative clause	A **relative clause** is used to identify someone or something, or give more information about them. It begins with *who, which, that*, etc.
The simple	The **simple** is the basic form of the verb: *I **agree** with you* (present simple), *He **agreed** with me* (past simple).
The subject	The **subject** is the word that shows who is doing the action of the verb: ***Jean** works here part-time.* It usually comes before the verb.
Tense	A **tense** is the form of the verb. It helps us to know the time at which an action or event happened (past, present or future). Academics sometimes have a more limited definition of the word 'tense', and they make a distinction between 'tense' and 'aspect'. *I **work** in the marketing area* (present simple tense), *I **worked** in the marketing area* (past simple tense).
Transitive verb	A **transitive verb** is a verb that has an object. The verb *make* is transitive, and in this sentence *a mistake* is the object: *They've **made** a mistake.* Compare with 'intransitive verb' on page 8.
Verb	A **verb** expresses an action or state: *He **arrived** at 10.30. He **knows** the market well.*

1 Present time 1

A Present simple: form

> *Peter Ratcliffe, the CEO of P&O Princess Cruises, **tends** to wake up early, at 6 am. The journey to work takes 75 minutes and he **uses** the time to call Europe. '**When I arrive** at my office I **sometimes sit** outside for half-hour,' he says, 'finishing my phone call.'*
>
> **(Sunday Times website)**

- The present simple is formed with the infinitive form of the verb. We add *s* for the third person singular *he/she/it*.
  I/you/we/they **work** *here.*
  He/she/it **works** *here.*

- Negatives are formed with *do/does not*. In speech and informal writing we use contractions.
  I/you/we/they **do not (don't) work** *here.*
  He/she/it **does not (doesn't) work** *here.*

- Questions are formed with the auxiliary verb *do/does* and the infinitive. Short answers to *yes/no* questions repeat the auxiliary.
  A: **Do** you **work** *here?*   A: **Does** she **work** *here?*
  B: *Yes, I* **do**. */No, I* **don't**.   B: *Yes, she* **does**. */No, she* **doesn't**.

B Present simple: uses

- We use the present simple for permanent facts.
  This machine **cuts** *the metal.*
  In finance, 'p/e' **stands** *for 'price/earnings ratio'.*

- We use the present simple for actions and situations that are generally true.
  We **offer** *a full range of financial products.*
  Liz **works** *in the Marketing department.*

- We use the present simple for actions which are repeated regularly over a long period of time, for example habits and routines.

  At Union Investment, a large Frankfurt fund manager, about half of the customers **invest** *a regular amount every month.* (Wall Street Journal Europe website)

C Present simple: time expressions

- We often use frequency adverbs with the present simple. Examples include:
  always, often, usually, normally, sometimes, occasionally, rarely, not often, hardly ever, never.

  Terry Smith, the chief executive of Collins Stewart, **usually rises** *at 6 am. He takes the train to London and arrives at his office by 8 am. Lunch* **is usually** *a sandwich with some Japanese green leaf tea.* (Sunday Times website)

- Note the position of frequency adverbs:
  Before the main verb: *I* **often take** *(I* **don't often take***)* the Eurostar to Brussels.
  After the verb *be*:   *I'm* **usually** *(I'm* **not usually***)* nervous before a presentation.

- Adverb phrases like *every day, once a year, most of the time, from time to time, now and then* come at the beginning or end of the sentence:
  Terry Smith travels to his New York office **once a month**. (Sunday Times website)

- **See unit 8** We also use the present simple after these future time expressions: *when, after, before, unless, in case, as soon as, until, by the time, the next time*

D Present continuous: form

● The present continuous is formed with the auxiliary verb *be* and the *-ing* form of the main verb.

*Things are also busy at Deutsche Post, which founded its E-Commerce Service (ECS) Internet division in mid-1999. ECS **is setting up** online stores, **handling** product delivery and even **administering** Internet customers' credit card numbers.* (FT.com website)

See appendix 3
for spelling rules

In speech and informal writing we use contractions. Negatives are formed with the verb *be + not*.

***I am (I'm)** working here.*	***I'm not** working here.*
***You are (you're)** working here.*	***You're not/You aren't** working here.*
***She is (she's)** working here.*	***She's not/She isn't** working here.*
***We are (we're)** working here.*	***We're not/We aren't** working here.*
***They are (they're)** working here.*	***They're not/They aren't** working here.*

Notice that there are two alternatives for the negatives of *you/he/she/it/we/they*.

● Questions are formed by inverting the subject and the auxiliary *be*. Short answers to *yes/no* questions repeat the auxiliary.

A: ***Are you** working here?*
B: *Yes, **I am**/No, **I'm not**.*

A: ***Is he** working here?*
B: *Yes, **he is**/No, **he isn't**.*

E Present continuous: uses

● We use the present continuous to talk about temporary actions and situations that are happening now.

● The action or situation may be in progress now, at the moment of speaking:
*Sorry, Mr Clark can't see you at the moment. **He's talking** to a customer.*

● The action or situation may be happening 'around now', even if it is not happening exactly at the moment of speaking:
*America's powerful online merchants **are moving** eastward, to the new Net market in Europe. They**'re opening** offices in London's Canary Wharf ... and **buying** billboards in Barcelona.* (BusinessWeek website)

● The action or situation may be a current trend:
*Computer games **are getting** better every year. The application of physics **is making** movement more realistic and artificial intelligence **is causing** players to become more emotionally involved.* (Economist website)

F Present continuous: time expressions

● The present continuous is often used with these time expressions: *now, at the moment, nowadays, currently, these days, right now.*

*Franchising in the United States has been growing steadily since the 1950s and this concept **is now providing** business opportunities in more than 75 different industries.* (worldtradeonline magazine)

1 Practice

Exercise 1 A D

Underline the correct words.

1 *You often work/Do you often* work at the weekend?

2 I *don't know/not know* why your invoice hasn't been paid. I'll try to find out.

3 Excuse me, *does you know/do you know* if this is the way to the IT seminar?

4 Sorry, that projector *don't work/doesn't work*. Use this one instead.

5 A: Do you know our new sales rep Marta?

   B: *Yes, I do./Yes, I know.*

6 A: Is that Linda Napier over there?

   B: Yes, *she works/she do work* here.

7 *I writing/I'm writing* the report at the moment. It should be ready tomorrow.

8 *They not replying/They're not replying* to my emails. I'll have to phone them.

9 Why is there such a long delay? What *is happening?/is happen*?

10 *You are enjoying/Are you enjoying* this conference?

11 Can Karen call you back? *She's speak/She's speaking* on another line.

12 A: Is Sarah Kennedy expecting me?

    B: *Yes, she's expecting./Yes, she is.*

Exercise 2 B E

Match sentences 1–5 with their uses a)–e).

a) permanent facts

b) habits and repeated actions

c) actions in progress at the moment of speaking

d) temporary actions happening 'around now'

e) current trends and changing situations

1 These days we're selling more and more of our products abroad. `e`

2 Look! They're selling malt whisky at 20% discount in duty free! ☐

3 We're selling the new model, but we don't have any in stock right now. ☐

4 We usually sell around 40% of our annual total at Christmas time. ☐

5 We sell a full range of consumer electronics, from TVs to cameras. ☐

Exercise 3 C

Decide which word order is the most usual, a) or b). Put a tick (✔) by the correct answer.

1 a) I every day arrive at the office at about nine. ☐

   b) Every day I arrive at the office at about nine. ✔

2 a) I always check my email before doing anything else. ☐

   b) Always I check my email before doing anything else. ☐

3 a) This takes a lot of time usually as I receive so many. ☐

   b) This usually takes a lot of time as I receive so many. ☐

4 a) Most of the time the emails are not very urgent. ☐

   b) The emails are most of the time not very urgent. ☐

5 a) I quite often get junk email from companies I don't know about. ☐

   b) I get quite often junk email from companies I don't know about. ☐

6 a) I about once a month delete all my junk email. ☐

   b) I delete all my junk email about once a month. ☐

Exercise 4 A B

 01   Jane introduces Claude to João in London. Complete the dialogue by putting each of the verbs in brackets into the correct form of the present simple.

JANE: Claude, (1) ....**Do you know**...... (you/know) João? João (2) ....(be) from Brazil, but he worked with me in Paris last year. He (3) .... (know) a lot about your line of work.

CLAUDE: Really! Well I (4) .... (be) very pleased to meet you, João.

JOÃO: Pleased to meet you too, Claude.

CLAUDE: So, what exactly (5) .... (you/do)?

JOÃO: I (6) .... (work) in the oil industry as a market analyst.

CLAUDE: Oh, so you (7) .... (make) decisions about levels of production?

JOÃO: No, I (8) .... (not make) any decisions really. My job (9) .... (involve) studying market trends and giving advice on levels of production.

CLAUDE: Still, that's a lot of responsibility.

JOÃO: Well, yes, but Brazil (10) .... (not/be) a major producer like Saudi Arabia. What about you?

CLAUDE: I work for a French company that (11) .... (supply) specialised equipment to the oil industry. We (12) .... (be) one of the biggest companies in our market.

JOÃO: Oh, really? And (13) .... (you/often/come) to London?

CLAUDE: Yes, quite often. My company (14) .... (have) an office here. It (15) .... (not/take) long to get here now, if you travel by Eurostar. Could I give you my card?

Exercise 5 D E

02   Complete this newspaper article about the Brazilian company Gerdau by using the words from the list below. Each set of words fills two spaces.

~~is becoming/companies~~   is making/flexible   is attracting/attention   is approaching/market share
is getting/right   is raising/plants   is beginning/expectations   is modernising/law

Gerdau: a Brazilian success story

Gerdau, the Brazilian steel maker, (1a) ......**is becoming**.... one of Latin America's most successful (1b) ......**companies**...... . It (2a) .... productivity in its (2b) .... ; it (3a) .... the price and timing of its takeovers of smaller companies (3b) .... ; and, most important, it (4a) .... to understand investors'

(4b) .... Investors want a firm that's focused and transparent, with a simple share structure, and that's exactly what Gerdau gives them.

The only problem in the short term is a problem of success. Gerdau (5a) .... a 50% (5b) .... in its domestic market, and so it (6a) .... the

(6b) .... of Cade, the monopolies authority.

These days it's much easier to do business in Brazil. The government is simplifying the company-tax structure, it (7a) .... the labour market more (7b) .... by changing the restrictive labour laws, and it (8a) .... company (8b) .... in general.

2 Present time 2

PCCW is building a $1.6-billion residential and office center for technology companies in Hong Kong. It also invests in Internet start-ups in Asia and elsewhere.
(Asiaweek website)

A Present simple or continuous?

● The present simple and present continuous are explained in unit 1. Compare:

Present simple	Present continuous
permanent	temporary
habits and routines	in progress now
facts that are always true	events happening at the moment
general situations	a particular situation
*I **live** in Budapest.* (all the time)	*I'm **living** in Budapest.* (for a few months)
*This plane **lands** in Frankfurt.* (routine)	*Look! **We're landing**.* (in progress now)

*NTL **dominates** the UK cable-television market (general situation). It **is doing** very well in the rest of Europe, too, with about 4m customers (at the moment).* (International Herald Tribune website)

*Canada **continues** to be the most popular country for franchise expansion among US-based companies (general situation), but **that is changing** (trend in progress).* (worldtradeonline magazine)

B Present continuous or present perfect continuous?

See unit 6
for the present perfect continuous

● The present continuous is used for a temporary action happening now.
The present perfect continuous describes an action in progress from the past up to the present.
*Sue **is working** on the new design.* (in progress now, and will continue)
*Sue **has been working** on the new design.* (in progress up to now, and may or may not continue)

C Other uses of present tenses

PRESENT SIMPLE

See unit 8 ● The present simple can be used to refer to timetables and schedules. When we speak about timetables we are often thinking about the future.

*British Airways flight BA729 **leaves** Geneva at 16.40 and **arrives** in London at 17.20.*

● The present simple can be used to make a story appear more immediate and interesting. This is common in journalism.

On a grey November day in New England the mood inside EMC's headquarters is sunny and bright. Executives of the data-storage market leader see no limits to the world's expanding appetite for their storage machines. CEO Michael Ruettgers calls EMC recession-proof.
(Business Week website)

PRESENT CONTINUOUS

See unit 7 ● The present continuous can be used to describe a fixed future arrangement. There is usually a future time expression.

*HSBC **are moving** to new premises next year.*

● We can use *always* with the present continuous. This is often used for exaggerating or complaining. We emphasise *always* in speech in this case.
*This photocopier is **always** breaking down!*

D State verbs

- Some verbs describe states, not actions. Nothing 'happens'. Verbs like this are not normally used in the continuous form of any tense.

  I **notice** that you've moved your desk. (NOT ~~I'm noticing~~)
  Sorry, I **don't understand**. (NOT ~~I'm not understanding~~)
  How much **does** it **cost**? (NOT ~~How much is it costing?~~)
  It **weighs** 4kg with the packaging. (NOT ~~It is weighing~~)

  These examples are in the present simple even though we are talking about temporary situations.

- State verbs include:

the senses:	*appear, hear, look like, notice, see, seem, smell, sound, taste* (= have a flavour)
feelings:	*dislike, fear, hate, like, love, prefer, want, wish*
thinking:	*agree, believe, doubt, expect* (= believe) *feel* (= believe), *forget, imagine, know, realise, recognise, suppose, suspect, think* (= believe), *understand*
possession:	*belong to, contain, have* (= possess), *include, own, possess*
being:	*be, consist of, exist*
other verbs:	*cost, depend on, fit, involve, matter, measure* (= have length), *mean, need, satisfy, surprise, weigh*

  Analysts **expect** *that shares in the demerged P&O Princess Cruises will trade initially at about 400p a share, which* **means** *that P&O is currently undervalued. However some analysts* **think** *that the arrival of new cruise ships on the market will produce a fall in profits.* (Telegraph website)

- Some of the verbs in the previous list can have a 'state' meaning and an 'action' meaning. Examples include *be, have, taste, think.*

  Our suppliers are usually very helpful. (state)
  Our suppliers are being very helpful at the moment. (action)
  I have two sisters. (state)
  I'm having problems with this computer. (action)
  This soup **tastes** salty. (state)
  I'm tasting the soup to see if it needs more salt. (action)
  I think you're right. (state)
  I'm thinking about changing my job. (action)

- State verbs are not normally used in the imperative.

**"What do you think . . . should we get started
on that motivation research or not?"**

2 Practice

Exercise 1 A

Underline the correct words.

1 A: What <u>*do you do*</u>/*are you doing*?

   B: I'm an executive secretary.

2 A: What *do you do*/*are you doing*?

   B: I'm looking for the details on the computer.

3 A: Where *do you work*/*are you working*?

   B: Paris this month, then Bonn the next.

4 A: Where *do you work*/*are you working*?

   B: At our head office in Paris.

5 My name's Walter, and *I come*/*I'm coming* from Frankfurt.

6 *I come*/*I'm coming* to Frankfurt next Thursday – I can call in to your office.

7 *I deal with*/*I'm dealing with* Andrew's clients while he's on holiday.

8 *I deal with*/*I'm dealing with* the paperwork and general administration.

9 A: Who *do you go*/*are you going* to the Trade Fair with?

   B: This year with Stefano.

10 A: Who *do you go*/*are you going* to the Trade Fair with?

   B: Usually with Stefano.

Exercise 2 A D

Complete the sentences by putting the verbs in brackets into the present simple or present continuous.

1 I ...*am looking at*... (look at) the details on the screen right now.

2 I .... (look at) the sales results in detail every month.

3 The production line .... (not, work) at weekends.

4 The production line .... (not, work) at the moment.

5 Yes, I agree. I .... (think) it's a good idea.

6 I .... (think) about it. I'll let you know tomorrow.

7 Helen .... (stay) at the Astoria while she's in Madrid this month.

8 Helen .... (stay) at the Astoria when she's in Madrid.

9 We .... (take) a sample for testing once a day.

10 We .... (take) a big risk if we go ahead with the project.

11 They .... (be) usually very flexible if we need to change the order.

12 They .... (be) flexible about giving us credit for a few more months.

Exercise 3 D

Some of the following sentences are right and some are wrong. Put a tick (✓) next to the right ones, and correct the wrong ones.

1 Which wine are you going to have?   ....✓........................

2 Which wine ~~are you preferring~~?   ....*do you prefer*........

3 That's ridiculous – I'm not believing it!   ....

4 That's ridiculous – I'm not doing business with them again!   ....

5 I'm sorry, I'm not following what you're saying.   ....

6 I'm sorry, I'm not understanding what you're saying.   ....

7 This building is containing all the printing machines.   ....

8 This building is getting very old – soon we'll have to move.   ....

Exercise 4 A D unit 1

 03 Complete this dialogue by putting each of the verbs in brackets into the correct form of the present simple or present continuous.

MATT: (1) ....*Are you looking*.... (you/look) for someone?

JENNIFER: Yes, I (2) .... (need) to speak to Kim Bryant but she isn't in her office.

(3) .... (you/know) where she is?

MATT: Oh, I'm sorry, she isn't here today. She (4) .... (work) at home trying to finish an urgent report. I (5) .... (think) she'll be back at her desk tomorrow. Perhaps I can help you?

JENNIFER: Oh, thanks. I (6) .... (work) for Pritchard Evans. We

(7) .... (organise) corporate hospitality …

MATT: Oh, yes.

JENNIFER: Well, Kim Bryant contacted us last week. Apparently you

(8) .... (expect) a visit by a Korean trade delegation next month.

MATT: Yes, that's right.

JENNIFER: Kim asked me to call in and give her some information on our service. Um, I

(9) .... (have) a list of suggestions with me. It

(10) .... (give) you information on where you could take your visitors, and details of extra services that we can offer, like our pick-up service from the hotel in a chauffeur-driven limousine.

MATT: Well, that sounds great. I'm sure Kim would be really interested to see this.

JENNIFER: How long (11) .... ? (your visitors/stay)?

MATT: Oh, I'm sorry, I (12) .... (not/know) exactly. You really need to speak to Kim, she (13) .... (deal) with this conference. I'll tell her to give you a ring tomorrow. What's the best time to call?

JENNIFER: I (14) .... (not/work) in the office in the mornings … anytime after two. Or she can call me on my mobile, on 0777…

Exercise 5 A D

 04 Complete this article about the magazine *Time Out* by using words from the list below. Decide whether to put the verbs into the present simple or present continuous.

~~own~~   look for   move   investigate   rely   want   provide   try to

Time Out: time to **expand**

Time Out, the London entertainment magazine, has plans for expansion. It already (1) ....*OWNS*......... the monthly magazine Paris Passion, and now it (2) .... beyond France to other markets such as Argentina and Japan. Tony Elliott, *Time Out's* founder, says he (3) .... local people to initiate and run the magazines, as *Time Out's* London office doesn't have the cash or management time. Elliott also has plans for the website, Timeout.com, which was launched in 1995 and (4) .... information about more than 30 cities. It (5) .... on advertising revenue and a small amount of money from ticket sales to survive. But as *Time Out* changes and expands, Tony Elliott (6) .... persuade advertisers in the printed version to take more space on the Internet site. Also, he (7) .... the possibility of charging visitors to the site for access to some information. Despite these expansion plans, Elliot says that a flotation on the stock market is out of the question. He (8) .... to keep control of the business he has built up.

3 Past time 1

A Past simple: form

● The past simple of regular verbs is formed by adding -ed to the infinitive. Verbs ending in -e simply add -d. Common irregular verbs are listed on page 240.

check-check**ed**: I **checked** the figures.
like-like**d**:   They **liked** his idea.
Irregular: eat – **ate**   drink – **drank**   go – **went**   etc.

● Negatives are formed with *did not* and the infinitive. This is contracted to *didn't* in speech and informal writing.
I **didn't like** his idea.
I **didn't go** to the meeting.

● Questions are formed with the auxiliary verb *did* and the infinitive. Short answers to *yes/no* questions repeat the auxiliary.
A: **Did you check** the figures?
B: Yes, **I did**. /No, **I didn't**.

● The verb to *be* is irregular and follows a different pattern. In negatives there is no *did*. In questions there is no *did* and the subject and verb are inverted:

I/he/she/it **was** late.	I/he/she/it **wasn't** late.	**Was** I/he/she/it late?
You/we/they **were** late.	You/we/they **weren't** late.	**Were** you/we/they late?

B Past simple: uses

● We use the past simple to describe actions and states in a completed period of time. We know when the action happened, and this may be mentioned or clear from the situation.
I **checked** the figures very carefully **last week**.
I'm sorry, I **wasn't** in the office **yesterday**.

*American ISP Juno **designed** an easy-to-use email service and user interface and then **outsourced** everything else. It **leased** phone lines from a dozen companies and **hired out** customer service.*
(BusinessWeek website)

● The past simple is also used to describe habitual actions in the past.
*Every evening we **went out** and **ate** in a different restaurant.*

C Past simple: time expressions

See unit 40
for more time expressions

● Time expressions used with the past simple include:
at twelve o'clock/the end of the year
in the morning/June/1998/the sixties
on Friday/the second of April
no preposition last week/yesterday/ago

"Productivity is up nine per cent since I made everyone a vice-president."

D Past continuous: form

See appendix 3
for spelling rules

● The past continuous is formed with the past of *be* and the *-ing* form of the main verb. Negatives are formed with the verb *be + not*. In speech and informal writing we use contractions.

*I/he/she/it **was** work**ing** yesterday.*   *I/he/she/it **wasn't** work**ing** yesterday.*
*You/we/they **were** work**ing** yesterday.*   *You/we/they **weren't** work**ing** yesterday.*

● Questions are formed by inverting the subject and the auxiliary verb *be*. Short answers to *yes/no* questions repeat the auxiliary.

A: ***Was he*** *working yesterday?*
B: *Yes,* ***he was****./No,* ***he wasn't****.*
A: ***Were they*** *working yesterday?*
B: *Yes,* ***they were****./No,* ***they weren't****.*

E Past continuous: uses

● The past continuous is used to describe a situation in progress in the past.
I was waiting *in the departure lounge for more than two hours.*

● There can be several situations in progress, happening at the same time:
*The early 1970s was a time when IBM **was beginning** to lose its way and many skilled people **were leaving** to set up their own businesses. Computing **was entering** a new age.* (The Times website)

● The past continuous is used to give information about the background situation. The separate, completed actions that happen during or after this period are in the past simple:
*'I **came in** to Oracle as **it was recovering** from the recession of the early 1990s. The business unit I **joined** had an ageing product line that **was declining** by 30 per cent a year in sales. Within a year we completely **turned** that unit around.'* (Eurobusiness website)

If we do not mention the background situation then the separate actions are in the past simple in the normal way:
*When I **arrived** I **registered** at reception and **went** straight to the conference hall.*

F Past continuous: time expressions

● We can use *when, while* or *as* with the past continuous to mean 'during the time that something was happening':
While *Plattner and Dietmar Hopp **were developing** the first real-time order processing system at SAP, Claus Wellenreuther **was writing** the financial software.* (Eurobusiness website)

But if we mean 'at the time that' then we only use *when* with the past simple:
*He wasn't very happy **when I told** him the news.* (NOT ~~while I told him~~ ...)

G Past simple or continuous?

● Sometimes the past simple or past continuous can be used. The past simple suggests a separate, complete action or event. The past continuous emphasises the duration of the action.
We discussed *the report and agreed that Peter should prepare some detailed figures before the next meeting.*

We were discussing *the report for over an hour. Eventually we agreed that Peter should prepare some detailed figures before the next meeting.*

3 Practice

Exercise 1 A

Underline the correct word/s.

1   A: Did you *get*/*got* the email I sent you yesterday?

    B: Yes, thanks, I *did*/*got*.

2   How *you felt*/*did you feel* when they *told*/*did tell* you about moving offices?

3   A: Did you *tell*/*told* him about the change of plans?

    B: Yes, *I told.*/*I did.*

4   I *didn't see*/*didn't saw* the reason for the delay, so I *got*/*did get* angry.

Exercise 2 A

 05 Complete the dialogue using the verbs from the list below in the past simple. There is a mixture of affirmative, negative and question forms. There is one negative question.

    ~~go~~   take   think   sell   like   have (x2)   make (x2)   be (x4)   buy

DALE: Hi, Jill. You (1) ....**went**........ to the Milan Fashion Show last week, didn't you?
(2) .... you .... a good trip?

JILL: Yes, it was great.

DALE: (3) .... you .... any useful contacts?

JILL: Well, there (4) .... loads of people at the show, and I (5) .... a lot of good
contacts but we (6) .... nearly as many orders as last year.

DALE: Oh, why was that? (7) .... they .... our new styles?

JILL: No, no, that (8) .... the problem. The shoes (9) .... really well, but we
(10) .... so successful with some of our other products, like handbags, for example, and
there (11) .... much more competition this year.

DALE: Who from?

JILL: Well, the Paul Smith stand was really busy.

DALE: Oh, but his clothes are expensive … Um, (12) .... people at the show
.... our prices were too high?

JILL: Possibly. But we (13) .... the authority to lower them at the time.

DALE: Oh, what a shame. So it was a waste of a trip then?

JILL: Well, not exactly … I (14) .... this great pair of Prada shoes and this Gucci handbag …

Exercise 3 B E

Underline the best continuation of the conversations.

1   A: What was she doing this morning?

    B: She *interviewed*/*was interviewing* candidates for the sales job.

2   A: How did Brenda spend her holiday?

    B: Most days she *went*/*was going* to the beach.

3   A: What happened after you launched the product?

    B: While we *promoted*/*were promoting* it, our main competitor *dropped*/*was dropping* their prices.

4   A: I didn't see you in the office last week.

    B: No, I *worked*/*was working* at home for a few days.

5   A: What did Pat do when she saw the artwork?

    B: She *called*/*was calling* the designers and *said*/*was saying* it wasn't suitable.

6   A: Why did Renata take so long to get here?

    B: She said they *mended*/*were mending* the road and so the traffic *moved*/*was moving* very slowly.

Exercise 4 A

06   Complete this article about Vivendi by putting each of the verbs in brackets into the past simple. Most of the verbs are irregular (see Appendix 2).

Vivendi: *150 years of history*

Vivendi, the French utilities and communications group, has a long history going back to 1853. In that year the Government (1) ....*created*.... (create) Compagnie Generale des Eaux. The founders (2) .... (have) two objectives: to irrigate the countryside for farming and to supply water to towns and cities in France.

In 1880 a treaty (3) .... (give) Generale des Eaux the right to supply water to Venice, and then Constantinople and Oporto (4) .... (come) soon after. By the time of the centenary celebrations in 1953 Generale des Eaux (5) .... (supply) water to eight million people in France.

In the 1960s and 1970s the company (6) .... (begin) activities in the area of civil construction and (7) .... (build) a large tower block in the La Defense business district of Paris.

During the 1980s Generale des Eaux (8) .... (join) with the Havas media group to create Canal Plus, a pay TV channel. They also (9) .... (take) a controlling stake in the civil engineering giant, SGE. In the 1990s they (10) .... (win) major contracts in the Asia Pacific region and in Latin America.

Jean-Marie Messier (11) .... (become) CEO in 1996 and (12) .... (run) the company along American lines.

He (13) .... (sell) $5 billion in assets and (14) .... (cut) the workforce by 10%. All this (15) .... (mean) that an annual loss of $600 million (16) .... (turn) into a profit of $320 million. In 1998 he (17) .... (change) the name of the group to Vivendi and soon after (18) .... (make) a series of partnerships and acquisitions in the telecommunications industry.

Operations in North America (19) .... (grow) very quickly after this and in 2000 Vivendi (20) .... (buy) Seagram to become a truly international media and communications company. ■

Exercise 5 B E

Complete the sentences by putting the verbs in brackets into either the past simple or past continuous. Sometimes the same tense is used twice; sometimes different tenses are used.

1   What .....*did you eat*.... (eat) when you ....*went*........... (go) to Paris?

2   While I .*was negotiating*. (negotiate) the contract, my boss ....*phoned*.......... (phone) me to say that he wanted completely different conditions.

3   The last time something like this .... (happen), she .... (call) a press conference immediately.

4   Anne .... (explain) her proposal when Pedro .... (interrupt) her.

5   We never got the chance to interview him. While we .... (investigate) the incident, he .... (resign).

6   When he .... (finish) reading the article, he .... (give) it to me.

7   Everyone .... (wait) for the meeting to begin when he .... (call) to say that he was stuck in a traffic jam.

8   When I .... (clean) the piece I .... (drop) it by mistake.

9   I .... (find) the missing file while I .... (look) for some other documents.

10   When Tim .... (arrive), we .... (tell) him what had happened.

4 Past time 2

A Past perfect: form

See appendix 2 for the past participles of irregular verbs

- The past perfect is formed with the auxiliary *had* and the past participle. In speech and informal writing *had* is contracted to *'d*.
  I had (I'd) already **decided** *what to do before he called me.*

- Negatives are formed with *not* and contractions are used (*hadn't*). Questions are formed by inverting the subject and *had*.
  *At that time **I** still **hadn't decided** what to do.*
  ***Had you** already **decided** what to do before he called you?*

B Past perfect: uses

- The past perfect is used to show clearly that one past event happened before another past event. We use the past perfect for the earlier event:

  *On the New York Stock Exchange the Nasdaq Index **had opened** higher, but **fell back** to 1,578 in morning trading.* (Yahoo News Service website)

  Compare these examples which describe exactly the same situation:
  1 *Sue **left** at 2 pm. We **arrived** at her office at 2.30.* (both verbs in past simple)
  2 *When we **arrived** at Sue's office, she **had left**.* (earlier action in past perfect)
  In example 1 the two actions are separate in the mind of the speaker. In example 2 there is a stronger connection between the two actions and the past perfect emphasises which happened first.

- It may not be necessary to use the past perfect if we use *before* or *after* to make the time clear. We can use the past simple for both actions.
  *Sue **left/had left** her office **before** we arrived.* (both forms possible)
  *We arrived at Sue's office **after she left/had left**.* (both forms possible)

  Many speakers still prefer to use the past perfect in this case, to show a strong connection between the two events.

- The past perfect is often used with verbs of thinking like *know, realise, remember, be sure, think*.
  *David **knew he'd seen** her somewhere before, but he couldn't remember where.*
  *When I got to the office **I realised I'd left** all my papers behind.*
  *Ellen **was sure they hadn't received** the invoice, but she checked one more time.*
  *I **thought we'd already chosen** the name for the new product!*

C Past perfect: time expressions

- The time expressions *after, once, by, already, just, never, meanwhile* are often used with the past perfect. The word *still* is often used with negative forms.
  *Around 1993 Korean corporations started turning to Park to acquire companies in the US or Europe. **By** this time, **he had built up** sufficient contacts to help them.* (Asia Inc website)

D Past perfect continuous: form

- The past perfect continuous is formed with the auxiliary phrase *had been* and the *-ing* form of the main verb. Contractions are used.
  *I'd been work**ing** on the project for two months before they decided to cancel it.*

- Negatives are formed with *had not been* and the *-ing* form of the main verb.
  Questions are formed by inverting the subject and *had*.
  ***I hadn't been** sleep**ing** well, so I was quite tired.*
  ***Had you been** work**ing** for a long time on the project before they cancelled it?*

E Past perfect continuous: uses

- The past perfect continuous is used to describe a situation that was in progress up to a certain point in the past. It often emphasises the duration of time.
  *Before he left IBM Plattner **had been putting together** a software package for the UK-based chemical company ICI. He **had been working** on this project during 1971 and 1972.* (Eurobusiness website)

- The past perfect and the past perfect continuous both look back from a point in the past. The past perfect looks back at an earlier event. The past perfect continuous looks back at a situation in progress.
  *The economic situation was quite healthy. The central bank **had lowered** interest rates because inflation **had been falling** steadily for several years.*

F *Used to/would* + infinitive

- *Used to* describes a habit or state in the past. There is no present form (for present habits we use the present simple).
  *'Price dictates what motorists put into their petrol tanks. Lots of people who **used to have** their doubts about diesel from biological sources are now regular users', says Dieter Enders, who owns an independent filling station in southern Germany. (Frankfurter Rundschau website)*

  Used to normally suggests that the action or situation is no longer true and so makes a contrast with the present:
  *I **used to work** in marketing.*   (= but now I work in another area)
  *He **used to be** really enthusiastic about his job.* (= but now he isn't)

- Note that *used to* is used for habits and repeated actions, not single events.
  *I **went** to the Milan Fashion Show for the first time last month.* (NOT ~~I used to go~~)

- With negatives and questions *used to* becomes *use to*.
  ***Did you use** to work in marketing?*   ***I didn't use** to work in marketing.*

- *Would* is used in the same way as *used to*, but it only describes repeated actions in the past, not states.
  *In the old days we **used to/would make** three copies of all documents for the files.*
  *Our company **used to belong** to an American multinational.* (NOT ~~would belong~~)

  Would is more common in descriptive writing than in speech.

4 Practice

Exercise 1 A B F unit 3

<u>Underline</u> the correct words. This exercise includes examples of the past perfect, *used to,* the past simple and past continuous.

1   While I *looked/<u>was looking</u>* for my keys, I suddenly remembered I *left/<u>had left</u>* them at home.

2   In those days the unions *used to/had used to* go on strike whenever there *was/was being* a problem.

3   After they *were buying/had bought* the company, they *started/were starting* to make a lot of people redundant.

4   Jack *used to have/was having* a Mac, but then he *used to change/changed* to a PC.

5   I asked about my package in reception, but they *said/were saying* that it still *hadn't arrived/wasn't arriving*.

6   I was sure that I *used to lock/had locked* the door to my office last night, but it *was/had* been open this morning.

7   I'm sure that the winters *used to be/had been* colder when I was a child. I remember that we *used to walk/were walking* to school in the snow every winter.

8   I *had gone/went back* to the restaurant to look for my umbrella, but *found/was finding* that someone *took/had taken* it.

9   When George *saw/was seeing* Diane at the seminar, he *knew/was knowing* that he *met/had met* her somewhere before.

10 While I *had/was having* breakfast I *looked/was looking* at the financial pages to see the share prices. I *saw/was seeing* that my original investment *grew/had grown* by over 40%.

Exercise 2 A B unit 3

Complete the sentences with the best form of the verb in brackets. In each sentence one verb will be in the past simple (unit 3) and the other in the past perfect.

1   After she ....had made.......... (make) a few notes, she ....started........... (start) writing the introduction to the Annual Report.

2   Gary .... (be sure) that he .... (set) the alarm before leaving the office.

3   I .... (call) my wife on my mobile because the meeting .... (still not finish).

4   Once I .... (speak) to him, I .... (realise) there had been a misunderstanding.

5   After Jill .... (give) her first presentation, she .... (feel) much less nervous.

6   Before Edite .... (become) Michael Edward's personal assistant she .... (already work) in the company for two years.

7   I .... (not see) the figures before the meeting, so it .... (put) me at a disadvantage during the discussion.

8   Sorry it took so long. I .... (have to) go down to the store room because we .... (run out of) paper for the photocopier.

9   The rain .... (stop) by the time I .... (get out of) the taxi.

10 I .... (be) surprised to find that she .... (already leave).

Exercise 3 B unit 3

 07   Complete this magazine article by putting the verb in brackets into either the past simple or past perfect. In one case only the past perfect can be used, in five cases only the past simple can be used and in six cases both are possible.

THE DANES SAY 'NO'

On 28 September 2000 the people of Denmark (1) ...*voted*... (vote) 'No' to joining the single European currency, the euro. All the main political parties, the trades unions, the employers and the media (2) .... (campaign) for a 'Yes' vote before the referendum. So why (3) .... (the Danes/reject) the euro?

Let's look first at the economic background. For many years the Danish central bank (4) .... (be) committed to keeping the value of the krone stable against the German mark, and this policy (5) .... (be) very successful in maintaining stability and prosperity. Then the euro was launched in January 1999. In the period after the launch the countries in the euro zone (6) .... (perform) relatively well in economic terms. How ever, by the time of the referendum the euro (7) .... (fall) significantly against the dollar, and the central banks of the USA and Japan (8) .... (be) forced to intervene in the foreign exchange markets to buy euros.

But the 'No' campaign (9) .... (focus) on national identity, not economic issues. In the end the Danes (10) .... (make) their decision because they (11) .... (fear) that economic integration would eventually lead to political integration. They (12) .... (want) to keep their independence and freedom.

Exercise 4 A B unit 3

 08   Alan is talking about his first job. Complete what he says with the best form of the verb in brackets. Choose between the past simple (unit 3), past continuous (unit 3) or past perfect.

INTERVIEWER: So, Alan, why did you quit your last job?

ALAN: Well, at the time I (1) ...*was working*... (work) as a financial officer for an International Accountancy firm in London. I (2) .... (be) in the same company for three years.

INTERVIEWER: How (3) .... (you/get) the job?

ALAN: Just after I (4) .... (finish) university I (5) .... (go) to a job fair. I still (6) .... (decide) what I wanted to do and I was interested to see what kind of jobs there (7) .... (be) at the fair. While I (8) .... (look) at information on one of the stands for a large international accountancy firm, someone (9) .... (give) me an application form to fill in. I thought this might be a good career opportunity for me as I (10) .... (already/take) some accountancy exams for my degree. So I (11) .... (complete) the form and (12) .... (send) it off. They (13) .... (interview) me the following week and I got job.

At first, I (14) .... (feel) satisfied with the job, but as time went by, things (15) .... (change) and I began to hate working there.

INTERVIEWER: So what (16) .... (go) wrong?

ALAN: Well, the situation was this: I (17) .... (work) for a person who was very difficult, er ... very demanding ... never satisfied. What's more, my job (18) .... (become) too repetitive and I really wanted to do something more creative. So, that's why I resigned ... I (19) .... (not have) another job to go to, but I knew I (20) .... (have) to make a change.

Exercise 5 F

Complete the sentences with *used to* or *used to/would*.

1   With my old boss we ..*used to / would*.. have meetings several times a week.

2   I .... own a BMW, but now I have an MG.

3   Before they built the new motorway it .... take me an hour to get to work.

4   I .... think I wanted to work for a large organisation. Now I want to be self-employed.

Since Ahold entered the US in 1977 with the purchase of Bi-Lo, it has reached the number one position for market share on the East Coast.
(Eurobusiness website)

5 Past and present 1

A Present perfect: form

See appendix 2
for the past participles of irregular verbs

- The present perfect is formed with the present tense of the auxiliary verb *have* and the past participle. In speech and informal writing we use contractions (*'ve* and *'s*).
  I/you/we/they **have ('ve) gone**.
  He/she/it **has ('s) gone**.

- Negatives are formed with *not*.
  I/you/we/they **have not (haven't) gone**.
  He/she/it **has not (hasn't) gone**.

- Questions are formed by inverting the subject and the auxiliary verb *have*. Short answers to *yes/no* questions repeat the auxiliary.
  A: **Have they** *gone?*   A: **Has he** *gone?*
  B: *Yes,* **they have**/*No,* **they haven't**.   B: *Yes,* **he has**/*No,* **he hasn't**.

B Present perfect: uses

- In general, we use the present perfect to talk about a present situation which is connected to the past.

- There may be a present situation that started in the past.
  I've lived *here for about ten years.*
  I've known *Mary since we worked together in Spain.*

- There may be a series of actions that happened in our life up to now.
  I've *often* **been** *to Singapore.*
  I've seen *a lot of changes around here.*

- There may be a result in the present of a past event.
  Sorry, I think **I've lost** *the file.*
  My computer **has crashed**.

  In this case we are explaining the current importance of the past event. When it happened is not important and is not mentioned.

C Present perfect: time expressions

- We use *ever* and *never* to ask and talk about our general life experience.
  Have *you* **ever spoken** *in front of a large audience?* (in all your life up to now)
  I've never worked *abroad, but next year I might be based in Paris.*

  If the answer to the question is *Yes* then we continue to give more information about the specific events by using verbs in the past simple.
  A: **Have** *you* **ever spoken** *in front of a large audience?*
  B: *Yes, I* **have**. *Last year I* **went** *to a sales conference in Berne and I* **gave** *a presentation.*

- The present perfect is often used with *already* and *yet*. *Already* is normally used in affirmative sentences:
  Knapp, CEO of US cable company NTL, insists that NTL **has already made** *75% of its planned investment to deliver broadband for mobile phone users.* (Telegraph website)

Yet is used in questions and negatives, and suggests that something has not happened, although we expect it to happen.

Have you **finished** the report **yet**?

Sorry, I **haven't finished** *the report* **yet**. *I'll try to finish it this afternoon.*

Shares in the two big telecoms stocks Colt and Energis continue to fall. Neither has **yet** *managed to convince investors that they can provide services attractive enough to earn a decent return.* (Guardian website)

- We use *just* to describe something that happened a short time ago.

  I've just spoken *to him on the phone and he says he'll be here at 9.30 tomorrow.*

- The present perfect is often used with time expressions that refer to unfinished time. In other words the time period includes the present. Common expressions are: *this morning, today, this month, so far, up to now, recently, during / in the past month, over the last few years,* etc.

  The Russian Central Bank announced on Thursday that its gold and currency reserves have increased **in the past week** *by $300 million.* (Delovoj Peterburg website)

  In the area of economic development, the Asia Pacific region has succeeded in achieving rapid growth, which has exceeded 7% annually **during the past few years**. (Asia Pacific Economic Review website)

- Some time expressions can be used with the present perfect or the past simple, depending on when you are speaking:

  Have you **spoken** to Sue **this morning**?   (It is now 11 am: the morning has not finished)

  Did you **speak** to Sue **this morning**?   (it is now 3 pm: the morning has finished)

- We use *for* and *since* with the present perfect to refer to periods of time.

  A: **How long has** Tom **worked** here?   B: He's **worked** here **for three months**. /

                                          B: He's **worked** here **since the beginning of May**.

  See also unit 40   *For* describes the length of the time period. *Since* describes the point when the time period started.

  'We **have been** *in business* **for 37 years**, *so the Internet to us is just another way of collecting orders' says Lands Ends' international vice president Sam Taylor.* (CNBC Business website)

  UPS became a worldwide Olympics sponsor in 1994, and **since then it has handled** *the Atlanta games in 1996 and the 1998 Japan winter games.* (worldtradeonline magazine)

- Frequency adverbs that are used with the present simple can also be used with the present

  See unit 1   perfect.

  *They***'ve often given** *us good advice.*

  Hollinger **has always been** *interested in buying newspapers, and we tend to look at most that come on to the market.* (Sunday Times website)

D *Been (to) and gone (to)*

- If we *have been to* a place, we went there and have now returned. If we *have gone to* a place we went there but have not yet returned.

  She's been *to visit our suppliers. Everything seems to be OK.*   (she has come back)

  She's gone *to visit our suppliers. I hope everything will be OK.*   (she is still there)

5 Practice

Exercise 1 A

Complete the sentences by putting the verbs in brackets into a form of the present perfect. Use contractions where possible.

1 Are you sure it isn't working?.....*Have you tried*..... (you/try) it?

2 I .... (never/see) such a boring presentation.

3 Luckily, our customers .... (not/complain) about the price rise.

4 We .... (already/spend) quite a lot of money on this project.

5 .... (they/reply) to your last email?

6 I .... (not/get) the figures to hand – can I call you back later?

7 Unemployment .... (go/up) by 2% since January.

8 I'm sorry, she's not here. She .... (just/leave).

9 Their shares .... (fall) by 15% since the merger.

10 .... (you/ever/take) the Eurostar to Brussels?

Exercise 2 B

Look at the paired sentences below. Match each one with situation a) or b).

1	Inflation has fallen by 1%.	b	a)	Two years ago it was 4%. Last year it was 3%.
2	Inflation fell by 1%.	a	b)	Last month it was 4%. This month it is 3%.
3	I think I've lost the file.	☐	a)	I can't find the file. I wonder where I put it?
4	Sorry, I lost the file.	☐	b)	The file has gone and I'll never find it.
5	Has Jane called this morning?	☐	a)	Jane promised to call this morning. It's 11 am.
6	Did Jane call this morning?	☐	b)	Jane promised to call this morning. It's 2 pm.
7	Sales improved.	☐	a)	Last year sales were poor. This year they are better.
8	Sales have improved.	☐	b)	Sales were poor initially. A year later they were better.
9	How long have you worked here?	☐	a)	In 1999.
10	When did you start working here?	☐	b)	Since 1999.

Exercise 3 C

Complete the sentences with a suitable time expression from the list below.

~~already~~   yet   ever   never   just   for   since   always

1 The goods will be with you soon. They've .... *already* .... left our warehouse.

2 I've .... had a great idea! Why don't we launch a new range of colours?

3 We've known each other .... more than twenty years.

4 I've .... used my credit card on the Internet. I don't think it's safe.

5 I haven't had a chance to speak to Magda ...., but I'm sure she'll agree.

6 I've .... worked in insurance, ever since leaving university.

7 I'm sorry he hasn't called you back. He's been in a meeting .... lunchtime.

8 Have you .... been to São Paulo? It's completely different from Rio.

Exercise 4 A B C

 09 Read this text about the performance of the Ford car company. Complete the text with the verbs from the list below, using the present perfect.

~~make~~ fall launch be have cut withdraw spend take perform

Ford: the road to recovery

Although Ford (1) ......*has*...... ......*made*...... operating profits of over $7 billion in its American market this year, the story in Europe (2) .... very different. Its market share (3) .... from 12% six years ago to only 9% now. The truth is that rivals like Volkswagen and Renault (4) .... much better over recent years. They (5) .... costs and (6) .... exciting and highly successful new models. In contrast, Ford (7) .... its large saloon, the Scorpio, which was not selling well. But Ford (8) .... a lot more success at the higher end of the market. Over the last few years it (9) .... a lot of money buying brands such as Jaguar, Aston Martin and Land Rover, and these models have much higher profit margins. It (10) .... some time to sort out the problems at Jaguar in particular, but it's now a successful part of the business.

Exercise 5 C D

Read this email from Steve, the Purchasing Manager of a UK importer, who is in Poland on a business trip. Complete the email by choosing the correct alternative from A, B, C or D below.

| Previous | Next | Reply | Reply All | Forward | Delete | Attachments | Print |

| From: | Steve McGinlay | To: | Mike Evans | Sent: | 18 May ... |
| Subject: | Poland | | | Cc: | |

Message:
Mike

Sorry I haven't contacted you (1) .....B..... last week, but I've been very busy. I've (2) .... to Katowice in the south-west of Poland (3) .... a few days, and I've (4) .... returned to my hotel in Warsaw, from where I'm sending this email. I visited several firms when I was in Katowice and one of them looks quite promising. I've (5) .... seen their factory, and I've got some product samples to show you.

Unfortunately I haven't met the guy in charge (6) .... He wasn't there – he's (7) .... to Gdansk and should be back next week.

So, the trip has been quite successful (8) .... Have you (9) .... been to Central Europe? Everything is changing very fast – I've (10) .... seen so much building work going on. Anyway, I'll email you again later in the week to let you know what's happening.

Regards, Steve

1	A for	B since	C just	D so far
2	A going	B gone	C being	D been
3	A for	B since	C already	D so far
4	A now	B been	C just	D so far
5	A yet	B already	C been	D gone
6	A just	B already	C now	D yet
7	A going	B gone	C being	D been
8	A so far	B yet	C just	D now
9	A yet	B since	C ever	D never
10	A yet	B since	C ever	D never

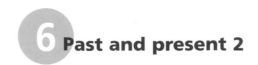

6 Past and present 2

A Past simple or present perfect?

● The past simple is used to describe actions in a completed time period.
The present perfect is used when the time period includes the present. This can be a situation which started in the past and continues to be true in the present, life experience until now, or the present result of a past action.

I **lived** in Milan many years ago.	(completed: now I live in another place)
I'**ve lived** in Milan since 1998.	(a situation that started in the past and continues in the present: I still live there)
I'**ve lived** in both Milan and Rome.	(life experience: the time when I lived in these cities is not mentioned and is not important)
I'**ve spoken** to my boss, and he'**s agreed**.	(present result of past action)

See unit 3 ● Time phrases used with the past simple refer to a particular point in the past: *yesterday, last month, a few years ago, in 2002.*

See unit 5   Time phrases used with the present perfect link the past to the present: *this month, ever, never, already, just, recently, since.*

Look at this example:

*Lojas Americanas, a chain of discount stores in Brazil, **has had** difficulties **since the mid–1990s**. Although the stores generate enormous traffic, profitability **has been** hard to achieve because of a low average purchase price. **In 1998** it **began** a rationalisation effort. It **reduced** the number of warehouses and **sold** 23 supermarket stores to Carrefour (France).* (ebusinessforum website)

● The time word *for* refers to a period of time. It can be used with either tense:
I **lived** in Milan **for four years** when I was at university.   (now I don't live there)
I **have lived** in Milan **for four years**.   (I still live there)

● The choice of tense often depends on the situation and where our attention is:
We'**ve won** the contract! (recent news: the event is present in my mind)
We **won** the contract.   (telling a story: the event feels distant in my mind)

B Present simple or present perfect?

● The present simple is used in two main ways: facts, and habits or states in the present. The present perfect makes a connection between past and present.
About two million people **live** in Milan. (a fact)
I **live** in Milan.   (a permanent state – I always live there)
I **have lived** in Milan for two years.   (I arrived there two years ago and still live there now)

C Present perfect continuous: form

● The present perfect continuous is formed with the present perfect of *be*, and the *-ing* form of the verb. Negatives are formed with *not*.
I'**ve been (haven't been) waiting** here for more than an hour.
She'**s been (hasn't been) waiting** here all morning.

● Questions are formed by inverting the subject and *have*.
I'm sorry I'm late. **Have you been waiting** long?

D Present perfect continuous: uses

● The present perfect continuous describes an action or situation in progress from the past up to the present.

*Trade between Slovenia and the Ukraine **has been increasing steadily** since 1992, when it totalled just US$9 million.* (Slovenia Business Week website)

● The present perfect continuous often emphasises the length of time of the action:
*I've **been trying** to contact her **all day**.*

● The action may be finished or continuing, we only know by the situation:
*I've **been waiting** for an hour! Why are you so late?* (the waiting is finished)
*I've **been waiting** for an hour and he hasn't arrived yet.* (I will continue waiting)

● The present perfect continuous can be used for repeated actions:
*I've **been phoning** her all morning, but she's always in a meeting.*

E Present perfect continuous: time expressions

● Typical time expressions that are used with the present perfect continuous include: *all day, for months, for ages, lately, recently, over the last few years, since, for.*

*Foreign life insurers **have been expanding** their business in Japan by about 15% annually **over the past four years**.* (BusinessWeek website)

F Present perfect or present perfect continuous?

● Often there is very little difference in meaning between the present perfect and present perfect continuous.
*I've **worked/been working** here for three years.*

● The choice of tense often depends on where our attention is. We use the present perfect if our attention is on the present result.
*I've **written** the report.* (the finished report is in my mind)

We use the present perfect continuous if our attention is on the action in progress.
*I've **been writing** the report.* (the act of writing is in my mind)

*In the global economic growth of recent years new companies **have been created** at an astonishing rate. Companies which **have been operating for many years** without franchising are now exploring the possibilities.* (worldtradeonline website)

● If we give details of how many or how much we do not use a continuous form.
*I've **written three reports** this week.*
*I've **done a lot of research** on this company.*

*The technology-heavy Nasdaq index has been falling for three weeks, and is now 34% lower than its March peak. Shares of companies announcing poor results **have fallen by a third or a half** after profit warnings.* (Washington Post website)

6 Practice

Exercise 1 A

<u>Underline</u> the correct words.

1 Yesterday *I phoned* / *I've phoned* the bank about my overdraft.
2 I *work here* / *have worked here* since the end of last year.
3 Your taxi *has just arrived* / *just arrived*.
4 We're enjoying our trip. We *have made* / *made* a lot of useful contacts.
5 *I've seen* / *I saw* Hugh Hopper a few days ago – he sends his regards.
6 We *went* / *have been* to an interesting seminar last week.
7 Today *has been* / *was* really busy – and it's only lunchtime!
8 Today *has been* / *was* really busy. It's 7 pm – I'm going home.
9 I'm afraid Patrizia *left* / *has left* the office an hour ago.
10 I'm afraid Patrizia isn't here – she *left* / *has left* the office.

Exercise 2 A B

Complete the sentences by putting the verbs in brackets into either the present simple, past simple or present perfect.

1 The company is doing very well. Last year sales ....**went up**........ (go up) by 15%, and so far this
   year they .....**have gone up**.... (go up) another 12%.
2 We .... (operate) all over Latin America. Recently we .... (set up)
   branches in Peru and Ecuador.
3 This .... (not look) like the right block. Are you sure we ....
   (come) to the right address?
4 .... (you/see) my laptop? I'm sure I .... (leave) it here earlier.
5 I .... (just/met) Andrew from Sales. .... (you/know) him?
6 I .... (never/speak) to him, but I .... (speak) to his assistant on the
   phone yesterday.
7 I .... (work) for WorldCom now – I .... (be) there for more than
   five years. .... (you/know) WorldCom?
8 I .... (work) for WorldCom since last year, but now I .... (want) to
   change jobs. .... (you/hear) of any vacancies?

Exercise 3 C D F

 10   Complete each mini-dialogue by putting the verbs in brackets into the correct form. One verb will be in the
present perfect and the other in the present perfect continuous. Use contractions where possible.

1 A: What's the matter? You look worried!
   B: Yes, I am. I ...**'ve been looking at**... (look at) the contract in detail, and I ....**'ve noticed**.........
   (notice) a lot of potential problems.
   A: Oh, such as?
2 A: I .... (phone) Carol all day, but there's no reply.
   B: I expect she .... (go) to Head Office.
   A: Oh, yes, I forgot.
3 A: 'Tosca' is coming to the Opera House. .... (you see) it?
   B: No, not yet. Shall we go? I .... (look forward) to it for ages.
   A: So have I. What about next week?
4 A: How long .... (you produce) cars at this site?
   B: About four years. We .... (invest) twenty million dollars in plant and machinery.
   A: Oh, and how long will it take to recoup your investment, do you think?

Exercise 4 A

 11 Complete this dialogue by putting the verbs in brackets into the correct form of the past simple or present perfect. Use contractions where possible.

VICTORIA: Hi, Sue. I (1) ......*haven't seen*...... (not/see) you for ages!

SUE: Hi. No, I'm sorry. I (2) .... (not/be) in touch with anyone recently ... I (3) .... (be) really busy.

VICTORIA: Oh, what have you been up to then?

SUE: Well, you know I (4) .... (leave) my job in January so that I (5) .... (can) go freelance as a graphic designer?

VICTORIA: Yes, I remember, you (6) .... (talk) a lot about that last year. How's it going?

SUE: Well, it (7) .... (be) a really difficult year so far. I (8) .... (never/do) anything like this before ... it's much harder work than I (9) .... (imagine). (10) .... (you/ever/be) self-employed?

VICTORIA: No, never, although I (11) .... (often/think) about it. So, why has it been so difficult?

SUE: Well, at the beginning I (12) .... (have) two or three good clients – and, you know, people that I (13) .... (know) for many years, like Tom Pierce. And since then I (14) .... (have) a lot of interest from different companies, but none of them (15) .... (become) regular customers.

VICTORIA: What about advertising in the specialist magazines?

SUE: I (16) .... (already/do) that. I (17) .... (put) an advert in Design Monthly a couple of months ago, but I (18) .... (not/get) any replies.

VICTORIA: Oh, dear, well, (19) .... (put) up a website with examples of your work?

SUE: Yes, I (20) ...., (just/finish) it. Would you mind having a quick look at it and tell me what you think of it?

Exercise 5 A

 12 Look at the graph and read the passage about technology stocks. Complete the text by putting the verbs in brackets into the correct form of the past simple or present perfect.

Market report: a rocky road for tech stocks

Dow Jones European Technology Index

J F M A M J J A S O

European investors (1) ......*have watched*...... (watch) US stock markets nervously over the last few months. The problems with US technology and telecomms stocks (2) .... (begin) last March, and since then share prices at companies like Intel, Apple and Dell (3) .... (crash). Over the summer all these giants (4) .... (announce) lower than expected profits, and investors fear that demand for PCs in the highly developed US market (5) .... (peak). Now it's the turn of European stocks. On Monday stocks in companies like Germany's SAP and Finland's Nokia (6) .... (fall) sharply. SAP (7) .... (be) down 3% in Frankfurt, and Nokia (8) .... (drop) 7% in Helsinki.

But there was some good news for investors yesterday. Yahoo! (9) .... (release) figures which showed that in the last quarter revenues (10) .... (rise) to $295 million, up from $115 million a year earlier. Yahoo! relies on online advertising for most of its income, and this year it (11) .... (gain) significant market share in Europe and (12) .... (manage) to achieve the position of top Web-navigation company.

Analysts believe that the market (13) .... (not/hit) the bottom yet. Earlier this year investors (14) .... (buy) any Internet stocks that were available, creating a stock market bubble. Now it's just the opposite. Investors (15) .... (become) so nervous that they are selling everything, even if the company is sound and the stock looks cheap.

7 Future 1

A *Will*

- We can use *will* + the infinitive (without *to*) to refer to the future. *Will* is usually shortened in speech and informal writing to *'ll*. The negative of *will* is *won't*.

- We use *will* to talk about future events that we see as facts:
  In June **we will** bring out two new models.
  Next year **I'll** be 45.

  The government **will** *soon* **impose** *an obligation on all electricity supply companies to buy a specified percentage of their power from renewable sources.* (Guardian website)

- We use *will* to talk about future beliefs:

  Lynch believes that globalisation and consolidation in the technology sector **will create** *a greater demand for large and powerful bourses. 'Stock markets* **will have to** *cover a lot more market capitalisation and smaller markets* **will have** *less of a role' says Lynch.* (Observer website)

- We can add *perhaps/maybe* or *probably* to make the belief less certain:

  The first wave of job losses resulting from the mergers in German banking **will probably be** *in the City of London.* (BusinessWeek website)

  Notice that *probably* comes after *will* but before *won't*:
  He**'ll probably** agree with you.
  He **probably won't** agree with you.

- We can use *will* with an introductory phrase to give other meanings. For example, a personal opinion (*I think*) or a hope (*I hope*):
  I think we**'ll probably** open a subsidiary in Russia next year.
  I hope he**'ll** agree with you.

See unit 11
for more information on this use of *will*

- *Will* can be used for instant decisions and thoughts that come into our head at the moment of speaking.
  I'll wait for you outside.
  I'll phone you tomorrow.
  I think **I'll stop** now.

B *Going to*

- We use the verb *be* + *going to* + the infinitive to make a connection between the present and the future.

- We use *going to* for plans and intentions. These are things we have already decided to do.

  I believe that Greenspan **is going to lower** *rates. There are some signs of liquidity problems in the credit markets at this point in time, and a smart central bank responds by easing credit.* (New York Times website)

  The time in the future can be near or distant:
  I'm going to call Fiona Clarke this afternoon.
  We**'re going to open** a factory in Hungary next year.

- We use *going to* to make predictions when there is some evidence in the present situation:
  Be careful! **It's going to fall.**   (I can see it)
  I think **we're going to lose** this deal.   (I've just heard some news)

C Present continuous

- We can use the present continuous tense to talk about things we have arranged to do in the future. There is nearly always a time expression.
  *Ann **is leaving** tomorrow morning.*
  *HSBC **are moving** to new premises next year.*

See units 1 and 2
for other uses of the present continuous

  The arrangements are often social arrangements or appointments.
  ***What are you doing** on Tuesday afternoon?*
  ***I'm seeing** Jack at two, and after that **I'm meeting** my bank manager.*

D *Will* or *going to*?

- *Will* is used for instant decisions. *Going to* is used for plans and intentions.
  Compare:
  *OK, I know what to do. **I'll call** Jane.* (an instant decision)
  *Do you have the information for Jane? **I'm going to call** her this afternoon.* (an intention)

- *Will* is used for general beliefs, opinions, hopes and things the speaker sees as facts.
  *I'm sure **they'll like** the new design.*
  *In the future, more people **will work** from home.*

- When *will* is used with a phrase like *I think* and/or words like *probably* then the belief/opinion becomes less certain, like a prediction.
  ***I think you'll** like this idea.*
  *The world **will probably** end in about five billion years.*
  But if there is strong evidence in the present situation then *going to* is usually used for predictions:
  *I think it**'s going to rain**.*   (I can see black clouds)
  *We**'re going to make** a loss on this project.* (I have the figures in front of me)

- There are occasions when we can use either form:
  *In my presentation **I'll talk**/**I'm going to talk** about three main areas. First, ...*
  Here the speaker could see it as a fact (*will*) or an intention (*going to*).

- *Will* is more usual in writing. *'ll* and *going to* are more usual in speech.

E *Going to* or present continuous?

- For future plans and arrangements there is often little difference between *going to* and the present continuous.
  ***I'm going to give**/**I'm giving** my presentation on Friday.*

- *Going to* can suggest that the details of the arrangement have not been finalised. The present continuous can suggest that the arrangement is more fixed, with a time and a place.
  ***I'm going to meet** him next week.* (just a plan – time and place are still unknown)
  ***I'm meeting** him at ten in my office.* (a definite, fixed arrangement)

F Time expressions

- Common time expressions for the future include: *tomorrow, the day after tomorrow, on Friday, at the weekend, next week, in a few days' time.*

7 Practice

Exercise 1 A B C

Match sentences 1–6 with their uses a)–f).

    a) a future fact   d) a future plan or intention

    b) an opinion about the future   e) a prediction with evidence in the present situation

    c) an instant decision   f) a future arrangement

1 I'm going to ask my boss for a pay rise next week.   `d`
2 I'm sorry to hear that. I'll find out what the problem is right now.   ☐
3 I'm sorry, but I won't be here tomorrow. I'll be in Paris.   ☐
4 I'm meeting Angela for lunch. Do you want to join us?   ☐
5 Their share price will probably rise when the market recovers.   ☐
6 With so much competition it's going to be difficult to increase sales.   ☐

Exercise 2 D E

13 Underline the correct words in each mini-dialogue.

1 A: Are you free next Tuesday morning?
   B: Sorry, *I'll have* / *I'm having* a meeting with Sue.
   A: Oh, right. Well, what about Thursday?

2 A: What are your plans for next year?
   B: *We'll open* / *We're going to open* a new factory in Hungary.
   A: That sounds interesting.

3 A: What do you think about their new marketing campaign?
   B: I think *it'll probably succeed* / *it's probably succeeding*.
   A: Do you really?

4 A: What about tomorrow at around five thirty?
   B: OK, *I'll see you then.* / *I'm seeing you then.*
   A: Bye.

5 A: So as you can see, I've been thinking about this problem quite a lot.
   B: Yes, I see. So, *what are you going to do?* / *what are you doing*?
   A: Resign!

6 A: It would be nice to see you next week.
   B: Yes, it would. *Are you doing anything* / *Will you do anything* on Wednesday?
   A: No, I'm free.

Exercise 3 A B C D E

Complete the sentences by putting the verbs in brackets into the most appropriate future form. Choose between *will, going to* and the present continuous.

1 Have you heard the news? Vetendi ....*is going to buy*........ (buy) Seagram.
2 I .... (meet) Andrea at nine next Thursday morning outside the station.
3 I've just had a call from Richard – he .... (be) late.
4 Next year .... (be) the company's centenary year.
5 This taxi driver is terrible. He .... (have) an accident.
6 In the future video-conferences .... (probably replace) many international meetings.
7 We .... (test) the new machine sometime next week.
8 I .... (go) to Manchester on Friday.
9 Would you mind waiting for a moment? I .... (not be) long.

Exercise 4 A B D

 14 Complete this dialogue by putting each of the verbs in brackets into the future. Choose between *will* and *going to*. Sometimes either answer may be possible, but decide which form is the most natural. Use contractions where possible.

JOANNA: Please, come in, have a seat. Would you like a drink? Coffee? Mineral water?

GREG: Oh, I (1) ....'ll have............... (have) a coffee please.

JOANNA: Lucy … could you make two coffees? (sighs) Well, thanks for coming this morning. I (2) .... (tell) you why I asked you here. Um, as you know, there (3) .... (be) some big changes in the company. In fact, we (4) .... (restructure) the whole department.

GREG: Yes, I know. When (5) .... (it/happen)?

JOANNA: Everything (6) .... (be) finished by the summer. Um, the thing is, under the new structure your job (7) .... (probably / disappear).

GREG: Really? Is that certain?

JOANNA: Well, we (8) .... (have) a meeting next week to finalise all the plans, and of course I (9) .... (let) you know what we decide. Anyway, you don't have to worry.

GREG: Oh?

  (coffee arrives)

JOANNA: Well, as I was saying, you don't have to worry. We (10) .... (offer) you a new job. You (11) .... (have) more responsibility, and the salary (12) .... (be) much better.

GREG: That's wonderful, thank you very much. What exactly (13) .... (the new job / involve)?

JOANNA: Well, we (14) .... (expand) the whole customer services area. If you accept the job, you (15) .... (be) responsible for the new team. Um, it (16) .... (mean) a lot more work, of course. What do you think?

GREG: It sounds great, but I (17) .... (need) a day or two to think about it.

JOANNA: Of course, no problem. Look, I (18) .... (not / be) in the office for the next few days – I (19) .... (visit) our subsidiary in Hungary. (20) .... (you/have) an answer for me by next week?

GREG: Yes, I (21) .... (give) you my decision on Monday.

Exercise 5 A C

Complete this email from a PA to her boss by putting the verbs in brackets into the future. Choose between *will* and the present continuous. Use contractions where possible.

From:	Mira Melisse	To:	Pierre Gaudard, Technical Director	Sent:	14 March ...
Subject:	Visit to Slovenia			**Cc:**	

Message:

I've booked your flight to Slovenia. You (1) ...'re leaving... (leave) on Tuesday 3rd at 8.45 in the morning, so you (2) .... (arrive) in Ljubljana before lunch. Someone (3) .... (be) at the airport to meet you. Your first meeting is with Aleksander Presekar, and you (4) .... (see) him at 1 pm at our local office. He (5) .... (probably/take) you out to lunch. After lunch you (6) .... (not/do) anything until 4 pm, so you (7) .... (have) time to go to the hotel. You (8) .... (stay) at the Intercontinental, which is in a very central location. I (9) .... (go) to the travel agents to pick up the tickets this afternoon, so I (10) .... (give) them to you tomorrow.

8 Future 2

A Future: time expressions

● We use the present simple or the present perfect (not *will*) to refer to the future after these words: *when, after, before, unless, in case, as soon as, until, by the time, the next time*:
When I **see** her, I'll tell her you called.
We'll discuss it again **after** you **get back**.
As soon as I**'ve** finished the report, I'll email it to you.
You can wait here **until** she **comes** back.

Notice that a future form (*will, can*) is used in the other part of the sentence.

B Present simple/continuous

● We often use the present simple (or present continuous) when we talk about events in the future based on a fixed timetable, programme or calendar:
Jim's plane **leaves (is leaving)** at 12.15.
Our boss **retires (is retiring)** next year.

C Future continuous

● The future continuous is formed with *will* + *be* + the *-ing* form of the verb:

One thing that is clear is that more and larger Taiwanese companies **will be investing** *in China and that the new government will allow them to.* (Asiaweek website)

● The future continuous describes an activity in progress in the future.
We often use it when we compare what we are doing now with what we will be doing in the future. There is nearly always a time expression.
Next year **I'll be working** in our São Paulo office.
Where **will you be working** in six months' time?

● The future continuous is often used to say that something will definitely happen:
We'll be holding a meeting soon, so we can make a decision then.

D Future perfect

● The future perfect is formed with *will* + *have* + past participle:
By the time I retire, **I'll have been** in banking for over thirty years.

By the year 2020 the volume of goods produced by traditional manufacturing worldwide will probably be at least twice what it is today. But in the US, the share of manufacturing in GDP, which is still around 15% or so, **will have shrunk** *to 5%.* (IndustryWeek website)

● We use the future perfect to look back from one point in the future to an earlier event or period of time. We often use *by* or *by the time* with the future perfect:
By the time we prepare our proposal they**'ll have found** another supplier.
By the end of the year we**'ll have sold** around 1,000 units.

● It is common to use a simple *will* form in place of the future perfect, although some people think this is not grammatically correct:
By the time we've prepared our proposal they**'ll find** another supplier.
By the end of the year we**'ll sell** around 1,000 units.

● We use the continuous form of the future perfect to look back from one point in the future at an activity in progress:
Next year we**'ll have been manufacturing** the same model for ten years.

E *Was going to*

- *Was/were going* to is not a future form. We use it to refer to something that we planned in the past but did not do:
  *I'm sorry, I **was going to phone you** this morning, but I had to see one of our clients.*

F Other ways to talk about the future

- We often use modals and related verbs like *should, be likely to, could, may, might* to refer to the future. See unit 13.

- We use the verbs *expect, hope, intend, would like, plan, want* followed by an infinitive (*to do*) to refer to the future:

  *German automaker BMW **is planning to build** a production plant in Central or Eastern Europe by the middle of 2001 – and the Czech Republic **is hoping to get** the contract.* (praguepost website)

  Notice the negative forms:
  *I expect/hope I **won't** ...*
  *We **don't** intend/plan/want to ...*
  *I **wouldn't** like to ...*

- We can use the verb *think* followed by *'ll*:
  *I **think/don't think** I'**ll** change my Internet Service Provider.*

- We can use *be due to* for things that we expect to happen:

  *Mr Welch, who hits GE's mandatory retirement age of 65 next month, has built GE into America's No. 1 company in stock market valuation. He **is due to name** the next chairman and chief executive of GE in the next few days.* (Wall Street Journal Europe website)

- We can use *be about to* for things that will (will not) happen very soon:

  *A look at the stock-market valuations of big software houses such as Cisco and Oracle show that the pace of development in new technology **is not about to** slow.* (Forbes.com website)

- **See unit 14** *for making suggestions* — In modern English *Shall I/we ...?* are used to make suggestions, not to refer to the future.
  ***Shall I** open the window?*
  ***Shall we** meet again next week?*

  Shall is still used for the future in formal situations, for example legal documents.

"I was just going to say, 'Well, I don't make the rules.' But, of course, I __do__ make the rules."

8 Practice

Exercise 1 A B C D E F

<u>Underline</u> the correct words.

1 Tomorrow *I'll interview/<u>I'll be interviewing</u>* candidates all morning.
2 We *will have moved/will be moving* to our new premises in August.
3 We *will have moved/will be moving* to our new premises by August.
4 What time *does your train/will your train* leave?
5 Don't forget to turn off the lights before *you are leaving/you leave*.
6 We can't send the goods until *we've received/we will receive* a firm order.
7 We *will be repaying/will have repaid* the bank loan by December.
8 Unless *they're/they'll be* more reasonable, we'll have to break off negotiations.
9 *I was going to write/was writing* to them, but I forgot.
10 *I hope/I will hope* to be able to speak at the press conference myself.
11 Our visitors are *due to arrive/due arriving* at 10.30.
12 *I hope I won't/I don't hope I'll* be late for the meeting.
13 I *think I won't/I don't think I'll* be late for the meeting.
14 When the contract *is/will be* ready, I'll let you know.
15 *Will we/Shall we* break for coffee now?
16 Sorry, I can't speak now, *I'll just have/I'm just about to have* a meeting.

Exercise 2 A C D

Complete each sentence 1–8. with an ending a)–h).

1	Please take a seat until	b	a)	you leave.
2	They won't accept our order unless		b)	Dr Rihal is ready to see you.
3	Helen wants to see you before		c)	you'll have left.
4	You won't see Helen. By the time she arrives		d)	we give a bank guarantee.
5	As soon as Helen arrives		e)	have finished and we can talk.
6	I can't wait! This time next week I'll		f)	I'll ask her to phone you.
7	I'll have a suntan next time we meet! I'll		g)	have just come back from Greece.
8	Sorry about this. In a few moments I'll		h)	be lying on a beach in Greece.

Exercise 3 A B C D

Complete the sentences by putting the verbs in brackets into the right tense. Choose between the present simple (*I do*), future continuous (*I'll be doing*) and future perfect (*I'll have done*).

1 By the time all the papers are ready, the deadline ....**will have passed**.... (pass).
2 The flight .... (leave) at 1 pm and .... (arrive) at 3.45.
3 I .... (see) Nick tomorrow, so I can give him your message.
4 This taxi is so slow. By the time we get there the meeting .... (finish).
5 Sorry, I can't see you on the 15th – I .... (play) golf with a client.
6 I won't do anything until I .... (hear) from you.
7 Hurry up! By the time we arrive, the play .... (start).
8 What .... (you/learn) by the end of your course?
9 .... (you/use) the conference room next Tuesday?
10 When I .... (see) him, I'll ask him.

Exercise 4 A C D F

An economist has prepared a short report about his country next year. Read it, then choose the correct alternative from A, B, C or D below to complete the report.

Executive Summary:

12 month economic forecast

The Central Bank (1) ...C.... keep interest rates low next year in order to stimulate economic growth, and so we (2) .... the economy to continue growing at about 4%. This means that unemployment (3) .... in most sectors of the economy next year. Exchange rates are very difficult to predict, but the currency (4) .... remain stable.

   Some important events are (5) .... take place in the political field. The president (6) .... call elections within the next twelve months, and so by the middle of next year the election campaign (7) .... The government (8) .... on a platform of honesty and competence, and it (9) .... introduce reforms to the legal system so that judges can investigate the misuse of public funds more easily. When that (10) .... , international investor confidence should increase rapidly.

1	A is wanting to	B is liking to	C would like to	D due to
2	A predict	B expect	C believe	D hope
3	A will be fallen	B will been falling	C will falling	D will fall
4	A probably will	B will probably	C probably is	D is probably
5	A about to	B soon	C being	D expecting
6	A dues to	B due to	C is due to	D is duing to
7	A will have begun	B will be begun	C has begun	D will begin
8	A will be fought	B will be fighting	C will fighting	D will have fight
9	A is planning	B planning to	C is planned to	D is planning to
10	A happening	B will happen	C happens	D happen

Exercise 5 A C D E

 15   The Human Resources Manager of a large company is explaining the appraisal system to a group of new employees. Complete his talk by putting the verbs in brackets into the right tense. Choose between the present simple (*I do*), future continuous (*I'll be doing*), future perfect (*I'll have done*) and *was going to*.

'Your appraisal interviews (1) ......are...... (be) in March. Er, I'm sorry, they (2) .... (be) in February but we had to postpone them. Sorry about that. Um, during February your line managers (3) .... (collect) all the information they need from you, and by the time you meet for the interview, they (4) .... (produce) a checklist of points for discussion.

   Right. Um, in the interview you (5) .... (discuss) your performance during the past year and any issues relating to your future needs, er, such as training. By the end of the meeting I hope that you and your line managers (6) .... (agree) on your personal objectives for next year, both in terms of sales targets and professional development. Is that clear? Yep, OK, good. Of course there is some flexibility in the targets, in case anything (7) .... (happen) to the market that we cannot predict. We may also have a budget for you to do some training, after you (8) .... (come) back from your summer holidays but before work (9) .... (get) really busy in September. Is that OK? Yeah. Good.

   After that, the next time that we all (10) .... (meet) again will be in October, when I'd like some feedback on your training, as by then any courses that you do (11) .... (finish). Is that OK? Yeah. I (12) .... (send) you feedback forms nearer the time. Well, er, unless you (13) .... (have) any questions, I think that's all. Oh, no. Er, yes – I (14) .... (have) a word with you about your holiday plans, but you probably don't know them yet. Could you email me with your request as soon as you know them.'

9 Passive 1

A Form

- To make the passive we use *to be* and a past participle:

Active	Passive
Intel **produces** millions of chips every year.	Millions of chips **are produced** every year.
Our supplier **is shipping** the goods next week.	The goods **are being shipped** next week.
The government **raised** interest rates by 1%.	Interest rates **were raised** by 1%.
He **was asking** me some difficult questions.	I **was being asked** some difficult questions.
They **have chosen** the new design.	The new design **has been chosen**.
Rosa **will give** a press briefing tomorrow.	A press briefing **will be given** tomorrow.
We **can arrange** a loan within six days.	A loan **can be arranged** within six days.
We **may give** you some new sales targets.	You **may be given** some new sales targets.

- The object in the active sentence (*millions of chips/interest rates*) moves to the front in the passive sentence and becomes the subject.

- We form negatives and questions in the same way as in active sentences:
  *The new design **hasn't been chosen**.*   ***Has** the new design **been chosen**?*

B Uses: focus on important information

- In the active sentences above the person or organisation who does the action (*Intel/The government/Rosa*) is important.

- In the passive sentences above the person or organisation who does the action is not mentioned. It might be:
  – unimportant
  – clear from the situation
  – unknown

  Instead, the important information is either the actions (*raised/chosen*) or the things affected by the action (*Millions of chips/The goods/A press briefing*).

- Study these examples:

  *A very large proportion of world oil production **is generated** in the Middle East.* (Gulf Business Magazine website.)

  Here the writer wants to emphasise the amount of oil. Who did the action (*generate*) is clear or not important.

  *The North American Free Trade Area (NAFTA) **was established** in 1993 to link the United States, Canada and Mexico in a free trade agreement.* (Latin Trade website)

  Here the writer wants to say when and why the action happened. Who did the action (*establish*) is not important.

  *Deutsche Post AG will offer investors share price discounts and bonus shares as part of its planned initial public offering. **These incentives will be offered** to retail investors in EU countries who make an early subscription.* (Wall Street Journal Europe website)

  Here the writer wants to give information about the incentives. Who will do the action (*offer*) is not important or not known.

C Uses: systems and processes

- We often use the passive to talk about systems, processes and procedures:

   *The barley used to make malt whisky takes about seven months to grow in the field. In August the barley **is harvested** and then **left** to rest for a couple of months. The next step is 'malting', an ancient chemistry full of tradition. It gives a rich, warm flavour to the whisky and causes the grain to produce starches, which **are converted** to sugars at a later stage of the process. The malted barley **is rested** for about three weeks then **ground** into flour and **placed** into huge vessels where it **is mixed** with hot water to make a 'wort'. The wort **is cooled**, then **run** into another vessel. Here, yeast **is added**, and the starch is turned into sugars, producing a clear liquid called 'the wash'. It is distillation that turns this wash into whisky. In distilling, the liquid **is heated** until the spirit turns to vapour, then condensed back into liquid. By law, Scotch whisky **must be aged** in oak barrels for at least three years.* (Adapted from Dewar's Scotch Whisky website)

See also unit 43 ● To show a sequence in a process we use words like: *Firstly/First of all, Then, The next step, Next, After that, Finally*:
   First of all *the finished products* **are checked** *for quality,* **then** *they* **are packed** *and* **sent out** *from our warehouse.* **After dispatch** *we allow customers to follow the progress of their order on our Intranet.* **Finally***, we get a digital image of the signature of the person who receives the goods, so that this* **can be checked** *later, if necessary.*

D Saying who does the action

- In all the passive examples above the person or organisation that does the action is not mentioned. If we want to say who does the action then we use *by*:
   The goods are being shipped next week **by our supplier in China***.*
   A press briefing will be given tomorrow **by our Information Officer, Rosa Mendoza***.*

   The factory is staffed **by the local people who worked there before***, but on a completely different basis.* (Business News Americas website)

E Transitive and intransitive verbs

See also unit 25 ● Verbs which usually take objects are called transitive verbs (eg: *help*). Verbs which do not usually take objects are called intransitive verbs (eg: *look*).
   A: *Can I* **help you**?
   B: *No, I'm just* **looking**.

   Dictionaries show this information with T or I. Some verbs can be both transitive and intransitive. Only transitive verbs can be made passive.

Raise *(T)*	*Interest rates were raised last month.*	possible
Increase *(T/I)*	*Interest rates were increased last month.*	possible
Go up *(I)*	*Interest rates* ~~were gone up~~ *last month.*	not possible

9 Practice

Exercise 1 A

Complete each sentence with a passive verb. You may need a negative form.

1 Somebody damaged the goods in transit.

The goods ....*were damaged*............ in transit.

2 Thousands of people see this advert every day.

This advert .... by thousands of people every day.

3 They will not finish the project by the end of the month.

The project .... by the end of the month.

4 They have closed fifty retail outlets over the last year.

Fifty retail outlets .... over the last year.

5 We are reviewing all of our IT systems.

All of our IT systems ....

6 We cannot ship your order until we receive payment.

Your order .... until we receive payment.

Exercise 2 B D

Decide if it is necessary to say who does the action. If it is not necessary, cross it out. If it is necessary, put a tick (✓).

1 I don't think your proposal will be accepted ~~by people.~~

2 The company was founded by the father of the present chairman. ✓

3 All our machines are serviced by highly trained technicians.

4 This machine isn't working again! It was repaired yesterday by a technician.

5 The conference was opened by someone from the London Business School.

6 I'll be shown round the factory by someone, and then I'll meet the sales team.

Exercise 3 A B D E

Rewrite these sentences using the passive if it is possible. You may need a negative form. If it is not possible (because the verb is intransitive) put a cross ✗.

1 Our R & D department have discovered a promising new drug.

   A promising new drug has been discovered by our R+D department

2 The inflation rate went down by 0.5% last month.

   ✗

3 One of our best young designers created this line.

   ....

4 I'm sorry, we can't do that.

   ....

5 Something very interesting happened to me last week.

   ....

6 We're spending more than a million dollars on advertising this year.

   ....

7 The Accounts Department may not authorise this payment.

   ....

8 I worked as a consultant for four years after my MBA.

   ....

Exercise 4 A B C

A marketing manager is writing a training manual that explains how the company uses questionnaires to do market research. Complete the text by putting the verbs from the list below into the present simple passive.

~~design~~   send back   distribute   offer   put   outsource   analyse

First, we carefully select a sample of people to ask. Then the questions (1) __*are designed*__ by a small team within the department. Next, the questions (2) .... into sequence and grouped together by topic. After that, we print the questionnaire and it (3) .... to everyone in the sample. Of course, not all the forms (4) .... to us, but we try to collect as many as possible.

Sometimes a small gift (5) .... to people who return the forms, as an incentive. Finally we enter all the results onto a spreadsheet, and the information (6) .... by the marketing department. If we are using a very large sample the distribution and collection (7) .... to an external company.

Exercise 5 A B

Helen is starting her own business. Look at the extract from her planning schedule, then complete her letter to a business advice service. Choose either the present perfect passive (*has/have been done*), present continuous passive (*is/are being done*) or a modal passive form (eg: *should be done*).

Contact bank to arrange loan.	✓
Find office space.	✓
Equipment needed? Order if necessary.	*In progress*
Print business cards, stationery, etc.	*In progress*
Decorate office, order furniture, etc.	*Finish end of month*
Place advertisements in local press.	✓
Review staffing needs for Christmas period.	*November*

Dear Sir or Madam

I am writing to arrange an interview with one of your business advisers to discuss my business start-up. I've analysed the market very carefully and I believe that I have a good business plan. I can give you a few details of my progress so far.

I've had several meetings with my bank, and a loan (1) _has been arranged_ (arrange). I've found some office space in a good location, although some work (2) .... (will / need) there before I can move in. I've reviewed my equipment needs and in fact some specialised items (3) .... (order) at the moment. My business cards (4) .... (print) and will be ready in a week or so. This week I'm busy decorating the office, and I (5) .... (should / finish) by the end of the month.

I know that soon I'll have to advertise in the local press, and perhaps you could advise me on this matter. Finally, I'd like some help planning my staffing needs – extra staff (6) .... (might / need) over the Christmas period.

Yours faithfully

Helen Chadwick

10 Passive 2

A Uses: linking to previous information

● The choice of active or passive often depends on how we want to continue from the previous sentence:

*Hasso Plattner is one of Germany's best known businessmen. He **founded** SAP in 1972 after working for IBM.* (active)

*SAP is a world leader in business software. It **was founded** by Hasso Plattner in 1972 after he left IBM.* (passive)

B Uses: being formal/impersonal

● The passive is often used in business correspondence where the writer wants to be impersonal. Compare:

ACTIVE more personal
*We **ordered** twenty filter units from you on the 16th March and the courier **delivered** them yesterday. Unfortunately, when we **opened** the package someone **had damaged** two of the units. Our production department **needs** these items urgently.*

PASSIVE more impersonal
*Twenty filter units **were ordered** from you on the 16th March and they **were delivered** yesterday. Unfortunately, when the package **was opened** two of the units **had been damaged**. These items **are needed** urgently by our production department.*

● Passives are frequent in formal writing generally, eg: reports and legal documents. Other language in the text will also be formal:

Contract of Employment

*(i) Offer of employment. The offer **may be expressed** directly or **it may be implied** by conduct. It **must be communicated** to the employee. The offer **can be withdrawn** at any time before acceptance. (i) Written Conditions. After the contract **is made**, every employee **must be given** a written statement of terms and conditions of employment.* (Business Link website)

See unit 22 ● Passives are used in phrases with *it* to report what people said in a formal way: *It was said/agreed that ... .*

● Try to find a balance between active and passive forms. Too many passive forms can make a letter or report difficult to understand.

C Passive + infinitive

● The verbs *believe, expect, know, report, say, think, suppose, understand* are often used in the present simple passive followed by an infinitive (*to do*). This use is common in news reports:

*The Hungarian economy **is expected to expand** 6% over the next two years as rising demand across Europe boosts demand for locally produced cars and refrigerators. Consumer prices **are predicted to rise** by an annual average of 7% next year.* (cebd website)

● To refer to the past we use *believe, expect*, etc with *to have done*.

*Many investment banks **are believed to have suffered losses** in the high yield, or 'junk', bond market in recent months.* (FT.com website)

● To refer to an activity in progress at the moment we use *believe, expect*, etc with *to be doing*.

*Ericsson **is known to be looking at** the possibility of outsourcing its low price, entry-level phones in Taiwan.* (Economist website)

D Verbs with two objects

See unit 25
for verbs with two objects

● Some verbs have two objects. We can:
give / lend / offer / promise / sell / send / take **something** to **somebody**
book / buy / keep / make / prepare / save **something** for **somebody**

● In active sentences we can use these verbs in two ways:
ABB **gave a large order to us** *last year.*   (with *to*)
ABB **gave us a large order** *last year.*   (without *to*)

The form without *to / for* is more usual.

● Each way can be made passive. One of the objects becomes the subject of the passive sentence, the other stays as an object.
A large order *was given* **to us** *by ABB last year.*   (with *to*)
We *were given* **a large order** *by ABB last year.*   (without *to*)

Again, the form without *to / for* is more usual.

E *Have* something *done*

● When a professional person, eg, a technician or accountant, does some work for us, we can use *have something done*:
We **have** *our accounts* **audited** *by KPMG.*
We **had** *our offices* **redecorated** *last year.*
We're **going to have** *a new air conditioning system* **installed**.
You **must have** *your computers* **checked** *for viruses.*

● We can use *get* in place of *have* in most cases. This is more informal.
We **got** *the contract* **checked** *by our lawyers.*

F *To be born*

● *To be born* is a passive form but does not have an obvious passive meaning.
I **was born** *in Uruguay.*

**"Some people, Remson, are born to push the envelope,
and some are born to lick it."**

10 Practice

Exercise 1 A

Read each statement 1–5 then choose which sentence a) or b) should follow. Put a tick (✔) by the correct answer.

1 Chevron and Texaco are going to merge via a $36 billion offer by Chevron.
    a) Senior executives first discussed it a year ago. ☐
    b) It was first discussed by senior executives a year ago. ✔

2 The process of economic union in Europe is progressing quickly.
    a) A commissioner from Spain called Pedro Solbes is directing it. ☐
    b) It is being directed by Pedro Solbes, a commissioner from Spain. ☐

3 Pedro Solbes is Europe's commissioner for economic and monetary affairs.
    a) He is directing the difficult process of economic union. ☐
    b) The difficult process of economic union is being directed by him. ☐

4 Novartis shares rose by 32 Swiss francs in Zurich yesterday.
    a) They are going to launch a new drug called Starlix later this year. ☐
    b) A new drug called Starlix is going to be launched by them later this year. ☐

5 Starlix is a powerful new drug for treating diabetes.
    a) Novartis are going to launch it later this year. ☐
    b) It is going to be launched by Novartis later this year. ☐

Exercise 2 C E F

<u>Underline</u> the correct words.

1 I had my car *be repaired/<u>repaired</u>* yesterday.
2 Profits are expected *grow/to grow* by 10% in the next quarter.
3 I *was born/born* in a little town just outside Dijon.
4 We're getting the machines *cleaned/to be cleaned* tomorrow.
5 The Board is thought to *be demanded/have demanded* his resignation.
6 We have the components *assembling/assembled* in Taiwan.
7 Where exactly *were you born/did you born*?
8 She is supposed *to been looking/to be looking* for a new job.

Exercise 3 D

Complete the second sentence so it has a similar meaning to the first sentence.

1 David Gill from Marketing lent me this book.
    ....I was lent.............. this book by David Gill from Marketing.

2 This sample was given to me at the Trade Fair.
    .... this sample at the Trade Fair.

3 They promised us delivery within two weeks of our order.
    We .... within two weeks of our order.

4 A textile firm near Milan made this fabric for us.
    .... for us by a textile firm near Milan.

5 This order was sent to us through our website.
    .... this order through our website.

6 My secretary booked the flight for me.
    .... for me by my secretary.

Exercise 4 B

 16 Complete the report by putting the verbs in brackets into the present perfect active (*has done*) or passive (*has been done*).

Investment opportunities: *Brazil*

Brazil (1) ....*has been transformed*.... (transform) from an economy based on sugar and coffee into a leading industrial power, and this (2) ....*has happened*........ (happen) over a relatively short time period. Over recent years inflation (3) .... (bring) under control, and foreign direct investment (4) .... (encourage).

The Government (5) .... (privatise) many state-owned companies, and they (6) .... (also / invest) a lot of money in advanced infrastructure. In an attempt to decentralise the economy, Campinas was chosen to be Brazil's IT capital, and car production (7) .... (move) away from traditional centres to states such as Rio Grande do Sul in the south. No one pretends that all the old problems (8) .... (solve), but Brazil is finally taking its place on the world stage.

Exercise 5 C

 17 Read the article about Manchester United, then complete it with the verbs in the brackets. Put the first verb in the present simple passive (*to be done*) and the second verb in a suitable form of the infinitive (*to do, to be doing,* or *to have done*).

Manchester United: just a game of football?

Manchester United is (1) ....*is supposed to have*.... (suppose / have) between 10 million and 30 million supporters throughout the world. In Norway, for example, one in every 140 people (2) .... (say / be) a registered supporter. Ticket sales and merchandising contribute over half of the club's revenue, with television contributing a further 20%.

But senior executives (3) .... (know / look at) other ways to generate income at the moment. For example, the club (4) .... (believe / develop) e-commerce initiatives through a series of alliances. Costs at the club continue to increase. A few years ago the club (5) .... (report / spend) £30m on a plan to expand

the capacity of the stadium from 55,000 seats to 67,400 seats. But this (6) .... (think / be) a good investment as it will generate nearly £7.5 million in additional turnover annually. The main costs at the club are the salaries of the players. Last year the team's captain (7) .... (understand / negotiate) a four-year contract worth over eight figures.

Exercise 6 B

The two emails below are very similar, but the one on the right is more impersonal. Complete it by using verbs from the first email in the correct form of the passive.

Thank you for your order for PCplus software which we received this morning. Our fulfillment team is dealing with your order, and we expect that we will deliver the package to you within 10 working days. I have included our current price list as an attachment. Please note we only guarantee these prices until 31 December. Thank you for choosing soft.com.

Thank you for your order for PCplus software which (1) ....*was received*.......... this morning. Your order (2) .... by our fulfillment team and we expect that the package (3) .... to you within 10 working days. Our current price list (4) .... as an attachment. Please note that these prices (5) .... until 31 December. Thank you for choosing soft.com.

11 Modals and related verbs 1

A Modal verbs: form

> *In the early stages of the Internet revolution, Midland Bank found it **could do** things with its online subsidiary First Direct that the computer systems of its mainstream bank were **not able to do**.*
> (ft.com website)

- Units 11–14 deal with modal verbs. Modal verbs are *can, could, will, would, may, might, shall, should* and *must*.

- Modal verbs are followed by the infinitive without *to*.

- Modal verbs have only one form. So there is no *-s* in the third person singular and there are no verb tenses with *-ing*, *-ed*, etc.

- Questions are made by putting the modal in front of the subject. Negatives are made by putting *not* immediately after the modal (often shortened to *-n't* in spoken English and informal written English).

Can I ...?	*I cannot (can't)*	*May I ...?*	*I may not*
Could I ...?	*I could not (couldn't)*	*Might I ...?*	*I might not*
Will I ...?	*I will not (won't)*	*Shall I ...?*	*I shall not (shan't)*
Would I ...?	*I would not (wouldn't)*	*Should I ...?*	*I should not (shouldn't)*
Must I ...?	*I must not (mustn't)*		

- Modal verbs are auxiliary verbs – they are used with other main verbs. Two modal verbs cannot be put together.

- Modal verbs have no infinitive form. Instead, we use other expressions like *be able to* (for *can*), *have to* (for *must*) and *be likely to* (for *might*).
  *I'd like **to be able to** speak better French.* (NOT ~~I'd like to can speak~~)

- Modal verbs show the speaker's attitude or feelings about a situation. For example, how probable or necessary something is, or that the speaker is offering or requesting something.

- The same modal verb can be used in different ways and with different meanings. You only know the meaning from the situation. For example, *could*:

*I **could** get to work in 30 minutes in my last job.*	(ability: past time)
***Could** you pass the salt, please?*	(request: present time)
*That **could** be difficult.*	(uncertainty: future time)

B Ability

- To talk about ability we use *can* and *can't* (or *cannot* in formal writing).
  *We **can get** that information from the Net.*
  ***Can you deliver** in two weeks? – No, we **can't**.*

  > *'If we **cannot** produce an image that both captures the essence of the Hungarian nation and is convincing, then others will produce it instead' said Hungarian Prime Minister Viktor Orbán in his speech yesterday.* (Central Europe Review website)

- See also unit 12 *Can't* is used for all things that we are not able to do.
  *I **can't speak** German.*

  For the special case of things that are prohibited (not allowed) by rules or laws we can also use **mustn't**.
  *I'm sorry, you **can't/mustn't smoke** in this area.*

- We sometimes use *be able/unable to* instead of *can*. They are common in writing.

  > *For the first time in years **we are now able to** generate growth internally, not just through acquisitions.* (International Herald Tribune website)

C Past ability

● To talk about general past ability (not limited to one occasion) we use *could*.
  I **could** *speak French quite well when I was at school.*

● To talk about one specific past action we use *was/were able to* and *managed to*.
  I **was able to/managed to** *install the new software quite easily.*

  Congress **managed to** *run through about $900 billion of the budget surplus in the three months or so leading up to this election; think of what it might do in two years.* (New York Times website)

  But to talk about a specific past action with a verb of the senses (*see, feel, hear, understand*) we can use *could*.
  I **could/was able to/managed to** *understand most of what he said.*

● In negative sentences and questions we can use *could*, *was/were able to* and *managed to*.
  I'm sorry I **couldn't/wasn't able to/didn't manage to** *come to the restaurant last night.*
  I **couldn't/wasn't able to/didn't manage to** *understand what he meant.*
  Could you/Were you able to/Did you manage to *deal with the problem?*

D *Will* and willingness

See unit 7
for *will* used for the future

See unit 13
for *will* used for making assumptions about the past

See unit 17
for *will* used in conditionals

● *Will* is an auxiliary verb used to refer to the future. But *will* also has modal uses that can refer to the present or the future.

● *Will* can be used for instant comments made at the moment of speaking.
  I think **I'll** *go home now.*   (a spontaneous decision)
  I'll *give you a lift to the station.*   (an offer of help)
  I'll *give you my full support in the meeting.* (a promise)
  I'll *have the roast lamb.*   (ordering food)

  Will can also be used in questions to make a request or offer something.
  Will *you hold the lift for me, please?*   (a request)
  Will *you have some more coffee?*   (offering something)

● In many of these examples where *will* refers to the present it expresses the idea of 'willingness'.

"Here at JM Networks, we recognize hard work and maybe someday we'll reward it."

11 Practice

Exercise 1 A

<u>Underline</u> the correct words.

1   *Do you can/Can you* come to the meeting next week?

2   *I can come/I can to come* to the meeting next week.

3   I won't *can't/be able to* come to the meeting next week.

4   Sorry that *I didn't could/I couldn't* come to the meeting last week.

5   Sorry that *I wasn't able to/I wasn't able* come to the meeting last week.

6   *Do you will/Will you* show me how to log on to the network?

7   What *we can do/can we do*?

8   I hope *to can/to be able* to fly directly to Dusseldorf.

9   *I must speak/I must to speak* with Mr Reiner as soon as possible.

10 *I managed to/I could* speak to Mr Reiner yesterday.

11 The hotel was OK, but *I managed to/I could* hear a lot of noise from the street.

12 *I managed to/I could* take a boat trip on Lake Leman when I was in Geneva.

Exercise 2 A B C

Complete the sentences with *can, can't, could, couldn't* or *be able to*.

1   I'm afraid I ....can't.......... help you at the moment.

2   I don't think I'll .... come to the meeting.

3   The negotiations broke down because we .... agree on the price.

4   I .... see you were having problems, so I didn't interrupt.

5   If you .... make a firm order today, we should .... ship by Friday.

6   I find Portuguese very difficult. I .... understand it, but I .... speak it.

7   Sorry, I .... see you next week, but I might .... make the week after.

8   A: Will you .... go to the training seminar?

    B: No, I .... – I'm very busy.

9   I'm sorry I .... come to your talk yesterday. I had to sort out a problem.

10 I .... ski really well when I was in my twenties, but now I'm out of practice.

Exercise 3 D   unit 7

Match sentences 1–8 with their uses of *will*.

a)   a future fact   e)   a promise

b)   a belief or opinion about the future   f)   ordering food

c)   an instant decision   g)   a request

d)   an offer of help   h)   offering something

1   I think sales will probably improve in the spring. `b`

2   I'll give you a hand with your bags.

3   Will you give me a hand with these bags?

4   OK, I'll phone them right now.

5   I'll have the pan-fried fish.

6   I'll be there at six o'clock. Don't worry, I won't be late.

7   In the spring we'll have two new products ready to launch.

8   Will you have another glass of wine?.

Exercise 4 B D unit 14

 18   Complete the telephone conversation using phrases from the list below.

can you send   can I call you   can you hear   can I help you   can't see
~~could I speak to~~   could you hold   could you repeat   could you speak   could you tell me
I'll need   I'll put one   I'll be on   I'll just go   I'll wait   I'll put you through   I'll get back to you

JON: Good morning, the Tech Store, this is Jon speaking.

SARA: (1) ...Could I speak to... someone in Customer Services, please?

JON: Er. Yes, of course, (2) ....

          ...

MARK: Customer Services, Mark speaking, how (3) .... ?

SARA: I'm calling about your new Samsung DVD players. (4) .... if you have
          any in stock?

MARK: (5) .... and see. (6) .... the line please?

SARA: Yes, no problem, (7) ....

          ...

MARK: Hello? I (8) .... any on the shelves. (9) .... to
          check the order status on the computer. (10) .... back?

SARA: Certainly. My name is Sara Hall and my telephone number is 0582 1067.

MARK: Sorry, (11) .... up? It's a terrible line.

SARA: Is that better? (12) .... me now?

MARK: Yes, that's much better. (13) .... the number please?

SARA: Of course. It's 0582 1067. (14) .... this number all morning.

MARK: Sorry, I can't tell you if we've got any DVDs in stock right now, but
          (15) .... as soon as I have the information. Was there anything else?

SARA: Er, yes, (16) .... me a copy of your latest catalogue?

MARK: Of course, (17) .... in the post to you today. What's your address?

SARA: It's 25 Ridley Lane, Lower ...

Exercise 5 A B D

This exercise introduces many of the modal verbs covered in the following units. Match each sentence 1–14
with a meaning a)–n).

1	I should do it.	g	a)	It's necessary to do it.
2	I shouldn't do it.		b)	It's not necessary to do it.
3	I can do it.		c)	Sorry, it's impossible.
4	I can't do it.		d)	It's forbidden.
5	I mustn't do it.		e)	I have the ability to do it.
6	I don't have to do it.		f)	I'm offering to do it.
7	I have to do it.		g)	It's a good idea.
8	I'll do it.		h)	It's a bad idea.

9	I'll do it.		i)	I'm inviting you.
10	I might do it.		j)	I'm asking permission.
11	Would you like to do it?		k)	I'm requesting that you do it.
12	Could you do it, please?		l)	I promise.
13	May I do it?		m)	Perhaps I will do it.
14	Shall I do it?		n)	I'm making a suggestion.

 Modals and related verbs 2

A Necessity (obligation)

- To say that something is necessary we use *have to, need to* and *must*.
  *I **have to/need to** speak to Jane before she leaves.*
  *We **must** finish the meeting by eleven at the latest.*

- All three forms are very similar, particularly in writing where they all express necessity (obligation).
  In speech there is a small difference:
  Have to and *need to* – the situation makes something necessary.
  *You **have to** pay the invoice by the end of the month.* (that's the company rule)

  Must – the speaker personally feels something is important.
  *You **must** stop working so hard.* (I'm telling you)

  *'We **must** recall that the economy is but one dimension of life as a whole, and it is by no means certain that it is the single most important one' said Prime Minister Orbán.* (Central Europe Review website)

- To make a question we normally use *have to* or *need to*. If we use *must* for a question we can sound annoyed, particularly if we stress *must* in speech.
  *Unfortunately, I **must/have to/need to** work this evening.*
  *Do you **have to/need to** work this evening?*
  ***Must you** work this evening?*

- *Have got to* and *'ll have to* are also used for necessity. They are more informal.
  *You've **got to/You'll have to** contact them as soon as possible.*

B No necessity, permission, prohibition

- When something is not necessary we use *don't have to* and *don't need to*.
  *You **don't have to** pay right now. We can give you credit.* (you are free to choose)

- When something is permitted we use *can* and *be allowed to*.
  *You **can** park your car here at the weekends, but not during the week.*

- When something is prohibited we use *can't, be not allowed to* and *mustn't*. *Mustn't* is more usual when we are telling someone what not to do.
  *You're **not allowed to** park on a double yellow line.* (that's the law)
  *You **mustn't talk about politics** if they invite you to dinner.* (I'm telling you)

- Notice that *have to* and *must* have similar meanings in their affirmative forms (section A above), but different meanings in their negative forms (this section).
  *I **have to/must** leave now.* (it's necessary for me to leave)
  *I **don't have to** leave now.* (it's not necessary, I have a choice whether to leave)
  *I **mustn't** leave now.* (it's prohibited, I cannot leave)

C Necessity, no necessity, permission, prohibition in the past

- To talk about necessity in the past, we use *had to* and *needed to*. There is no past form of *must*.
  *I **had to/needed to** speak to Emma about something, but I've forgotten what it was about.*

- To talk about no necessity in the past, we use *didn't have to/didn't need to*.
  *You **didn't have to/didn't need to** take a taxi. I could have picked you up in my car.*

- To talk about permission in the past, we use *could, was allowed to*.
  *In my last job I **could/was allowed to** use the phone for personal calls.*

- To talk about prohibition in the past, we use *couldn't, wasn't allowed to*.
  *In my last job I **couldn't/wasn't allowed to** use the phone for personal calls.*

D Opinions and advice

- We use *should, should not (shouldn't), ought to* and *ought not to (oughtn't to)* to give an opinion or recommendation about what is the best thing to do.
  *We **should/ought to** invest more heavily in marketing.*

  *By midnight Kennedy had 265 electoral votes, just four short of victory. Nixon wasn't ready to concede, but he thought he **should** make some kind of statement to his supporters in the ballroom downstairs. Kennedy watched this on TV. 'Why **should** he concede?' Kennedy said to his aides. 'I wouldn't.'* (Washington Post website)

- When we use *you* speaking to someone else our opinion becomes advice.
  *You **should** speak to your boss.* (it's my advice to you)

  Note that advice is like a weak type of necessity (section A).
  *You **should/ought to** go to the doctor.* (advice: it's the best thing to do)
  *You **must/have to** go to the doctor.*   (strong advice: it's really necessary)

- *had better (not)* is used for strong opinions. *Had* is usually contracted.
  *I**'d better not interrupt** him while he's on the phone.*
  *I think you**'d better call** them straightaway.*

E Past criticism

When we use the verbs in section D in the past (+ *have* + past participle) we mean that we didn't do the right thing and now we are making a criticism.
*We **should have seen** the dangers a long time ago.*
*We **shouldn't have spent** all the advertising budget on television spots.*
*You **ought to have mentioned** that earlier.*

F *Need to*

- *Need to* means the same as *have to* (sections A/B).
  *You **have to/need to** sign this form in two places, here and here.*

  *If you're going to jump into the UK market and become an important player, you **need to** have wine that retails in the £6–£7 price range.* (New York Times website)

- Notice the two possible negative forms.
  *You **don't need to/needn't** wait for me – I'll come along later.*

- In strict grammar the two negative forms have different meanings in the past.
  *I **didn't need to arrive** at seven.* (we don't know when I arrived – maybe seven or later)
  *I **needn't have arrived** at seven.* (we know when I arrived – seven – but it wasn't necessary)

  But in everyday speech we often use *didn't need to* for both cases.

12 Practice

Exercise 1 A B C D E

Match each sentence 1–12 with one of the formal sentences a)–l).

1	I can do it.	c	a)	It's necessary.
2	I mustn't do it.		b)	It's not necessary.
3	I don't have to do it.		c)	It's allowed.
4	I have to do it.		d)	It's not allowed.
5	I couldn't do it.		e)	It was necessary.
6	I didn't have to do it.		f)	It wasn't necessary.
7	I had to do it.		g)	It was allowed.
8	I could do it.		h)	It wasn't allowed.
9	I should have done it.		i)	Doing it would be a good idea.
10	I shouldn't have done it.		j)	Doing it would be a bad idea.
11	I shouldn't do it.		k)	Doing it was a bad idea.
12	I should do it.		l)	Not doing it was a bad idea.

Exercise 2 A

Complete the sentences with *must* or *have to*. Both are possible each time, but one is more natural in a spoken context.

1 I .... remember to email Steve and thank him for all his help.

2 Sorry, I .... go now, the meeting begins in five minutes.

3 You .... your tax form by 31 January.

4 You .... try to be more diplomatic when you're speaking to Tim.

5 I .... go the dentist next Friday morning, so I'll be a little late.

6 I really .... go the dentist. I've had this awful pain for two days.

Exercise 3 A B C D

Decide whether each pair of sentences has the same meaning. Write I for identical or nearly identical, S for similar or D for completely different. At the end there will be nine of I, two of S and three of D.

A		B	
1	You'd better go now.	You should go now.	..I..
2	We don't have to cut the budget.	We mustn't cut the budget.	......
3	You should have a rest.	You ought to have a rest.	......
4	You can't smoke here.	You're not allowed to smoke here.	......
5	We must sign the contract.	We should sign the contract.	......
6	You must be here before 8.30.	You have to be here before 8.30.	......
7	You mustn't touch that key!	You don't have to touch that key.	......
8	You didn't have to give a tip.	You didn't need to give a tip.	......
9	We have to work harder on this.	We must work harder on this.	......
10	I ought to leave now.	I have to leave now.	......
11	You shouldn't worry so much.	You ought not to worry so much.	......
12	I must write these letters now.	I'd better write these letters now.	......
13	I couldn't use the email.	I didn't need to use the email.	......
14	We don't have to decide yet	We don't need to decide yet.	......

Exercise 4 A B D

 19   Look at these notes that a Personnel Manager wrote to explain company rules. Then use the notes to complete a briefing he gave to some new employees on their first day at work. Choose from *have to, don't have to, can, can't, should* or *shouldn't*.

Necessary:	sign letter about working hours, leave building during fire drill
Not necessary:	send holiday form to personnel immediately
Permitted:	volunteer to work extra hours, take 3 weeks holiday, smoke outside building
Prohibited:	make staff work long hours, take all holiday time together
Good idea:	speak to head of department about excessive hours, give notice to head of dept. about holidays, read fire notices
Bad idea:	block fire exit

'Um. Excuse me. Good morning. Er, good morning. I've called you to this meeting to explain to you all some of the basic health and safety rules that we have here. Um, first of all, working hours: it's not our company policy to make staff work excessive hours – it makes people unproductive and can endanger health. Um, managers (1) ....**can't**.......... make any of their staff work more than an average of 48 hours per week, although anyone (2) .... volunteer to work more than these hours, but they (3) .... sign a letter from the company to say that they want to do this. Any member of staff who is worried that they are working too many hours (4) .... speak to their head of department about it.

Um, all employees (5) .... take a minimum of three weeks' paid holiday per year, but you (6) .... take all this holiday off in one block. Staff (7) .... give their head of department as much notice as possible about their holidays, although they (8) .... send their holiday form off to personnel until a few weeks before they go.

Next, er, fire drills. We have a fire drill about once a month – don't ignore it. You (9) .... leave the building immediately that you hear the bell, and of course you (10) .... block the fire exits. Fire notices are posted throughout the building. Employees (11) .... read these notices regularly. In the case of a real fire, don't panic and follow the fire procedures.

And lastly, for you smokers, I'm afraid that smoking is not permitted anywhere inside the building, although you (12) .... smoke just outside the front door.

I think that covers everything. Does anyone have any questions? No … Yes…'

Exercise 5 C E

 20   A businessman is describing his trip to Lagos. Complete the text with *had to, didn't have to, couldn't, should have* or *shouldn't have*. Each phrase is used twice.

'I (1) ...**should have**.... travelled on the 10 am flight, but when I got to the airport they told me that the flight was overbooked and I (2) .... catch a later flight. Then at the check-in desk they told me that I (3) .... take both my bags as hand luggage, so I (4) .... let one of them go in the hold, which was very annoying as I had my diary in it, and it delayed me by nearly an hour at baggage reclaim at the other end. When I got on the plane I wanted to use my laptop, but of course I (5) .... until after take off. The flight attendant told me to turn it off and said that I (6) .... known not to use it. To be honest I'd just forgotten, and he (7) .... been so rude. Er, it was quite late when I finally left Lagos airport, so it was lucky I (8) .... go to any meetings that afternoon. And, looking back at what happened, I (9) .... travelled with that airline – they have a lot of problems with overbooking. And my company was paying for the flight so I (10) .... choose the cheapest option.'

Modals and related verbs 3

A Degrees of probability

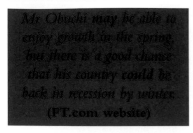

Mr Obuchi may be able to enjoy growth in the spring, but there is a good chance that his country could be back in recession by winter.
(FT.com website)

● We can use modals and other phrases to talk about the probability that something will happen in the future. See table and following sections.

100%	certainty	*will, be certain to*
95–100%	deduction	*must, can't*
80%	expectation	*should, ought to, be likely to, shouldn't, ought not to, be unlikely to*
30%–70%	uncertainty	*may, might, could, may not, might not*
0%	certainty	*won't*

B Certainty and deduction

● We use *will* and *be certain to* if we are certain that something will happen.
*The new Jaguar **will** be launched at the Paris Motor Show.*

● We use *won't* when we are certain something will not happen.
*I'm sorry, Christiane is on holiday. She **won't** be back until the 14th.*

See also unit 7 ● We can use *probably* and *definitely* with *will* and *won't*. Note the word order.
*She**'ll probably** be at the meeting.*   *She **probably won't** be at the meeting.*

● We use *must* and *can't* to show that something is very certain because it is logical. This is often called 'deduction'.
*There's no answer from her phone. She **must** be in a meeting.*
*Both the meeting rooms are empty. She **can't** be in a meeting.*

Note that *can't*, not *mustn't*, is used here.

C Expectation

● When we expect that something will happen we use *should, ought to* or *be likely to*.
*They **should/ought** to arrive at about 4.30.*
*Our profits **are likely to improve** next year.*

*Lisbon **should be** a turning point in European economic policy.* (Economist website)

● When we expect that something will not happen we use *shouldn't, ought not to* or *be unlikely to*.
*There **shouldn't/ought not to be** any problem.*

*Mr Blair's Lisbon strategy **is unlikely to be** enough to halt the deterioration in Britain's relationship with Europe.* (Economist website)

D Uncertainty

● When we are uncertain we use *may, might* or *could*. The meaning is 'perhaps'.
*We **may** be able to deliver in two weeks.*
*I **might** have some more news for you next week.*
*It **could** take a long time to arrange the finance.*

There is no important difference between these modals in this context.

● The negative forms are *may not* and *might not*.
*Friday is not a good day for the meeting. I **may/might not** be in the office on that day.*

See unit 11
for *could not*
Note that *could not* is not used with this meaning.

E Degrees of probability in the past

● For different degrees of probability in the past we use: modal verb + *have* + past participle. See the table below.

● Notice in the table that *will/won't have* + past participle is an assumption (you think something is true although you have no proof). For certainty in the past we just use a normal past tense like the past simple.

assumption	*You**'ll have seen** our new model. It's in all the shops.*
deduction	*There was no answer from her phone. She **must have been** in a meeting.*
	*Both the meeting rooms were empty. She **can't have been** in a meeting.*
expectation	*They **should/ought to have arrived** by now. I hope they haven't got lost.*
uncertainty	*Yes, I see what you mean now. I **could have been** wrong about that.*
	*We're only five minutes late. The talk **might not have started** yet.*
assumption	*You **won't have seen** our new model. It's not in the shops yet.*

*Christmas **could have been** an unhappy one last year if you ordered presents online. Many customers were still waiting for gifts to arrive long after the holidays had ended.* (Industry Week website)

F 'Possibility'

● Be careful with the word 'possibility' because it refers to two different ideas in English: uncertainty and ability. Study these examples:

UNCERTAINTY (there is a chance that something will happen)
***It's possible** that the share price will recover.* (= the share price **might/could** recover)

ABILITY (the mental skill or physical power to do something)
***It's possible** for our factory to produce 800 cars a month.* (= our factory **can** produce ...)

For uncertainty see sections C and D of this unit. For ability see unit 11.

● To talk about a past possibility we use *could + have +* past participle.
***I could have booked** an earlier flight, but it left at 7.30 in the morning.*
This is an opportunity that didn't happen.

To talk about a past impossibility we use *couldn't + have +* past participle.
*I **couldn't have booked** the earlier flight – it was completely full.*

"Well we've tried everything else -
I suppose we could try and improve
the product."

13 Practice

Exercise 1 A B C D

<u>Underline</u> the correct words.

1   Look at those clouds. I think it *can/<u>might</u>/must* rain.
2   That's impossible. It *can't be/mustn't be/may not be* true.
3   Well done! You *may be/must be/might be* very pleased.
4   Next Thursday is a possibility. I *might be/can't be/must be* free in the afternoon.
5   I'm not sure. I *must not be/may not be/won't be* able to get there in time.
6   That *can't be/mustn't be/may not be* David. He's away at a conference.
7   Lisa isn't at her office. She *can be/must be/mustn't be* on her way here.
8   Lisa hasn't arrived yet. She *should be/can be/can't be* here soon.
9   There's someone in reception. It *can be/could be/mustn't be* the engineer.
10 Sorry, I *can't/may not/might* come to your presentation. I'm busy that afternoon.
11 I'm not sure where Sue is. She *could be/must be/can be* at lunch.
12 I've looked everywhere for Sue. She *could be/must be/can be* at lunch.

Exercise 2 A B C D

Match each sentence 1–7 with a similar sentence a)–g).

1	They're likely to do it.	c	a)	I'm sure that they'll do it.
2	They might/could do it.		b)	I'm nearly sure that they'll do it.
3	They're almost certain to do it.		c)	They'll probably do it.
4	They'll definitely do it.		d)	Maybe they'll do it.
5	They're unlikely to do it.		e)	I'm sure they won't do it.
6	They're very unlikely do it.		f)	They probably won't do it.
7	They definitely won't do it.		g)	They almost certainly won't do it.

Exercise 3 A B D F

Complete the second sentence so it has a similar meaning to the first sentence using *must, might, can* or *can't*.

1   Deliver by the end of the month? Yes, I think it's possible to do that.
    Deliver by the end of the month? Yes, I think we ....*can*............ do that.
2   It's possible that we will lose this client.
    We .... lose this client.
3   I'm sure this isn't the right road.
    This .... be the right road.
4   I'm sure you work late most nights.
    You .... work late most nights.
5   It's possible that I'll see you tomorrow, but I'm not sure.
    I .... see you tomorrow.
6   It's possible for the new printer to print 20 sheets per minute.
    The new printer .... print 20 sheets per minute.
7   I'm afraid that I'm unable to go to the Trade Fair this year.
    I'm afraid that I .... go to the Trade Fair this year.
8   I suppose you are Kate Perry. How do you do?
    You .... be Kate Perry. How do you do?

Exercise 4 **E** **F**

Match each sentence 1–8 with its meaning a)–d).

1	He won't have arrived yet.	
2	He'll have arrived by now.	☐
3	He can't have arrived yet.	☐
4	He might have arrived by now.	☐
5	He could have arrived by now.	☐
6	He should have arrived by now.	☐
7	He must have arrived by now.	☐
8	He couldn't have arrived yet.	☐

a) 95–100% probability of his arrival.
b) 80% probability of his arrival.
c) 40–60% probability of his arrival.
d) 0% probability of his arrival.

Exercise 5 **A** **B** **C** **D**

21 Complete the article with the words and phrases from the list below. The graphs and ideas in the text will help you.

definitely won't   is almost certain to   ~~is likely to~~   is unlikely to   might   will definitely

Since the beginning of this year unemployment has fallen from 2.5 million to 1.8 million, and (1) ...*is likely to*... drop below 1.5 million by the end of the year. This (2) .... be good news for the government as unemployment is a very important issue in the country at the moment. By the time of the next election unemployment (3) .... even fall below 1 million – it all depends on the world

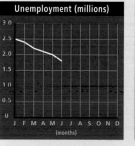

economy and is impossible to predict with any certainty. Unfortunately inflation is going up steadily. It (4) .... reach 6% by the end of the year. However, the government (5) .... take panic measures as inflation is similar to that of its trading partners and (6) .... return to levels of the 1980s when rates of 30% or 40% a year were quite common.

Exercise 6 **A** **B** **D** **E**

22 Martin and Anne have arrived at check-in at Heathrow Airport. Complete their dialogue with *must, might, can't, must have, might have* or *can't have*. Use each word once only.

MARTIN: Oh no, I can't find my passport.

ANNE: You're joking.

MARTIN: No, really, it's not in my briefcase.

ANNE: Well, it (1) .....*must*...... be in your other bag. Quick have a look.

MARTIN: It's not there. Where on earth is it?

ANNE: Well, I don't know. Do you think you (2) .... left it at home?

MARTIN: That's impossible. I (3) .... done. I checked I had it with me four times before I left the house.

ANNE: OK, calm down. What about checking your coat pockets? You never know, it (4) .... be there.

MARTIN: No, it isn't. This is ridiculous. We're going to miss our flight.

ANNE: Look, you (5) .... be looking in the right place.

CHECK-IN ATTENDENT: Excuse me, sir. Is that your passport there on the ground?

MARTIN: Oh, yes, so it is. Ah, I (6) .... dropped it when I was looking for the tickets.

14 Modals and related verbs 4

> *Would you mind providing our readers with an overview of Endemann Internet AG? ...*
> *Could you explain some of your other competitive advantages?*
> **(The Wall Street Transcript website)**

A Direct/indirect language

- Choice of language often depends on the social situation. Direct language is typical of informal situations, for example conversations between colleagues. Indirect language is typical of formal situations, for example first meetings where we have to be polite. In general:
  - present forms (*can, will*) are more direct than past forms (*could, would*)
  - short forms (*Can you*) are more direct than long forms (*I wonder if you could*)

B Requests

- To make a request (ask someone to do something) we *use can, could, will, would*. We can add the word *possibly* to make the request more polite.
  Could you (possibly) *open the window, please?*
  Will/Would you *give me a hand with these suitcases?*

  Question: My profession involves much socialising with middle/upper-class people. **Can you recommend** *a small book in good modern manners and etiquette?* (The Times website)

- **See unit 16** We use an indirect question to make the request more polite.
  Do you think you could *open the window?*
  I'd be grateful if you could *open the window.*

- We can reply by agreeing to or refusing a request.
  Agreeing: *Sure. No problem/Yes, of course./Yes, certainly.*
  Refusing: *Actually, it's a bit inconvenient right now./I'm sorry but that's not possible.*

C Requests with *mind*

"Would you mind stepping outside while we tear your proposal to shreds?"

- We can make a request with *Would you mind ...* followed by an *-ing* form.
  Would you mind repeat**ing** *that?*

- Questions with *mind* mean *Is it a problem for you?* So, to agree to a request we say 'no'.
  A: **Would you mind** *opening the window?*
  B: **No**, *of course not.*

  To refuse we use a phrase like *Well, Actually, To be honest* and give a reason.
  A: **Would you mind** *opening the window?*
  B: **Actually**, *I'm feeling quite cold.*

D Permission

● To ask if we can do something we use *can, could, may*.
Can/Could/May I *change my ticket?*

Imagine a National Health Service in which patients are greeted at the door with a smile and a 'how ***may I*** *help you?' Fantasy? It may not be as far away as you think.* (Guardian website)

See unit 16 ● We can use an indirect question to ask for permission.
Is it all right if I *change my ticket?*
I wonder if I could *change my ticket?*

● We can ask for permission with *Do you mind if I ...?* or *Would you mind if I ...?*
See unit 17 Notice the form of the verb that follows.
– conditionals
A: ***Do you mind if*** *I* **smoke**?   A: ***Would you mind if*** *I* **smoked**?
B: ***No***, *of course not.*   B: ***Actually***, *I'd rather you didn't.*

● We reply like in replies to requests. We often repeat the modal in the reply, but notice that when we reply to *Could I ... ?* we say *can* not *could*.
A: ***Can/Could I speak*** *to you for a moment?*
B: *Yes, of course* ***you can***.

E Offers and invitations

● To offer help we use *Can/Could/Shall I, Would you like me to, I'll* and *Let me*.
Shall I *make a copy for you?*
Would you like me to *give you a lift?*
I'll *give them a ring if you like.*
Let me *give you a hand.*

● To offer things we use *Would you like* or short phrases with choices. We reply by expressing a preference.
A: ***Would you like*** *tea or coffee?*   A: ***What would you prefer***?
B: ***I'd rather have*** *coffee, please.*   B: ***I don't mind.***
A: *Anything to drink? Tea or coffee?*
B: ***I'll have*** *coffee, please.*

● To invite somebody to do something we use *Would you like to ...?*
Would you like to *come with us to the restaurant tonight?*

● We can reply to offers and invitations by accepting or rejecting them.
Accepting: *Thank you very much. / Thanks. I'd appreciate that. / That's very kind of you.*
Rejecting: *That's very kind of you, but ... / Thanks, but I can manage.*

F Suggestions

● To make a suggestion we use *Could, Shall, What about, How about, I think we/you should/could* and *Let's*. Notice the different forms:
We could/I think we should/Let's have *a short break now.* (statement)
What/How about *hav***ing** *a short break now?*   (question + verb with *-ing*)
Shall we have *a short break now?*   (question)

● We often use the form of a negative question.
Couldn't we/Why don't we/Why not *try to renegotiate this part of the contract?*

'Describing my life takes hours. ***Why don't you*** *buy the business-school case history about us? Everything is there.'* – *Nicolas Hayek, CEO of Swatch.* (Sunday Times website)

● We can reply to suggestions by accepting or rejecting them.
Accepting: *Yes, I think we should do that. / That's a good idea. / Yes, let's do that.*
Rejecting: *I'm not really sure about that. / That sounds like a good idea, but ...*

14 Practice

Exercise 1 B C D E F

Underline the correct words.

1 I'm very busy. Would you mind *to give/giving* me a hand?

2 *Would you/Should you* help me carry these boxes, please?

3 *Do you like/Would you like* some more soup?

4 *May I/Would I* ask you a personal question?

5 How about *we talk/talking* to another supplier?

6 Are you having problems? *Will I/Shall I* help you?

7 Are you having problems? *Let me/I shall* help you.

8 *Would I/Could I* borrow your copy of the FT?

9 I think *you should/you can* spend less time playing golf.

10   Excuse me, *could you/may you* tell me which street this is?

11   Do you think *could I/I could* open the window?

12   Do you mind if I *open/opened* the window?

13   Would you mind if I *open/opened* the window?

14   *Would you sign/Please to sign* your name here?

Exercise 2 E

Match the forms 1–3 with the uses a)–c).

1 Would you like a/some … ☐	a)	offering help
2 Would you like to … ☐	b)	offering something
3 Would you like me to … ☐	c)	inviting somebody to do something

Exercise 3 B D E F

Match situations 1–6 with questions a)–f).

1 Making a request ☐d☐	a)	Would you like a coffee?
2 Asking for permission ☐	b)	Would you like me to carry your coffee for you?
3 Offering help ☐	c)	Would you like to come with us for a coffee?
4 Offering something ☐	d)	Could you get me a cup of coffee from the canteen?
5 Inviting somebody ☐	e)	Shall we break for coffee now?
6 Making a suggestion ☐	f)	Is it all right if I help myself to coffee?

Now match situations 7–13 with replies g)–m). You can look back at the questions in the previous part to help you.

7 Agreeing to a request ☐	g)	Actually, I think I'd rather have water if you don't mind.
8 Refusing a request ☐	h)	Of course, no problem.
9 Expressing a preference ☐	i)	Actually, I'm really busy at the moment.
10 Accepting an offer of help ☐	j)	I'm not sure that's a good idea.
11 Accepting a suggestion ☐	k)	OK, let's do that.
12 Rejecting an offer of help ☐	l)	Thanks, I'd really appreciate that.
13 Rejecting a suggestion ☐	m)	Thanks, but I can manage.

Exercise 4 C D E F

23 George is visiting Fernando in São Paulo. Complete the dialogue with the phrases from the list below.

~~Let me~~   shall we   I should   would you like   would you like to   would you like me to   do you mind
would you mind   I don't mind   of course   of course not   I'd appreciate that

FERNANDO: Please, come in. (1) .... Let me .... take your coat. It's good to see you!

GEORGE: It's very nice to be here in São Paulo. Thank you so much for your invitation to come and see your company. It was very kind.

FERNANDO: Not at all. It's my pleasure. (2) .... some coffee? Or mineral water perhaps?

GEORGE: I'd prefer mineral water, please.

FERNANDO: Still or sparkling?

GEORGE: Oh, (3) .... , either would be fine. (4) .... if I just make a quick call – I didn't get a chance earlier.

FERNANDO: (5) .... Go right ahead.

GEORGE: Oh, there's no signal. Never mind. Um, you have a wonderful building here. It looks really impressive from the outside.

FERNANDO: It's very new – we only moved in last year. It's designed by one of our most famous architects, Cesar Pelli. (6) .... show you around later?

GEORGE: Thanks. (7) ....

FERNANDO: Now then, (8) .... get down to business? (9) .... telling me a little about your interest in our market? What exactly are your long-term objectives here in Brazil?

GEORGE: Er, perhaps (10) .... begin by explaining a little about the history of our company. I have a short presentation on my laptop. (11) .... see it?

FERNANDO: (12) ....

Exercise 5 B C D E

Read the following impolite dialogue between a hotel receptionist and a guest.

Receptionist	**Guest**
1 Give me your name.	2 It's Jessop.
3 Spell it.	4 It's J-E-S-S-O-P.
5 Leave your passport.	6 OK. I want an early morning call.
7 Of course.	8 When is breakfast?
9 It's from seven thirty until ten.	10 Also, I must leave a message for a colleague.
11 Do you want a pen?	12 Thank you.

Now rewrite the following lines from the dialogue. The words in brackets will help you.

Line 1 (May/have/name please) ...... May I have your name, please? ......

Line 3 (Could/spell/that/me please) ....

Line 5 (Would/mind/your passport) ....

Line 6 (Do/think/book me/early morning) ....
....

Line 8 (I wonder/you/tell me when) ....
....

Line 10 (Would/mind if I/message/colleague) ....
....

Line 11 (Would/like me/lend/a pen) ....
....

Questions 1

A Yes/no questions and answers

- Questions with the answer *yes* or *no* are formed with an auxiliary verb + subject + main verb. The auxiliary can be *do, be, have* or a modal verb like *can, will, would*. Short answers repeat the auxiliary.

Present simple	A: **Do** you **speak** French?	B: Yes, I **do**./No, I **don't**.
Present continuous	A: **Are** you **staying** at the Metropole?	B: Yes, I **am**./No, I**'m not**.
Past simple	A: **Did** you **check** all the invoices?	B: Yes, I **did**./No, I **didn't**.
Past continuous	A: **Were** you **living** in Rome at the time?	B: Yes, I **was**./No, I **wasn't**.
Past perfect	A: **Had** you already **left** when I phoned?	B: Yes, I **had**./No, I **hadn't**.
Present perfect	A: **Have** you **seen** my new PalmPilot?	B: Yes, I **have**./No, I **haven't**.
Will	A: **Will** you **be** back before lunch?	B: Yes, I **will**./No, I **won't**.
Can	A: **Can** you **speak** French?	B: Yes, I **can**./No, I **can't**.

> **Have** Yale's applications **been rising** over the past couple of years? **Do** you **accept** people into your MBA program without any work experience? **Can** you **give** applicants any advice on the best ways of securing scholarships? (BusinessWeek website)

- The main verb *be* comes before the subject in a question.

  Is it time for the meeting?   **Are you** ready?   **Was it** a useful trip?

B Question word questions

- Question words are: *what, when, where, which, who, whose, why* and *how*.

> The key to production in the future will be partnership. One does not begin with the question '**What do I want?**' and then '**How do I persuade** these people?' One begins with the question '**What do they want?**' and then '**How can** this **be** made to fit into our common purpose?' – Peter Drucker (IndustryWeek website)

- After the question word we use the same structure as a *yes/no* question: auxiliary verb + subject + main verb.

Present simple	**When do** you usually **leave** work?
Present continuous	**Which projects are** you **working on** at the moment?
Past simple	**Whose car did** you **borrow**?
Past continuous	**Where were** you **living** at the time?
Past perfect	**How much research had** you **done** before the product launch?
Present perfect	**Why have** you **decided** to cut back on investment this year?
Will	**When will** you **be** back?
Can	**What languages can** you **speak**?

C Question phrases

- We often use *what* and *which* with a noun:
  What time are you arriving?
  What areas do we need to cover in the meeting?

> **What sectors** look promising at this time? **What implications** would there be if the price of oil continues to rise? (Business Week website)

---

*The price of oil reflects many, many factors. **Has** an oil field **shut down**? **Has** a cold spell **hit** northern Europe? **What is** the International Energy Agency **forecasting**? **What are** the major oil producers **forecasting** in terms of production?* (Gulf Business Magazine website)

Which is more usual with people and organisations, and when there is a limited number of possible answers:
Which customer service representative *were you speaking to?*
Which courier service *did we use last time?*
Which way *is it?*

- We can use *which of* or *which one*:
  Which of the proposals *did you accept?*
  Which one *did you accept?*

  We cannot use *what* in this way.

- We can make phrases with *how: how many, how much, how old, how far, how often, how long, how fast.*
  How often *do you travel abroad on business?*
  How long *will the meeting last?*

  ***How important** are the municipal elections?* ***How much** will the Brazilian economy grow next year and in what areas?* (LatinTrade website)

D Question words as the subject

- Sometimes the question word is the subject of the sentence:
  Who did you meet *in Argentina?* (*you* is the subject)
  Who met *you at the airport?*   (*who* is the subject, *you* is the object)

- When a question word is the subject of a question do not use *do/does/did*.
  What happened?   *Who works here?*   (*What* and *Who* are the subjects)
  *What **did** you do?*   *Who **do** I pay?*   (*you* and *I* are the subjects)

- Note that auxiliaries other than *do/does/did* can be used, but there is no subject pronoun because the question word is the subject.
  What has *happened?* (NOT ~~What it has ...~~)
  What will *happen?* (NOT ~~What it will ...~~)

E Negative questions

- We use negative questions to disagree politely.

  *But **don't you think** that different societies have a different appetite for social cohesion or social disruption? **Isn't there** a limit in what one can introduce from the US to Europe in terms of the new economy?* (Economist website)

- We use negative questions when we expect the answer to be 'no'. In social English this makes it easier for the other person to reply politely.
  A: **Do you like** *Japanese food?*
  B: *No, not really.* (the answer seems very strong)
  A: **Don't you like** *Japanese food?*
  B: *No, not really.* (the answer seems more polite)

- We use negative questions to show surprise.
  Don't you accept *American Express?*

15 Practice

Exercise 1 A B D

Underline the correct words.

1 *Spoke you/Did you speak* with Lara yesterday?

2 What did Lara *say/said* when you spoke to her?

3 A: Do you like Scotch whisky?

   B: *Yes, I like./Yes, I do.*

4 How *works this machine?/does this machine work*?

5 Who *set up Microsoft/did set up Microsoft*?

6 When *set up Microsoft/did Microsoft set up*?

7 Who *did telephone me/telephoned me* this morning?

8 Who *you telephoned/did you telephone* this morning?

Exercise 2 A

Expand the *And you?* questions to make full *yes/no* questions.

1 I've seen the news today. And you?   Have you seen the news today?

2 I work from home. And you?

3 I can understand German. And you?

4 I've already had lunch. And you?

5 I'll be back in time for lunch. And you?

6 I'm enjoying the conference. And you?

7 I agreed with her. And you?

8 I've never spoken to Pierre. And you?

Exercise 3 B

Expand the *And you?* questions to make full question word questions.

1 I know Jim from university. And you?   How do you know Jim?

2 I've invited Mary. And you?   Who _____?

3 I'm going on Monday. And you?   When _____?

4 I parked at the front. And you?   Where _____?

5 I'm here for the talk on optics. And you? Why _____?

6 I'll have the steak. And you?   What _____?

Exercise 4 B

Write a question for each answer.

1 When do you get to work?   Get to work? At about 8.30 usually.

2 _____   Done! I haven't done anything!

3 _____   The report? I put it over there.

4 _____   Here? I stay here because the pay is good.

5 _____   Yesterday? I was feeling awful.

6 _____   Staying? I'm staying at the Ritz.

7 _____   Report to? I report to Bob Taylor.

8 _____   This bag? I think it's Helen's.

Exercise 5 A B

Rearrange the words in each group from the list to make questions. Then match them to the answers below to make a complete dialogue.

~~you business here are on~~   you did do that what before   are for how you staying long
like what's it   been how have long there you working   arrive did when you   you what do do
to is first this Lyon your visit   staying you where are   involve travelling job does much your

1 A: Are you here on business?

   B: Yes, I'm here on a sales trip.

2 A: _____

   B: I work for a small biotech company.

3 A: _____

   B: About four years, I suppose.

4 A: _____

   B: I was in pharmaceuticals.

5 A: _____

   B: Yes, quite a lot. I travel all over Europe, but especially in France.

6 A: _____

   B: No, I've been here once before.

7 A: _____

   B: A couple of days ago.

8 A: _____

   B: Until Friday, then I go back to the UK.

9 A: _____

   B: At the Holiday Inn.

10 A: _____

   B: It's very comfortable actually, and the restaurant is good.

Exercise 6 B C E

 24   Complete the dialogue with question words and question phrases from the list below.

~~what kind of~~   how often   how far   how long   how many   how much
what (x2)   which (x2)   whose

SAM: So, tell me about your new job. (1) ..... What kind of ..... work is it?

JOE: It's in sales, like my last job, but it's a bigger company.

SAM: Really? (2) .... people work there?

JOE: I suppose there's about 60 people in our office.

SAM: Oh, yeah. And (3) .... holiday can you take a year?

JOE: Twenty-four days a year plus public holidays.

SAM: Oh, that's much better than your last job. And (4) .... is it from your home?

JOE: Well, it's really not that far and I don't have to catch the train to work every morning, which is great.

SAM: Oh, lucky you. So, (5) .... does it take you to get to work in the morning now?

JOE: About 20 minutes by car.

SAM: Wow. It sounds perfect. (6) .... time do you start work in the mornings?

JOE: About nine. But sometimes I have to go on sales trips at the weekends as well.

SAM: Oh? (7) .... idea was that?

JOE: I don't know, it's just something you have to do.

SAM: And (8) .... do you have to do it?

JOE: About once a month I think. They're going to give me a company car.

SAM: Really! (9) .... model are they going to give you?

JOE: A Golf, I think – and I can choose the colour.

SAM: Oh, and (10) .... colours are there?

JOE: Well, I can choose between black and dark blue.

SAM: Only two! So, (11) .... one do you prefer?

JOE: Well, dark blue sounds better than black.

SAM: Hmm, yeah. Well, congratulations, I'm sure you'll do really well.

16 Questions 2

A Question tags: form

● A question tag is a short phrase at the end of a statement that turns it into a question. It invites the other person to reply.

● Question tags are formed using auxiliaries (*do, be, have* or a modal). An affirmative statement usually has a negative tag, and vice-versa.

You **speak** French, **don't you?**	You **don't speak** French, **do you?**
You **went** to the conference, **didn't you?**	You **didn't go** to the conference, **did you?**
You **can meet** him tomorrow, **can't you?**	You **can't meet** him tomorrow, **can you?**
He's here, **isn't he?**	**He isn't** here, **is he?**

B Question tags: use

● Here are five possible uses of question tags presented in a dialogue:

A: **You haven't** got the sales figures yet, **have you?**   (request for information)
B: **They don't** have to be ready till Friday, **do they?**   (confirmation)
A: **You're not** going to leave it until the last minute again, **are you?** (attack)
B: Well, **I haven't** had any time, **have I?**   (defence)
A: So **it wasn't** you going home early yesterday, **was it?**   (sarcasm)

● If we use a negative statement with an affirmative tag, we often expect the answer to be *no*.
A: *I'm going to need an interpreter.*
B: *Of course. You* **don't** *speak French,* **do you?**

This form can be more polite because it is easier for the other person to reply *no*.
A: *You* **don't** *speak French,* **do you?**
B: *No, sorry, I don't.*

● A negative statement with an affirmative tag can also be used to ask people for things in a polite way.
You **couldn't** give me a hand, **could you?**
You **haven't** got any change for the parking meter, **have you?**

C Question tags: other points

● If the main verb in the statement is *have*, you make a tag with *do*.
You **had** a meeting this morning, **didn't** you?

When *have* is the auxiliary the tag is with *have* (as normal):
You**'ve** just been to Austria, **haven't you?**

● The tag with *I'm/I am* is *aren't*.
I'm a fool, **aren't** I?

● The tag with *Let's* is *shall*. This is a suggestion.
Let's break for coffee now, **shall** we?

● After an imperative we can use *will you?* or *won't you?*
Have a seat, **will you?**
Give me a call later, **won't you?**
If the imperative is a request we can use *can you?* or *could you?*

Hold the lift for me, **can you?**
Pass me that file, **could you?**

D Reply questions

● We can use a short question to reply to what someone says. We do this to show interest, surprise or uncertainty. The meaning is like *Really?* or *Is that true?*
A: *I went to Head Office last week.*
B: ***Did you?*** (interest)
A: *I can't install the new software.*
B: ***Can't you?*** (surprise)
A: *I think they're arriving at ten.*
B: ***Are they?*** (uncertainty)

● The reply question uses an auxiliary verb like in a question tag, but there is no change of affirmative to negative.

E Indirect questions

● We can be more polite or tentative by beginning a question with a phrase like *Do you know, Do you think/feel, Do you mind telling me, Could you tell me, Could I ask you, I'd like to know, I was wondering.*

__Do you feel__ this rise in interest is a result of increased recruiting? __Can you give me__ Yale's profile for the Class of '99 (ie minority, non-US, female)? Also, you mentioned that Yale has been working hard to strengthen its interview program. __Could you tell me a bit more about__ what the school is doing on that front? (Business Week website)

● The word order of an indirect question is like a normal statement.
direct: ***Could you*** *call me a taxi?*   indirect: *Do you think* ***you could*** *call me a taxi?*
direct: *How old* ***are you?***   indirect: *Could I ask you how old* ***you are?***

● Where there is no question word or modal verb we use *if* or *whether.*
direct: ***Does*** *Jane still* ***work*** *here?*   indirect: *Do you know* ***if*** *Jane still* ***works*** *here?*

F Prepositions in questions

● The preposition comes in the same place as in a statement, following the main verb, and this is often at the end.
Who are you waiting ***for?***
What are you looking ***at?***
Where do you come ***from?***
What were they talking ***about*** *in the meeting?*

G *What is it for* and *what was it like*

● We use *what ... for?* to ask about a purpose. The meaning is 'why'.
What is this switch for? (= Why is this switch here?)

● We use *what ... like?* to ask if something is good or bad. The meaning is 'how'.
What was the conference like? (= How was the conference?)

16 Practice

Exercise 1 A C

Add a question tag to each sentence.

1 We're nearly there, *aren't we?*
2 You know the Brazilian market, ... ?
3 You went to Brazil in March, ... ?
4 You haven't been to Brazil, ... ?
5 He's never been to Brazil, ... ?
6 You won't be late, ... ?
7 Harry isn't going to retire, ... ?
8 We had a good meal last night, ... ?
9 I'm late, ... ? Sorry.
10 Let's meet again soon, ... ?

Exercise 2 B

Make a question with a question tag.

1 Ask a colleague if he sent the fax. You expect the answer to be 'no'.
   You *didn't send the fax, did you?*
2 Ask a colleague if he sent the fax. You expect the answer to be 'yes'.
   You .... ?
3 Ask a stranger at the airport if his name is Mr Peters. You're not sure his name is Mr Peters.
   Your name .... ?
4 You recognise someone. You are sure his name is Mr Peters.
   Your name .... ?
5 You guess that Biotec have cancelled their order.
   Biotec .... ?
6 You are very surprised that Biotec have cancelled their order.
   Biotec .... ?

Exercise 3 E

Underline the correct words.

1 Could you tell me what *are your terms of payment/<u>your terms of payment are</u>?*
2 Do you know where *the marketing seminar is/is the marketing seminar*?
3 I'd like to know how *can we/we can* finance this project.
4 Could I ask you why *you left/did you leave* your last job?
5 Do you think *could I/I could* use your fax machine?

Exercise 4 F G

Rearrange the words to make questions.

1 to where are going you   *Where are you going to?*
2 from who did get you the information ....
3 in which funds do invest you ....
4 like what the weather was in Sweden ....

Exercise 5 A B C

25   Complete these dialogues with question tags.

A JOHN: Hi, Martha, we're due to meet next week (1) ...._aren't we_........ ? Well, I've just
remembered that I'm on holiday then. Can you make another time?

MARTHA: Yes, when are you free?

JOHN: Um, let's meet a fortnight on Tuesday, (2) .... ?

MARTHA: Let me look in my diary. Yes, that's fine − a fortnight on Tuesday.

B DAN: Luis will be arriving at the office at two, (3) .... ?

FRANK: No, at three.

DAN: Oh, right. Well, he's been here before, so he should know how to find the office,
(4) .... ?

FRANK: But that was before we moved buildings, (5) .... ?

DAN: Oh, yeah. I'll email him with directions to get here, then.

C STAN: These designs need to go to Norton Smith's office in Guildford today. They've got a
fax machine there, (6) .... ?

NICOLE: Yes, but it's not working. I'll send the document to them by first class post.

STAN: It'd be quicker if you sent it by courier, (7) .... ?

NICOLE: Oh, yes. I'll sort that out now.

D BRIDGET: This quote for the parts is much cheaper than the other one we had,
(8) .... ?

SERGE: Yes, much. It's very strange. They haven't forgotten to include delivery costs,
(9) .... ?

BRIDGET: No, everything is included in the price.

SERGE: Really? It all looks too good to be true, (10) .... ?

BRIDGET: Um, yes, well, let's give them a try anyway.

Exercise 6 B

Choose the most likely reply in each situation. Put a tick (✔).

1   If I go to Italy, I'm going to have problems with the language.
   a) Of course. You speak Italian, don't you? ☐
   b) Of course. You don't speak Italian, do you? ✔

2   In the meeting you said that our competitors had a better product than us.
   a) What! I said that, didn't I? ☐
   b) What! I didn't say that, did I? ☐

3   I haven't seen Ann for ages. I think she's working abroad.
   a) Yes, that's right. She's got a job in Spain, hasn't she? ☐
   b) Yes, that's right. She hasn't got a job in Spain, has she? ☐

4   The deadline for the project is Friday and there's still so much work to do.
   a) It's not looking good. We're going to make the deadline, aren't we? ☐
   b) It's not looking good. We're not going to make the deadline, are we? ☐

5   Do you mind if I help myself to some more couscous?
   a) No, of course not. You like Moroccan food, don't you? ☐
   b) No, of course not. You don't like Moroccan food, do you? ☐

6   We have to be at the airport at nine.
   a) You will be late, won't you? ☐
   b) You won't be late, will you? ☐

Conditionals 1

A Conditions and results

> *If you **buy** a personal computer today, there's a good chance that something **will** go wrong with it over the next couple of years. If your computer is dead on arrival, **try** to avoid getting involved with service departments. Instead, take it back and ask for a new one.*
> **(International Herald Tribune website)**

- Compare these sentences. The 'If ...' clause is the condition, and the other part of the sentence is the result.
  1 *If sales **increase** (generally), we **make** more profit.*
  2 *If sales **increase** (next quarter), we**'ll make** more profit.*
  3 *If sales **increased** (next quarter), we**'d make** more profit.*
  4 *If sales **increased** (last quarter), the Director **should** be happier.*
  5 *If sales **had increased** (last quarter), the Director **would have been** happier.*

- Sentence 1 is about something that is always true. See section B below.
  Sentence 2 is about something that is reasonably likely to happen in the future. See section C.
  Sentence 3 is about something that is imaginary or unlikely in the future. See section D.

- Sentences 4 and 5 are about the past. See unit 18.

- With all types of conditionals the *If* clause can come second.
  *We**'ll make** more profit if sales **increase**.*
  *We**'d make** more profit if sales **increased**.*

B *If we sell ... (always true)*

This is often called a 'zero' conditional

- When we want to talk about things that are always or generally true, we use:
  If/When + present,   present simple or imperative
     (condition)   (result)
  In this type of conditional we are not referring to one specific event.

  > *If people **understand** that change is necessary, **they have** an appetite for it. ... If you **don't get** the best people into the company, your product **suffers**.* (Business Week website)

- In the condition clause there can be a variety of present forms.
  ***When** you **fly** business class, you get much more legroom.*   (present simple)
  ***If** interest rates **are rising**, bank loans become more expensive.* (present continuous)
  ***When** you**'ve finished** the course, you get a certificate.*   (present perfect)

  In the result clause there can be a present simple (last examples) or an imperative.
  *When you fly business class, **don't drink** too much of the free alcohol.*

- Notice that we can use either *if* or *when* where the meaning is 'every time'.

C *If we sell ... (likely future)*

This is often called a 'first' conditional

- When we want to talk about future events that will happen, or are likely to happen, we use:
  If + present,   future or imperative
  (condition)   (result)

  > *If the compromise deal **fails**, who knows what **will happen** at Equitable Life?* (Telegraph website)

- In the condition clause there can be a variety of present forms.
  ***If** you **increase** your order, we'll give you a bigger discount.*   (present simple)
  ***If** you**'re meeting** her at three, I'll join you later at about four.* (present continuous)
  ***If** I**'ve made** any mistakes, I'll correct them later.*   (present perfect)

In the result clause *'ll* is common (last examples). We can also use other future forms or an imperative.

*If you increase your order, you**'re going to get** a bigger discount.*   (*going to* future)
*If he doesn't get the job, he**'ll have done** a lot of work for nothing.* (future perfect)
*If anyone from Head Office calls, **say** I'm in a meeting.*   (imperative)

● The examples above are about two actions in the future. If the result clause refers to the present we use a present tense.
*If anyone calls, **I'm** in a meeting all morning.*
*If you need me, **I'm working** in the room at the end of the corridor.*

D *If we sold ...* (imaginary future)

This is often called a 'second' conditional ● When we want to talk about future events that are imaginary, unlikely or impossible, we use:

If + past simple or continuous,   *would/could/might* + infinitive
         (condition)   (result)

*'Outsourcing is the only solution. **If we did** all of this stuff ourselves, **we would have to** have at least 1,000 people working here,' estimates Ardai.* (Business Week website)

● In the condition clause we can use a past simple or past continuous.
*If you **wanted** a quantity discount, you'd have to order at least 1,000 units.*
*If you **were still speaking** after an hour, the audience would probably be bored.*

● Note the past form in the condition clause, but the future time reference.

E *Unless*

● *Unless* means the same as *If ... not.*

*Polish attitudes are dominated by the belief that **unless** Poland joins the European Union, things **can** only get worse.* (Le Monde Diplomatique website)

Compare these sentences which have the same meaning:
***If** he does**n't** arrive soon, he'll miss the start of the presentation.*
***Unless** he arrives soon, he'll miss the start of the presentation.*

F Other modals

See unit 18 ● The modals used in this unit are mainly *will* and *would.* We can use all other modals like *can, could, must,* etc, with their normal meanings.

"On second thought, don't correct me if I'm wrong."

17 Practice

Exercise 1 B C D E

<u>Underline</u> the correct words.

1 If *we're*/*we would* be late, *they'll start*/*they'd start* without us.
2 If we *will take*/*take* a taxi, *we'll arrive*/*we arrive* sooner.
3 If we *worked*/*would work* for ADC, *we'll get*/*we'd get* a better salary.
4 When inflation *will go*/*goes* up, there *would be*/*is* usually pressure on salaries.
5 If we *don't hurry*/*won't hurry*, *we would be*/*we'll be* late.
6 If you *change*/*are changing* your mind, *give me*/*you will give me* a ring.
7 Unless you *click*/*would click* on that icon, *it didn't*/*it won't* print out.
8 If you *ordered*/*order* on the Net, we always *will send*/*send* an email confirmation.
9 If I *lend*/*will lend* you this book, when *do you return*/*will you return* it?
10 If you *heard*/*hear* anything in the next few days, *let me*/*letting me* know.

Exercise 2 C D

Read these sentences and decide if the events are likely or imaginary. Complete the sentences by putting the verbs in brackets into the present simple + *will* or the past simple + *would*. Use contracted forms where possible.

1 It's not far. If you ....*follow*........ (follow) this road, you ....*'ll come*...... (come) to the station.
2 If I ....*was*.......... (be) on the Board of this company, I ....*'d argue*..... (argue) against the merger.
3 If you .... (have) any questions, I .... (deal) with them at the end of my presentation.
4 If the council .... (ban) all cars from the city centre, there .... (not be) so much pollution.
5 A: I have no idea what the other side are going to propose in the negotiation tomorrow.
   B: Neither do I. If I .... (know), I .... (tell) you.
6 A: My train leaves in forty minutes.
   B: It only takes ten minutes to the station by taxi. If you .... (leave) now, you .... (catch) it.
7 A: Is that the time? I really should be going.
   B: If you .... (wait) a moment, I .... (give) you a lift.
8 A: Would you like to go to English evening classes with me?
   B: I'm sorry, but I can't. I'm really busy. If I .... (have) more time, I .... (love) to.

Exercise 3 B C D

Complete the sentences with the correct pair of possible forms, a) or b).

1 If the bank lends us the money, ...*a*... it in new machinery.
   a) *we'll invest*/*we're going to invest* b) *we'd invest*/*we were investing*
2 When .... a lot of orders, we always employ extra staff in the factory.
   a) *we'll get*/*we got* b) *we get*/*we've got*
3 If .... this project again, I think I'd do it differently.
   a) *I was starting*/*I started* b) *I'll start*/*I've started*
4 If the computer crashes, ... someone from the IT department.
   a) *you'd call*/*you are calling* b) *call*/*you'll have to call*

Exercise 4 B C D E

 26 Paula, a marketing manager of a car manufacturing company, is talking to her colleague Luis, a production manager. Complete their conversation with the words from the list below.

> will (x2)   won't (x2)   would (x2)   wouldn't   unless (x2)   be   is   is going to be   don't   didn't

PAULA: Luis. Aren't you worried about the proposed strike?

LUIS: Well, sure …

PAULA: You see, if the factory workers go on strike, we (1) ....`ll........... lose a lot of production. If we lose production, we (2) .... be able to supply all our customers.

LUIS: Yes, I know, but …

PAULA: And if we (3) .... supply our customers, they'll probably buy other makes of car. If that happens, our market share (4) .... go down. It's not looking good.

LUIS: Well, that's right, but …

PAULA: And what's more, in my experience, when workers go on strike there (5) .... a bad atmosphere for months afterwards.

LUIS: Yes.

PAULA: So, (6) .... you can come to an agreement with the workers soon, there (7) .... a lot of trouble ahead. If you want my advice, (8) .... very careful.

LUIS: Look, don't worry.

PAULA: Don't worry?

LUIS: Yes. Look, the workers know that the success of the company depends on this new model. (9) .... they're stupid, they (10) .... go on strike.

PAULA: Oh?

LUIS: Now, just imagine – if it sold really well, we (11) .... increase our market share and our profits. If that happened, we (12) .... need to make so many job cuts. And if we (13) .... have to cut jobs, the trade unions (14) .... be much happier.

PAULA: Well, I suppose you've got a point.

Exercise 5 B C D

You are talking to a friend about your new job. Use your thoughts to complete the sentences you say. Put the verb in brackets into either the present simple, past simple, imperative, *will* + infinitive or *would* + infinitive.

You think: *People say that hard work usually results in promotion in this company.*
You say: (1) They say that if you ..work... (work) hard, you .get. (get) promoted.
You think: *I want to show them that I'm good at my job so that I can have more job security.*
You say: (2) I hope that if I .... (do) my best, they .... (give) me a permanent contract after a few months.
You think: *I've been late in the morning a few times. I wish I could work at the Leiria site which is nearer my home.*
You say: (3) I'm sometimes late for work. If I .... (work) at the Leiria site, it .... (not be) such a problem.
You think: *One thing worries me. I had a health problem a few years ago, but it's very unlikely that it will reoccur.*
You say: (4) I wonder what .... (happen) if my health problem .... (reoccur)?
You think: *Maybe it's not a problem. In general they seem to be very reasonable about illness.*
You say: (5) Actually, if you .... (miss) one or two days because of illness, they .... (not seem) to mind.
You think: *Goodbye. I hope I'll see you soon.*
You say: (6) If you .... (fancy) a drink one evening, just .... (give) me a ring.

If these countries **had remained** outside the euro, they **wouldn't have had** the same degree of economic stability.
(**Economist website**)

18 Conditionals 2

A *If we sold ...* (possible past)

- When we want to talk about past events which possibly happened, we use *If* + past simple in the condition clause, and any tense or modal in the result clause.
  If you went to the meeting yesterday, you probably **heard** the news.
  If you missed the TV programme last night, you **can borrow** the recording I made.

B *If we had sold ...* (imaginary past)

This is often called a 'third' conditional

- When we want to talk about past events that are different to what really happened, we use:
  If + past perfect,   *would* + *have* + past participle
      (condition)   (result)

  *If Clinton and Gore **had won** the election, they **would have promoted** free trade agreements with other nations in the same way as Bush.* (Yahoo Business News website)

  There is often a suggestion of criticism or regret:
  *If the economic situation **had been** better, we **wouldn't have lost** so many customers.*

- A contracted *'d* in speech can be *had* in the condition or *would* in the result.
  *If **I'd done** an MBA, **I'd have had** more opportunities.*

- The examples above are about two actions in the past. If the result clause refers to the present we use *would* + infinitive.
  *If **I had done** an MBA, **I would be** on a higher salary now.*

C Conditionals without *if*

- We use *if* for something that might happen in the future, or something imaginary. We use *when* for something that we know will happen.
  *I'll call you **if** I get a chance.* (I'm not sure if I will phone you)
  *I'll call you **when** I arrive.*   (I will definitely phone you)

  We can use either *if* or *when* where the meaning is 'every time'.
  ***If/When** anyone rings my mobile, I get a photograph of the person on the screen.*

- In informal speech we sometimes use *imagine* or *supposing* in place of *if*.
  ***Imagine/Supposing you had** a million dollars, how **would** you invest it?*

- We can use *provided that, providing, on condition that, as long as* and *so long as* for emphasis. The meaning is 'if and only if'.
  As long as there is new technology, consultants will continue to be in demand. (Sunday Times website)

- We can use *in case* to talk about doing something to avoid a possible problem later. The result clause usually comes first and often uses *going to*.
  *I'm going to give you my mobile number **in case** you need to contact me.*

See unit 17
- We use *unless* to mean *If not*.

D *Wish*

- We use *I wish* to express regret or dissatisfaction.

- For the present and future, use *I wish* followed by the past simple or continuous.
  I wish we ***didn't*** *have so many meetings.*
  I wish *I* ***wasn't working*** *next weekend.*

- For the past, use *I wish* followed by the past perfect.
  I wish *we* ***had advertised*** *on television.*
  I wish *I* ***hadn't eaten*** *the oysters.*

- If the wish is a good one, use *I hope* followed by the present simple or *will*.
  I hope *your presentation* ***goes*** *well.*
  I hope *the merger* ***will*** *be a success.*

- If the wish is about doing something that is difficult or impossible, use *I wish I could*.
  I wish *I* ***could*** *contact him, but he hasn't got a mobile phone.*

- We can replace *I wish* with *If only* for emphasis. We stress *only* in speech.
  If only *I* ***hadn't*** *eaten the oysters.*
  If only *I* ***could*** *contact him.*

E Modal verbs in conditionals

See units 11–14
for modal verbs
- The examples in unit 17 were with *will*. But other modal verbs like *can, could, may, might, must* and *should* are common in conditional sentences and have their normal meanings.

  ***If you deal with** the Middle East **you must be** available to your customers on Saturdays and Sundays.* (Overseas Trade magazine)

  ***If** the euro **were** weak in the long term, companies **might** slow down their drive to increase productivity and governments **might** put the brake on their structural reforms.* (Le Monde diplomatique website)

  *Compaq CEO Michael Capellas commented on the recent decline of dot.com firms, which were so popular on the U.S. stock market a few months ago. '**If you don't have** a sound business plan, **you cannot succeed**.'* (International Herald Tribune website)

- We often use present forms like *will* and *can* with likely futures, and past forms like *would* (*'d*) and *could* with imaginary futures.
  *If you **sign** now, we**'ll/can** deliver by Friday.*   (likely future)
  *If you **signed** now, we**'d/could** deliver by Friday.* (imaginary future)

- But it is also common to find mixed tense sequences because modals keep their normal meanings:

  ***If** Hungarian farmers **respond** to competition by improving productivity and becoming more efficient at marketing, they **could have** a bigger share of the market.* (Business Central Europe website)

  With a present form (*respond*) we might expect *can*. However *could* is used here with its normal meaning of uncertainty (*can* does not express uncertainty).

F *If I were you, ...*

- We can use *If I were* in place of *If I was* in imaginary futures, particularly when we give advice with the phrase *If I were you*.
  If I were you, *I'd wait until tomorrow.*
  *I'd be more careful, **if I were you**.*

18 Practice

Exercise 1 B F unit 17

<u>Underline</u> the correct words. This exercise includes revision of imaginary futures.

1 If you *phoned*/<u>*had phoned*</u> me yesterday, *I had told*/<u>*would have told*</u> you.

2 If you *took*/*would have taken* more exercise, you *might feel*/*had felt* better.

3 If Tim *would have listened*/*had listened* more carefully, he *wouldn't have made*/*didn't make* that mistake.

4 If *we'd found*/*we found* suitable premises, *we'd have moved*/*we had moved* earlier.

5 If people *kept*/*had kept* their offices more tidy, it *might present*/*presented* a better image to our visitors.

6 If *I'd known*/*I would know* about their financial problems, I *wouldn't do*/*wouldn't have done* business with them.

7 If our side *had been*/*was* better prepared, we *succeeded*/*could have succeeded* in the negotiations.

8 I *wouldn't*/*won't worry* if I *am*/*were* you.

Exercise 2 C

Complete the sentences with the words from the list below. Each word is used twice.

> when   as long as   in case   unless

1 I'll speak to you again ....**when**...... I've looked at the contract in detail.

2 Leave your return flight open .... the negotiations take an extra day.

3 We can start the project next week .... everyone agrees.

4 We can start the project next week .... anyone disagrees.

5 The Board will be happy .... our share price remains high.

6 Keep your receipt .... you need to return the goods.

7 The new stock will arrive .... the Christmas sales are finished.

8 We'll probably make a loss this year .... sales improve in the last quarter.

Exercise 3 D

<u>Underline</u> the correct words.

1   I wish I <u>*hadn't drunk*</u>/*didn't drink* so many whiskies last night.

2   There's so little space in here. I wish I *have*/*had* a bigger office.

3   I don't feel well. I wish I *could stay*/*will stay* in bed this morning.

4   I hope you *enjoyed*/*enjoy* yourselves at the theatre tonight.

5   I've been waiting thirty minutes for the bus. I wish I *took*/*had taken* a taxi.

6   I must get in touch with Sue. If only I *know*/*knew* her number!

7   I'm not a good typist. I wish I *could type*/*would type* better.

8   I wish Jim *didn't interrupt*/*doesn't interrupt* so often in meetings.

9   I have to finish this report by tomorrow. If only I *would have*/*had* more time.

10 Enjoy your holiday. I hope you *have*/*could have* a good time.

11 That presentation was a disaster! I wish I *could do*/*would do* it all again!

12 I'm disappointed with this camera. I wish I *didn't buy*/*hadn't bought* it.

Exercise 4 B C E

27 Patrick and Jurgen are discussing a negotiation that went wrong. Complete the dialogue with words from the list below.

~~if~~   as long as   in case   unless (x2)   'll   'd (x2)   can   would have   'd have   wouldn't have

PATRICK: Jurgen, (1) ....if.......... you've got a moment, (2) .... I have a word with you?

JURGEN: Sure. (3) .... it doesn't take too long, I've got a meeting in five minutes. Is it about that contract that we lost?

PATRICK: Yes. What went wrong? Do you think we (4) .... got the deal if we (5) .... offered a better price? Maybe we (6) .... lost the business.

JURGEN: No, I don't think the problem was the price.

PATRICK: No? Well, was it a problem with the delivery time? If we (7) .... given a shorter delivery time, (8) .... we .... been more successful?

JURGEN: No, the delivery time was OK.

PATRICK: Hmm, this is strange. We really should find out what went wrong (9) .... a situation like this happens in the future. You know, (10) .... we learn from our mistakes, we (11) .... lose more orders. Now, Jurgen, tell me what do you think could really have happened?

JURGEN: Well, nothing, (12) .... they didn't like our sales rep.

PATRICK: Oh?

JURGEN: Do you know who it was?

PATRICK: Er, it was me.

Exercise 5 B E unit 17

A supplier is thinking about a negotiation in the future. Match his thoughts 1–4 with his words a)–d).

1 We're likely to offer a lower price. If we do, success is possible.	**b**	a) If we offer a lower price, we'll get the contract.
2 We're likely to offer a lower price. If we do, success is certain.	☐	b) If we offer a lower price, we might get the contract.
3 Perhaps we'll offer a lower price. If we do, success is possible.	☐	c) If we offered a lower price, we'd get the contract.
4 Perhaps we'll offer a lower price. If we do, success is certain.	☐	d) If we offered a lower price, we might get the contract.

The same supplier is thinking about a negotiation in the past. Match his thoughts 5–8 with his words e)–h).

5 We offered a lower price. That's why we succeeded.	☐	e) If we'd offered a lower price, we'd have got the contract.
6 We offered a lower price. That's probably why we succeeded.	☐	f) If we'd offered a lower price, we might have got the contract.
7 We didn't offer a lower price. That's why we failed.	☐	g) If we hadn't offered a lower price, we'd have lost the contract.
8 We didn't offer a lower price. That's probably why we failed.	☐	h) If we hadn't offered a lower price, we might have lost the contract.

19 Verb + *-ing* or infinitive 1

A Verb + *-ing*

- Some verbs are followed by an *-ing* form. Some of the commonest verbs follow below:

  As manufacturers **consider automating** their distribution channels, they should not lose sight of the effectiveness of personal contact. (IndustryWeek website)

  Auto manufacturers are concerned consumers will **postpone buying** cars until after next July, when the current 22% sales tax on autos is expected to fall. (Business Review Weekly website)

  Van der Hoeve, CEO of Royal Ahold, **spends** 50 per cent of his time **travelling** and **getting onto** the sales floor as much as possible. As he explains: 'I usually get a good feel for the store as I walk around'. (Eurobusiness website)

saying and thinking	admit*, consider*, deny*, describe, imagine*, mention*, suggest*
liking and disliking	dislike, enjoy, fancy, (not) mind*
phrasal verbs	carry on, give up, keep on, put off
phrase with *can't*	can't bear, can't help, can't resist, can't face, can't stand
other common verbs	avoid, delay, finish, involve, keep, miss, postpone, practise, risk
common phrases	It's not worth ..., spend/waste time/money ...
	It's no use/good ..., There's no point (in) ...,

- Some of the verbs in the list can also be followed by a noun. These include: *admit, deny, imagine, suggest, dislike, enjoy, fancy, keep, mind, practise*.
  The Minister **admitted taking** a bribe.   and   The Minister **admitted** his **mistake**.
  What do you **fancy doing** this evening?   and   I **fancy** a nice, cold **beer**.

  The group of verbs with *can't* can also be followed by a noun.
  I **can't bear** avant-garde **jazz**.

- We use *mind* in questions and negative sentences.
  A: Do you **mind waiting** a moment?
  B: No, I **don't mind**.

- *Go* and *come* plus *-ing* form are often used for sports and outside activities.
  I often **go skiing** in the winter.
  Do you want to **come shopping** with me?

- Some verbs and verb phrases have *to* as a preposition. These include: *look forward to, object to, be used to, get used to, respond to*. Prepositions are always followed by the *-ing* form.
  I'm **looking forward to seeing** you next week. (NOT ~~to see~~)
  After a few months in the UK I **got used to driving** on the left. (NOT ~~to drive~~)

B Verb + *to* + infinitive

- Some verbs are followed by *to* + infinitive.

  'PCCW has openly stated that it **wishes to become** the biggest broadband player in Asia,' says Richard Ferguson, a telecom analyst in Hong Kong. 'That means it cannot **afford to stand still**.' (Asiaweek website)

  'And by working together with the guys at IBM, Kodak and so on, we're actually **managing to improve** the local supply base for all of us.' says Jaime Reyes, head of Hewlett-Packard's printer operations. (Global Business Magazine website)

plans and decisions	*aim, arrange, choose, decide*, intend, plan*, prepare*
expectations	*demand*, deserve, expect*, hope*, want, wish*, would like*
promises and refusals	*fail, guarantee, offer, promise*, refuse, threaten*
other common verbs	*agree*, can/can't afford, learn*, manage, pretend*, seem*, tend, train, wait*

● Note that verb + *to* + infinitive is also used in these cases:

See unit 42 1 To explain why we do something (the 'infinitive of purpose')

*I'm calling **to find out** if you stock spare parts.* (NOT ~~for to find out~~)

2 After a question word

*Can you show me **how to get on** to the Internet on this computer?*

See units 4, 7, 11, 12 3 With *used to, be going to, be able to, be allowed to, have to, need to* and *ought to*.

C Verb + object + *to* + infinitive

● The following verbs are followed by an object + *to* + infinitive.

advise*, allow, ask, cause, encourage, expect, forbid, force, help, invite, order, pay, prefer, persuade, remind*, teach*, tell*, train, want, warn*

*Russia will **ask the Paris Club of creditors to postpone** the signing of bilateral agreements on the repayment of debt.* (Delovoj Peterburg website)

*Li also **persuaded four banks**, including HSBC Holdings and Bank of China, **to lend** him $11 billion, a record in Hong Kong.* (Asiaweek website)

D *Make* and *let*

● After *make* and *let* we use the bare infinitive without *to*.

*I **made** them **check** everything very carefully.* (NOT ~~I made them to check~~)

*They **let** us **have** all these free samples.* (NOT ~~They let us to have~~)

E Verb + *that* clause

● The verbs marked with an asterisk* in sections A, B and C can also be followed by a *that* clause. In everyday speech we can leave out the word *that*.

*I suggested **speaking** to Eliza about it.*	*I suggested **(that) we could** speak to Eliza about it.*
*We decided **to cancel** the meeting.*	*We decided **(that) we would cancel** the meeting.*
*They told us **to wait**.*	*They told us **(that) we should wait**.*

"Gentlemen, I've called this meeting
to discuss absenteeism."

19 Practice

Exercise 1 A B

Underline the correct words.

1　We can't afford *to miss*/*missing* this opportunity.
2　Do you fancy *to go*/*going* for a drink after work?
3　Are you waiting *to use*/*using* the phone?
4　It's not worth *to spend*/*spending* any more time on this.
5　We decided *to close down*/*closing down* the factory in Belgium.
6　You promised *to deliver*/*delivering* by April, and it's now May.
7　I considered *to call*/*calling* him, but I decided it was better to write.
8　If we don't decide soon, we risk *to lose*/*losing* the whole contract.
9　She agreed *to prepare*/*preparing* some figures before the next meeting.
10　I'm sorry, there seems *to be*/*being* a misunderstanding here.
11　Is Mr Messier busy? OK, I don't mind *to wait*/*waiting* for a few minutes.
12　He refused *to sign*/*signing* the contract until he'd spoken to his boss.
13　May I suggest *to postpone*/*postponing* the meeting until next week?

Exercise 2 A B

Complete these sentences with the verbs from the list below. Choose either the *-ing* form or *to* + infinitive.

~~give~~　write　fly　receive　make　recognise　advertise　help　think　speak

1　They agreed ....*to give*....... us thirty more days to pay the invoice.
2　He pretended .... me, but I don't think he knew who I was.
3　There's no point .... this brand on TV, it would cost too much.
4　We're expecting .... some more stock early next week.
5　I'll join you later. I need to finish .... this report.
6　I learnt .... Portuguese when I worked in Brazil.
7　I work in public relations. My job involves .... contact with the media.
8　I can't help .... that something is going to go wrong.
9　I can't afford .... business class all the time.
10　I can't promise .... you with this problem, but I'll do my best.

Exercise 3 C

Complete the following sentences with verbs from the list below. Include an object in every case.

~~advise~~　remind　persuade　expect　help　encourage　force

1　I'm sorry I missed work yesterday. The doctor ...*advised me to*... stay in bed.
2　I tried to .... come with us tonight, but he said he was busy.
3　Could you .... call Head Office later? I might forget.
4　If you employ a secretary, it will .... deal with all the paperwork.
5　She hasn't called yet, but I .... contact me some time today.
6　I didn't feel very confident, but she .... apply for the job.
7　The fall in demand has .... make some of our best workers redundant.

Exercise 4 A B C

 28   Complete the mini-dialogue by putting the verbs in brackets into the correct form, using *-ing* or *to +* infinitive.

ISABEL: Oh, no, not again.

FERNANDA: What's wrong?

ISABEL: My computer's crashed. It keeps (1) .....doing..... (do) it. I have to save my documents every few minutes or I risk (2) .... (lose) all the work I've just done.

FERNANDA: Have you got enough disk space?

ISABEL: Yeah, I have. I really don't know what's causing it (3) .... (crash) so often. Look, you're good at computers. What do you advise me (4) .... (do)?

FERNANDA: Well, I don't know. I haven't been trained (5) .... (fix) them. You'll have to ask an IT technician (6) .... (come) and have a look at it.

ISABEL: Hah. You know, there's no point (7) .... (call) a technician – they'll be ages and I … I really can't afford (8) .... (wait) all day for someone to come, I'm really busy.

FERNANDA: Why don't you phone the helpdesk then? They'll advise you what (9) .... (do) over the phone.

ISABEL: Oh, yeah. I suppose so.

FERNANDA: And if you're really that busy, have you considered (10) .... (ask) Sophie to help you, she hasn't got a lot of work at the moment.

ISABEL: Oh, hasn't she? That's great. I'll ask her (11) .... (type) up this report. Thanks.

Exercise 5 A B

Complete this email that circulated in a company that makes mobile phones. Choose a verb from the list below and use the correct form, *-ing* or infinitive with *to*.

~~interview~~   be   pay   pretend   receive   refer   show   take   talk   worry

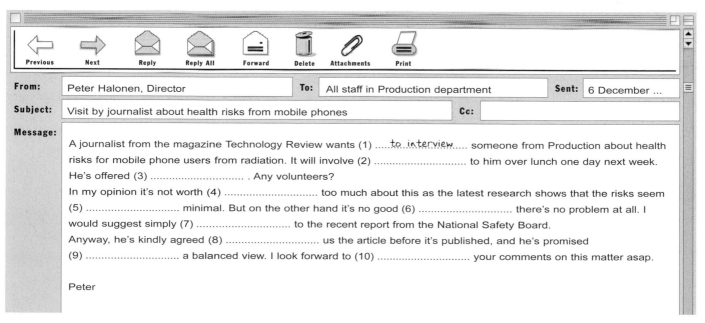

From: Peter Halonen, Director   **To:** All staff in Production department   **Sent:** 6 December …

Subject: Visit by journalist about health risks from mobile phones   **Cc:**

Message:

A journalist from the magazine Technology Review wants (1) .....to interview..... someone from Production about health risks for mobile phone users from radiation. It will involve (2) .... to him over lunch one day next week. He's offered (3) .... Any volunteers?

In my opinion it's not worth (4) .... too much about this as the latest research shows that the risks seem (5) .... minimal. But on the other hand it's no good (6) .... there's no problem at all. I would suggest simply (7) .... to the recent report from the National Safety Board.

Anyway, he's kindly agreed (8) .... us the article before it's published, and he's promised (9) .... a balanced view. I look forward to (10) .... your comments on this matter asap.

Peter

 20 Verb + *-ing* or infinitive 2

A Verb + *-ing* or infinitive: change in meaning

> *The 21st century may see the emergence of a kind of 'welfare capitalism', in which corporations **try to recruit** and **retain** employees by providing services that in another era were provided by government agencies or families:*
>
> **(Business Week website)**

- Some verbs can be followed by *-ing* or *to* + infinitive and the meaning of the verb changes.

- REMEMBER AND FORGET We use *remember/forget doing* for memories of the past (the action happens before the remembering). We use *remember/forget to do* for actions someone is/was supposed to do (the remembering happens before the action).

*I definitely **remember posting** the letter.*	post	◄——— remember
*I must **remember to post** the letter.*	remember	———► post
*I'll never **forget flying** into Taipei airport.*	flying	◄——— forget
*Sorry, I **forgot to turn off** the lights.*	forget	———► turn off

- REGRET We use *regret doing* when we are sorry about something that happened in the past.
  *I **regret saying** no to the job in Paris.*
  We use *regret to inform/to tell* when we are giving bad news.
  *I **regret to inform** you that we are unable to ...*

- TRY We use *try doing* when we do something and see what happens. We use *try to do* when we make an effort to do something, but don't necessarily succeed.
  *I'll **try talking** to him and maybe he'll change his mind.* (I'll do it and see what happens)
  *I'll **try to talk** to him but I know he's very busy today.* (I may not be successful)

  *Last September, Breuer **tried to negotiate** a cost-cutting merger of Deutsche's and Dresdner's retail operations. However, he was unsuccessful.* (BusinessWeek Online website)

- STOP We use *stop doing* when we end an action. We use *stop to do* when we give the reason for stopping.
  *We **stopped buying** from that supplier.* (now we don't buy from them)
  *I **stopped to buy** something for my wife.* (I stopped in order to buy something)

- MEAN We use *mean doing* when one thing results in or involves another. We use *mean to do* to express an intention.
  *Globalisation **means being** active in every major market.* (= involves)
  *I **meant to phone** you, but I forgot.* (= intended)

- GO ON We use *go on doing* when we continue doing something. We use *go on to do* when we move on to do something else.
  *They **went on trading** even though they were nearly bankrupt.* (= did the same thing)
  *After leaving IBM he **went on to start** his own company.* (= did something else)

B Verbs of perception

- Verbs of perception include: *feel, hear, listen to, notice, see, watch*. These verbs can be followed by an object + *-ing* or a bare infinitive (without *to*) and the meaning of the verb changes.

- If we see or hear only part of the action, or it continues, we use the *-ing* form. If we see or hear the whole action from beginning to end, we use the bare infinitive without *to*. Compare:
  *I **saw** her **giving** her presentation.* (I saw part of the presentation)
  *I **saw** her **give** her presentation.* (I saw the whole presentation)
  *I **heard** the machine **making** a strange noise.* (I heard the noise and it continued)
  *I **heard** the machine **make** a strange noise.* (I heard the noise and it stopped)

C Verb + -*ing* or infinitive: little change in meaning

● Some verbs can be followed by -*ing* or *to* + infinitive and there is little change in meaning. These include: *begin, continue, intend, start.*
*What do you **intend doing/to do** about it?*

*In the second quarter, when the market **began to go down**, we **began selling**, dropping our equity position in the fund to around 70% and holding the remainder in cash. This way, I was able to minimize the impact of the downturn.* (Asiaweek website)

*The number of German jobless **continued to fall** in February.* (Wall Street Journal website)

● We do not usually have two -*ing* forms together.
*It **was starting to get** dark.* (NOT ~~starting getting~~)

*The business community is again **starting to pay** very close attention to the country's economic health.* (Global Business Magazine website)

● The verbs *like, love, prefer, hate* can be followed by either form. *To* + infinitive suggests something is a good/bad idea. The -*ing* form shows your feelings.
*I **like to do** my tax returns early, but I **don't like doing** them.*

When we use the modal *would* with these verbs we must use *to* + infinitive.
***I'd prefer to do** it myself, if you don't mind.*

Like followed by *to* + infinitive can mean that we do something because we think it is a good idea, even though we don't enjoy it.
*I **like to write** several drafts before I write the final report.*

D Passive forms: -*ing* or infinitive

● Unit 19 gave lists of verbs that are followed by either an -*ing* form or *to* + infinitive. Only the active forms were given.

● The passive form of 'verb + -*ing*' is verb + *being* + past participle.
*If the share price falls any more we **risk being taken over** by a larger company.*

● The passive form of 'verb + *to* + infinitive' is verb + *to be* + past participle.
*I think I **deserve to be given** a pay rise.*

"Actually, the boss is away on vacation - but he likes
to remind everyone he's still in charge."

20 Practice

Exercise 1 A

Underline the correct words.

1   I'm sorry I forgot *to call*/*calling* you, but I was really busy.
2   I stopped in Paris for a few days *to meet*/*meeting* Henri.
3   We've stopped *to meet*/*meeting* so often. It was a waste of time.
4   Learning a language means *to be*/*being* interested in the culture as well.
5   I meant *to make*/*making* some more photocopies, but I didn't have time.
6   Please remember *to speak*/*speaking* to Josie when you see her.
7   I don't remember *to say*/*saying* anything like that.
8   I tried *to open*/*opening* the window, but it was too high to reach.
9   I tried *to open*/*opening* the window, but it was still too hot in the room.
10   I'll never forget *to give*/*giving* my first presentation to the Board.
11   Don't forget *to look at*/*looking at* the audience when you speak.
12   We regret *to announce*/*announcing* the death of our founder, Mr Obuchi.
13   I regret *to quit*/*quitting* my MBA course.
14   The new product is doing really well. I think we should go on *to sell*/*selling* it for another six months at least.
15   First I'll say a little about the history of the company, then I'll go on *to describe*/*describing* our new range of products.

Exercise 2 B

Match the situations a)–d) to the sentences 1–4 below.

a)   I heard part of your conversation.
b)   I saw your whole presentation.
c)   I saw the whole tour.
d)   I passed them in the corridor.

1   Sorry to interrupt, but I heard you talking about e-books. ☐
2   I heard you talk about e-books at the Internet seminar. ☐
3   I saw Barbara showing the visitors round the factory. ☐
4   I saw Barbara show the visitors our new production line. ☐

Exercise 3 D unit 19

Complete the sentences with *being* or *to be*.

1   I enjoy ....*being*.... taken out for expensive meals.
2   The Minister denied .... given a bribe.
3   The Minister refused .... questioned about the bribe.
4   I expect .... asked some tough questions after my presentation.
5   Do you mind .... picked up at the airport by a taxi?
6   How awful! Imagine .... asked to give a presentation on a topic like that!

Exercise 4 A C

 29   Complete the mini-dialogue with the correct form of the verb in brackets. On two occasions both forms are possible.

THOMAS: Hi, Carla. I've been meaning (1) ...to speak... (speaking / to speak) to you all day. We're trying (2) .... (booking / to book) a table at that new Chinese restaurant tonight. Would you like to come too?

CARLA: Oh, thanks, I'd really like to, but I was intending (3) .... (starting / to start) work on my monthly sales report tonight.

THOMAS: Really? Wouldn't you prefer (4) .... (coming / to come) out with us? Just this once?

CARLA: Of course I want (5) .... (going / to go) out with you tonight, but I really have to get this report done. I'm sorry it means (6) .... (missing / to miss) dinner with you guys tonight.

THOMAS: Well, perhaps next time then.

CARLA: Yeah. And next time don't forget (7) .... (giving / to give) me as much notice as possible beforehand so I can keep the evening free.

THOMAS: Oh, the trouble with you, Carla, is that you never stop (8) .... (working / to work). You should remember (9) .... (having / to have) some fun sometimes.

CARLA: Look, Thomas, you know I'd really love (10) .... (joining / to join) you, but I just …

THOMAS: Well, if you go on (11) .... (working / to work) like you do at the moment, you'll start (12) .... (getting / to get) really stressed, and then you'll regret (13) .... (missing out / to miss out) on your social life. It happened to a friend of mine – in the end he went on (14) .... (having / to have) a nervous breakdown.

CARLA: Oh, come on. Stop (15) .... (being / to be) so dramatic. I don't enjoy (16) .... (taking / to take) work home, it's just that I like (17) .... (finishing / to finish) my reports on time.

Exercise 5 A unit 19

Complete this letter by putting the verbs in brackets into the correct form, -*ing* or *to* + infinitive.

Dear Audio World

I am writing to complain about the poor service that I received when I was in your store last week. Recently you decided (1) ...to remove.. (remove) listening facilities in your stores, and your sales staff encouraged customers (2) .... (take) home their choice of CDs without (3) .... (hear) them first. You invited us (4) .... (return) any CDs that we did not like, as long as we kept the receipt as proof of purchase. In my opinion this was an excellent policy as it allowed customers (5) .... (risk) (6) .... (buy) things that were a little different.

A consequence of your policy is that customers will buy more CDs, and this means (7) .... (return) more that they don't like. In fact last week I brought back eight CDs, from the fourteen I had bought on the previous visit. Your salesman refused (8) .... (accept) such a large number, and accused me of (9) .... (take) the CDs home just (10) .... (copy) them. I strongly objected to (11) .... (be) treated like this as I had remembered (12) .... (bring) the receipts with me and my actions were within the terms of your guarantee.

I can't help (13) .... (think) that you will lose a lot of business if your staff go on (14) .... (behave) in this way, and I advise you (15) .... (train) your staff (16) .... (deal) with customers in a more polite manner.

Yours sincerely

Ian Carr

21 Reported speech 1

A Reported speech

Czech central bank Governor Josef Tosovsky **said** on Thursday that **he had withdrawn** his candidacy to become a vice president of the European Bank for Reconstruction and Development (EBRD).
(czechtoday website)

● We often tell people what other people have said. This is called reported or indirect speech. We very rarely try to report the exact words that someone says. Usually we give the general meaning with a summary.

'Look, I've been phoning all day and he's always in a meeting. Can you tell him that I'll give him a call sometime next week, please?' (actual words)

→ *Sandra phoned. She said she'd call you next week.* (report)

'From what I can see, the advertising campaign is a great success.' (actual words)

→ *He said the campaign was a success.* (report)

● Note the change of tense in the above examples: *will* to *would* and *is* to *was*.

It is not always necessary to change tenses. If the statement is still true we can keep the same tense as the original.

He said the campaign was a great success. (the campaign is finished)

He said the campaign is/was a great success. (the campaign is still happening)

See sections B and C below for more details.

● In writing we can repeat the exact words using speech marks (' ... ').

'I have no further comment to make at this stage,' said the company press officer when he spoke to our reporter yesterday.

● This unit uses *said* as the reporting verb. See unit 22 for other reporting verbs.

B Tense changes

● When the verb tense changes it 'moves back' in time.

Actual words	Report (Indirect speech)
*'I **work** for IBM'*	*She said she **worked** for IBM.*
*'I'm **working** for IBM'*	*She said she **was working** for IBM.*
*'I've **worked** for IBM'*	*She said she **had worked** for IBM.*
*'I've **been working** for IBM'*	*She said she **had been working** for IBM.*
*'I **worked** for IBM'*	*She said she **had worked** for IBM.*
	OR *She said she **worked** for IBM.*
*'I **had worked** for IBM'*	*She said she **had worked** for IBM.*
*'I'm **going to work** for IBM.'*	*She said she **was going to work** for IBM.*
*'I **can/will/may work** for IBM.'*	*She said she **could/would/might work** for IBM.*

*Kiwwi, a Vienna-based telecoms company, said on Friday **it was entering** the Czech market by offering cheaper voice services through the Internet.* (czechtoday website)

*Earlier in the week, a labor union report said that 751 deaths **had occurred** 'on the job' in Italy during the first six months of this year, up from 621 for the same period last year.* (International Herald Tribune website)

*The Shading Aluminum Industry Co. said last week it **would issue** 160 million shares for listing on the Shanghai Stock Exchange.* (Shanghai Daily website)

● There is no change for *must, might, could, should, would*.

● Note that if the actual words were in the past simple (*worked*), the report can change or stay the same.

● Note that there is no change for the past perfect (*had worked*).

C No tense change

● We do not need to change tense if the information is still true.
   *'The sales team **are doing** very well at the moment.'*
   *He **says/said** the team **are** doing very well.*

● We do not need to change tense if we report something which is always true.
   *'There **is** always a period of uncertainty after a merger.'*
   *He **says/said** there **is** always a period of uncertainty after a merger.*

D People, places, times and things

● In reported speech references to people, places, times and things often change, because the point of view changes.

   *'**I**'ll see **you here tomorrow**,' said Sue.*   *'**I**'ve read **your** report about **this** project,' he said.*

   *Sue said **she**'d see **me there the next day**.*   *He said **he**'d read **my** report about **the** project.*

● The examples in the previous paragraph show some of these typical changes:

People:	*I*	→ *he/she*
	you	→ *me*
	my	→ *his/her*
	your	→ *my*
Place:	*here*	→ *there, at the office*
Times:	*now*	→ *then, at that time*
	today	→ *that day, on Monday*
	yesterday	→ *the day before, the previous day*
	tomorrow	→ *the next day, the following day, on Monday*
	this afternoon	→ *that afternoon*
	last week	→ *the week before, the previous week*
	next week	→ *the week after, the following week*
	a few days ago	→ *a few days before, a few days earlier*
Things:	*this project*	→ *the project*

"Remember when I said I was going to be honest with you, Jeff? That was a big, fat lie."

21   Practice

Exercise 1 B

Write the actual words that each person says. Use contractions where possible.

1   Anna said that she had already finished.
   (Anna's actual words) ' I've already finished .... '

2   She said he would be back after lunch.
   (Her actual words) ' .... '

3   He said she was going to contact the printers.
   (His actual words) ' .... '

4   Paul said that he wanted to make a phone call.
   (Paul's actual words) ' .... '

5   She said she was meeting the bank manager at eleven.
   (Her actual words) ' .... '

6   Pierre said he had found out about the problem a long time ago.
   (Pierre's actual words) ' .... '

7   David said he had to be back in the office by three thirty.
   (David's actual words) ' .... '

8   Jan said she would let me know.
   (Jan's actual words) ' .... '

Exercise 2 D

Look at the actual words spoken. <u>Underline</u> the correct words in the reported version.

1   (Helen's words) 'I won't do it until tomorrow.'
   Helen said I/<u>she</u> wouldn't do it until the previous/<u>following</u> day.

2   (Peter's words) 'It's very busy in here. I'll call you later.'
   Peter said it was very busy here/there, and he'd call me/him later.

3   (The sales manager's words) 'We received your order last week.'
   He said they'd/we'd received our/their order the week after/before.

4   (Mel Bowen's words) 'I'm sorry about the delay, I'll deal with this now.'
   She said she/I was sorry about the delay, and she'd deal with it right then/later.

Exercise 3 B D

Rewrite the sentences in reported speech. Use contractions where possible.

1   'I won't put it in the sales because it's selling very well,' she said.
   She said she wouldn't put it in the sales because it was selling very well.

2   'I've read the report and I don't understand section 4,' he said.
   He said ....

3   'When I finish my presentation, I'm going to have a drink,' he said.
   He said that when ....

4   'I'm preparing the figures but I won't be long,' she said.
   She said ....

5   'I like playing tennis, but I don't do it very often,' she said.
   She said ....

6   'I'm going to visit our Polish subsidiary, but I'm not sure when,' she said.
   She said ....

Exercise 4 B C

Read the words spoken in a conference presentation about the role of the Chief Executive Officer.

> *'Jack Welch, one of the most famous CEOs of all time, was head of General Electric for twenty years. But he was an exception. In fact, two-thirds of all major companies worldwide have replaced their CEO over the last five years. What's the reason? The reason is that expectations of CEO performance are far too high. Boards of companies look at their CEO as a kind of superhero who can solve all the company's problems. This process started in the 1980s, and the prototype was Lee Iaccoca, "the man who saved Chrysler Corp". Then in the 1990s, we had CEOs from the technology sector, like Microsoft's Bill Gates, or Cisco's John Chambers, who managed to produce constantly rising share prices. But the situation is very different now and economic growth is slowing down.'*

Now look at ways to report the words to a colleague. By each sentence write P/TC (if the sentence is Possible because of Tense Change rules), P/ST (if the sentence is Possible because it is Still True) or I (if the sentence is Incorrect).

The speaker said that ...

1. Jack Welch was CEO of General Electric for twenty years. ...P/TC...
2. Jack Welch had been CEO of General Electric for twenty years. ....
3. Boards of companies look at their CEOs as superheroes. ....
4. Boards of companies looked at their CEOs as superheroes. ....
5. Boards of companies had looked at their CEOs as superheroes. ....
6. Lee Iaccoca started it all in the 1980s. ....
7. Lee Iaccoca had started It all in the 1980s. ....
8. Lee Iaccoca had been started it all in the 1980s. ....
9. The situation is different now. ....
10. The situation was different now. ....

Exercise 5 B D

On Friday morning you had a meeting with someone from your advertising agency at his offices. The words he spoke are on the left. The next week you tell a colleague about the discussion. Underline the correct words on the right.

The advertising person's words:

'Did you get my email I sent yesterday about this campaign we've been working on? I hope so. I'm sorry to ask you to come here at such short notice, but it's quite urgent. The situation is this: we use an outside printing company, and a few days ago the workers there went on strike. I'm having a meeting with a union representative this afternoon, but I thought I should talk to you first.'

What you say to your colleague:

'He said he (1) *hopes/hoped* I'd got (2) *his/my* email that (3) *he'd send/he'd sent* (4) *yesterday/the day before* about (5) *the/this* advertising campaign (6) *they've/we've* been working on. And he apologised for asking (7) *me/you* to go (8) *here/there* at such short notice – he said it (9) *is/was* urgent. Well, apparently a few days (10) *ago/before* the printers they use (11) *have gone/had gone* on strike, and he (12) *is/was* meeting them (13) *this/that* afternoon. He said he thought he should talk to (14) *me/you* about it first.'

22 Reported speech 2

A Say or tell

It was announced yesterday that the chief executive of the Dublin Chamber of Commerce, Mr Jim Miley, had resigned in order to join a dot.com company.
(Irish Times website)

● We *say* something and we *tell* somebody.
  Simon **said** he was confident about the success of the Beta project.
  Simon **told me** the project was going well.

● We never use *to* between *tell* and the object.
  He **told me** what happened in the meeting. (NOT ~~told to me~~)

  We can use *to* after *say*, especially when the actual words are not reported.
  What did he **say to** you?
  I think the boss wanted to **say** something **to** Susan.

B Other reporting verbs

● There are many verbs to report what people say. Each verb has one or more possible patterns.
  Common reporting verbs include:

Verb + *-ing* form (unit 19)	*admit, deny, mention, propose, suggest*
Verb + *to* infinitive (unit 19)	*agree, ask, demand, decide, offer, promise, refuse, threaten*
Verb + object + *to* infinitive (unit 19)	*advise, ask, convince, encourage, invite, order, persuade, remind, tell, warn*
Verb + *that* clause	*admit, agree, announce, answer, claim, complain, confirm, deny, explain, mention, promise, propose, reply, say, suggest*
Verb + object + *that* clause	*advise, assure, convince, inform, notify, persuade, promise, reassure, remind, tell*

They **denied doing** anything wrong.
I **suggested changing** our export agency.

She **promised to call me** tomorrow.
They **refused to lower** their price.

He **advised us to wait** until next year.
They **invited me to come** for lunch.

They **agreed (that)** they'd wait.
She **promised (that)** she'd call me tomorrow.

I **reminded them (that)** they had to pay a 25% deposit.
I **told him (that)** I couldn't make the meeting next week.

● We use the same tense change rules as in unit 21.

  *Greek telecom giant OTE won the privatisation contract with RomTelecom. OTE **promised** that 70 per cent of the telephone system **would** be digital within three years.* (Bucharest Business Week website)

● We can also report what people think or know. Verbs include: *know, notice, think, realise,* etc.
  Sorry, **I didn't realise** you were busy. **I thought** you had finished.

C *It* + passive of a reporting verb

- We use *It* + passive of a reporting verb + *that* to report what people in general feel or believe. This is a formal use, for example in a newspaper story, a scientific report or a written summary of a meeting.

  It was announced at the conference that Argentina was losing Pesos $3,000 million per annum on grain prices compared with the average in the last ten years. It was pointed out that international prices had not improved in two years, but this stability had allowed an increase in production. (LatinTrade website)

  Verbs that are often used in this way are:
  be agreed, be announced, be believed, be claimed, be confirmed, be considered, be decided, be estimated, be expected, be feared, be felt, be found, be pointed out, be proposed, be reported, be rumoured, be said, be shown, be suggested, be thought.

D Reporting questions

- The word order in reported questions is like a normal statement (this is the same rule as for indirect questions in unit 16). Tense changes follow those given in unit 21.
  *'Where **is it**?'*   →   *He asked me where **it was**.* (NOT ~~where was it~~)

- When we report question word questions (*when, what, why, where, how,* etc) we use the question word.
  *'When **will** the goods **arrive**?'*   →   *They asked me **when** the goods **would arrive**.*
  *'Why **have** your sales **gone down**?'* → *I was asked **why** our sales **had gone down**.*

  *'A year ago, I was asked **how** this wonderful merger between Daimler and Chrysler **would work**, and I said I was waiting for the interpersonal problems. They were bound to happen, as our experiences with Seat had shown.' – CEO of Volkswagen*   (Der Spiegel website)

- When we report *yes/no* questions (*Do you, Did you, Are you,* etc) we use *if* or *whether.*
  *'**Do you speak** French?'*   → *She asked me **if I spoke** French.*
  *'**Are you** going to pay in cash?'*   → *He asked me **whether I was** going to pay in cash.*

- Notice in the examples that reported questions have no question mark in writing.

E Reporting commands and requests

- Commands are reported with *tell* and the infinitive.
  'Take us to the airport.'   →   *She **told** the driver **to take** us to the airport.*
  'Don't worry. I'll deal with it.'   →   *She **told** me **not to worry**.*

- Requests are reported with *ask* and the infinitive.
  'Would you mind waiting for a moment?'   *He **asked** me **to wait**.*
  'Please don't wait for me, I'll come along later.'   *He **asked** us **not to wait**.*

22 Practice

Exercise 1 A

Underline the correct words.

1   Sally *told*/*told me* that she had lost the catalogue.
2   This is confidential, please don't *say*/*tell* anything about it.
3   This is confidential, please don't *say*/*tell* anyone about it.
4   Chris *said*/*said me* he must leave early.
5   I *said*/*told* them about the meal, and they *said*/*told* they would come.
6   'You see,' *told*/*said* Steve, 'I always *told*/*said* you'd get a promotion.'
7   'You see,' *told*/*said* Steve, 'I always *told*/*said* you you'd get a promotion.'
8   'Look,' I *told to*/*said to* her, 'why don't you *tell*/*say* me what you mean?'

Exercise 2 B

Match the actual words in sentences 1–12 with the reported statements a)–l).

1	'Well done! You've done it!'	c	a)	He advised me to do it.	
2	'Who me? No, I never did it.'		b)	He apologised for not doing it.	
3	'I'm really sorry I didn't do it – I just forgot.'		c)	He congratulated me on doing it.	
4	'If I were you, I'd do it.'		d)	He invited me to do it.	
5	'Would you like to do it?'		e)	He denied doing it.	
6	'Don't forget to do it!'		f)	He mentioned that he'd done it.	
7	'Oh, I see that you've done it.'		g)	He didn't realise I'd done it.	
8	'Oh, by the way, I've done it.'		h)	He promised that he'd do it.	
9	'Oh! I thought you hadn't done it!'		i)	He noticed that I'd done it.	
10	'I really wouldn't do it. It could be a disaster.'		j)	He refused to do it.	
11	'I'll do it, you can count on me.'		k)	He reminded me to do it.	
12	'No, I won't do it. It's out of the question.'		l)	He warned me not to do it.	

Exercise 3 D unit 21

Rewrite each sentence in reported speech.

1   'Are you on holiday for the whole of August?' she asked me.
    She asked me *if/whether I was on holiday for the whole of August.*
2   'What do the letters 'URL' mean?' I asked him.
    I asked him ....
3   'Have you prepared the figures?' my boss asked me.
    My boss asked me ....
4   'When is your birthday?' I asked Francesca.
    I asked Francesca ....
5   'Did you remember to back up the file?' she asked him.
    She asked him ....
6   'Why have you turned off the air conditioning?' Ellen asked me.
    Ellen asked me ....
7   'Do you speak Italian?' they asked me at the interview.
    They asked me at the interview ....
8   'How much did you pay for your car?' I asked Pablo.
    I asked Pablo ....

Exercise 4 C

 30   Read the extract from a meeting, chaired by Claudia. Then <u>underline</u> the most appropriate reporting verbs in the written summary below.

CLAUDIA: Oh, hi. Take a seat … Um, I'd like to hear your views on the talks we're having with BCP about the possible merger. Do you think we should go ahead with the discussions?

NIGEL: Well, no actually. I don't think we should. Our company cultures are totally different, and I can't see many opportunities to cut costs in a combined operation. I'm sorry, but I'm against it.

TONY: But, Nigel, can't you see that we're too small to stand alone in the global economy. There's going to be rationalisation in our market and now is the right time to act.

CLAUDIA: Um, right. How long do you think it would take to integrate the two companies?

TONY: Probably about six months, maybe more.

NIGEL: That's six months of complete chaos and falling investor confidence. It's just too risky.

CLAUDIA: Well, I don't think we have enough information at the moment. Perhaps we could set up a task force to look into the whole issue in more detail?

TONY: Hmm.

CLAUDIA: Tony – would you be willing to chair it?

TONY: OK, I'll chair a task force, but I'll need representatives from the other departments as well.

CLAUDIA: That shouldn't be a problem. When do you think you'll be able to get the report done?

TONY: Um, in about six weeks.

NIGEL: Six weeks! That's ridiculous.

TONY: OK, we'll try to get all the information together in four weeks.

CLAUDIA: Right, that's settled. We'll meet again a month from today, same time same place.

1   It was *estimated*/*announced* that it would take about six months to integrate the two companies in the event of a merger.

2   It was *rumoured*/*suggested* that we could set up a task force to produce a report on the implications of the merger.

3   It was *proposed*/*claimed* that the task force would be chaired by Tony, with representatives from other departments.

4   It was *shown*/*agreed* that the task force should produce its report in four weeks.

5   It was *claimed*/*decided* that the next meeting would be on July 28th at 9 am in the main conference room.

Exercise 5 A B D

Nigel (from Exercise 4) is talking to a colleague about the same meeting later in the week. <u>Underline</u> the correct words in his report.

'Claudia asked us (1) *that we give*/*to give* our opinions about the merger talks. I (2) *told them*/*told to them* that I thought the whole thing was a bad idea, but they refused (3) *to listen*/*listening*. Of course Tony disagreed, as usual. He (4) *told*/*said* that we were too small for the global market. Then Claudia asked how long (5) *would it*/*it would* take to integrate the two companies, and Tony claimed it would (6) *take*/*to take* six months. Claudia suggested (7) *setting up*/*to set up* a task force to look into the whole thing. I decided (8) *not saying*/*not to say* anything. Tony offered (9) *to chair*/*that he would chair* the task force. He proposed that the task force (10) *reporting*/*should report* back in six weeks, but I (11) *reminded them that*/*reminded that* we'd need the report much sooner. Anyway, we decided (12) *to meet*/*meeting* again in a month.'

23 Phrasal verbs 1

A Understanding phrasal verbs

Financial entrepreneurs figured out years ago they could make a profit by taking on some of the tasks that businesses don't like – managing an employer's payroll, for instance, keeping up with tax payments, benefits deductions and the like.

(cnn financial website)

● Verbs are often followed by particles like *back, off, through, up,* etc, (the word 'particle' means adverb or preposition). Sometimes both verb and particle have their normal meanings. Other times there is a new meaning when the verb and particle are put together. Compare:
*It took 20 minutes to **go through** passport control.* (normal meaning)
*Can we **go through** your proposal again?* (new meaning = 'look at carefully')

The term 'phrasal verb' is used for the second type, where the verb + particle together has a special meaning. Phrasal verbs are common in informal English.

● Sometimes a phrasal verb has the same meaning as a one-word verb.
find out = discover   *go back* = return   *go on* = continue
The phrasal verb is usually more informal than the one-word verb.

● Often one phrasal verb can have several different meanings and the correct one is only clear from the situation.
1 *Don't worry, I'm **dealing with** it now.* (= taking the necessary action)
2 *We **deal** mainly **with** Taiwanese companies.* (= do business with)
3 *The report **deals with** our future strategy.* (= is about)

B Separable phrasal verbs

● With some phrasal verbs we can separate the two parts and put the object before or after the particle.
*Could you **fill** this form **in**, please?* OR *Could you **fill in** this form, please?*
*I'll **print** the spreadsheet **out** now.* OR *I'll **print out** the spreadsheet now.*

*Mario Monti, the EU's competition commissioner, says he will use EU rules to **keep** consumer prices **down** following the 'astronomic' sums paid for 3G licences in Europe.* (International Herald Tribune website)

● When the object is a pronoun (*me, you, it,* etc) it must come before the particle.
*Could you **fill it in**, please?* (NOT ~~fill in it~~)
*I'll **print it out** now.* (NOT ~~print out it~~)

● When the object is a long phrase it must come after the particle.
*Could you **fill in the form that's over there on the desk**, please?*
*I'll **print out the spreadsheet with last month's sales figures** now.*

● Here is a list of common separable phrasal verbs:
*Have you **backed** the data **up**?* (= made a copy on your computer)
*Will you **back** me **up** in the meeting?* (= support, provide evidence for)
*They had to **cut** their advertising budget **back**.* (= spend less on)
*Our lawyers will **draw** a new contract **up**.* (= think about and then write)
*Can you **drop** me **off** at the station?* (= take me in your car and leave me)
*Could you **fill** this form **in**, please?* (= complete by writing information)
*I'm trying to **give** smoking **up**.* (= stop doing it, quit)
*The Central Bank is trying to **keep** inflation **down**.* (= control it to stop it increasing)
*They had to **lay** 100 workers **off** last month.* (= dismiss, make redundant)
*I **looked** their number **up** in Yellow Pages.* (= searched for it in a reference list)
*Can you **pick** me **up** at the station?* (= collect me in your car)
*I'll **print** the details **out** for you.* (= print from a computer onto paper)
*I need to **ring/call** the printers **up** this afternoon.* (= telephone)

*We've **set up** a subsidiary in Estonia.*　(= established)
*We're trying to **sort** it **out** now.*　(= organise it, put it right, deal with it)
*He's stressed because he's **taken on** too much.*　(= accepted responsibility for)
*His son will **take over** the firm when he retires.*　(= take control)
*The new CEO will be **taking over** in January.*　(= taking responsibility)
*Can I **throw** this newspaper **away** now?*　(= get rid of it, dispose of it)
*We **turned down** their offer. It was too low.*　(= refused, said 'no' to)

C Inseparable phrasal verbs

● With some phrasal verbs we cannot separate the two parts. The object must come after the particle.

*Enery Quinones, Head of the Anti-Corruption Unit at the OECD, told us that she hopes Singapore will soon sign its anti-bribery protocol. 'Governments would prefer to **deal with companies** from countries that are signatories to the convention,' she said.* (Business Times Singapore website)

● Here is a list of common inseparable phrasal verbs:

*I have to **call on** a client this afternoon.*　(= visit)
*Have you **come across** a company called TMN?*　(= discovered by chance)
*Can you **deal with** this invoice, please?*　(= take the necessary action)
*We've been **dealing with** FedCo for a long time.*　(= doing business with)
*The report **deals with** e-commerce in SE Asia.*　(= is about)
*I couldn't **do without** my personal assistant.*　(= function/manage without)
*Can you **look after** the office while I'm out?*　(= take care of)
*I've **looked through** my files and I can't find it.*　(= examined carefully)
*I'm sorry to **take up** so much of your time.*　(= use an amount of time or space)

See also unit 25 ● Many inseparable phrasal verbs are intransitive. They do not have objects.

*The photocopier has **broken down** again.*　(= stopped working)
*You must **check in** one hour before departure.*　(= register, report your arrival)
*Can I just **come in** for a moment, please?*　(= interrupt the discussion)
*The negotiations **fell through** at the last moment.*　(= failed)
*I think we can **get by** with a smaller budget.*　(= manage to do things)
*Will you just **hold/hang on** for a moment?*　(= wait)
*He had to **step down** after the corruption inquiry.*　(= leave the job, resign)
*She might **turn up** at any moment.*　(= arrive unexpectedly)

"Could you go over that once again, Gene? Just in case any of us don't understand it."

23 Practice

Exercise 1 B C

Choose the best verb each time from A, B, C or D below.

1 Banca di Roma ..C.. up an online banking service with Telecom Italia.

   A created   B put   C set   D took

2 It's not just my own personal opinion. Here are some figures that ...... up everything I've been saying.

   A put   B back   C support   D turn

3 This is a great opportunity. We can't just ...... it all away.

   A remove   B get   C put   D throw

4 I might need some help. I've never .... across a situation like this before.

   A come   B been   C found   D discovered

5 Their long-term strategy is in crisis. The merger has ...... through.

   A gone   B fallen   C collapsed   D passed

6 It's great having you in the team. I don't know how we ...... by without you!

   A survived   B came   C went   D got

Exercise 2 A B C

Complete each sentence with a phrasal verb that means the same as the words in brackets. The particle has been given to help you.

1 Did you ....find........ out ... why they haven't paid their invoice? (discover)

2 Can you .... on ... a minute until I find the information? (wait)

3 You need to .... in ... this customs declaration. (complete by writing)

4 Any more questions? OK, I'll .... on ... with my presentation. (continue)

5 You need determination to succeed. Don't .... up ... now. (quit)

6 In my job I .... with ... a lot of paperwork. (take the necessary action, handle)

7 If you like, I can .... up ... the parcel on my way home. (collect)

8 Can I .... back ... to what you were saying a few moments ago? (return)

9 This job is going to .... up ... most of the morning. (use an amount of time)

10 If Mike Pinker arrives, could you .... after ... him until I return? (take care of)

Exercise 3 B C

<u>Underline</u> all the possible word orders from the four alternatives. Sometimes two are possible, sometimes three are possible.

1 I'm too busy to <u>*deal with this*</u>/*deal this with*/<u>*deal with it*</u>/*deal it with* right now.

2 I'm going to *look up the information*/*look the information up*/*look up it*/*look it up* on the Internet.

3 In the current economic climate we're trying to *keep down our costs*/*keep our costs down*/*keep down them*/*keep them down* as much as possible.

4 I couldn't *do without my mobile phone*/*do my mobile phone without*/*do without it*/*do it without*.

5 He proposed a new product line to the Board but they *turned down the idea*/*turned the idea down*/*turned down it*/*turned it down*.

6 I'll call you back tomorrow morning. We're just trying to *sort out the problem*/*sort the problem out*/*sort it out*/*sort out it* right now.

Exercise 4 A B C

Complete the email using phrasal verbs from the list below that mean the same as the words in brackets.
Three verbs need to be put into an *-ing* form.

back up   break down   call on   check in   draw up   drop off   find out   get by

keep down   look through   ~~pick up~~   print out   ring up   sort out   turn up

From: David R.   **To:** Simon   **Sent:** 28 May ...

Subject: Things to do   **Cc:**

Message:

1 Mr Yamanaka

Mr Yamanaka will be arriving at the airport at 10.30 tomorrow morning. Can you (1) .... pick .... him

.... up .... (collect by car) from there and (2) .... him .... (leave) at his hotel?

He's staying at the Marriott. I won't be able to (3) .... (arrive) there until about 1 pm, so perhaps you

could stay with him and make sure there are no problems (4) .... (registering) etc. Then I'll be with

Mr Yamanaka for most of the afternoon, so Mike and Kath will have to (5) .... (manage) without me in

the sales meeting.

2 Spain trip

I'm trying to (6) .... (organise) the itinerary for my trip to Spain next month. Can you

(7) .... (think about then write) a list of all our Spanish customers by (8) .... (examining)

our customer accounts database? I'd like to know exactly who I need to (9) .... (visit). Also the flight

needs to be booked – can you (10) .... (telephone) the travel agency and check flight times and prices?

We're trying to (11) .... (control to stop them increasing) travel expenses at the moment so just

(12) .... (discover) prices for Eurotraveller class.

3 March Spreadsheet

The printer keeps (13) .... (stopping working), and I didn't have a chance to (14) ....

(print) the spreadsheet for last month's figures. Can you do it and then (15) .... (make a copy) the file

onto a disk for me to use on my laptop?

Thanks

Exercise 5 B C

 31   Complete this newspaper article by choosing the correct adverb from those in brackets.

TRAVEL ON THE NET

Larry Diller, Chief Executive of e-travel, stepped (1) ..... down ..... (off/~~down~~/out) yesterday in a dramatic move for the on-line travel agency. Revenues at e-travel are currently 15% down on the same period last year, and they've had to cut (2) .... (off/up/back) their advertising budget severely. Earlier in the year e-travel laid (3) ....

(off/up/out) a quarter of its staff in a bid to keep costs (4) .... (off/down/out), but these measures were not enough to make the company profitable. Diller had been in negotiations with the Internet portal YoHo to get exclusive rights to advertise on their site, but the deal fell (5) .... (off/through/out) at the last minute. It seems that this news finally forced investors

to call for Mr Diller's resignation. E-travel's finance officer Martha Piper will now take (6) .... (through/up/on) the task of trying to sort (7) .... (over/up/out) their problems, but the most likely outcome is that e-travel will be taken (8) .... (over/up/out) by another company, perhaps online rival HiFly.com. ■

24 Phrasal verbs 2

*Steel companies around the world will soon start to **cut back** heavily **on** production, causing prices to rise again next year.*
(Business Day South Africa website)

A Phrasal verbs + preposition

● Like other verbs, many phrasal verbs can be used either alone without an object, or followed by a preposition + object.
*Any more comments? OK, shall we **move on**?*   (phrasal verb used alone)
*Shall we **move on to the next item** on the agenda?* (phrasal verb + preposition + object)

● Here is a list of common phrasal verbs of this type:
*Can we **bring** the meeting **forward to** Monday?* (= move it to an earlier time)
*You go on ahead. I'll **catch up with** you later.* (= reach the same place as)
*We need to **cut back/down on** our spending.* (= reduce)
*Let's **drop in on** David while we're in London.* (= make a short, informal visit)
*I **get on with** my colleagues very well.* (= have a friendly relationship with)
*Let's **get on with** the meeting.* (= continue after stopping)
*I couldn't **get through to** directory inquiries.* (= contact someone by telephone)
*It's hard to **keep up with** developments in IT.* (= know about all the changes in)
*OK, I'll **move on to** my next slide.* (= change to a new subject)
*Can we **put** the meeting **back to** Friday?* (= move it to a later time, delay)
*Can we **put** the meeting **off until** Friday?* (= move it to a later time, delay)
*Can you **put** me **through to** Sales, please?* (= connect someone by telephone)
*I think the photocopier has **run out of** toner.* (= there is none left)

B Three-part phrasal verbs

● A few phrasal verbs have three parts and all three must be used. The parts are not separable.
*I **look forward to** seeing you next week.*

*You have mastered email, your mobile phone sends faxes and you have spoken out in a chat room. Now the next big executive decision – do you wear a tie? Europeans are giving up their suits to **fit in with** dress codes in the Internet industry.* (China Daily website)

● Here is a list of common phrasal verbs of this type:
*It's time to **face up to** your responsibilities.* (= not avoid)
*If it's not successful, we can **fall back on** plan B.* (= use if necessary)
*Does the course **fit in with** your holiday plans?* (= be accepted without problems)
*I'll **get back to** you tomorrow.* (= telephone you again)
*I'll **get on to** our suppliers right away.* (= contact)
*I'll try to **get round to** reading your report today.* (= find the time for)
*I **look forward to** seeing you next week.* (= think ahead with pleasure)
*I can't **put up with** such rude behaviour.* (= tolerate)

"Coles, we've decided to cut back on people named Coles."

C Particle meanings

● Often the meaning of the phrasal verb is related to the meaning of the particle.

*Several applicant countries have criticised the EU for **sending out** confusing signals about its intentions. Candidates complain that they cannot **carry on** indefinitely with the costly reforms needed to qualify for membership without some firm date for entry. They suspect some EU governments want to **put off** enlargement for fear that it will be unpopular with their voters, or that the new entrants will monopolise EU spending.* (Economist website)

● Study these examples, and note that a particle can have several meanings.

back	*I'll **call** you **back**.* (= telephone again)
	*I'll **pay** you **back** tomorrow.* (= repay the money I borrowed)
behind	*We mustn't **fall behind** our competitors.* (= be slower than)
	*I'm **getting behind** with my work.* (= not doing as much as I should)
down	*Inflation has **come down** by 2%.* (= become less)
	*I'm trying to **cut down** on fatty foods.* (= reduce)
	*The factory will **close down** next year.* (= stop operating)
	*They **turned down** our offer.* (= said 'no' to)
	*Can I **take down** one or two details?* (= write on paper)
	*I **noted down** some questions to ask you.* (= write on paper)
forward	*She **put forward** an interesting idea.* (= suggested)
	*The meeting's been **brought forward**.* (= moved to an earlier time)
into	*I'd like to **go into** finance after my MBA.* (= start working in an area)
	*He**'s** really **into** windsurfing.* (be into = like and be interested in)
off	*I should be able to **get off** at about five.* (= leave work)
	*Can you **drop** me **off**?* (= take me in your car and leave me)
	*I'm sorry, I think we were **cut off**.* (= lose the signal in a phone call)
	*They'll **cut off** my electricity if I don't pay this bill.* (= stop supplying)
on	*I **leave** my computer **on** all the time.* (= operating, working)
	*It looks cold outside, I'll **put** my coat **on**.* (= wear)
	*I'm going to **carry on** working until about seven.* (= continue)
	*Shall we **move on**?* (= change to the next topic)
out	*I'll **hand out** some catalogues at the end.* (= give to everyone)
	*We **share out** the profits equally.* (= divide between people)
	*I'll just **work out** the price for you.* (= calculate)
	*We're trying to **sort out** the problem now.* (= put it right)
over	*Can we just **go over** the details again?* (= check/summarise)
	*I'm not sure. I need to **think** it **over**.* (= think about it carefully)
through	*Can you **go through** your proposal again?* (= explain)
	*I've **looked through** the files, but it's not there.* (= examined)
up	*They **put up** the price last month.* (= increased)
	*I was **brought up** in the country.* (= looked after from child to adult)
	*I must **write up** that report.* (= write using notes made earlier)
	*The company was **set up** last year.* (= established)

24 Practice

Exercise 1 A B

Complete the sentences with one word from list A and one word from list B.

A: back ~~forward~~ down in on out up up

B: on of ~~to~~ to to to with with

1 I'm sorry, I can't make that date. Can we bring the meeting ..**forward**.. ...**to**.... this week?

2 I'm sorry, I can't make that date. Can we put the meeting .... next week?

3 I'm starting to get a bit overweight. I'm going to have to take more exercise and cut .... alcohol and fatty food.

4 We really have to make the decision this week. We're beginning to run .... time.

5 First I'll talk a little about the current market situation, then I'll move .... outline the Board's thinking about future strategy.

6 It's not just a question of choosing a candidate with the right experience. They also have to fit .... the company culture.

7 Everyone in the R & D department does a lot of reading outside work hours. Things are moving so fast you really have to keep .... the field.

8 We might have to withdraw this product from the market and face .... the fact that it hasn't been the success we had hoped for.

Exercise 2 A B

Match the beginnings of sentences 1–5 with their endings a)–e).

1 I'll look into it right away and get back [d]	a) to Philip Jenkins on extension 3177 but there's no answer.
2 I'm so busy dealing with the day-to-day crises that I never get round ☐	b) with my colleagues much better.
3 Switchboard? I'm trying to get through ☐	c) to our local office and try to get a clearer picture of the situation.
4 I'm not sure what's happening. I'll get on ☐	d) to you this afternoon.
5 Yes, I'm a lot happier now. I get on ☐	e) to thinking about the future.

Exercise 3 C

Study three possible meanings of the adverb *up* a)–c). Then decide which meaning is most closely related to the use of *up* in the underlined phrasal verbs.

a) in a high/noticeable position   b) increase, become more   c) completely

1 A key goal for Allianz is to <u>build up</u> its asset management business.   [b]

2 Many technical issues have <u>come up</u> in the negotiations.   ☐

3 I could <u>sum up</u> the situation by saying that we're in big trouble.   ☐

4 I'd like to <u>bring up</u> the question of financing the operation in Croatia.   ☐

5 I need a new PC. I've nearly <u>used up</u> all the space on my hard disk.   ☐

6 We need more capital to <u>speed up</u> our plant modernisation programme.   ☐

Exercise 4 A B C

Complete this email sent by a financial adviser to his client by choosing the correct particle from the list below.

back   behind   ~~down~~   in   of   off   on   on   out   through   to   up   with   with

From:	Brendan Murphy	To:	Charlotte Taylor	Sent:	8 October ...
Subject:	Market update			Cc:	

Message:

Stocks in the US have come (1) .....down.... a little since I last contacted you, but in general the economy is healthy and the Fed will put (2) .... interest rates if growth is too fast. I think they'll probably put this decision (3) .... until the third or fourth quarter. The real danger is with telecomms, which have really fallen (4) .... the other sectors. Basically, the telecomm sector has run out (5) .... steam, at least in the short term. We recommend that you cut (6) .... on your exposure to this sector and switch to energy and retailing, which will fit in nicely (7) .... the rest of your portfolio. Institutional investors are likely to fall back (8) .... these areas if the current market volatility carries (9) .... I've attached a document with specific suggestions for your portfolio. When you've had a chance to go (10) .... it let me know. If you agree with my recommendations I'll get on (11) .... our brokers and they'll work (12) .... the commission for buying and selling the stocks. By the way, thanks for dropping (13) .... the other morning. Now I'll let you get on (14) .... your work.

Exercise 5 A B C unit 23

 32   Complete the telephone call with phrasal verbs from the list below that mean the same as the words in brackets. Some are from unit 23.

call back   cut off   get back to   get through   breaking up   go ahead   go over   hold on   look into
~~put through~~   rang up   sort out   speak up

RECEPTIONIST: Good morning, Media Solutions, how can I help you?

DEREK: Can you (1) ..put.. me ...through... (connect) to Christine Moreau, please?

RECEPTIONIST: Of course, hold the line ... I'm sorry, caller, I can't (2) .... (make contact) at the moment, the line's busy. Shall I ask her to (3) .... you .... (telephone again)?

DEREK: It's OK, I'll leave a message.

RECEPTIONIST: OK, (4) .... (wait) just a second while I look for a pen. ... Right, (5) .... (continue).

DEREK: My name is Derek Richardson, from Weston Security. Ms Moreau (6) .... me .... (telephoned) yesterday. She wanted me to (7) .... (investigate) the cost of installing an alarm system for your premises. I said I'd (8) .... (telephone again) her today.

RECEPTIONIST: I'm sorry, Mr Richardson, the line is very bad, can you (9) .... (talk louder) please? Hello? Hello? I'm sorry, you're (10) .... (having problems with the signal). Hello? ...

DEREK: Sorry about that. I'm on a train using my mobile and we were (11) .... (disconnected) in a tunnel. Er, yes, as I was saying, I've managed to (12) .... something .... (organise). Can you tell her that I'll send her a quotation along with all the other details in the post?

RECEPTIONIST: Oh, right, er, can I just (13) .... (check) that again? Your name is Derek Richardson, from Weston Security, and you're going to send some details about an alarm system in the post.

DEREK: That's right. Er, thank you for your help. Goodbye.

25 Verbs and objects

A Transitive and intransitive verbs

● Verbs in English can either be transitive or intransitive. This information is shown in dictionaries with the letters T or I.

B Transitive verbs

● Transitive verbs are followed by an object. The object can take a variety of forms:
noun: *Do you sell **stamps**?*
pronoun: *It's too expensive. I can't afford **it**.*
reflexive pronoun: *I enjoyed **myself** at the cocktail party yesterday afternoon.*
clause: *I decided **that it was too risky**.*

● A transitive verb is not complete without an object.

C Intransitive verbs

● Intransitive verbs do not take an object.
Her flight has arrived. / Her flight arrives at Heathrow. / Her flight arrives before mine.
(But NOT ~~Her flight arrives Heathrow.~~)
Our sales in Turkey fell. / Our sales fell last year. / Our sales fell dramatically in the US.
(But NOT ~~Our company fell its sales last year.~~)

● Intransitive verbs include: *ache, appear, arrive, come, depart, disappear, exist, fall, go, happen, live, occur, rain, remain, rise, sleep, speak, wait, walk, work.*

D Verbs with both transitive and intransitive forms

● Many verbs can have both a transitive and intransitive form.
I opened the door.   The door opened.
We began the meeting.   The meeting began.

● Often you can leave out the object if it is obvious because of the situation or because you have already mentioned it.
*I parked (**my car**) in front of your office.*
*OK, I think I understand (**it**) now.*

● Verbs with both forms include: *accept, answer, ask, begin, break, change, choose, close, cook, decrease, drop, eat, end, explain, finish, forget, grow, help, improve, increase, know, learn, leave, meet, move, open, park, phone, read, remember, see, start, stop, turn, understand, watch, win, write.*

● Many verbs are transitive with one meaning and intransitive with another.
He took off his jacket.   (take off (T) = to remove an item of clothing)
The plane took off at 3 pm. (take off (I) = to leave the ground and start flying)
I've recovered the files from the hard disk. (recover (T) = to get back something that was lost)
The economy is recovering slowly.   (recover (I) = to return to normal after some trouble)

E Verb + two objects

- Some verbs can have two objects, an indirect object (a person who receives something) and a direct object (the thing someone gives).
  After a lot of negotiation they offered (IO) ***us*** (DO) ***a better deal***.
  They paid (IO) ***the consultants*** (DO) ***a lot of money***.
  She sends (IO) ***you*** (DO) ***her best regards***.

  Verbs like this include: *award, bring, buy, cause, cost, email, fine, give, hand, leave, lend, make, offer, owe, pass, pay, post, promise, read, refuse, sell, send, show, take, teach, tell, write.*

- Notice that in the examples above we do not use *to*.
  NOT ~~they offered to us a better deal~~.
  NOT ~~they paid to the consultants a lot of money~~.

- You can often put the direct object first, and in this case you use *to* + indirect object. This happens when we want to give special importance to the indirect object.
  They offered (DO) ***a better deal*** (IO) ***to our competitors***.
  They paid (DO) ***a lot of money*** (IO) ***to the consultants who came here last month***.
  She sends (DO) ***her best regards*** (IO) ***to you and your family***.

  Banks lend (DO) money (IO) to those businesses that explain how the funds will be repaid.
  (Business Advisor Zone website)

  This structure is also common when both objects are pronouns.
  They offered (DO) ***it*** (IO) ***to us***.

- Some verbs must have *to* + indirect object. They cannot have the structure in the first paragraph above.
  She explained (DO) ***the situation*** (IO) ***to me***. (NOT ~~explained me the situation~~)
  I recommend (DO) ***the fish*** (IO) ***to you***. (NOT ~~recommend you the fish~~)
  He suggested (DO) ***another solution*** (IO) ***to us***. (NOT ~~suggested us another solution~~)

  The spokesman for Metro AG didn't mention (IO) to reporters (DO) their plans to sell part of the department store chain Kaufhof. (Frankfurter Allgemeine website)

  Verbs in this group include: *admit, announce, demonstrate, describe, explain, introduce, mention, propose, prove, recommend, repeat, report, say, suggest.*

F Verb + two objects using *for*

- With some verbs we use *for* to introduce the indirect object instead of *to*.
  *I've brought **you a present**.*   *I've brought **a present for you**.*
  *I've left **you the report**.*   *I've left **the report for you** on your desk.*
  *I'll reserve **us a table**.*   *I'll reserve **a table for six people**.*

- Verbs with two objects that use *for* include: *book, bring, build, buy, call, change, charge, choose, cook, cut, do, fetch, find, fix, get, keep, leave, make, order, prepare, reserve, save.*

Practice

Exercise 1 A B C

Tick (✓) the sentences that are complete and cross (✗) the ones that are incomplete.

1   You need.   ✗
2   My head aches.   ☐
3   The box contains.   ☐
4   It's finally happened.   ☐
5   I've really enjoyed.   ☐

6   I got.   ☐
7   What did you get?   ☐
8   The company is trying to cut.   ☐
9   I am trying to work.   ☐
10   He reminded.   ☐

Exercise 2 A B C

Tick (✓) the sentences that are correct and cross (✗) the ones that are incorrect.

1   We've redesigned the reception area to look more modern.   ✓
2   I'll wait the reception area for you.   ✗
3   I've been studying Accenture on my MBA course.   ☐
4   I've been working Accenture for five years.   ☐
5   What will happen the company if the CEO leaves?   ☐
6   Who will run the company if the CEO leaves?   ☐
7   I've lived London all my life.   ☐
8   I've liked London all my life.   ☐
9   The airport bus leaves the hotel at eight.   ☐
10   The airport bus arrives the hotel at eight.   ☐
11   They told us last month that the delivery was going to be late.   ☐
12   They said us last month that the delivery was going to be late.   ☐
13   Last year we had to fall our advertising budget.   ☐
14   Last year we had to cut our advertising budget.   ☐

Exercise 3 D

Each pair of sentences has the same verb. Mark the sentence T if it is used transitively or I if it used intransitively. Underline the object in the transitive sentences.

1   a) Can you **see** the woman in the blue suit over there?   T
    b) So you're going to cancel your order. I **see**.   I

2   a) I had to **run** to the post office.   ☐
    b) He **runs** the marketing department.   ☐

3   a) Our family has **managed** this hotel for three generations.   ☐
    b) We **managed** very well while our boss was on holiday.   ☐

4   a) She **lost** her job last month when they restructured the company.   ☐
    b) Real Madrid **lost** by two goals to one.   ☐

5   a) The sales target was set at 8 million this year but I think we'll **miss**.   ☐
    b) I enjoy working abroad, but I **miss** my family and friends.   ☐

6   a) Our sales **dropped** by 12% last year.   ☐
    b) I **dropped** my laptop on the floor, but I don't think it's broken.   ☐

7   a) Susan, do you **know** Dr Goschel from our Munich office?   ☐
    b) It's going to be more expensive. I **know**.   ☐

8   a) You must invest if you want your business to **grow**.   ☐
    b) Farmers who **grew** olives used to get a lot of subsidies from the EU.   ☐

Exercise 4 E

Underline the correct words.

1 He *lent me*/*lent to me* the article about Turkey from *The Economist*.
2 I'm going to *suggest them*/*suggest to them* that we postpone the meeting.
3 They *promised me*/*promised to me* a full refund if I wasn't satisfied.
4 I *explained them*/*explained to them* that I was just following company policy.
5 This delay is *causing us problems*/*causing problems to us*.
6 I recommend *you the chicken*/*the chicken to you*. It's usually very good in here.
7 I reported *the fault to the technician*/*to the technician the fault* yesterday.
8 In the end I *sold them*/*sold to them* the more expensive model.
9 I described *them the whole situation*/*the whole situation to them* in great detail.
10 She *told me*/*told to me* that your trip to Seoul was very successful.
11 Jennifer, can I *introduce you Joseph Lee*/*introduce you to Joseph Lee*?
12 I *showed the visitors*/*showed to the visitors* our new assembly line.

Exercise 5 E

Put the words and phrases into the correct order to make a sentence.

1 I/to Jackie from the marketing department/lent/the article
   I lent the article to Jackie from the marketing department.

2 I/Jackie/lent/the article about marketing
   I ....

3 I/an email/them/sent/yesterday
   I ....

4 I/an email/to their customer services department/sent/yesterday
   I ....

5 I/the display model that's been in the window/sold/him
   I ....

6 I/the display model/sold/to a woman who came in this morning
   I ....

7 I/my report/her/this morning/gave
   I ....

8 I/my report/gave/to her secretary/this morning
   I ....

Exercise 6 E F

Complete the sentences with either *to* or *for*.

1 They emailed their reply ...**to**.. us this morning. I've left a copy ..**for**.. you on your desk.
2 Could you give this .... my secretary and ask her to make some coffee .... our visitors?
3 I've prepared a report .... the Board meeting. Here, I'll show it .... you.
4 Please write a letter ....our suppliers in Lodz and save a copy .... our files.
5 If you leave a message .... her on this notepad, I'll take it .... her when the meeting ends.
6 I'll bring some samples .... the office .... you.
7 It'll cause damage .... the company if we choose the wrong location .... our new factory.
8 Mary has just left. Hand the documents .... me and I'll keep them .... her.

The *-ing* form

> *Some 38% of those asked said that the best aspect of working from home is **having freedom and flexibility** and 12% say **being their own boss** is the key advantage. A further 9% say **not having to commute** is a great benefit.*
> **(Guardian website)**

This unit covers uses of the *-ing* form that are not mentioned in units 1–8 and 19–20.

A *-ing* form as a noun

- The *-ing* form can be used as a noun (in this case it is also called a gerund).
  *Marketing requires careful **planning**.*

- It can also be part of a noun phrase.
  ***Combining two financial groups successfully** is always a difficult task.* (BusinessWeek Online website)

  *The reality now is thousands of emails, fax messages, telephone calls and Internet orders coming into a company everyday. **Intergrating that information intelligently so that the customer gets what it needs** is a very complex task **demanding a very complex solution**.* (Eurobusiness website)

B *-ing* form as an adjective

- The *-ing* form can be used like an adjective, before a noun.
  *My **working day** starts at nine and finishes around six thirty.*
  *We are a small **manufacturing company** with about 50 employees.*

- A small group of adjectives can have either an *-ing* form or an *-ed* form.
  Adjectives ending *-ing* describe something we are reacting to (outside us).
  See also unit 36 Adjectives ending *-ed* describe our feelings (inside us).
  *The meeting was very **interesting**. I was **interested** in your comments about Cisco.*
  *My work is quite **tiring** at the moment. Last night I was really **tired**.*

  Other examples are: *bored / boring, excited / exciting, surprised / surprising.*

C *-ing* form after prepositions

- We use the *-ing* form after prepositions.
  *Wal-Mart became successful **by selling** high volumes at low prices.*
  *We never launch a new product **without doing** extensive market research.*
  ***Instead of buying** telecom shares, I suggest you look at the biotechnology sector.*
  ***After washing** the fruit, we sort it according to size and put it into boxes.*
  ***Before starting** work at UBS, I worked at CreditSuisseFirstBoston.*

- **See unit 46** There are many verb + preposition combinations.
  *We need to **invest** heavily **in** manufacturing.*

- **See unit 47** There are many adjective + preposition combinations.
  *I'd be very **interested in** hearing your suggestions.*

- **See unit 48** There are many noun + preposition combinations.
  *I need some **advice on** doing business in the Balkans.*

● Be careful with the word *to*. For verbs followed by *to* + infinitive see unit 19:
*We've **decided to use** an outside company.*

And we use *to* + infinitive to explain why we do something (this is called 'the infinitive of purpose'):
*We're doing this **to reduce** costs.*

But we use *to* + *-ing* when *to* is a preposition:
*Outdoor posters are an alternative **to using** expensive TV advertisements.*

● Some verbs have *to* used as a preposition. Examples include: *look forward to, object to, be used to, get used to, prefer ... to ..., respond to.*
*I'm **looking forward to seeing** you next week.* (NOT ~~to see~~)
*He seems to **respond** well **to working** under pressure.* (NOT ~~to work~~)
*I'm not **used to having** such a short lunch break.* (NOT ~~to have~~)

D *-ing* form used to begin a clause

● An *-ing* clause can give more information about a noun.

*Very few farms are in a position to benefit from the EU market. Look at Poland, where there are two million **farms employing over a quarter of the population**, to see the problem at its worst.*
(Business Central Europe website)

*UK-based workers have been told that internal meetings with overseas colleagues must now be conducted through videoconferencing. Only **sales staff travelling to essential customers' meetings** will be allowed to fly.* (Sunday Business magazine)

See also unit 29
This type of *-ing* clause is like a defining relative clause.
*A lot of the small Internet companies **operating in Europe** are likely to be taken over.*
(= which are operating in Europe)
*The woman **talking to Robert Wilkinson** is the Chief Finance Officer at Accor.*
(= who is talking)

● An *-ing* clause can give the reason for an action in the past.
*I went over to him, **thinking he was the manager**, but he said he was a sales assistant.*
(= because I thought he was the manager)

The negative is formed with *not*.
***Not being used to the company culture**, I found it hard to fit in.*

● An *-ing* clause can describe a background situation for another action.
***Walking into work this morning** I met Celia who used to work in Personnel.*
(= as I was walking into work)

The negative is formed with *not*.
*I started the job **not knowing what to expect**.*

"All those in favour of moving the decimal point one place to the right?"

26 Practice

Exercise 1 A B

Match the beginnings of sentences 1–8 with their endings a)–h).

1	Manufacturing in the UK has been	[d]
2	In the UK, the service sector is now much more important than the	[ ]
3	In the UK, services are now much more important than	[ ]
4	Our manufacturing process	[ ]
5	We're going to invest heavily	[ ]
6	Car manufacturing in Poland is	[ ]
7	Developing and promoting Poland's manufacturing base will	[ ]
8	Developing manufacturing in Poland will need	[ ]

a) manufacturing sector.
b) is now almost completely automated.
c) manufacturing.
d) in decline for many years.
e) need a lot of investment.
f) concentrated in the Katowice area.
g) in manufacturing over the next few years.
h) a lot of investment.

Exercise 2 A B

For each sentence in exercise 1 above, decide if the word *manufacturing* is a noun or an adjective.

Noun: ..1..   ....

Adjective: ..2..   ....

Exercise 3 B

Complete the sentences with adjectives formed from the verbs in the list below in their -*ing* form.

~~tire~~ welcome confuse last interest wear cut shop sell meet

1 It's been a very ....tiring......... day, I need a drink to help me relax.
2 There's a .... point in front of the ticket office. I'll see you there at six.
3 They're building a new .... centre by the motorway exit.
4 Her presentation was very .... , although perhaps a little .... for people who were new to the subject.
5 This carpet is very hard- .... , and so it will be very long- ....
6 The new reception area should be .... , not cold and formal like before.
7 This is .... -edge technology, you won't find it anywhere else in Europe.
8 Its design is one of its strongest .... points.

Exercise 4 C

Underline the correct words.

1 Thanks for calling, and I look forward to *meeting*/*meet* you at the conference.
2 Thanks for calling, and I hope to *meeting*/*meet* you at the conference.
3 I'm expecting to *taking*/*take* the train to work when I move into the new house.
4 I don't object to *taking*/*take* the train, but I prefer coming to work by car.
5 I can help you with your spreadsheet, I'm used to *working*/*work* with Excel.
6 When I was in my twenties I used to *working*/*work* as a sales consultant.

Exercise 5 C

Complete each sentence by choosing a preposition from list A followed by an *-ing* form from list B.

A: ~~after~~   without   by   of   before   instead of

B: ~~leaving~~   using   being   going   increasing   taking over

1   ....*After*........ ....*leaving*........ university I worked in IT recruitment for a while.

2   I was aware .... very nervous at the start of my presentation.

3   Vodafone grew .... local operators.

4   .... on, I'd just like to look at this graph in a little more detail.

5   If it's urgent I could take it there myself .... a courier.

6   The Fed is hoping to reduce inflation .... interest rates.

Exercise 6 D

Cross out two unnecessary words in each sentence.

1   A lot of the firms ~~which are~~ developing Bluetooth are based in Cambridge.

2   The woman who is replacing Kay Walker used to work at Saachi.

3   The thing that is worrying me most is the fluctuation in oil prices.

4   The visitors who are coming this afternoon are a Japanese Trade Delegation.

Exercise 7 D

Match the beginnings of sentences 1–6 with the most appropriate ending a)–f).

1	Speaking to Mike,	b	a)	he gave his credit card to the waiter.
2	So, concluding my presentation,		b)	I realised that the situation was hopeless.
3	Insisting that he be allowed to pay,		c)	I'd just like to sum up the main points again.
4	Of course I didn't say anything,		d)	not regretting my actions for one moment.
5	I just took it all for granted,		e)	not wishing to offend him.
6	I resigned the next week,		f)	not appreciating the work that was involved.

Exercise 8 D

Rewrite the underlined part of each sentence using an *-ing* clause. Note that in some examples there is a negative form.

1   I got to the airport at ten <u>because I expected the flight to arrive on time</u>.

I got to the airport at ten, ...*expecting the flight to arrive on time*........ .

2   <u>I didn't understand the language</u> so I found it hard to get around on my own.

........*Not understanding the language*........ , I found it hard to get around on my own.

3   I invested £5,000 in a China fund <u>because I hoped that the market would go up.</u>

I invested £5,000 in a China fund, ...

4   <u>As I wasn't an experienced negotiator</u> I think I made too many concessions.

.... , I think I made too many

concessions.

5   <u>I assumed she wouldn't mind so</u> I asked her about her annual salary.

.... , I asked her about her annual

salary.

6   I said yes <u>because I didn't know it would create so many problems</u>.

I said yes, ...

27 Make, do, get, have

A Make and do

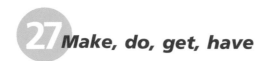

'The job of the Fed is to make sure that there is lots of liquidity in the system', said economist David Orr. 'There's a fairly good probability that we'll get a small increase in retail sales in the next few months', he said. (Yahoo News Service website)

● There are many common expressions based on *make* and *do*. There is no general rule, although often *make* is used for a product or result and *do* for a process or activity.

You make ...   *an appointment with sb. / an arrangement with sb. / sb. angry, sad, etc. / an attempt to do sth. / sth. better, lighter (comparative adjectives) / a bid for sth. / a call to sb. / sth. clear / a complaint against sb. / contacts / a decision / a difference to sth. / an exception / an effort / inquiries / an excuse / a good impression on sb. / an investment / a loss / a mess / a mistake / money / a noise / a note of sth. / a plan / sth. possible / a profit / a promise / progress / sb. redundant / sense of sth. / a start / a suggestion / sure / yourself understood*

You do ...   *the accounts / your best / business with sb. / the cleaning, shopping, etc. / a course in sth. / damage to sth. / economics at university / everything you can to help / sb. a favour / a job for sb. / nothing / overtime / research / something about it / a test on sth. / well, badly at sth. / without sth. / work for sb.*

Note: *sth.* = something and *sb.* = somebody.

● We use *make* to mean 'produce' or 'manufacture'. Products are *made in* a country, *made by* a company and *made of* a material like plastic/leather, etc.

● We use *do* to mean 'perform an action' when we are speaking generally.
*Can I **do** anything to help you?*
*What did you **do** at the weekend?*

*'The stock market is what it is. You live with that,' says Ollila, CEO of Nokia Corp, 'You just **do** the best you can on a daily basis, try to get the right balance of short-term and long-term actions. That's the only attitude to have to avoid losing sleep unnecessarily.' (IndustryWeek website)*

B Get

● *Get* has the following basic meanings:

1 obtain/buy   *I **got** this shirt from Harrods.*
2 receive/be given   *I **got** an email from Frank yesterday.*
3 become   *It's **getting** late. Shall we stop now?*
4 move/arrive somewhere *I **got** into Sales many years ago. I **get** to work at nine.*
5 bring sth. to a place/fetch *Can I **get** you anything from the drinks machine?*
6 understand   *I'm sorry, I didn't **get** that.*
7 persuade sb. to do sth. *We tried to **get** them to agree, but they refused.*
8 travel by/catch (transport) *I **got** a taxi from the airport.*

*Tiny cameras are a favorite spy-movie gadget. And soon you'll be able to **get** one of your own. And it's digital. (Forbes.com website) (get = obtain)*

*Need to **get** connected to the Internet in Moscow? You'll probably have to deal with Anatoly Karachinsky. (Forbes.com website) (get = become)*

*Mr. Bezos said Amazon lost a lot of money on its investments in both living.com and Pets.com. 'The idea was to **get** in quickly and stake your claim to a particular market sector.' (Wall Street Journal Europe website) (get = move)*

*Make sure your promises won't **get** you into trouble. (Quicken.com website) (get = bring)*

*Is the business community mature and confident enough to **get** what went wrong in the dot com crash? I have my doubts. (Irish Times website) (get = understand)*

C *Have*

- We use the verb *have* either like 'possess' or as an action (= do something).
  *I **have** a Ferrari and a VW Golf* (= possess)
  *I **had** an interesting conversation yesterday.* (action)

See unit 2
for state verbs

  When *have* is used like 'possess' it is a state verb and so does not form continuous tenses.
  *I **have** a good job in the City.* (NOT ~~I'm having~~)

- We can use *have got* in place of *have* when it means 'possess'. This is very common in British English.
  *I**'ve got** a good job in the City.*
  *He**'s got** an MBA from Insead.*

- Here are some examples of *have* used like 'possess':

things / people	*have a new car/job, have two sisters, have a baby* (= to give birth)
appearance	*have long hair, have glasses*
personal qualities	*have a good sense of humour, have a lot of energy*
ideas	*have an idea, have an/no alternative, have a/no doubt*
illness / injuries	*have a cold, have a headache, have a bad back*

- Here are some examples of *have* in its other use as an action verb:

eat / drink / smoke	*have a coffee, have a glass of wine, have a meal, have lunch/dinner, have the steak, have a cigarette*
have + noun (instead of verb)	*have a meeting* (= meet), *have a drink* (= drink), *have a look* (= look), *have a wash* (= wash), *have a break* (= break), *have a rest* (= rest)
other phrases	*have an accident, have an appointment, have a chance, have a day off, have difficulty (in + -ing), have a guess, have a holiday, have milk (in your coffee), have time, have second thoughts, have trouble (+ -ing), have a word*
imperatives	*Have fun! Have a good time! Have a nice day! Have a go! Have a try! Have a rest and you'll feel much better.*

*Mr Legendre said Profilium won't **have trouble** raising money because of its track record at working with big-name customers like Nortel Networks and Sun Microsystems.* (Financial Post website)

"Mr. Herman, you made me laugh and you made me cry, but you didn't make me money."

27 Practice

Exercise 1 A

Complete the sentences with *make* or *do*. You may have to use a past simple form.

1 I'm sorry, the President is busy. You'll have to ......make...... an appointment.
2 The insider dealing scandal .... a lot of damage to his reputation.
3 I think France Telecom are going to .... a bid for Telecel.
4 Could you .... me a favour? Could you .... some more coffee?
5 I think we should use another agency to .... the cleaning.
6 Don't worry, just .... your best. We all .... mistakes.
7 OK, shall we .... a start?
8 The builders .... so much noise that it was difficult to .... any work.
9 We .... business in the Ukraine for three years before we .... a profit.
10 We .... some tests last week and I think we .... progress.
11 We have to .... a decision. We can't just .... nothing.
12 I hope we can send a technician to .... the job this afternoon.

Exercise 2 B

Match the uses of *get* in the following sentences with meanings a)–h).

a) obtain/buy   e) bring/fetch
b) receive/be given   f) understand
c) become   g) persuade
d) move/arrive   h) travel by/catch

1 What time do you usually get to the office? | d |
2 You might be able to get it a little bit cheaper if you go to a larger store.
3 I'm sorry, I didn't quite get the last point. Could you explain it again?
4 The factory is very busy. We got a large order from Taiwan last week.
5 Can I get you a coffee while you are waiting?
6 This new software is so hard to use. I don't think I'll ever get used to it.
7 I flew to Heathrow and then got a train to Reading.
8 I couldn't get her to sign the contract. She needs more time to decide.

Exercise 3 C

Look at the form of the word *have* in the sentences below. Put a tick (✓) if the sentence is possible. Put a cross (✗) if it is not possible.

1 It's OK, I don't need any help, I'm just having a look. | ✓ |
2 I'm having one brother and one sister. | ✗ |
3 She's a good team member – she's having a lot of energy.
4 Why not join us later? We'll be having a drink in the bar.
5 OK, I've decided. I'm having the steak.
6 You'll easily recognise Anna. She's having short brown hair and glasses.

Exercise 4 C

In three examples in exercise 3 the word *have* can be replaced by *have got*. Write the sentence numbers below.

....

Exercise 5 C

Complete the sentences with a word or phrase from the list below.

> alternative   appointment   chance   conversation   break   day off   difficulty   doubt
> the fish   go   headache   holiday   look   lunch   ~~meeting~~   time   word

1   I'm having a ....**meeting**.... with my bank manager this afternoon.
2   Did you have a good .... ? You went to Greece didn't you?
3   Did you have a good .... ? You went to that Greek restaurant didn't you?
4   If you have a .... , could you have a .... at these figures?
5   I didn't have any .... to look at the report yesterday. I'll do it today.
6   I'm sorry, we have to stop your credit. We have absolutely no ....
7   It's been a long meeting. Let's have a short .... and then meet back here in twenty minutes.
8   Good morning. I have an .... with Catherine Booth at ten o'clock.
9   Let me see. I think I'll have .... It's normally very good in here.
10   I have no .... at all that he's telling the truth. He's a very honest person.
11   I had a lot of .... understanding the technical details in his presentation.
12   I've got a bit of a .... I think I'll take an aspirin. If it gets worse I might have to have the .... tomorrow.
13   I'd like to have a quick .... with you about the new product launch.
14   Have a .... ! I'm sure you can do it!
15   I had a very interesting .... with Tony over lunch yesterday.

Exercise 6 A B

 33   Complete the dialogue with a correct form of *make, do* or *get*.

IAN: Helen, you've been (1) ...**doing**... a lot of overtime recently! Are you hoping to (2) .... promoted?

HELEN: No, it's just that I haven't been (3) .... this job very long and I really want to (4) .... a good impression. In the last place I worked they (5) .... a lot of people redundant, including me.

IAN: Really, why was that?

HELEN: Well, the company just wasn't (6) .... very well. Basically they (7) .... into difficulties by expanding too quickly. They (8) .... a big investment in Latin America but they hadn't (9) .... their market research properly. So they just couldn't (10) .... enough money.

IAN: So what did you (11) .... then?

HELEN: Well, it was difficult for a while, although the company was very good to us and we (12) .... a lot of help in applying for new jobs.

IAN: Well, at least that's something.

HELEN: And the redundancy package was quite good and I (13) .... some money on some shares I'd sold, so I had enough money to last me a few months while I applied for other jobs.

IAN: So, how long was it before you got this job?

HELEN: Well, about two months. I put my CV on the web, and I (14) .... quite a few replies. At the time having the Internet at home (15) .... a big difference.

IAN: Yeah, it's great, isn't it. I couldn't (16) .... without it. I even (17) .... my shopping on the Internet now ...

HELEN: Then I (18) .... an interview here, and they (19) .... me an offer the next day, and I accepted it straightaway.

28 Relative clauses 1

A Relative clauses

> *Any City expert who would rather talk than listen has forgotten what made him an expert in the first place.*
> (The Economist, 19.0200)

● Relative clauses are short phrases beginning with words like *who, that* and *which* that define or describe people and things. There are two types:

● Defining relative clauses: we use these to identify exactly which person or thing we mean.
The candidate who we interviewed on Friday *is better than this one.*

The relative clause is part of the noun phrase. The information is necessary for the sentence to make sense.

● Non-defining relative clauses: we use these to add extra information about a person or thing.
Capellas, **whose father was a Greek immigrant who entered the United States after World War II**, *returned yesterday to Greece on a business trip.* (International Herald Tribune website)

The information may be interesting, but it is not a necessary part of the sentence. To show this in writing we use commas.

Non-defining clauses are more common in writing. In speech, we often give the same information by just using two short sentences. Compare:
The salesman, **who was very helpful**, *said this model was in stock.* (writing)
'The salesman was very helpful. He said this model was in stock.' (speech)

● Look again at the previous example. Remember that we are just adding extra information about a salesman. If there is more than one salesman and we want to say which one we are talking about, then we use a defining relative clause.
'The salesman **who I spoke to on the phone yesterday** *said this model was in stock, but now you tell me that you don't have any. I've come all the way here to buy it.'*

B Relative pronouns

● The words *who, which, that, whom* and *whose* can begin a relative clause. They are called relative pronouns.

● For people both *who* and *that* are used, but *who* is more common.
The candidate **who** *they chose for the job has a finance background.*

● For things or ideas both *which* and *that* are used, but *that* is more common, especially in speech.
The products **that** *you ordered were sent today.*

The food sector faces another problem. In order to participate in the EU's single market it will have to conform to the Common Agricultural Policy, **which makes up 40% of all EU regulations.** (Business Central Europe website)

The fight for survival of daily business will be won by the organizations **that adapt** *most successfully to the new world* **that is developing.** (BusinessWeek website)

● The relative pronoun *whose* shows that something belongs to someone or something.
I've invited to the meeting everyone **whose work is relevant to this project.**
The European Union is an organisation **whose policies change quite slowly.**

He owns 100 per cent of this company, **whose sales hit close to $3 million in 1998.** (Asia, Inc. website)

● In formal English it is possible to use *whom* instead of *who* where *who* is the object of the sentence. But in modern English most speakers only use *who*.
The candidate **who/whom** *we chose for the job has an MBA in corporate finance.*

C Leaving out the relative pronoun in a defining relative clause

● We can leave out *who, which, that* (but not *whose*) in a defining relative clause if they are followed immediately by a noun or pronoun.
*The technician **(who) Tony** spoke to said the network was working fine.*
*The salad **(which/that) I** had for my starter was superb.*
This is usual in spoken English.

● We must keep the relative pronoun if it is followed immediately by a verb.
*The technician **who spoke** to Tony said the network was working fine.*
*The salad **which/that came** with the fish was superb.*

D Non-defining relative clauses

● We must keep the relative pronoun in non-defining clauses. We cannot leave it out (it makes no difference whether it is followed by a noun or a verb).
*The technician, **who my colleagues** know well, said the network was working fine.*
*The technician, **who spent** over an hour here, said the network was working fine.*
*The salad, which **he**'d spent hours preparing, was superb.*
*The salad, **which** had avocado in it, was superb.*

● *That* is never used in a non-defining relative clause.
*Chile, **which** is an important market for us, is having some currency problems.*

E Relative pronouns and prepositions

● Normally we put prepositions at the end of the relative clause.
a) *The person **(who) I got these figures from** said they were accurate.*
b) *Unilever is a company **(that/which) we know quite a lot about**.*
c) *The person **(who) I spoke to** was called Pam.*

● But in formal English it is possible to put prepositions in front of *whom, which* and *whose* (but not *who* or *that*). Compare with the previous examples:
a) *The person **from whom** I got these figures said they were accurate.*   (formal, rare)
b) *Unilever is a company **about which** we know quite a lot.*   (formal, rare)
c) *The person ~~to who~~ I spoke was called Pam.*   (incorrect)

● We do not put another pronoun after the preposition.
(NOT *Unilever is a company that we know quite a lot about ~~it~~.*)

"Miss Dugan, will you send someone in here who can distinguish right from wrong?"

28 Practice

Exercise 1 A

Decide whether the words in italics are defining or non defining relative clauses. Write D or ND.

1   The man *who is in reception* has been waiting for ten minutes.   D

2   The food, *which was very nice*, was served at the bar.   ☐

3   The projector, *which has a new bulb*, is over there.   ☐

4   The projector *which has a new bulb* is over there.   ☐

5   The train *which leaves at 8 am* doesn't stop at Bath.   ☐

6   The train, *which leaves at 8 am*, doesn't stop at Bath.   ☐

Exercise 2 B

Complete the sentences with *who, whose* or *that*.

1   The customer ...**whose**... company I visited is phoning this afternoon.

2   The manual .... they sent explains everything.

3   It's difficult to say .... this fax was sent by.

4   The candidates .... CVs I looked at this morning were all very good.

5   I don't remember .... I spoke to when I called yesterday.

6   Your colleague, ... I met this morning, had a different opinion.

7   Toyota is a manufacturer .... reputation is excellent all over the world.

8   The contract .... you showed me before was different to this one.

9   I can't remember .... I invited to the meeting.

10   Do you know .... Catherine works for?

11   The consultant, ... seems very young, is speaking to Martin Sommer.

12   They promoted the manager .... sales team was most successful.

Exercise 3 C D

Put a bracket around the relative pronoun if you can leave it out. Put a tick at the end if you must keep the relative pronoun.

1   The book (that) you lent me about e-commerce is really interesting.

2   The company which is our main competitor is Apollo.   ✓

3   The name which they chose for the new model is Prima.

4   The meeting room, which wasn't very large, became hot and stuffy.

5   In the end, the sales campaign was the best that we'd ever had.

6   These are the people whose names appear on the database.

7   The people who attended the presentation found it very useful.

8   The supplier who we visited last week had better quality than this one.

9   Richard Branson, who started with almost nothing, is a typical entrepreneur.

10   *Newsweek* is the English-language magazine that I read most often.

Exercise 4 **E**

Rewrite the formal sentence as everyday informal sentences, beginning as shown.

1   These are the colleagues with whom I went to the conference.

These are the colleagues I ....*went to the conference with*.... .

2   This is the breakthrough for which we have been waiting.

This is the breakthrough we ....

3   That's the hotel at which I stayed.

That's the hotel I ....

4   When I call the accountants, Richard is the person with whom I usually deal.

When I call the accountants, Richard is the person I ....

5   This is the catalogue from which we choose the samples.

This is the catalogue we ....

6   This is the area for which I am responsible.

This is the area I ....

Exercise 5 **B C E**

Decide whether each sentence is possible or impossible. Write P or I.

1   This is the customer we received the complaint from. ☐ P

2   This is the customer who we received the complaint from. ☐

3   This is the customer from whom we received the complaint. ☐

4   This is the customer from who we received the complaint. ☐

5   This is the product which we're depending on. ☐

6   This is the product we're depending on. ☐

7   This is the product on whom we're depending. ☐

8   This is the product on which we're depending. ☐

9   The consultants with who we deal are called AlphaCom. ☐

10   The consultants with whom we deal are called AlphaCom. ☐

11   The consultants who we deal with are called AlphaCom. ☐

12   The consultants we deal with are called AlphaCom. ☐

Exercise 6 **A B C D**

34   Read this newspaper article which includes four relative clauses a–d. Then decide whether each statement below is True or False about each relative clause. Write T or F at the end.

Yesterday, the Federal Reserve made the cut in interest rates (a) *which the markets had been expecting*. The Fed Chairman, (b) *who was back at his desk yesterday after a short trip to Japan*, made the announcement after trading on Wall Street had closed. The reaction (c) *which will follow on the currency markets* is difficult to predict, as the dollar – (d) *which has been trading at around 0.93 euros* – has had a lot of bad news over the last few days.

	a	b	c	d
1 The relative clause identifies a person, event or thing.	☐	☐	☐	☐
2 The relative pronoun can be replaced with 'that'.	☐	☐	☐	☐
3 You can leave out the relative pronoun.	☐	☐	☐	☐

29 Relative clauses 2

> *The company **that made the DAX index jump** was Deutsche TeleKom. Traders said that big shareholders **who received hundreds of millions of shares as part of TeleKom's** purchase of US-based VoiceStream intended to hold on to their TeleKom shares.*
> **(Frankfurter Allgemeine website)**

A Combining sentences

● Look at this example of two short separate sentences.
I'm taking a flight. It goes via Frankfurt.

We can combine the sentences using a relative clause. There are two ways, but the meanings are the same.
a) *I'm taking a flight **that goes via Frankfurt**.*
OR
b) *The flight **(that) I'm taking** goes via Frankfurt.*

See unit 34 ● Note that articles often change when sentences are combined.
a) has **a** *flight*, like the original short sentence, because the flight is mentioned for the first time and there are several of them.
b) has **the** *flight* because there is only one in the speaker's mind.

See unit 28 ● Remember that we often leave out the relative pronoun (*that*) in spoken English in cases like this.

● When we combine sentences we do not add another pronoun.
a) NOT I'm taking a flight that ~~it~~ goes via Frankfurt.
b) NOT The flight that I'm taking ~~it~~ goes via Frankfurt.

B Use of *what*

● We can use the relative pronoun *what* to mean *the thing(s) that*.
*I didn't understand **what** she said.* (= the things that she said)
***What** we need is a better marketing strategy.* (= the thing that we need is)

*Having a few huge corporations control our outlets of expression could lead to less aggressive news coverage and a more muted marketplace of ideas. Conglomeration affects **what** the media companies do and, in turn, **what** you read, watch, and hear.* (Brillscontent website)

C Use of *where, when* and *why*

● We can use the relative adverbs *where, when* and *why* with their normal meanings to identify which thing we are talking about.
*Analysts said it was difficult to understand **the reason why the European Central Bank had cut rates**.* (Observer website)

● We can leave out *when* or *why*, or use *that*.
*Do you remember the day **(when) I started working here**?*
*Do you remember the day **that I started working here**?*

● We must keep *where*, except when there is a preposition at the end of the clause. In this case we leave it out or use *that*.
*The hotel **where I stayed** was quite cheap.*
*The hotel **(that) I stayed in** was quite cheap.*

D Relative clauses with a participle (-ing, -ed)

● The relative clause can have a continuous verb form (with an -ing ending) or a passive verb form (with an -ed ending).

*The people **who are making the real decisions** are all at Head Office.*

*The products **that were attracting most interest** were the smaller, lighter models.*

*Passengers **who are seated in rows J–P** can now board the aircraft.*

*Food **which is sold in supermarkets** needs a relatively long shelf-life.*

● In these cases we can simplify the sentence by leaving out both the relative pronoun and the verb *be*.

*The people **making the real decisions** are all at Head Office.*

*The products **attracting most interest** were the smaller, lighter models.*

*Passengers **seated in rows J–P** can now board the aircraft.*

*Food **sold in supermarkets** needs a relatively long shelf-life.*

*Asda, **now owned by Wal-Mart**, is keen to increase the space in its stores devoted to household goods, electricals and entertainment products.* (Independent website)

"David, as head of our acquisitions division, your annual bonus is 10 million dollars, from which we deduct 2 million for the coffee fund."

29 Practice

Exercise 1 A

Combine each pair of sentences by including the word given in brackets.

1   Last year we introduced a new line. It's aimed at the youth market. (that)
    The new line ....*that we introduced last year*......... is aimed at the youth market.

2   I'd like you to meet a colleague. He could be a useful contact for you. (who)
    I'd like you to meet a colleague ....

3   A candidate's CV is on your desk. She deserves an interview. (whose)
    The candidate .... deserves an interview.

4   A visitor is coming next week. She's from our Paris office. (who)
    The visitor .... is from our Paris office.

5   Tom took me to a restaurant. It was called 'Noodle Heaven'. (that)
    The restaurant .... was called 'Noodle Heaven'.

6   I heard a man's presentation. He was an investment banker. (whose)
    The man .... was an investment banker.

7   Here is a mobile phone. I was telling you about it. (that)
    Here is the mobile phone ....

8   Over there is a site. They're going to build a new factory. (where)
    The site .... is over there.

Exercise 2 A

If the sentence is correct put a tick (✓) at the end. If the sentence has a word which should not be there, write the incorrect word at the end.

1   The woman who I asked didn't know the way.   ....✓........

2   The firm whose their stand was at the back had very few visitors.   *their*

3   That was the longest meeting I've ever been in.   ....

4   The train which it goes to Brussels leaves from here.   ....

5   The products which sell best they are those with nice packaging.   ....

6   This model, which it was launched last year, is selling very well. ....

7   Everyone that I spoke to advised me to try again.   ....

8   The company where I used to work it was called Interlink.   ....

Exercise 3 B C unit 28

Underline the correct words. This exercise includes some revision of unit 28.

1   The flight *which*/*who* I'm taking leaves from Terminal 2.

2   She's from the company *which*/*whose* products we distribute.

3   Everyone *who*/*which* was at the meeting will receive a copy of the minutes.

4   Message. To *whom*/*who* it may concern: please do not leave dirty coffee cups here.

5   There were some interesting ideas at the meeting *that*/*what* I went to.

6   It's not the first time *that*/*what* they've done this.

7   *That*/*What* I like best about my job is the contact with people.

8   Has anybody seen the folder *what*/*that* I left on this desk?

9   The room *where*/*that* I work has very little natural light.

10 The room *where*/*that* I work in has very little natural light.

Exercise 4 B D

Complete the sentences with *what, which* or *who*, or tick (✓) the space if the sentence is already correct.

1   There's a lot of noise from the builders ......✓........ working next door.

2   Mike doesn't really know .....*what*.... he wants in his career.

3   I was talking to a man .... going to the same conference as us.

4   I was talking to a man .... is going to the same conference as us.

5   I asked her .... she was thinking.

6   This is a new drug .... was developed at our Cambridge laboratories.

7   This is a new drug .... developed at our Cambridge laboratories.

8   This drug, ... was developed at our Cambridge laboratories, is fantastic.

9   This drug, ... developed at our Cambridge laboratories, is fantastic.

10   .... we need now is better brand recognition.

11   The 'assets' include everything .... owned by the company.

12   I didn't really understand .... he was talking about.

Exercise 5 A

 35   Complete the article by writing relative clauses based on the notes below. Begin with either *who* or *which*.

The Battle for
GUCCI

In 1999 Bernard Arnault's LVMH fought a battle to take over Gucci, (1) *which was run by Domenico De Sole* . De Sole received news that LVMH, (2) .... , had bought 5% of Its shares. This was going to be the battle (3) .... De Sole gathered together a team of people (4) .... It included American lawyer Allan Tuttle and Bob Singer, (5) .... There were two options: either negotiate with Arnault and sell the business, or defend Gucci by finding a friendly 'white knight' to rescue them. They decided to fight. The models at the Gucci men's show in January 1999 had white faces and teeth like Dracula, (6) .... Meanwhile Arnault had accumulated shares (7) .... The white knight (8) .... arrived in the form of Francois Pinault, (9) .... PPR was very successful in Europe, but Pinault wanted a chance to build a global group. Pinault agreed to invest US$3 billion, (10) .... ,

In return Pinault's group gained representatives on a new strategic committee, but he agreed to leave control of the company with De Sole and the senior Gucci team.   ■

1   LVMH fought a battle with Gucci. Gucci was run by Domenico De Sole.

2   LVMH had bought 5% of Gucci's shares. LVMH was the largest luxury goods company in the world.

3   This was going to be a battle. It would decide the future of the industry.

4   De Sole gathered together a team of people. He could trust them.

5   Bob Singer was in the team. Bob Singer was the chief financial officer.

6   The models looked like Dracula. This was meant to be a message for Arnault.

7   Arnault accumulated shares. They represented 34% of Gucci's total stock.

8   A white knight arrived. Gucci had been looking for one.

9   Francois Pinault was the white knight. He was the head of a non-food retail group called PPR.

10   Pinault invested US$3 billion. This was a 42% share in Gucci.

30 Countable and uncountable nouns

> *Toulouse is **the home** of French aerospace **research** and has been considered **a center of innovation** for many years. Recently, thanks to explosive **growth** in the biotech and computer **industries**, it has become one of Europe's most fashionable **hubs** for young tech **workers**.* (TheIndustryStandard website)

A Countable nouns

- A countable noun has a singular and a plural form. We can use numbers with it.

  one **bank**, three **banks**   one **solution**, two **solutions**   one **metre**, five **metres**

  one **person**, two **people**   one **child**, three **children**   one **foot**, two **feet**

B Uncountable nouns

- An uncountable noun only has one form. We cannot use numbers with it.

  *With OPEC cutting **oil production** and **demand** still outpacing **supply**, it would seem oil prices have nowhere to go but up.* (Yahoo Business News website)

  Here are more examples:

substances, materials	*water, rice, air, oil, coffee, money, steel, electricity, food*
abstract ideas	*life, fun, freedom, progress, health, time, trouble*
activities	*work, travel, sleep, football, help, music, research*
human qualities/feelings	*honesty, patience, sadness, hope, respect, courage*

- The following nouns are uncountable in English, although they may be countable in other languages:

  accommodation, advice, baggage, behaviour, business, cash, English (language)*, equipment, furniture, health, homework, information, knowledge, luggage, machinery, money, permission, rubbish, scenery, traffic, travel, weather, work*

- A few uncountable nouns end in *-s*:

  athletics, diabetes, economics, gymnastics, measles, news, politics

- Uncountable nouns cannot be counted directly. However, we can count them using phrases like *a piece of, a bit of, an item of, a cup of, a glass of, a bottle of, a kilo of, a barrel of,* etc.

  a piece/two pieces of advice   **a bit/two bits** of information   **an item/two items** of news

  a bottle/two bottles of water   **a kilo/two kilos** of rice   **a barrel/two barrels** of oil

C Singular or plural?

- Countable nouns can be singular or plural.

  *The new model **is** a big improvement.*

  *The new model**s are** a big improvement.*

  Uncountable nouns are always singular.

  *The new equipment **is** a big improvement.*

- Some singular nouns can be followed by either a singular verb or a plural verb.

  *The company **is/are** doing very well at the moment.*

  It depends whether we think of the group as a whole (singular verb), or its individual members (plural verb). Examples are:

  army, audience, board, committee, company, data, family, government, group, management, media, press, public, staff, team, union

● Some nouns only have a plural form and take a plural verb. Examples are:
clothes, contents, earnings, expenses, feelings, goods, jeans, police, remains, scissors, surroundings, trousers.

D *A/an, some, a lot of, any, many, much, few, little*

● We use *a/an* with singular countable nouns only.
*This is **a** good **product**.*   (NOT ~~This is an interesting information~~.)

With uncountable nouns we use *some* in place of *a*, or simply the noun by itself.
*There is **information/some information** here that is important.*

● Study this table for words before plural and uncountable nouns.

Used with both plural and uncountable nouns	*some/a lot of/lots of/any*
Used with plural nouns only	*many/few/a few*
Used with uncountable nouns only	*much/little/a little*

*We don't have **many customers**/We only have **a few customers** at this time of year.*
*There isn't **much information**/There's very **little information** about this budget item.*

● *Some* is common in affirmative statements, and *any* is common in negative statements and questions.
*I've seen **some** things I like, but I don't have **any** money.*

But we can use *some* in a question if it is an offer or request.
*Would you like **some/any** information about our investment funds?*

And we use *any* in affirmative sentences where we mean 'it doesn't matter which'.
See unit 31 for more details on *some* and *any*
*I'm free all day. Call **any time** you like.*

● *Many* and *much* are often used with the words *how* and *not*.

How many people *will have Internet access in the coming years?* **How much revenue** *will a single industry, like travel, earn from the Web?* (Brillscontent website)

*There's **not many jobs/not much work** in the manufacturing sector at the moment.*

E Specific and general meanings

● Some nouns can be either countable or uncountable. The countable form has a specific meaning, and the uncountable form has a general meaning.

*The machine is making **a** strange **noise**.*	**Noise** *inside factories can be a problem.*
*This is **a** new **business**.*	**Business** *is going well at the moment.*
*There aren't **many spaces** in the car park.*	*There isn't **much space** in my office.*
a coffee (a cup of coffee)	**coffee** (the substance)
a paper (a newspaper, conference paper)	**paper** (the material)
a glass (for drinking)	**glass** (the material)

30 Practice

Exercise 1 A B C D

<u>Underline</u> the correct words.

1   *How much/<u>How many</u>* pages are there on your website?
2   *Is/Are* there *many/much* banks with a head office in Geneva?
3   *Is/Are* there *many/much* traffic in Geneva?
4   *How much/How many* information have we got about this company?
5   Where *is/are* the goods we ordered?
6   There *is/are* some people waiting for you in reception.
7   We bought some new *equipment/equipments* last month.
8   We bought some new *machine/machines* last month.
9   This is *an equipment/a piece of equipment* that controls the speed of rotation.
10 This is *a machine/a piece of machine* that controls the speed of rotation.
11 He gave me *an/some* advice which *was/were* really useful.
12 I'm afraid we haven't got *much/many* time.
13 The news *is/are* on at nine. There may be *an/some* information about Davos.
14 We have *some/any* blue ones in stock, but we don't have *some/any* red ones.
15 You can choose *some/any* colour you want.

Exercise 2 A D

Complete the sentences with the word *a, an, some, much* or *many*.

1   That's ......*a*...... good idea.
2   Well, that's .... progress, I suppose.
3   We do some business in Poland, but not ....
4   We have a few customers in Poland, but not ....
5   I'd like to make .... inquiry about training courses you offer at your college.
6   Can I have .... information about trains to Paris?
7   I'll see you in an hour. I don't have .... more emails to write.
8   I'll see you in an hour. I don't have .... more work to do.
9   Do you have .... trouble with the unions in your factory?
10 Do you have .... difficulties with the unions in your factory?
11 I need to claim .... expenses for my trip last month.
12 We didn't study .... economics at university, just a little.

Exercise 3 E

Look at the <u>underlined</u> noun in each sentence. Write *S* if it has a specific, countable meaning, or *G* if it has a general, uncountable meaning.

1   a) Do you see this material? This is unbreakable <u>glass</u>.   G
    b) What a beautiful wine <u>glass</u>! Where did you get it?   S
2   a) In this job, <u>experience</u> is more important than qualifications.   ☐
    b) This is going to be an <u>experience</u> I'll remember for a long time.   ☐
3   a) Claire runs a <u>business</u> designing company websites.   ☐
    b) It's not good for <u>business</u> when interest rates are too high.   ☐
4   a) You should meet Mark – he's had a very interesting <u>life</u>.   ☐
    b) <u>Life</u> is complicated sometimes.   ☐

Exercise 4 A B C D

How many possibilities are there with the phrases below. Put a tick (✓) if the phrase is possible.

		car	food	clothes	work	job	money	dollars	expenses	idea
1	I haven't got many			✓						
2	I haven't got much		✓							
3	I haven't got a/an	✓								
4	There are some									
5	There is some									
6	There is a/an									
7	There's									
8	They're									
9	It's a/an									

Exercise 5 B

Match each phrase on the left with the best phrase on the right.

1	a cup of	b
2	a glass of	
3	a bottle of	
4	a barrel of	
5	a sheet of	
6	a slice of	

a) wine is acceptable at a business lunch, but no more.
b) coffee is a good way to start the day.
c) paper can sometimes get stuck in the photocopier.
d) whisky costs less at the airport.
e) wholemeal bread goes well with tomato soup.
f) oil can cost US$15–30 on the commodity markets.

Exercise 6 A B C D E

 36   Underline the correct words in this dialogue.

ANGELA: Jack, have you got (1) *a / some* moment for a chat?

JACK: Of course, go ahead. Now's a good time.

ANGELA: There (2) *is / are* (3) *an / some* important work that we need to do over the next few months.
It should be (4) *an / some* interesting job, and I think you're the best (5) *person / people* to do it.

JACK: Oh, really?

ANGELA: Yes. Well, (6) *an / a* piece of empty land has come onto the market on the other side of town.

JACK: Uh, huh …

ANGELA: And, as you know, we haven't got (7) *many / much* space at our present site. Well, we think it's
(8) *an / some* ideal opportunity to expand.

JACK: Yeah. We don't have much room here.

ANGELA: Well, we're thinking about building completely new offices. We'd like you to do (9) *a / some*
research on the whole idea, and then write (10) *a / some* report on whether to go ahead or
not. Are you interested?

JACK: Well, I haven't got (11) *much / many* experience of this kind of thing. I …

ANGELA: I know, but there really isn't anyone else here who is suitable.

JACK: Oh …

ANGELA: And we need to make (12) *a progress / progress* on this as quickly as possible. We're taking on
fifteen new people in March.

JACK: Um, right, but there (13) *is / are* (14) *many / a lot of* (15) *information / informations* to collect. I …

ANGELA: Well, with this new responsibility we might consider reviewing your salary.

JACK: Well, OK, it sounds like (16) *an / a* interesting challenge. I'll do it.

31 Pronouns

A Indefinite pronouns

● Words like *everyone, anything*, etc, are called indefinite pronouns. They refer to people, things or places without saying exactly who, what or where they are.

People:	*someone/somebody*	*anyone/anybody*	*everyone/everybody*	*no one/nobody*
Things:	*something*	*anything*	*everything*	*nothing*
Places:	*somewhere*	*anywhere*	*everywhere*	*nowhere*
Time:	*sometime*	*anytime*	(all the time)	(never)

● There is no difference between the *-one* forms and the *-body* forms.

● Indefinite pronouns are followed by a singular verb, but we refer back to them in a sentence with *they/them/their*.
*Someone **is** waiting for you in reception. I told **them** you wouldn't be long.*
*Well, I suppose that **everyone is** ready for **their** coffee break now?*

B *Someone/anyone*, etc

● Words with *some-* and *any-* follow the rules given in unit 30. In more detail:
AFFIRMATIVE SENTENCES
Some- is very common in affirmative sentences:
*There's **someone** waiting in reception.*

Any- is also common, particularly when we want to show that there is no limit to the possibilities:
*You can fly **anywhere** you want from here.*

*Despite Amazon's refusal to comment on the Best Buy report, the company's executives have said they remain open to partnerships with other retailers. 'We'll talk with **anyone**,' said Warren Jenson, Amazon's chief financial officer, two weeks ago.* (Wall Street Journal website)

Compare with 'some':
*We can bring it to your office **sometime** tomorrow.*   (we don't know yet, but we'll tell you)
*We can bring it to your office **anytime** tomorrow.*   (there's no limit – you decide)

Any- is common in sentences with *if*:
*If there is **anything** you want to know, just ask.*

QUESTIONS
Any- is very common in questions:
*Does **anyone** understand the new software?*
Some- is common with offers and requests:
*Can I give you a lift **somewhere/anywhere**?*

Compare *any-* and *some-*. *Any-* emphasises that there is no limit to the possibilities:
*Is there **something** I can do to help?* (a normal offer)
*Is there **anything** I can do to help?*   (I'll do whatever I can)

NEGATIVE SENTENCES

Not ... any- is very common and means the same as *no-*:
*There is**n't anybody** here with that name.*   =   *There is **nobody** here with that name.*

Not ... some- is rare and has a different meaning to *not ... any-*. Study the examples:
*He is**n't someone** I feel comfortable talking to.*   (= He isn't a person I feel ...)
*That is**n't something** I'd thought about before.*   (= That isn't a thing I'd thought ...)

C *Everyone/no one, etc*

- Words with *every-* mean all the people, things or places in a group.
  *A big 'thank you' to **everyone**. You all did a wonderful job.*
  *We handle **everything** for you, from design to delivery.*

- *Every one* (with two words) has a different meaning. It means *each single one* and is used to give emphasis. In pronunciation, both words have equal stress.
  ***Every one** of our clients is important, even the smallest companies.*

- Words with *no-* mean no people, things or places.
  ***Nobody** phoned while you were out.*

  *Meanwhile, Allianz tried to bring Dresdner together with HVB, in which Allianz also has a large stake. Initially, the idea went **nowhere** because HVB board members opposed it.* (BusinessWeek Online website)

  Double negatives are not used.
  *There **is nothing** we can do.*   OR   *There **isn't anything** we can do.*
  (NOT ~~There isn't nothing we can do.~~)

D Reflexive pronouns

- The reflexive pronouns are: *myself, yourself, himself, herself, itself, ourselves, yourselves, themselves*. Note that there is a plural 'you' form.

- We use a reflexive pronoun if the object of the verb is the same as the subject.
  Compare:
  I'm enjoying the trip.   *I'm enjoying **myself**.*
  Jill introduced me to her boss.   *Jill introduced **herself** to me.*

- Some verbs may be reflexive in your language, but are usually not in English. Examples include:
  change (clothes), *complain, decide, dress, feel, hurry, meet, relax, remember, rest, sit down, stand up, wake up, wash, wonder, worry*.
  Note that actions that we do to ourselves do not have a reflexive pronoun.
  *When I got home I **washed** and **changed** quickly before going out again.*

- We can use a reflexive pronoun for emphasis. In pronunciation, we stress *self* or *selves*.
  *I **myself** haven't seen the new design, but I believe it's very good.*

- If the meaning is 'without help' or 'alone' we can use *by* + reflexive pronoun.
  *Are you doing all the research **(by) yourselves**?*   (without help)
  *I wanted to travel to the conference **by myself**.*   (alone)

- Compare *themselves* and *each other/one another*:
  *Andrew and Jessica emailed **each other/one another**.*
  (Andrew sent an email to Jessica, and Jessica sent an email to Andrew)
  *Andrew and Jessica emailed **themselves**.*
  (Andrew sent an email to himself, and Jessica sent an email to herself)

  *Not long ago companies were falling over **each other** trying to 'dot com' **themselves**. AudioNet became Broadcast.com ... and Sun Microsystems spent millions trying to convince us all that it was 'the dot in dot com,' whatever that means. Ah, but those days are gone.* (money.com website)

31 Practice

Exercise 1 A B C

Complete the sentences using the most appropriate words from the list below.

anyone anything anything everyone everything no one nothing someone
~~something~~ something

1 It's just not right. _Something_. is worrying me about this.
2 The office is empty. There's .... here except me.
3 I'm sorry, I don't think there's .... I can do to help you.
4 (the telephone line is dead) Hello? Is there .... there?
5 .... seems to be wrong with the printer. It's not working.
6 There's .... to see you. Shall I ask them to wait?
7 I see that .... has a copy of the agenda, so let's begin.
8 (before moving on to the next point in a meeting) Is there .... else?
9 Good, ... is going according to plan.
10 No, I've decided. .... you could say would make me change my mind.

Exercise 2 B C

Underline the correct words.

1 We can't blame _anyone_/no one but ourselves for this mess.
2 There's _anything_/_nothing_ in the post for you this morning.
3 There isn't _anything_/_nothing_ in the post for you this morning.
4 _Anyone_/_Someone_ called for you earlier, but I don't know who.
5 Isn't there _anywhere_/_nowhere_ to go that's open at this time of night?
6 Can I ask you _anything_/_something_?
7 There's _anyone_/_someone_ on the phone to speak to you.
8 You can do _anything_/_something_ you want, it won't make any difference.
9 Sorry, I don't know _anything_/_nothing_ about it.
10 _No one_/_Someone_ knew what to do, so I used my own initiative.

Exercise 3 D

Complete the sentences with a word from the list below, in a suitable form, and a reflexive pronoun.

~~ask~~ blame enjoy express help hurt introduce make prepare teach

1 I keep ....._asking_..... ....._myself_.... what I would do in his situation.
2 It was a great holiday. We really ....
3 James .... Spanish by listening to cassettes while driving to work.
4 Be careful! It's very heavy! Don't .... !
5 Paula knows a lot of French, but she can't .... very easily.
6 Ladies and Gentlemen, please .... to more coffee.
7 Mary, ... for a shock. I'm going to resign.
8 Let me .... My name is Susan Conway.
9 It wasn't your fault. Don't ....
10 Ann and Nick! Great to see you. Come in and .... at home.

Exercise 4 **A B C D**

Underline the correct or most appropriate words.

1 No one *like*/*likes* to discover hidden costs, *does he*/*do they*?

2 I *felt*/*felt myself* quite nervous at the start of the presentation, but after a few minutes I *relaxed*/*relaxed myself*.

3 We'll deliver your pizza *sometime, somewhere*/*anytime, anywhere*.

4 I *remember*/*remember myself* when I first started working here. I always used to *worry*/*worry myself* if I was doing the right thing.

5 The figures in this spreadsheet don't correspond to the ones on the invoices. We're going to have to check *everyone*/*every one*.

6 Everyone *has*/*have* to meet in the lobby at nine o'clock to collect *his*/*their* conference registration forms.

7 Rome isn't *somewhere*/*anywhere* near Milan.

8 Rome isn't *somewhere*/*anywhere* I'd like to go for holidays in August. It's too hot for me then.

9 Your two colleagues introduced *themselves*/*each other* to me yesterday. First I met Peter, then later I met Susan.

10 Your two colleagues introduced *themselves*/*each other* to me yesterday. Peter told me a little about what Susan does, and Susan told me a little about Peter.

Exercise 5 **B C**

 37 Complete the dialogues with the words from the list below.

anyone   anything   anywhere   everyone   everything   ~~everywhere~~   someone
something   somewhere

A

DAVID: I can't find my mobile phone. I've looked (1) ...**everywhere.**... I must have put it down (2) .... , but I just can't remember where. Oh, how annoying! It could be (3) ....

RITA: Perhaps (4) .... has picked it up by mistake? (5) .... in the company has the same type of mobile phone. (6) .... could have picked it up.

B

GUY: Sales have dropped by 50% in Asia over the last 12 months.

PETRA: There must be (7) .... we can do to increase sales.

GUY: But what? I've tried (8) .... I can't think of (9) .... else we can do.

Exercise 6 **D**

 38 Vicky and her husband Charles are staying in a hotel. Complete what Vicky says by using the verbs in brackets with or without a reflexive pronoun.

'Charles, come on, try to (1) ...**enjoy yourself**... (enjoy)! (2) ....**Remember**...... (remember) you're on holiday! Look, why don't you (3) .... (help) to another drink, go on … Goodness me, there's Daniel Westlake over there. What on earth is he doing here in Marrakech? Er, have you two (4) .... (met) before? You know, you'd have a lot in common with Daniel. Why don't you go over there and (5) .... (introduce) to him? While you do that I'll go back to the room and (6) .... (change) in time for dinner. I don't know. Sometimes I (7) .... (ask) whether you can ever (8) .... (relax) when you're away from the office.'

32 Determiners

> *Most of the top automakers have made agreements with **either** Sirius **or** XM to install satellite radios in their cars. But **neither** company has earned any revenues yet, and the technology may not deliver on its promise of CD-quality sound anywhere, anytime.*
> **(Fortune website)**

A Determiners

- A determiner is a word used in front of a noun to show which thing you mean, or to show the quantity of something. Determiners include: *a/the, my/your, this/that, all/most/some/any, no/none, much/many/a little/a few, each/every, both/either/neither.*

- Units 30, 34 and 35 also deal with determiners: *some* or *any? much* or *many?* (unit 30), *a* or *the?* (units 34 and 35).

- We do not use a determiner if we are talking generally. See units 30 and 35.
  Our/Those/Some computers *are expensive.*   (particular computers)
  Computers *are a part of everyone's life.*   (computers in general)

B *All, most, many, some, a few*

- Before a plural noun we can use *all/most/many/some/a few*. Note the structures:
  *All/most/many/some/a few **employees** have 25 days' paid holiday.*
  *All/most/many/some/a few **of the employees** have 25 days' paid holiday.*
  *All **the employees** have 25 days paid holiday.* (NOT ~~Most the …/Many the … etc.~~)

- We can use *my, your*, etc, in place of *the*, and we can use pronouns:
  *All/most/many/some/a few **of our employees** have 25 days' paid holiday.*
  *All/most/many/some/a few **of them** have 25 days' paid holiday.*

See also unit 30
- Before an uncountable noun similar structures are possible. We use *much* in place of *many*, *a little* in place of *a few*, and *it* for the pronoun.
  *All/most/**much**/some/**a little of the information** in this report is useful.*
  *All/most/**much**/some/**a little of it** is useful.*

- With singular nouns we do not use the words above, except for a few special expressions:
  all day, all night

C *All* meaning 'everything' or 'the only thing'

- We can use *all* + subject + verb to mean 'everything' or 'the only thing':
  *That's **all** I know about it.*   (all = everything)
  ***All** we need is a signature.* (all = the only thing)

- In modern English it is unusual to use *all* as a single-word subject or object. Instead we use *everything*.
  ***All the preparations are/Everything is** going well.* (NOT ~~All is going well.~~)
  *I want to hear **all your news/everything**.* (NOT ~~I want to hear all.~~)

D *No, none*

- We can use *no* with a singular noun, plural noun or uncountable noun.
  No employee has more than 25 days' paid holiday.
  No new ideas were put forward at the meeting.
  There was no useful information in the report.

- We do not use *no* if there is another negative word. In this case we use *any*.
  We have**n't** dismissed **any** employees. (NOT ~~We haven't dismissed no employees~~.)

- We do not use *no of*. Instead, we use *none of* or *none* on its own as a pronoun.
  None of the employees have more than 25 days' paid holiday.
  None have more than 25 days' paid holiday.

- To emphasise the idea of *none* we can use *None at all* or *Not one* or *Not a*:
  A: *How many people came?*
  B: **None** *at all!/***Not one***!/***Not a** *single person!*

  Germany's Neuer Markt All Share index dropped below the 1,500 mark for the first time yesterday. **Not a single** *stock in the top 20 stocks showed a gain.* (Yahoo Business News website)

E *Each, every*

- The meaning of *each* and *every* is similar and often either word is possible. They are both followed by a singular noun.

- We use *each* when we think of the members of a group as individuals, one by one. It is more usual with smaller groups and can mean only two.
  Make sure that **each parcel** *has a label.*

  Samsung and Globetronics know they have to raise their brand profile. Management consultants will debate **each** *firm's stategy, but in the end consumers will determine whether these companies are successful in a more globalized world.* (asiaweek website)

- We use *every* when we think of all the members together, and it is usual with a larger number.
  Sales have increased **every year** *for the last five years.*
  I believe **every word** *he says.*

- We can use *each of*, but we cannot use *every of*.
  Each of the parcels *needs a label.*

- *Each* can be used after the subject, or at the end of a sentence.
  The parcels **each** *need a label.*
  The parcels need a label **each***.*

F *Both, either, neither*

- We use *both, either* and *neither* to refer to two things.

- *Both* means 'the one and the other'. Note the structures:
  Both emails/both the emails/both of the emails/both of them *are important.*
  The emails are **both important***.   I've read* **them both***.*

- *Either* means 'the one or the other'. *Neither* means 'not the one or the other'.
  Monday or Tuesday? Yes, **either day/either of the days** *is fine.*
  Monday or Tuesday? I'm sorry, but **neither day/neither of the days** *is convenient.*

  This is a hell of a gamble — one that may pay off for **both***, one, or* **neither** *of the two companies.* (Fortune website)

32 Practice

Exercise 1 A

Match the phrases from the list below with an approximate value.

~~none of them~~   most of them   a few of them   many of them   some of them   all of them

1 0% _none of them_

2 5–25% ....

3 25–50% ....

4 50–75% ....

5 75–95% ....

6 100% ....

Exercise 2 B C D E F

<u>Underline</u> the correct words.

1 There were *none/no* messages on the answering machine.

2 The key account managers *each/every* have their own list of clients.

3 *Not one/Not no* question has been answered.

4 *Some of/Some* the restaurants have service included in the price.

5 *Some of/Some* restaurants have service included in the price.

6 Sorry, but I can't hear *either/neither* of you properly.

7 *Each our customers/Our customers each* have a separate file on the database.

8 I can't come at the weekend. I'm busy *both days/every day*.

9 *All of/Every of* the files are corrupted by the virus.

10 I can't see *no/any* solution to the problem, I'm afraid.

11 The flight and hotel are booked. *All/Everything* is organised.

12 We gave the sales reps *each a mobile phone/a mobile phone each*.

13 *Every option has been/Every options have been* explored.

14 OK, I think that covers *all/everything* on that point. Shall we move on?

Exercise 3 B C D E F

Complete the sentences with a word or phrase from the list below.

all (x2)   any   no   ~~not one~~   none   each (x2)   every (x2)   both   either (x2)   neither

1 We sent letters to sixty customers, but _not one_ replied!

2 I can't go. There are only two flights, and there are .... seats left on .... of them.

3 I can't go. There are only two flights, and .... of them has any seats left.

4 .... I want is a bit of peace and quiet to finish writing this report.

5 I've phoned .... store in the Yellow Pages and they are .... out of stock.

6 We have three models, and .... one has its own special features.

7 I was nervous at the start of my talk, but after that I enjoyed .... minute.

8 I got three letters, but there were .... for you, I'm afraid.

9 I got three letters, but there weren't .... for you, I'm afraid.

10 The Trade Fair is important. We need .... Sue and Mike on the stand.

11 Both roads lead to the city centre. You can take .... one.

12 You've been six of the best trainees that we've ever had on this course. The best of luck to .... of you in your future careers.

Exercise 4 B C D E F

Rewrite the second sentence so it has a similar meaning to the first sentence and contains the word/s in brackets. Some sentences have two possible answers.

1 We only have a week left. (all)
   .... *All we have left is* ...... a week.

2 All the participants will be sent an agenda. (every)
   .... will be sent an agenda.

3 Nobody at all asked a question. (single person)
   .... asked a question.

4 This idea won't work, and the other one also won't work. (neither)
   .... will work.

5 Not all the audience understood his talk. (some)
   .... understand his talk.

6 Not one of my colleagues speaks German. (none)
   .... speak German.

7 We only want a weaker dollar. (all)
   .... a weaker dollar.

8 No documents were inside this parcel. (any)
   There .... inside this parcel.

9 The hotels were both unsuitable. (neither)
   .... suitable.

10 The two proposals are interesting. (both)
   .... interesting.

11 These items aren't expensive. (none)
   .... expensive.

12 I'm sorry, we have absolutely none. (all)
   I'm sorry, we have ....

Exercise 5 B C E F

 39   Complete this article by choosing the correct alternative A, B or C below.

TRANSLATION ON THE NET

The world of online translation is dominated by Amsterdam-based Aquarius.net and California-based Proz.com (1) ...... maintain a list of translators who bid for jobs posted on the site, but (2) ...... has a d i f f e r e n t business plan. (3) ...... charges clients to post translation jobs on the site, but Aquarius has started charging translators to register, and also charges transaction fees of up to 7.5% to the translator who gets the job. Meanwhile Proz is still a free site, and gets (4) ...... revenue from advertising. (5) ...... trying to deal with the problem of quality assurance, and (6) ...... translator has their diplomas and qualifications online. And what about the Old Economy off-line translation agencies? They offer better guarantees of quality and (7) ...... them haven't looked to the Internet for a solution yet, but (8) ...... is changing very fast, and the Net offers significant cost benefits to clients. ■

1	A Both them	B Both of them	C Every of them
2	A each one	B every one	C all of them
3	A Either of them	B Neither of company	C Neither company
4	A all its	B most its	C much its
5	A Each they are	B Both they are	C They are both
6	A all	B all of	C every
7	A most	B most of	C every of
8	A all	B the only thing	C everything

33 Possessives and compound nouns

> Small companies, with a market capitalisation of less than £350,000, could provide the greatest value for investors this year. The advice comes from David Rough, Legal & General's investment director. Mr Rough said yesterday there were a number of factors that pointed to the success of smaller companies this year.
> **(Independent website)**

A Possessive adjectives and pronouns

- *My, your*, etc, are adjectives and come before a noun.
  *This was **my/your/her/his/our/their** suggestion.*
  *I'm looking for a street, but I can't remember **its** name.*

  Mine, yours, etc, are pronouns and we use them on their own.
  *This suggestion was **mine/yours/hers/his/ours/theirs**.* (no 'its' form)

- We can add *own* to a possessive adjective for emphasis.
  ***My own** view is that we should go ahead with the project.*

B 's (apostrophe s)

- We use *'s* to show that something belongs to a person or organisation. Many other languages use *of* in these cases. We add *'s* even if the name ends in *s*.
  *Helen**'s** idea   The CEO**'s** office   Ford**'s** cars   Charles**'s** address*

  With plural nouns we add the apostrophe only.

  *The **Chinese government's National Audit Office** held a press conference in December to report on its work and **auditors' investigations** in the country. The auditors are among **the central authorities' most important weapons** in their efforts to clear up malpractice by business people and officials.* (Business Beijing Online website)

- We can use the *'s* form without a following noun if the meaning is clear.
  *The project was a team effort, but the original idea was **Helen's**.   (= Helen's idea)*

- A special use of *'s* is to refer to someone's home, a shop name or a place name.
  *I'll be at **Jack's** this evening.   (Jack's house)*
  *I'm going to **Smith's**. Do you want anything?   (the shop called Smith)*
  *I must go to the **chemist's/doctor's/dentist's**. (the place where they work)*

- If there is no possession, we do not use an apostrophe.
  Epson printers on special offer!   (NOT ~~Epson printer's~~)

- There is no apostrophe in possessive adjectives or pronouns (section A).
  (NOT ~~I like it's colour~~)
  Apostrophes can be a short form of *is* or *has*.
  ***It's** a lovely day. (= It is)   **It's** been a pleasure meeting you. (= It has)*

C Of

● We use *of* to show that one thing belongs to or with another thing.
*The end **of the street**.* (NOT ~~the street's end~~)
*The time **of the meeting**.* (NOT ~~the meeting's time~~)
*The last two pages **of the report**.* (NOT ~~the report's last two pages~~)

● Here are some common phrases with *of* and examples of nouns that follow:

a choice of (flights)	*a method of* (payment)	*the strength of* (the Euro)
an error of (judgement)	*a number of* (factors)	*a stroke of* (luck)
a flood of (complaints)	*the pace of* (change)	*the success of* (the project)
a lack of (funds)	*a piece of* (advice)	*the time of* (arrival)
the level of (commitment)	*a range of* (colours)	*a waste of* (time)

● Section B said that we use *'s* for people. There are some exceptions to this rule. We normally use *of* with long phrases.
*This is the email address **of the sales representative who came yesterday**.*
(NOT *This is* ~~the sales representative who came yesterday's email address.~~)

And we can use *a ... of ...* + possessive form to show a connection between people.
*She's **a colleague of mine**.* OR *She's my colleague.*
*She's **a friend of Stephen's**.* OR *She's Stephen's friend.*

● We can use *of* or apostrophe for places and organisations.
*The historic centre **of Prague*** OR ***Prague's** historic centre*
*the future **of the company*** OR ***the company's** future*

D Compound nouns

● A compound noun is two nouns together. Compound nouns are common in English, and are particularly common in business language.

*'I can also report that manufacturing — despite the ... **exchange rate** — grew last year by 1.6 per cent; **manufacturing productivity** grew by 4.4 per cent and **manufacturing exports** by 11.8 per cent.' — Chancellor Gordon Brown's budget speech.* (The Times website)

● When we use two nouns together, the first noun is like an adjective and describes the second noun.
*It was a **management decision**.*
*These **research results** are very interesting.*
*Have you seen this **sales report**?*
*The whole **company strategy** is wrong.*

*Transforming traditional **ordering** and **distribution processes** into **e-commerce solutions** leads to significant **cost reductions**.* (Connectis website)

The first noun is usually singular:
*reductions in **costs*** * **cost** reductions*
*the law relating to **companies*** * **company** law*

● We can use more than two nouns. To understand the meaning start at the end.
*an **executive search company*** (a company that searches for executives)
*a **government training course*** (a course of training provided by the government)
*a **stock market launch*** (a launch in the market for stocks)

● In certain fixed phrases we cannot use a compound noun. We have to use *of*.
*lack **of** confidence* *freedom **of** choice* *the price **of** success* *the cost **of** progress*

● Some compound nouns are written as one word.
database *timescale* *salesman* *network* *workshop* *bookshop*

33 Practice

Exercise 1 A

Underline the correct words.

1 They offer reasonable prices, but I'm not sure about <u>*their*</u>/*theirs* quality.
2 Excuse me, is this *your*/*yours* seat?
3 Excuse me, is this seat *your*/*yours*?
4 Is this pen *yours*/*your's* or mine?
5 We do all *ourselves*/*our own* design and printing.
6 We do all the design and printing *ourselves*/*our own*.
7 The office at the end of the corridor is *my*/*mine*.
8 *My*/*mine* office is at the end of the corridor.
9 It's not really *her*/*hers* decision.
10 The committee had *its*/*it's* final meeting yesterday.

Exercise 2 A B

Rewrite the sentences with apostrophes where necessary.

1 Susan should know that its Marys decision, not hers.
   Susan should know that it's Mary's decision, not hers.

2 Alices friends names Bill. Hes one of Merrill Lynchs top analysts.
   ....

3 Toyotas deal on its company cars is better than ours.
   ....

4 I went to my doctors and hes computerised all the patients records.
   ....

5 Its important to recognise that every company has its own particular culture, however ...
   ....

6 My bosss PA reads all the customers letters.
   ....

7 Look at those two Mercedes. Ones our directors and the others a visitors.
   ....

Exercise 3 D

Make two compound nouns from the nouns in each group.

1 profits course training company	company profits	training course
2 staff forecast meeting sales	....	....
3 card store credit department	....	....
4 Internet sale summer access	....	....
5 figures price inflation range	....	....
6 survey market hour rush	....	....
7 technology keys car information	....	....
8 assistant shop failure power	....	....
9 shopfloor working worker lunch	....	....
10 insurance loan contract bank	....	....
11 features costs production product	....	....
12 market marketing budget leader	....	....

Exercise 4 C

Complete the sentences with phrases from the list below.

> error of   flood of   lack of   level of   method of   pace of   piece of
>
> range of   stroke of   ~~waste of~~

1   I went there, but they were closed. It was a complete ....*waste of*.......... time.
2   The product launch is a disaster. There's a complete .... interest.
3   You shouldn't have told them that information. It was an .... judgement.
4   Our hotel offers a wide .... facilities for the business traveller.
5   We have a relatively low .... unemployment in our country, just 4%.
6   I heard a very interesting .... information the other day.
7   We arrived just at the right time. What a .... luck!
8   The advertisement has been very successful. There's a .... inquiries.
9   The results must be correct. We used a very reliable .... data analysis.
10 Things are moving so quickly in this field. The .... change is very fast.

Exercise 5 A B C D

Rewrite the second sentence so it has a similar meaning to the first sentence.

1   I'll see you in the room we use for meetings in ten minutes.
    I'll see you ....*in the meeting room*.... in ten minutes.
2   This pen doesn't belong to me.
    This isn't ....
3   This pen doesn't belong to me.
    This pen isn't ....
4   These documents belong to James.
    These are ....
5   Margaret met one of her colleagues at the conference.
    Margaret met a .... at the conference.
6   What is your boss called?
    What .... name?
7   You should consult an expert in law about companies.
    You should consult .... law.
8   This graph shows the figures for sales for last year.
    This graph .... for last year.
9   I just sent an email to one of our customers.
    I just sent an email to a ....
10 I'm going on a course to train managers.
    I'm going on .... course.

Exercise 6 D

Cross out the one word in each group that does not make a common compound noun with the first word in bold.

1   **sales**   forecast/figures/~~trade~~/target
2   **market**   forces/sector/check/share
3   **price**   offer/list/range/rise
4   **brand**   image/leader/loyalty/process
5   **tax**   relief/benefits/output/allowance
6   **product**   manager/range/features/share
7   **advertising**   slogan/campaign/line/agency
8   **production**   market/line/capacity/target
9   **working**   conditions/trend/hours/lunch
10 **stock**   option/decision/market/exchange

34 Articles 1

> Is a shark responsible for cutting **Internet access** to millions of people across **China**? It's one possible explanation for how **a $1.4 billion cable** linking China to **the western U.S.** was cut. Another possibility is that **a fisherman** may have cut **the cable** by mistake.
> (Yahoo Business News website)

A Articles

- *A/an* is called the indefinite article, and we use it to introduce new information.
  The is called the definite article, and we use it when the listener knows which person or thing we are talking about.
  'No article' is the noun by itself, without an article. We use no article when we want to speak generally.

- Compare:
  *I read **an interesting report** last week.*   ('report' is mentioned for the first time)
  *Have you read **the report** I gave you?*   (the listener knows which report)
  ***Reports** are sent out four times a year.*   (speaking generally)

B *A/an*

- We use *a/an* to introduce new information. The listener does not know which person or thing we are talking about.

- We use *a/an* to refer to something for the first time.
  *We must have a **meeting** next week.*
  *I have **an idea** I'd like to discuss.*

- We use *a/an* to refer to one of a group of things.
  *Can you pass me **a paper clip** from that box by your side?*

- We use *a/an* to describe someone's job, but not areas of business.
  *Fiona used to be **a teacher**, but now she's in management training.*

- We use *a/an* to describe something.
  *It's **an interesting idea**.*   *Cairo is **a very big city**.*   *This is **a better product**.*

- We use *a/an* in expressions of measurement. *Per* can also be used.
  twice a/per month   *3,000 units an/per hour*   *We charge £100 an/per hour*

- *A/an* mean 'one', so we cannot use *a/an* with plurals or uncountable nouns.
  *Can you give me **some information**?* (NOT ~~an information~~)

C *A* or *an*?

- We use *a* in front of a consonant sound, and *an* in front of a vowel sound.
  consonant sounds: *a manager, a job, a university, a one-way street, a European law*
  vowel sounds: *an idea, an employer, an hour, an MBA*

- In a similar way, *the* is pronounced /ðə/ before a consonant sound and /ðiː/ before a vowel sound.

D *The*

● We use *the* for old information. It is clear which person or thing we are talking about.

*Six banks are interested in buying a stake in Peru's Banco Latino. Three are North American banks, one is a major Spanish institution, another is Ecuadorean and the other is Peruvian. **The six** have been invited to study Latino's books and bid by the end of March.* (Business News Americas website)

● We often know which one because we mentioned it before, using *a/an*.
*We must have **a meeting** next week. **The meeting** should focus on the auditors' report.*
*I went to **an interesting show** last week. It was **the Paris Spring Collection**.*

● Sometimes we know which one because it is clear from the situation, or it is shared knowledge from the lives of the speaker and listener.
*Where's **the newspaper**?*   (we know which one from the situation)
***The meeting** will begin at ten.* (both the speaker and listener know which meeting)

Note that in this case we can use *the* to refer to something for the first time.

● We use *the* when there is only one of something. It is clear which one we are talking about.
*I'll speak to **the boss** when he gets back.*

● We use *the* with nationalities and other groups.
*I really admire **the Italians** for their sense of design.*
*The government is trying to do more to help **the poor**.*

See unit 37 ● We use *the* with superlatives.
*This is **the best** quality material we have in stock.*

E No article

● No article is used when we are talking generally.

*The first issue of the Agency Magazine features an article called '**Health** and **safety** at work – A question of **costs** and **benefits**?'.* (European Agency for Safety and Health at Work website)

● **PLURAL NOUNS**
Compare:
*I sent **the emails** this morning.* (we know which emails)
*I usually reply to **emails** within 24 hours.* (emails in general)

● **UNCOUNTABLE NOUNS**
Compare:

***The information** in this report gives us **the power** to target our advertising.*	(we know which information and power)
***Information** is **power**.*	(information and power in general)
***The insurance business** is doing well.*	(we know which business)
***Business** is going well at the moment.*	(business in general)
***The negotiating** was a lot easier last time.*	(we know which negotiating)
***Negotiating** with suppliers takes a lot of time.*	(negotiating in general)

● A common mistake is to use *the* with plural nouns and uncountable nouns used in a general way.
Small companies often grow faster. (NOT ~~The small companies~~)
For me, football is like life. (NOT For me, ~~the football is like the life~~.)

See unit 35 ● We use no article for most companies, countries, states and cities.
*I work for **HBSC** in **Hong Kong**.*
***Los Angeles** is in **California**.*

34 Practice

Exercise 1 A B D

Underline the correct words.

1 Where's *a/the* fax they sent this morning? I can't find it.

2 I have *an/the* appointment at *a/the* bank.

3 I had *a/the* very good holiday. *A/The* weather was marvellous.

4 I've been working so hard that I need *a/the* break.

5 They are *a/the* largest manufacturer of light bulbs in *a/the* world.

6 *A/The* presentation was *a/the* great success.

7 Can I give you *a/the* lift to the station?

8 I think I need *a/the* new pair of glasses.

9 We need to reach *a/the* decision as soon as possible.

10 There must be *an/the* answer to *a/the* problem.

11 Mike is *an/the* accountant. He works on *another/the other* side of town.

12 His office is *a/the* biggest one in *a/the* building.

13 Where is *a/the* document that we were looking at just now?

14 *The Portuguese/The Portuguese people* are very good negotiators.

Exercise 2 A B C E

Put either *a/an* or a dash (–) to show no article.

1 .....─..... money makes the world go round.

2 Sheila drives .... French car.

3 Rita works in .... insurance agency in .... Lisbon.

4 .... health is the most important thing in .... life.

5 This is .... good time for .... sales of new cars.

6 This is the number to call for .... information.

7 I've got .... colleague who is .... systems analyst.

8 .... product knowledge is very important for .... sales representative.

9 He is .... engineer. He studied .... engineering at university.

10 We produce .... full sales report four times .... year.

Exercise 3 A B C D E

Put either *a/an, the* or a dash (–) to show no article.

1 *The*.. Italians have given us ...*a*... lot of ...─... business.

2 .... most people thought that it was .... very good product.

3 I like to drink .... glass of .... wine in .... evening.

4 I wish I could speak .... English like .... English.

5 As soon as .... Helen gets off .... plane, ask her to give me .... call.

6 .... smoking is not permitted in this area.

7 There's .... visitor at .... reception desk.

8 When I arrived at .... airport, I had .... drink and waited for .... flight.

9 I want .... action, not .... words.

10 .... person with .... MBA usually gets .... good job.

11 I'll get you .... coffee from .... machine.

12 Marie comes from .... France.

Exercise 4 A B C D

 40 Complete this article with either *a/an, the* or a dash (–) to show no article.

HOW CLEAN IS THEIR MONEY?

'Money laundering' is (1) ...*the*... name given to one of (2) .... world's biggest financial problems: moving money that has been obtained illegally into (3) .... foreign bank accounts so that (4) .... people do not know where it has come from. Putting (5) .... value on money laundering is of course very difficult, but the International Monetary Fund estimate that it is huge – perhaps $1 trillion

(6) .... year, equivalent to about 4% of gross world product.

(7) .... problem has grown hand-in-hand with (8) .... globalisation, and particularly with (9) .... lifting of capital controls and (10) .... development of (11) .... international payment systems. These allow money to be moved in (12) .... seconds between banks in different parts of the world

who know very little about each other. (13) .... international payment system is crucial to (14) .... stability of the world's financial markets, but it also provides (15) .... opportunity for criminals to hide their money.

Private banking is (16) .... best-known laundering channel. Clients of these banks are wealthy people who want their affairs handled with discretion,

especially because they want to minimise (17) .... amount of (18) .... tax they pay. In these banks there is (19) .... culture of 'don't ask; don't tell'. And (20) .... biggest problem within (21) .... private banking is offshore banks. There are around 5,000 offshore banks controlling about $5 trillion in assets, and some have no physical presence in any location.

Exercise 5 A B C D E

 41 Complete this interview between a journalist and the CEO of Biotec, a biotechnology company. Use either *a/an, the* or a dash (–) to show no article.

JOURNALIST: Can you begin by telling me (1) ...*a*... little about (2) ..*the*. recent changes at (3) ..*–*... Biotec?

CEO: Well, as you know, last year we made (4) .... decision to move our operations to (5) .... Cambridge, because it's very important for (6) ...... biotechnology companies to recruit (7) .... scientists from (8) .... best universities. Er, we're in (9) ...... very competitive jobs market here in Cambridge, and we motivate our employees by offering them (10) .... attractive salaries and (11) .... excellent working conditions. We've built up (12) ...... excellent team, and we're doing some very important research in (13) .... field of (14) ...... gene therapy.

JOURNALIST: Many people say that (15) .... biotechnology promises more than it delivers. Is that true at Biotec?

CEO: That may be true in general, but (16) .... biotechnology that we do is already producing (17) .... results. Last year we made (18) .... small profit for (19) .... first time, and (20) ...... revenue is increasing rapidly. Also, we've recently made (21) .... distribution deal with (22) .... large pharmaceutical company. They have the marketing skills that we lack, and (23) .... partnership is working well for both sides. Our aim next year is to enter (24) ...... American market, and we're confident of (25) ...... success.

35 Articles 2

> *What will be the impact of global warming? Sea levels will probably rise six to 37 inches, threatening to flood islands from the Bahamas to the Maldives in the Indian Ocean. The risk of tidal waves could rise in Florida and other coastal states. (Fortune website)*

Unit 34 gives some basic rules for articles. This unit gives additional points.

A Place names and no article

● In general, no article is used for continents, countries, states, islands, mountains, lakes, cities, parks, roads, streets, squares, palaces, castles, cathedrals, stations and airports.

Europe/Asia   France/China   California/Lazio   Crete/Madeira
Mont Blanc/Mount Everest   Lake Lucerne/Lake Michigan   Tokyo/Budapest
Central Park/Hyde Park   Fifth Avenue/Church Street   Trafalgar Square/Times Square
Buckingham Palace   Windsor Castle   Milan Cathedral   Grand Central Station   Orly Airport

B Place names and *the*

● Note that all the following use *the*:

Plurals:	*the Alps, the Bahamas, the Netherlands*
Adjective + place:	*the Red Sea, the Middle East, the West End*
	(But NOT if the place is the name of a country or continent: *France, South-East Asia*)
Phrases with 'of':	*the Houses of Parliament, the South of France*
Political constitutions:	*the Irish Republic, the United Kingdom (the UK), the US*
Rivers and canals:	*the Amazon, the Loire, the Suez Canal*
Oceans and seas:	*the Pacific, the Atlantic, the Mediterranean*
Roads with numbers:	*the M6 (motorway), the A1*
Theatres and galleries:	*the Globe (Theatre), the Uffizi (Gallery)*
Hotels:	*the Marriott (Hotel)*
Famous buildings:	*the Eiffel Tower, the Taj Mahal, the White House*

C Special uses of *the*

● We use *the* with:

International institutions:	**The United Nations, The World Bank, The IMF**
Adjectives to refer to a group:	**The unemployed** *do not receive enough help.*
the ... of a/the ... :	**the** *end* **of an** *era,* **the** *start* **of the** *project*
Some time phrases:	*in* **the past***, at* **the moment***, in* **the future** *(but at present),* **the 1960s** *(decades),* **the 21st century** *(centuries)*
Points of the compass:	*in* **the north/east/south/west***, in* **the south-west**
Playing instruments:	*I play* **the piano/guitar***.*
Job titles and official titles:	**The Marketing Director, the Prime Minister** *said ...*
	(But NOT title + name: *Prime Minister Tony Blair said ...*)

City Snapshots: a monthly guide for **the** *business traveler.* (asia-inc magazine website)

Hypo Alpe–Adria–Bank *has been highly successful in* **Croatia** *over the past four years. According to* **Dr. Wolfgang Kulterer, the Chairman of the Board***, this success is due to concentrating business activities on* **the Alpine–Adriatic market** *and choosing good business partners.* (cebd website)

D Special uses of 'no article'

● We use no article with:

Company names:	*I work for **Accenture**.*
Years, months, days:	*in **2001**, in **July**, on **Thursday***
Special times of the year:	*at **Christmas/Easter***
Some parts of the day:	*at **night/midnight/sunset*** (BUT *the morning, the afternoon*)
Means of transport (in general):	*by **car/taxi/train/bus**, on **foot*** (BUT *on the train to Rome*)
Meals (in general):	***Dinner** is at 7.30.* (BUT *There was a dinner at the conference*)

● Note the use of 'preposition + no article' with certain buildings, when the purpose of the building is more important than the place itself. Compare:

*I spent two days **in hospital**.* (the speaker is not interested in which one)
*My company supplies equipment for **the hospital**.* (one specific hospital)

Other words of this type which use 'preposition and no article' are:
in/to *hospital/prison/bed/class/court*
at/to *work/school/university/sea/home*

Note how we use 'home':
be at home, go home (NOT ~~go to home~~)

E General and specific meanings

● When we use a plural noun or an uncountable noun on its own it has a general meaning. When we put *the* in front it has a specific meaning.

***Cars** are much safer these days.*	***The cars** we make are built to last.*
*I don't understand **spreadsheets**.*	***The spreadsheets** for March and April are here.*
***People** can be difficult.*	***The people** in my office are all very friendly.*
*I prefer **fish** to **meat**.*	***The fish** I had for lunch was superb.*
***Money** makes the world go round.*	*Have you got **the money** I gave you?*
*How's **business**?*	***The clothing business** is very competitive.*

*****Taxis** in Singapore are abundant and reasonably priced, but hard to find during rush hours, when it rains and between 11 pm and midnight. **The taxis from the airport to the central business district** cost around $12.* (asia-inc magazine website)

"We reward top executives at the agency with a unique incentive program. Money."

35 Practice

Exercise 1 A B C D

Underline the correct words.

1　We went to *Pisa*/*the Pisa* and saw *Leaning Tower*/<u>*the Leaning Tower*</u>.

2　*Crete*/*The Crete* is very beautiful at this time of year.

3　My son is in *hospital*/*the hospital* and can't go to *school*/*the school*.

4　You can go from *Heathrow*/*the Heathrow* by *underground*/*the underground*.

5　*Helmut Kohl*/*The Helmut Kohl* was *Chancellor*/*the Chancellor* who helped to reunite *Germany*/*the Germany*.

6　We flew over *Alps*/*the Alps* and saw *Mont Blanc*/*the Mont Blanc*.

7　In *near future*/*the near future* videoconferences will replace many meetings.

8　I'm tired! Thank goodness it's time to go *home*/*to home*.

9　*New York*/*The New York* is in *United States*/*the United States*.

10　I usually have *lunch*/*the lunch* at about one.

11　I used to work for *Deutsche Bank*/*the Deutsche Bank* in *City of London*/*the City of London* at *start*/*the start* of my career.

12　My son wants to go to *university*/*the university* after his exams.

13　Do you know *Lake Windermere*/*the Lake Windermere*? It's in *Lake District*/*the Lake District,* in *north-west*/*the north-west* of *England*/*the England*.

14　I bought this suit from *Bond Street*/*the Bond Street*.

15　The Government should do more to help *the poor*/*the poor people*.

16　On our trip to *UK*/*the UK* we toured around *south-east*/*the south-east* and visited *Canterbury Cathedral*/*the Canterbury Cathedral*.

17　They wouldn't pay, so we took them to *court*/*the court*.

18　*John*/*The John* is at *work*/*the work* at *moment*/*the moment*.

19　We travelled to *Italy*/*the Italy* by *car*/*the car*.

20　*Danube*/*The Danube* is the main river in *Central Europe*/*the Central Europe*.

Exercise 2 E

In each pair of sentences, fill in one space with *the* and the other space with a dash (–) to show no article.

1　a)　...−.... profits are increasing across every division of the company.

　　b)　..The.. profits we made last year were up in comparison to the year before.

2　a)　.......... information in your report will be very useful to us.

　　b)　.......... information about the Kazakh market is hard to find.

3　a)　.......... visitors should sign their name in the book at reception.

　　b)　.......... visitors from Germany will be arriving at ten.

4　a)　This magazine article gives .... advice about which stocks to buy.

　　b)　Thank you for .... advice you gave me last week.

5　a)　.......... bonds I have are all long-term investments.

　　b)　.......... bonds are a safe investment when interest rates are falling.

6　a)　.......... French exports to the rest of Europe are up 4% this year.

　　b)　.......... French are world leaders in the luxury goods market.

7　a)　.......... management is an art, not a science.

　　b)　.......... management are blaming the unions for the breakdown in negotiations.

Exercise 3 B C D

Complete the second sentence so it has a similar meaning to the first sentence.

1 Tracey is the team leader.

   Tracey _is the leader_ of the team.

2 Your goods are on a ship at the moment.

   At the moment your goods are .... sea.

3 The meeting has ended.

   This is .... meeting.

4 Brighton is at the bottom of a map of England.

   Brighton is .... south of England.

5 Do you have the Internet at your house?

   Do you have the Internet .... home?

6 We walked to the station.

   We went to .... foot.

7 We employ 250 people at the moment.

   We employ 250 people .... present.

8 Daniel is still in his office.

   Daniel is still .... work.

Exercise 4 A B C D E unit 31

Complete the following texts with either *the* or a dash (–) to show no article. This exercise includes some revision of unit 31.

A

(1) ..–.. Argentina is one of (2) ...... most deregulated markets in (3) ...... world. (4) ...... privatisation process started in (5) ...... 1990s, and has included sectors such as (6) ...... telecommunications, (7) ...... utilities and (8) ...... financial services.(9) ...... Argentine telecoms market was fully deregulated in (10) ...... November 2000 and there are now (11) ...... five million cellular lines and six million homes with (12) ...... cable television services. (13) ...... water was decentralised before being privatised. (14) ...... Aguas Argentinas, (15) ...... local water supply company for (16) ...... city of Buenos Aires and all (17) ...... municipalities in (18) ...... Greater Buenos Aires, is (19) ...... largest privatised water utility in (20) ...... world.

B

Imagine a country that continues for 4,200 km from (21) ...... dry deserts in (22) ...... north, through (23) ...... industrial and agricultural heartland in (24) ...... centre, to (25) ...... lakes and forestry plantations in (26) ...... south, and finally to (27) ...... ends of (28) ...... earth in (29) ...... Patagonia and Antarctica. Welcome to (30) ...... Chile! It's a very diverse country, with (31) ...... Pacific Ocean to one side and (32) ...... Andes to (33) ...... other – you can swim in (34) ...... sea and ski in (35) ...... mountains all in (36) ...... same day. There are (37) ...... business opportunities in many areas, and (38) ...... financial services sector is (39) ...... most sophisticated in (40) ...... Latin America.

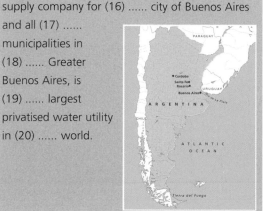

36 Adjectives and adverbs

A Adjectives and adverbs

> *How you succeed at business hasn't become radically different because of the New Economy. We've seen that trying to grow a company really fast usually doesn't work, and it's better to grow quite gradually to give it a solid foundation.*
> (e-business advisor website)

- An adjective describes a noun.
  Last year we had a significant increase in profits.
  Last year profits were much better than this year.

  If you want big gains on the stock market you need a long-term view. (TheStreet.com website)

- An adverb says how (*quickly*), when (*tomorrow*) or where (*over there*) something happens.

- Adverbs can come in different positions. 'How' adverbs usually come after the verb.
  We planned everything very carefully.
  The economy is growing slowly.

  Frequency adverbs (unit 1) come after *be* and auxiliaries, but before other verbs.
  She is never late.
  She has never arrived late.
  She never goes there.

  Other 'when' adverbs can come before or after the verb.
  Last year our profits rose slightly.   *Our profits rose slightly last year.*

  If we have several adverbs together, the usual word order is:
  HOW – WHERE – WHEN
  Our profits rose slightly in Germany last year. (NOT ~~last year in Germany~~)

- As well as describing verbs, adverbs can also describe adjectives and other adverbs.
  It's relatively expensive. (adverb + adjective)
  He arrived extremely late. (adverb + adverb)

- Adverbs are also covered in units 1, 3, 5 and 7 (time expressions); 39 (*too, enough*); 40 (time words like *in/on/at, for/since, by/until*); units 43 and 44 (linking words, which include 'sentence adverbs': *firstly, actually, in general, clearly, anyway*); and unit 49 (trends: *sales grew steadily all last year*).

B Form of adverbs

- Many 'how' adverbs are formed by adding *-ly* to an adjective. A few add *-y*, *-ally*, or *-ily*, depending on the spelling of the original adjective.
  slow – slowly   slight – slightly   careful – carefully
  full – fully   dramatic – dramatically   steady – steadily

- Some adverbs and adjectives have the same form. Examples include *fast, hard, early, late, high, low, right, wrong, daily/weekly/monthly/quarterly.*
  This is a fast machine. (adj.)   *This machine goes very fast.* (adv.)
  It's a hard decision. (adj.)   *He's working very hard at the moment.* (adv.)

- Note that the adverb *hardly* is not related to the meaning of *hard*.
  It's so noisy I can hardly think. ('hardly' = almost not)

- Note that *good* is an adjective and *well* is an adverb.
  She's a good negotiator.   *She negotiates well.*

C Gradable and non-gradable adjectives

● Look at these sequences:

boiling ◄─────────────── hot, warm, mild, cool, cold ───────────────► freezing

excellent/fantastic ◄─────────────── good, bad ───────────────► awful/terrible

enormous ◄─────────────── large/big, small, tiny ───────────────► minute

● Adjectives in the middle of the sequence are 'gradable'. We can make them stronger or weaker with words like *very, a bit, quite, reasonably, relatively, extremely*.
*The weather was **quite** hot/cold.* (NOT ~~quite boiling/freezing~~.)
*The meal was **very** good/bad.* (NOT ~~very excellent/awful~~.)

● Adjectives at the end of the sequence are 'non-gradable' or 'extreme'. With these adjectives we use *absolutely*.
*The talk was **absolutely** excellent/awful.* (NOT ~~very excellent~~.)

D Order of adjectives

● When we have more than one adjective we use this order:

Opinion	*wonderful, lovely, nice, difficult, important*
Size	*large, small, long, short*
Other qualities	*cheap, clean, quiet, fast*
Age	*new, old, second-hand*
Shape, pattern, colour	*circular, flat, striped, red, black*
Origin, nationality	*French, Japanese, American, Scandinavian*
Material	*wooden, metal, plastic, steel*
Type (what kind?)	*third-generation (phone), economic (policy), safety (device), investment (bank), face (cream)*

● Words in the final two categories can be nouns used as adjectives.

● Here are some examples:
*a **10-page American legal** contract*   (size, nationality, type)
*a **fast new sports** car*   (quality, age, type)
*an **efficient worldwide distribution** network* (opinion, size, type)
*a **cheap clean energy** source*   (quality, quality, type)

E Adjectives ending *-ing* and *-ed*

● Adjectives ending *-ing* describe something we are reacting to (outside us).
Adjectives ending *-ed* describe our feelings and reactions (inside us).
*The meeting was very **interesting**. I was **interested** in your idea about outsourcing.*

*Asia Online president Kevin Randolph says he does not concentrate on the number of customers because he is not really **interested** in mass marketing. 'I am **interested** in quality marketing,' Randolph says. 'We have 100,000 customers, which is an **interesting** number, but I am not managing the business based on that.'* (business review weekly website)

Other pairs like this are: *bored/boring, confused/confusing, excited/exciting, fascinated/fascinating, surprised/surprising, tired/tiring*
*I found her comments quite **surprising**. I was **surprised** by her comments.*

"It's worse than you think, it goes down to the third floor."

36 Practice

Exercise 1 A B

Complete the second sentence so it has a similar meaning to the first sentence.

1 There was a slight fall in profits in April.
   In April profits ....*fell slightly*................. .

2 There was a dramatic improvement in our share price last month.
   Last month our share price ....

3 There has been a significant drop in demand for oil over the last few months.
   Demand for oil .... over the last few months.

4 Let's have a brief pause for coffee.
   Let's .... for coffee.

5 There has been a steady improvement in the inflation figures.
   The inflation figures ....

6 There was a slow recovery in consumer confidence last year.
   Consumer confidence .... last year.

7 There has been a gradual rise in unemployment.
   Unemployment ....

8 There has been considerable growth in Korean GDP over recent years.
   Over recent years Korean GDP ....

Exercise 2 C E

Underline the correct adjective.

1 I couldn't do any more work last night. I was just so *tired/tiring*.
2 I don't think the audience liked the talk. They looked *bored/boring*.
3 I don't think the audience liked the talk. It was a bit *bored/boring*.
4 Your new multimedia project sounds really *excited/exciting*.
5 You look *worried/worrying*. Is anything the matter?
6 Their profits last year were extremely *large/enormous*.
7 Their profits last year were absolutely *large/enormous*.
8 The sales figures last month were very *bad/terrible*.
9 Warsaw is absolutely *cold/freezing* at this time of year.

Exercise 3 A

Complete the sentences with one word from the list A and one word from list B.

A: badly   completely   easily   extremely   heavily   quite   unexpectedly   ~~well~~

B: delayed   designed   helpful   illegal   late   ~~made~~   promoted   recognisable

1 This suitcase is very ....*well made*.......... . It will last for years and years.
2 The new product is being .... You see the adverts everywhere.
3 This website is very .... I can't find the information I need.
4 You've been .... I really appreciate it.
5 Our offices are .... Look out for the large flags at the front.
6 I'm sorry, my flight has been .... I'll call you when I arrive.
7 Taking bribes is .... You'll lose your job if they catch you.
8 I arrived at the presentation .... and missed the first part.

Exercise 4 D

Put each group of words into the best order.

1 old-fashioned a large machine cutting   .... *a large old-fashioned cutting machine* ....
2 wooden square two cartons   ....
3 new package an amazing software   ....
4 period a transition three-month difficult   ....
5 chips computer Taiwanese high-quality   ....
6 a strategy well-planned investment   ....
7 access cheap Internet high-speed   ....
8 a new revolutionary computer handheld   ....
9 a powder washing new wonderful   ....
10 awful plastic cheap souvenirs   ....

Exercise 5 A B

Complete the sentences with a word from the list below. At the end of each sentence write *adj.* (adjective) or *adv.* (adverb) to show how the word in the gap is being used.

good   well   fast   fast   hard   hard   hardly   late   late   ~~monthly~~

1 We're going to introduce a ... *monthly* ... newsletter for all employees.   ..... adj .....
2 I'm sorry, your goods are going to arrive about a week ....
3 That flight time is too .... Haven't you got anything earlier?   ....
4 Everything's fine. The meeting is going very ....
5 I was so tired that I could .... keep my eyes open.   ....
6 The hotel was .... , but we didn't like the food in the restaurant.   ....
7 It's a .... choice, but I think Carla is the better candidate.   ....
8 I had to work very .... to get everything finished on time.   ....
9 I'm sorry, I don't understand. You're talking too ....
10 We'll have to make a .... exit if things start going wrong.   ....

Exercise 6 A B

 42 Read this report about the convergence of mobile phones and handheld computers. Underline either the adjective or adverb each time.

The Net: anywhere, anytime, in the palm of your hand

It seems (1) *strange/strangely*, but some people are walking around with a mobile phone, a handheld computer like a Palm, a pager, and even a notebook computer with a (2) *conventional/conventionally* keyboard as well. These digital devices are converging (3) *rapid/rapidly*, but manufacturers are finding it difficult to get all the parts to integrate (4) *proper/properly*. Contemporary mobile phones look (5) *good/well*, are relatively (6) *good/well* at sending short text messages, but don't work (7) *good/well* as handheld computers. They lack memory, synchronise (8) *bad/badly* with desktop PCs, and are not (9) *easy/easily* to use for writing emails. Searching for an address-book entry or scrolling through a contact list is (10) *slow/slowly*, although once you find the name you can call the person (11) *direct/directly* by just touching the phone number. Of course the big issue in the future is Internet access – it needs to be fast, (12) *easy/easily* and (13) *cheap/cheaply*, but still allow phone companies to make a profit. Things are moving very (14) *quick/quickly* in this area, and the manufacturers who succeed in getting everything (15) *right/rightly* are going to make (16) *huge/hugely* profits. ∎

Consumer prices for goods and services rose just 0.2% in February, the smallest jump for many years. But this follows a larger than expected rise of 0.6% in January.
(Business Week website)

37 Comparing 1

A Comparatives and superlatives

- We use the comparative form of an adjective to compare two separate things.

  Comparative: *Model C400 is **more powerful than** model C200.*

  *Model C200 is **less powerful than** model C400.*

  We use the superlative form to say that one thing in a group has more or less of a quality than all the others.

  Superlative: ***The most powerful** model that we make is the C600.*

  ***The least powerful** model that we make is the C200.*

B Form

- The form depends on the number of syllables in the word and the spelling.

	Adjective	Comparative	Superlative
One syllable	cheap	cheap**er**	the cheap**est**
	nice	nice**r**	the nice**st**
One syllable ending vowel – consonant	big	big**ger**	the big**gest**
	hot	hot**ter**	the hot**test**
One/two syllables ending -y	risky	risk**ier**	the risk**iest**
	easy	eas**ier**	the eas**iest**
Two or more syllables	modern	**more/less** modern	**the most/least** modern
	expensive	**more/less** expensive	**the most/least** expensive

  *A franchising contract is one of **the longest** and **most sophisticated** that investors will ever sign.*
  (Entrepreneur International website)

- Note that one-syllable adjectives ending in single vowel – single consonant double the final consonant, and that -y becomes i.

  bi**g** – big**ger**   fl**at** – flat**ter**   w**et** – wet**ter**

  eas**y** – eas**ier**   nois**y** – nois**ier**   happ**y** – happ**ier**

- Some two-syllable adjectives can form in either way. Examples include *clever, common, narrow, polite, quiet, simple, tired.*

  common   common**er**/**more** common   the common**est**/the **most** common

- Note that long adjectives have both *more/most* and *less/least*, but short adjectives only have -er/-est.

- Note the following irregular forms:

good	better	the best
bad	worse	the worst
far	farther/further	the farthest/furthest

  *Japan's economy is weakening. Its chances of recovery from **the worst** slowdown since World War II are getting smaller and smaller every day.* (Yahoo Business News website)

C Other points

- We use *than* to link the things we are comparing.
  *This year's profits will be a little higher **than** last year's.*
  *It's a lot more difficult **than** I thought at first.*

See units 35 and 37
- Before a superlative we use *the* or a possessive form.
  *This is **the/our/Digicom's** most powerful model.*

- Comparative and superlative adjectives can be used without a noun if the meaning is clear from the context.
  *Their level of service is good, but ours is **better**.*
  *Digicom produces a range of models, but this one is **the most powerful**.*

- The present perfect with *ever* is often used with superlatives.
  *This is **the most powerful machine** that we **have ever produced**.*
  *This is **one of the best** meals I **have ever eaten**.*

  *The Brazilian supermarket chain Pão de Açucar reported a profit of US$167.3m last year, **the largest** it **has ever made**.* (Business News Americas website)

D Comparing equal things

- We can compare two equal things with *(just) as ... as*. We say that two things are not equal with *not as ... as*. The adjectives do not change.
  *The C600i is **(just) as powerful as** the C600.*
  *The C400 is **not as powerful as** the C600.*

  *Trends in oil prices are about supply and demand fundamentals. It really is **as simple as** that.* (Gulf Business Magazine website)

  *It's still good to be king of your corporation – just **not as good as** it used to be.* (BusinessWeek website)

E Comparing actions

- When we compare actions we can use an auxiliary at the end of the sentence.
  The C600 runs faster than the C400.   OR   *The C600 runs faster than the C400 **does**.*
  You've done more work than me.   OR   *You've done more work than **I have**.*

37 Practice

Exercise 1 A B C D

<u>Underline</u> the correct words.

1 The new line should be *so profitable as/as profitable as* the old one.

2 This handset is *the most profitable/the more profitable* we've ever made.

3 This version of the programme is the most *recent/recenter*.

4 The guarantee is a year longer *than/that* with our older models.

5 Nothing is *worse/worst* than missing a flight because of traffic.

6 This printer is one of the *best/better* on the market.

7 The meeting wasn't *long as/as long as* I thought.

8 Today the share price is *more bad/worse* than it was yesterday.

9 I'm sorry, the journey took *longer than/the longest* we expected.

10 We'll be there soon. It's not much *farer/further*.

Exercise 2 A B C D

Complete the sentences with a comparative or superlative form of the adjective in brackets. Include any other necessary words like *the, more, less, as* or *than*.

1 Coca-Cola is ...*the biggest*... (big) soft drinks manufacturer in the world.

2 This keyboard is quite difficult to use. It's .... (small) the one I'm used to.

3 The conference was a little disappointing. It was .... (interesting) I expected.

4 Yesterday was one of .... (hot) days of the year.

5 I think this suggestion is .... (good) the other one.

6 It's impossible to choose between these two products. One is .... (good) the other.

7 The first round of negotiations was easy. The next will be .... (difficult).

8 We're only a small company. We're not .... (large) the market leader in our sector.

9 This year our sales figure are .... (bad) last year.

10 This is .... (bad) case of corruption we've seen for years.

Exercise 3 A B C D E

Put <u>one</u> suitable word in each space.

1 We are bigger ....*than*.... GNC, but Satco are ......*the*..... biggest in the market.

2 I can see you either day. One day is .... good .... the other.

3 Nobody knows more about electronics .... Tina ....

4 Of course I'll speak to him. It's the .... I can do after all your help.

5 Sorry, 5% discount is my best offer. It's the .... I can do.

6 He is one of the .... difficult customers I have ever dealt with.

7 Everyone else had worked a lot longer on the project .... I ....

8 I don't think that this market is .... risky .... it was.

9 The restaurants are the same. This one is .... as expensive .... that one.

10 This restaurant is better for us. It's .... as expensive .... that one.

Exercise 4 A B C D

Complete the second sentence so it has a similar meaning to the first sentence.

1 David is a better technician than Paul.

Paul is not ....*as good a technician as*........ David.

2 Nobody at KBN is a better investment analyst than Carol.

Carol is the .... at KBN.

3 I haven't read as many sections of the report as you.

You've read ....

4 I expected the meeting to last longer.

The meeting didn't last ....

5 Our training budget isn't as big as yours.

Your training budget is ....

6 No presentation I've given is more important than this one.

This is the ....

7 This speaker is more interesting than the last one.

The last speaker was not .... this one.

8 I ate less than George did.

I didn't .... George.

9 No one in the team has better communication skills than Jane.

Jane has .... in the team.

10 I have rarely met a more interesting person.

He is one of ....

Exercise 5 A B

 43   Complete the magazine article about investment options with the comparative or superlative forms of the adjectives in brackets.

Investment choices: risk and reward

In this report we're going to look at the three main types of investments: cash (in bank accounts), bonds (long-term loans that give a fixed rate of return) and stocks (equities). The (1) ....*safest*........... (safe) is cash, and the fact that this has less risk than the others means that it also has a (2) .... (low) return. If you want a (3) .... (good) return you should consider bonds. These are fixed interest investments, and are a (4) .... (attractive) option than cash, particularly when interest rates are falling. The (5) .... (risky) form of investment is stocks. They offer the chance of much (6) .... (great) profits over the long term, but you might make a loss if the company does badly. The (7) .... (bad) case scenario is that the company goes bankrupt and you lose everything. You can reduce the risk by investing in a fund rather than individual stocks. Funds that invest in developed economies are a (8) .... (sensible) choice for most people, as the markets have more liquidity and it is (9) .... (easy) for the fund manager to buy and sell. But there are also emerging market funds that invest in countries like China, India or Turkey. These markets are only for the (10) .... (aggressive) investors of all as they have much (11) .... (high) volatility.

So what is the (12) .... (good) solution? Most financial advisors recommend a balance. In the middle of your career you can afford to have a (13) .... (large) part of your investments as stocks, perhaps 60–80%, with some bonds for stability and cash for emergencies. As you get (14) .... (near) retirement you should consider switching most of your money to bonds, and increasing your available cash.

38 Comparing 2

The new Deutsche would be the largest bank in Europe, the second biggest in the world, and twice as big as the U.S.'s Citigroup. (Business Week website)

A Large and small differences

● We can using adverbs of degree (see unit 39) to talk about differences.

Product A	Product B	
		Using *more ... than*
$220	$200	A is *a bit/ a little bit/slightly* more expensive than B.
$300	$200	A is *considerably/much/a lot/far* more expensive than B.
		Using *as ... as*
$120	$200	A is *not nearly as* expensive as B.
$180	$200	A is *almost/nearly/not quite* as expensive as B.
$400	$200	A is *twice as expensive* as B.
$450	$200	A is *more than twice* as expensive as B.

*Foreign exchange markets are **far more** volatile and unpredictable **than** commodities markets.* (African Business magazine website)

● We can use *even* to emphasise the comparison.

*Japan is a country full of distributors, wholesalers and other middlemen. The dislocation caused by the Internet could be **even greater than** in the US.* (FT.com website)

B Other structures with comparatives

● We can say that something is increasing or decreasing by using two comparatives linked by *and*.
*The personal pensions market is growing **bigger and bigger**.*
*Investors are becoming **more and more** sophisticated.*

● We can say that one situation depends on another by using *the* and one comparative followed by *the* and another comparative.
The longer the strike goes on, **the more difficult** it will be to find a solution.

The bigger the company and **the larger** its costs, **the greater** the opportunity to see tremendous efficiencies. (BusinessWeek Online website)

● These phrases are also useful for comparing things:

exactly/just/almost/nearly/virtually/more or less/roughly	the same ... as ...
exactly/just/very/more/less/quite/a bit/a little	like
completely/quite/slightly	different from
very similar	to
compared to/in comparison with	

*Online retailers with 30 employees have to offer **exactly the same** service **as** trading companies with turnover in billions of euros.* (Connectis website)

C Phrases with superlatives

● These phrases are common with superlatives.

One of the	*largest retailing group**s** in Latin America.*
By far the/Easily the	*largest retailing group in Latin America.*
The second/third/fourth	*largest retailing group in Latin America.*

*The recession that followed the dollar crisis of 1994 was **one of the worst** in Mexican history.* (Global Business Magazine website)

D Comparing adverbs

- In general, adverbs follow exactly the same rules as adjectives.

  One syllable: *hard, hard**er**, the hard**est***

  Two syllables ending -*y*:   *early, earl**ier**, the earl**iest***

  Two or more syllables: *efficiently, **more/less** efficiently, **the most/least** efficiently*

- The adverbs *well* and *badly* are irregular.

  well, better, the best   badly, worse, the worst

- We can use the same structures as adjectives.

  *In the IT sector people are having to work **harder and harder** to get promotion.*

  ***The quicker** we can sign the deal, **the sooner** we can start production.*

  *Those arguing that the US slowdown is about to end **almost as** soon **as** it began miss the point entirely.* (BusinessWeek website)

- We often need comparative and superlative adverbs when the verb has the form of a present participle (*doing*) or a past participle (*done*).

  *Korea is one of **the most rapidly developing** countries in the world.*

  *This product is **more attractively designed** and **more solidly** built.*

  *The new Deutsche Bank will **be better placed** to use its strong corporate relationships to benefit from the restructuring and M&A boom currently happening across Europe.* (Business Week website)

E Comparing nouns

See unit 30 for countable and uncountable nouns

- We compare nouns using the words below.

  Countable nouns   (products, people, customers, banks)

  more, fewer, the most, the fewest, (not) as many ... as

  *We have far **more people** working for us now **than** two years ago.*

  *We don't have **as many products** on the market **as** two years ago.*

  Uncountable nouns   (time, money, information, progress)

  more, less, the most, the least, (not) as much ... as

  *I'm working as a freelancer now and I earn considerably **less money**.*

  *I do**n't** have nearly **as much time** for reading **as** I would like.*

38 Practice

Exercise 1 A B C D E

Underline the correct words.

1 The new design is considerably *more light/lighter* than the old one.
2 There are nearly twice as many people working here *as/than* last year.
3 The sooner they decide, *it's better/the better* for us all.
4 There's *each time more/more and more* investment in China every year.
5 We have *the nearly largest/the second largest* market share in Turkey.
6 This model might be better for you. It's *slightly/quite* less expensive.
7 This is our *faster/fastest* selling product.
8 Everything's getting *more and more expensive/expensiver and expensiver*.
9 If needed, could this production line go *more quickly/more quicker*?
10 It's a little more expensive, but the quality is *much better/more better*.
11 Our sales this year are virtually *the same as/the equal of* last year.
12 This is one of *the best/the well* organised conferences I've ever been to.

Exercise 2 A B

Write a word or phrase from the list next to a similar word or phrase below.

~~virtually~~   a bit   roughly   exactly   much

nearly/...**virtually**....   a little/......................   far/......................
more or less/......................   just/......................

Now complete these sentences by writing the pairs of words/phrases in the space.
1 They're similar. They're .....**roughly / more or less**..... the same.
2 They're very similar. They're .... the same.
3 They're identical. They're .... the same.
4 X costs $580 and Y costs $600. X is .... cheaper.
5 X costs $400 and Y costs $600. X is .... cheaper.

Exercise 3 D

Rewrite each sentence using a superlative with a present participle (*doing*) or a past participle (*done*).
1 Few credit cards are accepted as widely as Visa.
   Visa is probably ....**the most widely accepted**......... credit card.
2 No market is growing as fast as China.
   China is .... market.
3 Few watches on the market are designed as cleverly as the new Seiko.
   The new Seiko is one of .... watches on the market.
4 Few of our products are selling as well as this.
   This is one of our .... products.
5 Few facts about Oracle are less known than this.
   This is one of .... facts about Oracle.
6 No area of business is changing anything like as rapidly as biotechnology.
   By far .... area of business is biotechnology.

Exercise 4 **A** **B** **C** **E**

A company wants to move premises and there are several options. Read the details in the table.

Possible new premises	size (square metres)	rent per square metre	running costs per year	distance from city centre (km)
Docklands (converted warehouse)	285	$500	$120,000	4
City View Business Park	300	$350	$125,000	12
Newtown Industrial Area	310	$200	$105,000	30

Now complete the sentences with the phrases from the list below.

~~slightly~~   not nearly   by far   a lot   more than twice   roughly the same

slightly less   considerably less   almost as much   almost as many

1   The three options are all about the same size, but Newtown is ....*slightly*............ larger.
2   The running costs at Docklands and City View are ....
3   The running costs at Newtown are .... than the other two places.
4   There's .... square metres at Docklands as at City View.
5   There's .... space at Docklands as at City View.
6   The rent at Newtown is .... than at the other two places.
7   The rent at Docklands is .... the rent at Newtown.
8   Docklands is .... the closest to the city centre.
9   In terms of access to the centre, Newtown is .... as convenient as City View.
10   You'd have to travel .... further to get to Newtown.

Exercise 5 **A** **B** **C** **D** **E**

 44   Look at the table then complete the presentation extract with phrases from the list below.

~~in comparison with~~   twice as much   twice as many   a lot   a little

different   similar   by far   considerably more   roughly the same

	Sales $ mil.	% change	Profit $ mil.	% change
Chevron	50,000	42	5,000	150
Texaco	52,000	43	3,000	116
Exxon Mobil	210,000	29	16,000	102

'If we look at the figures for the oil sector last year, you can see that the three largest US companies all did very well (1) .*in comparison with*. the previous year.

Let's start by comparing Chevron and Texaco. Their sales were (2) .... , although Chevron made (3) .... profit. Looking at the year-on-year trend you can see that the percentage change in sales was very (4) .... between the two companies, whereas the change in profits was quite (5) .... In fact, Chevron's profits grew (6) .... faster – 150% compared to 116%.

Now let's look at Exxon Mobil, the market leader. The table shows that Exxon is (7) .... the largest company, with more than (8) .... sales as Chevron and Texaco combined, and exactly (9) .... profit. In terms of percentage growth, Exxon's figures were (10) .... lower than its two competitors.'

39 Adverbs of degree

So far, German economic growth hasn't been strong enough to translate into job growth. **(Wall Street Journal website)**
Profits were so good that the three partners decided they wanted their dividends in full. **(Asia, Inc. website)**

A Adverbs of degree

● Adverbs of degree show how big or important something is. They make the meaning weaker (small degree) or stronger (large degree).

Small degree:	*a little, a bit, slightly*
Medium degree:	*quite, fairly, pretty, rather, reasonably, relatively*
Large degree:	*extremely, really, very, absolutely, completely*

*Marc Faber is noted as a **slightly** eccentric but often **very** accurate market tipster.* (asia–inc magazine website)

● Look at these examples.

With adjectives:	*It was **a little** expensive/**rather** strange/**very** professional.*
With adverbs:	*It was done **a bit** late/**quite** quickly/**very** professionally.*
With verbs:	***I really** disagree.* *They've increased their offer **a little**.*
With comparatives:	*It's **a bit/slightly/considerably/much/a lot** cheaper.*

B *Too, enough, not enough*

● *Too* means 'more than is necessary or good'. *Not enough* means 'less than is necessary or good'. *Enough* means 'as much as is necessary' or 'sufficient'.

Adjectives:	*The salary is **too low**.*	*The salary is**n't high enough**.*
Adverbs:	*I'm sorry, it goes **too slowly**.*	*I'm sorry, it is**n't fast enough**.*
Nouns:	*There's **too much work**.*	*There is**n't enough time**.*

● Note the positions: *too* comes before adjectives, adverbs and nouns; *enough* comes after adjectives and adverbs, but before nouns.

● We use *too many/few* + plural nouns and *too much/little* + uncountable nouns.
*There are **too many people** involved in the project.*
*I think we spent **too much money** on the consultants.*

● We can leave out the noun if the meaning is clear.
*Just a little milk, please. Not **too much**.*
*There are six chairs. Is that **enough**?*

C Other structures with *too* and *enough*

● After *too* and *enough* we can use a phrase with *for*.
*Their delivery times are **too** long **for us**.*
*Have we got **enough** chairs **for everyone**?*

● After *too* and *enough* we can use a *to* infinitive.
*Sales are **too** slow **to make** much profit.*
*We don't have **enough** time **to do** everything.*

*Simply put, information technology is just **not** important **enough** on its own **to generate** a sustained recovery.* (FT.com website)

D *So* and *such*

- We use *so* and *such* for emphasis.

  So with adjectives and adverbs: *The meeting finished **so quickly**.*
  Such a with adjective + singular noun: *It was **such a quick meeting**.*
  Such/So many/So few with plural nouns: *You have **such friendly colleagues**.*
                                                          *We sold **so many policies** last month!*
  Such/So much/So little with uncountable nouns: *It was **such good advice**.*
                                                          *I have **so much work** to do.*

  *'**Such a big merger** has huge competitive implications,' says a senior German banking executive.*
  (BusinessWeek Online website)

- *So/such* and *too* are different. *So/such* express an opinion which can be either positive or negative. *Too* suggests a difficulty, that something cannot be done.
  *There are **so many people** involved in the project.*   (it's just my opinion)
  *There are **too many people** involved in the project.*   (we need to reduce the number)

  So/such can be used with *that* to express a result. *Too* cannot be used with *that*.
  *The meeting finished **so** quickly **that** I was home by 5.30.* (NOT ~~too quickly that~~)

E *Quite, fairly, pretty* or *rather*?

- *Quite, fairly* and *pretty* mean 'a medium amount'.
  *'Like most businesses, we're **fairly** cautious about what might come in the next couple of years, mainly because of the Asian situation.'* (business review weekly website)

- In American English *pretty* is a common way of saying 'very'.

- We can change the meaning of *quite* in British English by stressing the adjective in speech. The meaning changes to 'very'. This is called understatement.
  The restaurant was <u>quite</u> good. (normal meaning: it was OK)
  The restaurant was quite <u>good</u>. (understatement: it was very good)

- *Rather* also means 'a medium amount', but it often suggests that something is bad, surprising or unusual. It is more formal.
  It's rather late to do anything now. (It's a little too late, I'm afraid)
  The restaurant was rather good. (I enjoyed it, surprisingly)

- With a comparative we can only use *rather*, not *quite*.
  *The meeting took **rather longer** than I expected.* (NOT ~~quite longer~~)

- With some adjectives *quite* means 'absolutely' or 'completely'. These include: *absurd, certain, different, hopeless, impossible, ridiculous, right, sure, true, wrong.*
  *I'm **quite certain** about this.* (= absolutely certain)
  *Are you sure that's **quite right**?* (= completely right)

*"My fees are quite high, and yet you say you have little money.
I think I'm seeing a conflict of interest here."*

39 Practice

Exercise 1 A B E

Match each phrase 1–8 with the phrase a)–h) with the closest meaning. Be careful – some are similar.

1	It's a bit slow.	b	a) It's comparatively slow.
2	It's quite slow.	☐	b) It's slightly slow.
3	It's rather slow.	☐	c) It's fairly slow.
4	It's relatively slow.	☐	d) It's a little too slow, I'm afraid.
5	It's so slow.	☐	e) I want it to be even slower.
6	It's too slow.	☐	f) There's a problem. I want it to be faster.
7	It's slow enough.	☐	g) It really is very slow.
8	It's not slow enough.	☐	h) OK. That's as slow as it needs to be.

Exercise 2 B C D

Underline the correct words.

1   The salary they are suggesting sounds *so good/too good* to be true!
2   There were *so few/so little* customers that I went home early.
3   We can't pull out now. There's *too much/too many* money involved.
4   It was *such/so* a boring meeting that I nearly fell asleep.
5   The meeting was *such/so* boring that I nearly fell asleep.
6   I had to say 'no' – the cost was *so much/too much* for the budget I was given.
7   We had *so much/so many* new business that we needed extra staff.
8   I had *so much/so many* reports to write that I put the answering machine on.
9   We have *so few/so little* information that we can't make a decision.
10   The meeting was *so short/too short* to cover all the points properly.
11   Can you help me? I'm not *enough tall/tall enough* to reach the top shelf.
12   There isn't *enough money/money enough* in the budget for your idea.

Exercise 3 B C D

Complete the sentences with one of these words: *too, enough, so, such, much, many, little, few*.

1   Is your coffee ......too..... hot? Would you like a little more milk?
2   I had .... trouble finding somewhere to park that I arrived late.
3   I had .... problems finding somewhere to park that I arrived late.
4   There were .... replies to the last mailing that we won't do another.
5   I had .... cash on me that I couldn't even buy a sandwich.
6   The price of their shares is .... high to buy any more right now.
7   We're making .... progress that we should finish a week early.
8   We're expecting a lot of people. This room won't be large ....
9   I couldn't do any work on the train. I was .... tired that I fell asleep.
10   She speaks .... quickly for me to understand.
11   They pay .... late that we won't receive the money until June.
12   That's .... a good idea. It'll save us thousands of dollars.

Exercise 4 D

Look at the table below, then combine the sentences, using either *so ... that ...* or *such ... that ...* .

1	a) There was a big drop in their share price.	+ Investors became very nervous.
	b) The drop in their share price was very big.	
2	a) The advertising campaign was very successful.	+ Sales increased by 25% per month.
	b) The advertising campaign was a success.	
3	a) Our order processing system works very well.	+ Most goods are dispatched within 48 hours.
	b) We have a very good order processing system.	
4	a) That company has very large bank debts.	+ There's a risk it will have to close down.
	b) That company's bank debts are very large.	
5	a) The Internet connection is very fast.	+ Web pages appear almost instantly.
	b) There is a very fast Internet connection.	

1 a) There was *such a big drop in their share price that* investors became very nervous.
   b) The drop in their share price was *so big that* investors became very nervous.
2 a) The advertising campaign was .... sales increased by 25% per month.
   b) The advertising campaign was .... sales increased by 25% per month.
3 a) Our order processing system works .... most goods are
      dispatched within 48 hours.
   b) We have .... most goods are dispatched within 48 hours.
4 a) That company has .... there's a risk it will have to close down.
   b) That company's bank debts are .... there's a risk it will have
      to close down.
5 a) The Internet connection is .... Web pages appear almost instantly.
   b) There is .... Web pages appear almost instantly.

Exercise 5 B D

Complete the second sentence so it has a similar meaning to the first sentence and contains the word in brackets.

1 I didn't buy that laptop because the screen was too small. (enough)
   I didn't buy that laptop because *the screen wasn't large enough* .
2 The problem was so difficult that I referred it to my line manager. (such)
   It .... that I referred it to my line manager.
3 There weren't enough copies of the agenda. (few)
   There .... of the agenda.
4 There's not enough space on this spreadsheet for all the results. (little)
   There's .... on this spreadsheet for all the results.
5 It was such a good presentation that they gave us the contract immediately. (so)
   The .... that they gave us the contract immediately.
6 I sold too few units last month to get a bonus. (enough)
   I .... last month to get a bonus.
7 I've got such a busy schedule that I can't meet you until next Tuesday. (so)
   My schedule .... that I can't meet you until next Tuesday.
8 We've sent out lots of brochures and we'll need to print some more. (many)
   We've sent out .... we'll need to print some more.
9 I haven't got enough time to prepare for the meeting. (too)
   I've got .... to prepare for the meeting.

40 Time adverbs

A *In, on, at*, no preposition

The Shanghai Futures Exchange said **on Friday** that its copper stocks in warehouses had risen to their highest level **since November 1998**. Stocks hit a peak this year of more than 90,000 tons **in late July** … This compares with more than 60,000 tons **at the start of the year**.
(insidechinatoday website)

in ...	the morning/June/the summer/the third quarter/1998/the sixties/ the twentieth century
on ...	Friday/Friday morning/the 2nd of April/the second/Christmas Day
at ...	three fifteen/the weekend/the end of the week, month, etc./night/ Easter, Christmas, etc./breakfast, lunch, dinner
no preposition	this morning/yesterday afternoon/last night/the day before yesterday/a few days ago/last week/tomorrow morning/the day after tomorrow/next week

- The word *night* has some special forms:
  I woke up three times **in the night**. (= during the night)
  It happened **on Friday night**. (= one particular night)
  The hotel is quite noisy **at night**. (= in general when it is night)

- We can use *in* for the time it takes to complete something.
  This production line can produce 80 vehicles **in** a day.

- We can also use *in* to talk about 'time from now'.
  The new offices will be ready **in two months/in two months' time**.

B *On time* or *in time*?

- *On time* means 'at the right time'. *In time* means 'with enough time'.
  The plane took off exactly **on time**. (not late and not early)
  We arrived at the airport **in time** to have a meal. (early enough to do something)

  *Ensuring parcels are dispatched **on time** is the simplest task facing any logistics company.*
  (Connectis website)

C *For, since, during, ago*

See also unit 5
- We use *for* and *since* with the present perfect to talk about something continuing up to the present. We use *for* to talk about the period of time and *since* to say when it started.
  I've lived here **for six months**. (period of time)
  I've lived here **since January**. (point in time when it started)

- We can also use *for* with other tenses, and sometimes we can leave it out.
  I'm staying in the UK **for a year**.
  The training period lasted **(for)** six months.

- We can use *during* to talk about periods of time. *During* answers the question 'When?' *For* answers the question 'How long?'
  I didn't feel nervous **during my presentation**. (when?)
  She talked **for about thirty minutes**. (how long?)

- *Ago* means 'before the present'. It is used with the past simple.
  I came here **six months ago**. (NOT ~~since six months~~)

- To refer to a time before another time we use *before (that)* or *previously*.
  I came here six months ago. **Before that/Previously**, I lived in Rome.

D *During* or *while*?

● *During* is a preposition and comes before a noun phrase. *While* is a linking word and comes before a clause (subject + verb).
*I moved into the marketing area **during my time at Bacardi**.*
*I moved into the marketing area **while I was working at Bacardi**.*

E *By* or *until*?

● *By* means 'on or before'. *Until* means 'up to'.
*I need your report **by Friday**.* (on or before Friday – perhaps Thursday)
*She'll be away **until Friday**.* (all the time up to Friday)

*If things haven't changed dramatically **by 2006**, then Central Europe can wave goodbye to a large part of its agri-food business.* (Business Central Europe website)

When we use *by* we look back. When we use *until* we look forward.
***By ten** I had dealt with all my emails.*
*I waited **until ten** and then I left.*

F *Then, afterwards, after, later*

● *Then* and *afterwards* are very similar. *Then* is used like 'next' in a sequence. *Afterwards* is used like 'at a later time' or 'after something else has happened' and can come at the end of a sentence.
*First we discussed last months' sales, and **then** the advertising campaign.*
*We discussed the problem, and **afterwards** everything was OK.*
*It was a long meeting and we went for a drink **afterwards**.*

*Google was growing very, very fast at the time. We realized we needed a lot of disk space, and so we went out and bought 120 hard drives using all of our credit cards and our friends' credit cards. Pretty soon **afterwards**, we got some private investments through Stanford University.* (Business Week website)

● *After* is usually followed by an object.
***After the meeting** I need to speak to you.*
*We discussed the problem, and **after that** everything was OK.*

● *Later* means 'after some time'.
*Sarah James isn't here at the moment. Can you come back **later**?*

G Calendar references

● In the UK people say *the tenth of June* or *June the tenth* and write Day/Month/Year: *10/6/03*.

● In the USA people say *June ten* and write Month/Day/Year: *6/10/03*.

40 Practice

Exercise 1 A

Put *in*, *on* or *at*.

1 ......*in*........ + parts of day (*the evening*)
2 .... + longer religious holidays (*Easter*)
3 .... + meal times (*dinner*)
4 .... + special days (*my birthday*)
5 .... + long periods (*the nineteenth century*)
6 .... + clock times (*four thirty*)
7 .... + day + part of day (*Monday morning*)
8 .... + seasons (*the winter*)
9 .... + years (*1998*)
10 .... + days (*Monday*)
11 .... + dates (*5 May*)
12 .... + months (*August*)
13 .... *the weekend*
14 .... *the moment*
15 .... *that day*
16 .... *the end of the year*

Exercise 2 A

It is now Wednesday afternoon. Put these phrases into order, with 1 as the most distant in the past, and 14 as the most distant in the future.

1 ..*f*.. 2 ...... 3 ...... 4 ...... 5 ...... 6 ...... **NOW** 7 ...... 8 ...... 9 ...... 10 ...... 11 ...... 12 ...... 13 ...... 14 ......

a) a few days ago
b) tonight
c) in a few weeks' time
d) in a fortnight
e) in an hour
f) last night
g) last week

h) next week
i) this evening
j) this morning
k) the day before yesterday
l) tomorrow evening
m) yesterday morning
n) the day after tomorrow

Exercise 3 A B C D E F

Underline the correct words.

1 Sorry, I was out of the office *this morning*/*in this morning*.
2 I'll give you a call *next week*/*at next week*.
3 Bye. I'll see you *the day after tomorrow*/*the next day*.
4 We have a security guard to look after the premises *at the night*/*at night*.
5 It's very important to arrive at meetings *on time*/*in time* in this country.
6 If you arrive *on time*/*in time* we can talk a little before the meeting starts.
7 The joint venture has been operating successfully *for*/*during* three years.
8 We had one or two problems *for*/*during* the summer, but things are OK now.
9 I started working here *since two years*/*two years ago*.
10 The market crashed. Luckily I had sold my shares a few months *ago*/*before*.
11 *During*/*While* the meeting I made a lot of notes.
12 *During*/*While* she was talking I made a lot of notes.
13 It happened *during*/*while* dot-com shares were booming in 2000.
14 It happened *during*/*while* the dot-com boom of 2000.
15 We have to finish this project *by*/*until* the end of the month.
16 I have to work late. I'll be here *until*/*by* eight this evening.
17 We reviewed the training plans, and *after*/*then* talked about the cost.
18 We had lunch, and *afterwards*/*after* I showed them round the factory.
19 *Afterwards*/*After* lunch I showed them round the factory.
20 I can't talk now. I'll call you *later*/*afterwards* today.

Exercise 4 C

Make questions using *How long* and the present perfect. Make answers using *for* or *since*.

1 Q: (How long/you/work here?) .... *How long have you worked here?*

   A: (about six months) .... *For about six months.*

2 Q: (How long/you/have a subsidiary in Portugal?) ....

   A: (1998) ....

3 Q: (How long/Peter Middelhoff/be CEO?) ....

   A: (the start of last year) ....

4 Q: (How long/your company/have the same logo?) ....

   A: (twenty years) ....

5 Q: (How long/you/own your Telekom shares?) ....

   A: (privatisation) ....

6 Q: (How long/you/know Alex Scott?) ....

   A: (a long time) ....

7 Q: (How long/you/live in this town?) ....

   A: (I was born) ....

Exercise 5 C D F

 45   Complete the dialogue with one of these words: *for, since, during, while, ago, before, after, afterwards.*

INTERVIEWER: Well, perhaps you could begin by telling us a little bit about your career history? And (1) ...*afterwards*... we'll move on to your current job.

ALESSANDRO: Yes, of course. Well, I graduated from Bocconi University in Milan five years (2) .... I was at Bocconi (3) .... about six years, and (4) .... that period I worked briefly as an analyst in my uncle's consultancy firm.

INTERVIEWER: Uh, huh. And did you manage to find a job easily (5) .... you left university?

ALESSANDRO: Well, eventually I was offered a job in an Italian bank, but (6) .... that I had been looking for work (7) .... quite a long time. It wasn't easy finding jobs in Italy at that time, you know, but luckily the situation has got much better (8) .... then.

INTERVIEWER: Yes, like here. So how long did you work at the bank?

ALESSANDRO: Well, I worked there (9) .... about two years.

INTERVIEWER: Two years … and why did you leave?

ALESSANDRO: I enjoyed my time there a lot. And (10) .... I was there I learnt a lot of techniques for financial analysis, and important skills like teamwork, you know. But I wanted the chance to do something more challenging in an international environment. …

INTERVIEWER: Uh, huh.

ALESSANDRO: … It had been my dream to work in an international company (11) .... leaving school.

INTERVIEWER: Well, you've applied to the right place. So what did you do then?

ALESSANDRO: Well, I decided to take a risk and move to London. That was about two years (12) ....

INTERVIEWER: Did you have a job to go to in London?

ALESSANDRO: No. (13) .... I left Italy I sent my CV to a lot of different agencies, but I thought that it would be easier to find a job (14) .... I was actually living in London. Hah. I only realised (15) .... how much competition there was!

INTERVIEWER: Well, yes.

ALESSANDRO: Anyway, eventually, (16) .... some months, I found a job at a bank in the City. That's where I'm working now.

41 Linking words 1

PCCW has also formed Network of the World, a multimedia company that will source TV shows from overseas as well as engage in e-commerce and other Internet activities. **(Asiaweek website)**

A Linking words

- We use some linking words to join parts of sentences. They give a structure to the sentence. Examples include *and, but, because, so*. Units 41 and 42 deal with this kind of linking word.

- We use other linking words and phrases to make a link across sentences and paragraphs. They give a structure to our whole argument. Examples include *Firstly, In general, Actually, In other words*. Units 43 and 44 deal with this kind of linking word or phrase.

B Addition: *and, both, too, also,* etc

- We use *and* to join words or parts of sentences. To emphasise the fact that there are two things we can use *both ... and ...* .
  *I need to call Andy **and** find out when he's free to have a meeting.*
  *I need to call **both** Andy **and** Helen.*

- We use *too, as well, as well as* and *also* to add another fact or say that something happens at the same time. Note the positions.
  *I need to call Andy, Kate **and** Helen **too/as well**.*
  *I need to call Andy **and** Kate **as well as** Helen.*
  *I need to call Andy, Kate **and also** Helen.*

C Contrast: *but, yet* and *although*

- We use *but* and *although* to make a contrast. *Although* is typical of more careful or formal speech or writing.
  *In theory it seems like a good idea, **but** I don't think it'll work in practice.*
  *In theory it seems like a good idea, **although** I don't think it will work in practice.*

- The clause with *although* can come at the beginning.
  ***Although** it seems like a good idea, I don't think it will work in practice.*

  ***Although** the ministry insisted the reforms would still go ahead, it is unclear what shape they will take.* (FT.com website)

- We can emphasise *but* and *although* with *still* and *anyway*.
  *I wasn't feeling very well, **but I still** went to work.*
  *I wasn't feeling very well, **but** I went to work **anyway**.*
  *I **still** went to work, **although** I wasn't feeling very well.*
  ***Although** I wasn't feeling very well, I went to work **anyway**.*

- We can use *yet* in place of 'but' in writing.

D Contrast: *though* and *even though*

- We can use *though* in informal speech and writing like *although*.
  ***Though** it seems like a good idea, I don't think it'll work in practice.*

  ***Though** he owned a 40 percent stake, his partners outvoted him and unseated him from the board.* (Asia. Inc. website)

  With *though* we often use two separate sentences and put *though* at the end.
  *It seems like a good idea. I don't think it'll work in practice, **though**.*

- We can use *even though* like *although* to give a stronger contrast.
  ***Even though** I wasn't feeling very well, I **still** went to work.*

E Contrast: *whereas*

● We can use *whereas* in formal speech and writing to compare two facts and emphasise the difference between them. The clause with *whereas* can come at the beginning or end.
Indonesia has a lot of natural resources, **whereas** *Singapore has none.*
Whereas *Indonesia has a lot of natural resources, Singapore has none.*

F *Although* or *whereas*?

● *Although* in a sentence suggests surprise. But the clause with *although* does not always contain the surprising information – usually it is the clause that comes second that seems surprising.
We had a reasonable year in Asia, although **sales fell a little in Japan**.
Although sales fell a little in Japan, **we had a reasonable year in the rest of Asia**.

Whereas simply compares two facts. It makes a strong contrast, but there is less suggestion of surprise.
We had a reasonable year in Asia, **whereas** *sales in Europe were quite disappointing.*

● We can use *while* like *although* or *whereas*.
While *there are still some issues to resolve, I think we should go ahead.*   (like 'although')
Inflation rose by 3% last year, **while** *house prices went up 6%.*   (like 'whereas')

While some freelance workers will jump from job to job, companies like IBM and Sun Microsystems Inc. want to have a core of careerists to provide continuity. (BusinessWeek Online website)

G Contrast: *despite/in spite of*

● *Despite* and *in spite of* are like *although*, but they are followed by a noun or noun phrase.
Although I was ill, *I went to work.* = **In spite of my illness**, *I went to work.*
Although sales increased, *profits fell.* = **Despite the increase in sales**, *profits fell.*

Despite last year's Internet business slowdown, corporations today must still recognize the strategic value of adopting e-business processes and technologies. (e-business advisor website)

Remember that a gerund (verb with -*ing*) can act as a noun.
In spite of/Despite *feeling ill, I went to work.* (NOT ~~Despite I felt ill, I went to work.~~)

"And as your department representative,
let me just say that I am both proud
and honoured to be taking credit
for your accomplishments."

41 Practice

Exercise 1 C D E F G

<u>Underline</u> the correct words.

1 *Although/But* I like this company, I probably won't work here long.

2 *In spite of/Although* their shares are rising, their future is still uncertain.

3 Kate gave a good presentation, *although/despite* having very little time to prepare.

4 This year our earnings are close to $8m, *while/still* last year they were just $6m.

5 *Whereas/In spite of* these candidates all have an MBA, these other ones don't.

6 I read the book you suggested. I didn't enjoy it, *although/though*.

7 I didn't have much time, *but/whereas* I managed to visit the whole site.

8 Nowadays we have very few strikes, *but/whereas* ten years ago we had a lot.

9 We weren't sure whether to go ahead with the launch, but we did it *still/anyway*.

10 *Although/In spite of* the delay, we still arrived on time.

11 I didn't manage to close the deal, *although/whereas* I really tried.

12 *Although/Whereas* their share price is falling at the moment, the company is still a good long-term investment.

Exercise 2 B

Rewrite each sentence in two ways so it has a similar meaning to the first sentence each time. Use the word/s in brackets.

1 Paula visited both the Madrid office and the Barcelona office.

   a) (too) ...... Paula visited the Madrid office and the Barcelona office, too. ......

   b) (as well as) ....

2 We can handle the transport arrangements and the insurance.

   a) (also) ....

   b) (both) ....

3 I want the sales figures for October and November.

   a) (as well) ....

   b) (as well as) ....

4 We're setting up offices in Peru and Ecuador.

   a) (also) ....

   b) (too) ....

Exercise 3 C D E F G

Complete the sentences with one of these words or phrases: *although, anyway, but, in spite of, still, though, whereas*. Use each word or phrase once only.

1 Carol didn't recognise Mark Larner, ...*although*... she had met him before.

2 I don't like karaoke bars, ... I went with my Japanese clients anyway.

3 I offered my best price, but they .... didn't seem interested.

4 I think we'll have to change our suppliers. It's a pity, ...

5 .... the early problems, the project has been a great success.

6 Spain is a mature market, ... in Portugal there is still room for growth.

7 We haven't got all the facts, but it's worth discussing it ....

Exercise 4 `C` `D` `E` `F` `G`

Rewrite each pair of sentences using the words given. There are two ways each time.

1 It was raining. We got here on time.
    a) Although .... *it was raining, we got here on time.*
    b) Despite .... *the rain, we got here on time.*

2 I had a headache. I still went to the meeting.
    a) In spite of ....
    b) .... , but ....

3 Some analysts think that stocks will fall in value. Others disagree.
    a) ...., whereas ....
    b) Although ....

4 There were difficulties in the negotiations. We won the contract.
    a) Despite ....
    b) Even though ....

5 Oil prices rose slightly last year. This year they have gone down.
    a) Whereas ....
    b) .... , although ....

6 I've written twice. I still haven't received a reply.
    a) .... , yet ....
    b) Despite ....

7 He didn't use any notes. He gave an excellent presentation.
    a) Although ....
    b) .... He .... , though.

Exercise 5 `B` `C` `E` `F` `G`

 46 Complete the article about Formula One with a suitable word from the list below.

both (x1) as well (x1) as well as (x1) also (x1) yet (x1) although (x4) whereas (x1) despite (x2)

Formula One, Ferrari and Fiat

The growth of Formula One over the last ten years has been extraordinary. With 400 million people watching each race it is perhaps the world's number one sport, (1) *although* football (2) .... makes this claim. Formula One is the ideal marketing tool for companies, as shown by the fact that sponsors for Jaguar, like Ford, PAG and HSBC are very happy – (3) .... the fact that Jaguar is not actually very successful on the track.

Most years the sport is dominated by two teams, Ferrari and McLaren-Mercedes, (4) .... other teams like BAR Honda, BMW Williams and Benetton Renault are important (5) .... (6) .... Ferrari and McLaren-Mercedes have huge sponsorship deals. Ferrari's sponsors include Marlboro, Fiat and Shell, (7) .... McLaren-Mercedes have Mercedes, Mobil and Computer Associates. These two top teams each have a budget of over $300 million, and money comes in from direct sponsorship and trade support (8) .... merchandising, TV rights and prize money.

Ferrari have an unusual problem. Their brand name is very famous and the team is very successful, (9) .... they only sell around 6,000 cars a year. The problem is that they are not directly associated with a mass volume car producer, (10) .... all the other teams are. In reality Ferrari is controlled by Fiat, but (11) .... being the main owner Fiat gets little publicity when Ferrari wins. Many years ago Gianni Agnelli, the Fiat boss, wanted to rename the cars Fiat Ferrari. (12) .... he tried, he failed. A man called Enzo Ferrari, a legend in Italy, stood in his way. He died in 1989 and Agnelli respects his wishes, but things may change in the future.

42 Linking words 2

A Reason: *because, as, since*

- We use *because, as* and *since* when we want to explain the reason for something. *As* and *since* are more common in formal speech and writing.
  *I'm calling to complain **because** the goods are damaged.*
  *I am returning the goods **as/since** they were damaged on arrival.*

- *As* and *since* can come at the beginning of the sentence. Normally we do not begin sentences with *because*, but this is possible in informal speech.
  ***As/since** the goods were damaged on arrival, I am returning them.*
  ***Because** you're a first-time customer, I need to see your bank references.*

B Result: *so*

- We use *so* to express a result. Note the relation between *because* and *so*:
  *I'm calling to complain **because** the goods are damaged.* (reason)
  *The goods are damaged, **so** I'm calling to complain.* (result)

C Purpose: *to* and *for*

- We use the *to* infinitive to express purpose, to say why we do things.
  *He went to the airport **to meet** Mr Li.* (NOT ~~for to meet~~)
  *I'm calling **to talk** about the sales conference next week.*

  *Mr Zhu said the Government would work **to** improve China's unemployment insurance system and **to** speed up reform of the labour market.* (Australian Financial Review website)

- We can use *in order to* or *so as to* in place of *to*. They are more formal.
  *The CEO called a press conference **in order to** explain the merger.*

  We can use the negative *in order not to* or *so as not to*. We cannot use *not to* on its own.
  *I'll call a taxi **so as not to** miss my flight.* (NOT ~~I'll call a taxi not to miss my flight.~~)

- We can use *for* followed by a noun to say why we do something.
  *He went to the airport **for a meeting** with Mr Li.* (= to have a meeting)
  *Shall we go out **for some lunch**?* (= to have some lunch)

D Purpose: *so that*

- We can use *so (that)* to express purpose. After *so (that)* we use subject + verb.

  *I guess the question is how do you develop your company **so that** it can evolve in response to changing customer expectations.* (e-business advisor website)

- For a present purpose we use the present simple, *will* or *can*.
  *I'll send it by courier **so (that)** it **gets**/it**'ll get** to you on time.*
  *I'm calling you **so (that) I can check** your last order.*

- For a past purpose we use the past simple, *would* or *could*.
  *I sent it by courier yesterday **so (that)** it **got**/it**'d get** to you on time.*
  *I left work early **so (that) I could go** the doctor's.*

● If the subject of the first part of the sentence and the subject of the purpose clause are different, we can't use *to*. We have to use *so (that)*.

*I'm calling **to** talk about the sales conference.*   (same subject)

*I'm calling **so (that) we** can talk about the sales conference.*   (different subject)

***She** called a press conference **to** explain the merger.*   (same subject)

***She** called a conference **so (that) journalists** could ask questions.* (different subject)

E Manner: *as, as if* and *like*

● We can use *as* or *like* before a clause (subject + verb) to mean 'in the way that'. In this case there is no difference in meaning, but *as* is more formal.

*He runs the company **as/like** his father used to.*

*We'll have four people working on the stand, **as/like** we did last year.*

*As Central Europe looks for growth, it could learn a lot from countries like Ireland, Portugal, Spain and Greece. All of them started off their EU careers far poorer than the EU average, just **as** Central Europe will do.* (Business Central Europe website)

● We can use *as if* or *like* before a clause to say how someone or something feels, looks, sounds or behaves.

*I have a bit of a temperature. I feel **as if/like** I should go home.*

*It looks **as if/like** we're going to recover our costs by the end of the year.*

*For two decades, Friedel Neuber ran the giant German savings bank WestLB **as if** it were an arm of the government.* (Business Week website)

● We can use *as* and *like* before a noun or noun phrase. In this case *as* means 'something is something', and *like* means 'something is similar to something'.

*She works **as** a financial controller.*   (she is one)

*She thinks **like** a financial controller.* (she thinks in a similar way to one)

*We're using the Estonian market **as** a test.*   (it is a test)

*The Estonian market is **like** a test for Finnish market.* (it is not a test, but is it similar to one)

C Barsotti

"No, Hoskins, you're not going to do it just because I'm telling you to do it. You're going to do it because you believe in it."

42 Practice

Exercise 1 A B

Complete the second sentence so it has a similar meaning to the first sentence and contains the word in brackets.

1 It was inconvenient for everyone, so the meeting was postponed. (as)
   As *the meeting was inconvenient for everyone, it was postponed* .

2 I sent Karen a copy of the minutes because she missed the meeting. (so)
   Karen missed the meeting, ...

3 I had a lot of paperwork to do, so I finished work late. (because)
   I finished work late ....

4 I'll call you back. I have to go now because I have a meeting. (so)
   I'll call you back. I have a meeting, ...

5 He doesn't know, so I'll ask someone else. (since)
   Since ....

Exercise 2 C D

Underline the correct word.

1 We're not in this business just *to make*/*for to make* short-term profit.

2 I'll explain in more detail *so*/*that* our objectives are clear.

3 I wrote the date in my diary so *that*/*to* I wouldn't forget the meeting this morning.

4 He resigned *in order to*/*for* spend more time with his family.

5 Jack came to me *in order to*/*for* advice.

6 We'll agree to your offer so that we *can*/*could* close the deal.

7 We agreed to their offer so that we *can*/*could* close the deal.

8 She rechecked the figures so that the auditors *won't*/*wouldn't* find any errors when they came.

9 I'll recheck the figures so that the auditors *won't*/*wouldn't* find any errors when they come.

10 Many visitors come here *to see*/*for to see* our automated production line.

Exercise 3 C D

Match the beginnings of each sentence 1–16 with an ending a) or b).

1	I went to Barcelona to	b	a)	the Trade Fair.
2	I went to Barcelona for	a	b)	attend the Trade Fair.
3	I'm here for		a)	a meeting with Manuel Lopez.
4	I'm here to		b)	meet Manuel Lopez.
5	I think it's time to		a)	a short coffee break.
6	I think it's time for		b)	have a short coffee break.
7	It's worth shopping around for		a)	a better price.
8	It's worth shopping around to		b)	get a better price.
9	I left work early so that I		a)	can go the dentist.
10	I'll have to leave work early so that I		b)	could go to the dentist.
11	I kept his business card so that I		a)	would remember his name.
12	I'll keep his business cards so that I		b)	'll remember his name.
13	I'll deal with it personally so that there		a)	aren't any problems.
14	I dealt with it personally so that there		b)	weren't any problems.

Exercise 4 C D

Are these sentences in English possible or impossible. Write *P* or *I*.

1 I'll speak louder so that everyone can hear. <u>P</u>
2 I'll speak louder in order to everyone can hear.
3 Sorry, I'll explain my proposal again to avoid any confusion.
4 Sorry, I'll explain my proposal again so avoid any confusion.
5 Sorry, I'll explain my proposal again so we avoid any confusion.
6 We mail our clients regularly not to lose contact with them.
7 We mail our clients regularly so as not to lose contact with them.
8 I'll take an umbrella so I won't get wet.
9 I'll take an umbrella so I wouldn't get wet.
10 I'll take an umbrella so I don't get wet.

Exercise 5 E

Complete the sentences with *as* or *like*, or put *as/like* if both are possible.

1 While I was at university I sometimes worked ....as.......... a waiter.
2 The negotiations are going very slowly, ... I expected.
3 Anna's so funny! She's .... a comedian.
4 We'll send the order in two consignments, ... we agreed in the meeting.
5 This crisis is not .... the last one. It's worse!
6 I'm lucky. I have a small room at home that I use .... my study.
7 You look just .... your brother.
8 In a situation like this, you should do exactly .... it says in the book.

Exercise 6 A B C D E

47   <u>Underline</u> the correct word/s in this dialogue.

JACK: Oh, hi, Pamela. Could you give me some advice?
PAMELA: Yeah, sure.
JACK: It's about my laptop. I use it a lot when I'm out of the office, (1) *so / like* I wanted to talk to you about saving my files … I, er, don't want to lose everything if there's a problem.
PAMELA: Hmm. Do you back-up your files (2) *for / to* make sure your work is safe?
JACK: Oh yes. I have a small storage device that plugs into the USB port – it's (3) *as / like* a portable hard disk. And so if anyone stole my laptop it wouldn't be such a disaster (4) *because / for* I would still have all my files.
PAMELA: Well, that's OK then.
JACK: The problem is I often keep this device in the same place as my laptop (5) *for / so that* it's easy for me to find. And that's what worries me.
PAMELA: Oh?
JACK: Well, yes. It's easy for me to find, (6) *so / so that* it's easy for the thief too.
PAMELA: Ah, hah. It sounds (7) *as / as if* you're getting a little bit paranoid, Jack.
JACK: So, is there some kind of solution (8) *for / to* people (9) *as / like* me … who are worried?
PAMELA: Do you use your laptop (10) *to / for* access the Internet?
JACK: Of course.
PAMELA: Well, (11) *not to worry / so as not to worry* about losing your files how about using on-line storage?
JACK: Um, what's that?
PAMELA: It works (12) *as / as if* a hard disk, (13) *as / like* your portable device, but it's an Internet site.
JACK: Oh.
PAMELA: You can upload files to the site whenever you want (14) *so that / like* they are there to download on another occasion. It could be with another computer. I use it all the time (15) *so that / to* keep copies of my most important files.
JACK: Ah, I see. That sounds (16) *as / like* a really good idea. Well, thanks a lot. I'll do that.

43 Developing an argument 1

A Words meaning *and*, *but* and *so*

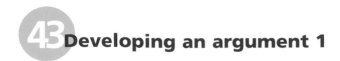

As a result of the reforms in the area of banking, trade, and investment, the economy grew significantly and achieved high annual growth rates. In fact, last year the economy grew by 8%.
(Asia Pacific Economic Review website)

● Units 41 and 42 gave words like *and, but* and *so* to join parts of sentences. We can use longer words and phrases with the same meaning to link both across sentences and within more complex sentences.

and: *In addition, Besides, Moreover, Furthermore*

but: *However, Nevertheless, On the other hand*

so: *Therefore, Consequently, As a result*

These words and phrases are typical of formal speech (for example presentations) and writing. They usually come at the start of a sentence and have a comma afterwards, but can come after a comma in the middle of a sentence.

Supplier A is cheaper, and their delivery times are good. **However**, *supplier B has better quality products and they have a good reputation in the market.*

This new process produces less waste, and **as a result** *it's much better for the environment.*

Our stocks are moving in a downwards spiral, **therefore** *the Fed must cut interest rates to boost our confidence. That, at least, is the theory among investors this week.* (Forbes.com website)

B Examples: *for example, for instance, such as*

● We can use *for example* or *for instance*. Note the possible positions.
Our costs have gone up. **For example**, *the cost of steel has nearly doubled.*
Our costs have gone up. The cost of steel, **for example**, *has nearly doubled.*

● We use *such as* in the middle of a sentence to give examples. It is the same as 'like'. *Such as* is followed by a noun phrase, not a whole clause.
Some delays, **such as** *strikes or bad weather, are beyond our control.*
Some delays are beyond our control, **such as** *strikes or bad weather.*

C Additional/real information: *in fact, actually*

● We use *In fact, Actually* or *As a matter of fact* to add a piece of information to what we just said. The second piece of information gives more details.
We have plenty in stock. **In fact/As a matter of fact**, *we could deliver tomorrow.*

● We also use these words to emphasise what the real situation is. This is surprising or different to what people imagine.
I thought we had some in stock, but **in fact/actually** *we don't.*

D Sequence: *first of all, as well as this, finally*

● We can use *First, Firstly, First of all* to begin a series of points in a formal argument. For other numbered points we say *Second, Secondly*, etc.
To add a point without numbering we can say *As well as this, Besides this* or *In addition*.
At the end we can say *Finally*.
Why choose the Czech Republic? Well, **first of all**, *it has lower labour costs than other neighbouring countries, and* **secondly**, *it has a stable currency.* **As well as this**, *it has a trained workforce with good labour relations, and* **finally**, *it has a strong local market.*

● To finish one point we can say *Overall* or *Taking everything into consideration*.

Overall, a record 67% of the adult population is employed or looking for work, mainly because female participation in the labor force has jumped over the last two decades. (Business Week website)

To finish a formal speech we can say *In conclusion*.
In conclusion, *I'd just like to thank you all very much for coming, and I look forward to seeing you again at our next meeting on 31 September.*

E Generalising: *in general, on the whole*

● There are many words and phrases we can use to talk generally: *In general, On the whole, As a rule, Typically, All in all, Basically, Overall, Broadly speaking.*

*Organisations **typically** have five 'customer' relationships: customers, business partners, suppliers, employees, and shareholders.* (e-business advisor website)

● If we want to make a balanced argument we often use one of these phrases followed by a contrasting idea with a word like *but* (see section A and unit 41).
In general *the Japanese economy has not been very dynamic over recent years.* **However**, *some technology and telecom companies are growing very fast.*
On the whole, *I think you're right,* **although** *I disagree with you about the level of risk.*

F Summarising: *so, to sum up, in summary*

● We can use *So, In short, To put it simply, To sum up* and *In summary* to summarise.
So, to sum up *the main points of my presentation so far, we are a truly international company offering a full range of services to corporate and private clients in the areas of finance, banking and insurance.*

To put it simply, *food processors will lose competitiveness as a direct result of EU membership.* (Business Central Europe website)

G *Either ... or ..., instead of, except for*

● We use *either* to begin a list of possibilities. We do not begin with *or*. The other possibilities are introduced with *or*.
Either *we could cancel the product launch,* **or** *postpone it.* (NOT ~~Or we could cancel~~)

But in speech we can begin with *or* to complete the other person's idea.
A: *'We could just cancel the launch.'*
B: *'**Or** perhaps postpone it.'*

● We use *instead (of)* to mean 'in the place of something else'. At the end of a sentence, *instead* is used without *of*.
*Can we have the meeting on Friday **instead** of Thursday?*
*Thursday is no good? OK, can we have it on Friday **instead**?*

● We use *except, except for* or *apart from* to mean 'not including'.
*I have contacted everyone **except (for)** Margaret.*

43 Practice

Exercise 1 A B C E G

<u>Underline</u> the correct words.

1   If registered mail is too slow, we could use a courier *instead*/*instead of*.

2   The fall in share prices has made investors nervous. On the other *side*/*hand*, it's an excellent buying opportunity if you're prepared to take a risk.

3   *As a rule*/*Therefore* I don't normally have a big lunch, but I'll come with you to the restaurant today.

4   All commodity prices rose last week, *also*/*except* gold.

5   We can *either*/*or* wait for a train, or go by taxi.

6   I know Madrid very well. *As a matter of fact*/*On the whole*, I worked there for a short time many years ago.

7   *As a matter of fact*/*On the whole* stocks are riskier than bonds, but stocks can give a better return in the long term.

8   It's convenient for me to come to work by car. *On the other hand*/*Besides*, the train would probably be quicker.

9   It's convenient for me to come to work by car. *On the other hand*/*Besides*, the company pays for the parking.

10   Investment in areas *for example*/*such as* biotechnology can be risky.

11   Investment in some areas, *for example*/*such as* biotechnology, can be risky.

12   Can we send an email *except for*/*instead of* a fax?

Exercise 2 A B C D E F G

Complete each sentence with a word or phrase from the list below.

~~actually~~   as well as this   either   except   instead   such as   therefore
nevertheless   so   in general

1   People think it's expensive, but ....**actually**......... over the long term it isn't.

2   The restaurant is open every day .... Monday.

3   She's out of the country and .... unable to attend the meeting.

4   I was going on Tuesday, but now I'm going on Monday ....

5   .... I think the meeting went very well, although we didn't manage to agree on the composition of the new team.

6   Some areas, ... recruitment, are outsourced to other companies.

7   I'm sorry. .... you accept this price, or we can't do business.

8   It's reliable, safe and easy to use. .... , it's excellent value for money.

9   It's reliable, safe and easy to use. .... , the maintenance costs can be quite high.

10   .... , in short, it's reliable, safe and easy to use.

Exercise 3 A B E

Put four commas in this short paragraph.

In general taking an MBA is a good idea for an ambitious young professional however you do have to make some sacrifices. You miss out on two years' valuable work experience for example and it can be very expensive.

Exercise 4 A B C D E F G

 48 Read this article about transport policy in city centres. Complete the article by choosing the correct alternative from A, B, C or D below. This exercise includes revision of unit 41.

Want to enter the city?
Sorry, you'll have to pay.

Traffic congestion in city centres is a big problem for both businesses and residents. Policy makers are being forced to think of solutions based on public transport, road pricing and restricted use of one kind or another (1) ....C.... unlimited access for cars at all times. What are the reasons for this? (2) .... , cars cause noise and pollution in areas where people walk, shop or go sightseeing, and (3) .... this they are of course quite dangerous. (4) .... , cars cause traffic jams and (5) .... many hours of work time are lost. (6) .... , people need incentives before they change their habits and alternatives to cars are often not available or of poor quality. The first thing is that public transport must become more reliable and more comfortable. (7) .... , bicycle use should be encouraged, (8) .... by having more cycle lanes. Some large cities, (9) .... Amsterdam, are already organised in this way. But the most radical measure is road pricing. Asking motorists to pay to enter city centres is controversial, but is an increasingly common solution. So, (10) .... , we can see that imaginative and sometimes unpopular measures will be needed to make the city centre a more pleasant place to work and live.

1	A but	B except for	C instead of	D such as
2	A As well	B First of all	C In fact	D As a result
3	A As well as	B Also	C For example	D Except
4	A For example	B However	C And	D Secondly
5	A either	B both	C as a result	D instead of
6	A However	B Therefore	C So	D In conclusion
7	A To sum up	B In addition	C Actually	D For example
8	A to sum up	B in addition	C actually	D for example
9	A such as	B as well as	C instead of	D except
10	A thirdly	B in conclusion	C instead	D also

Exercise 5 A C D E G

 49 Complete this speech made by the leader of a Korean trade delegation at the end of a trip to Wales with the words and phrases from the list below.

~~first of all~~   in conclusion   in addition   therefore   instead of   as a rule   however   in fact

'Could I just say a few words? Thank you. Well, (1) ...first of all... I'd like to thank everyone here at GNK for organising today's visit. We have enjoyed meeting all the staff, seeing your new products and looking round your factory. (2) .... , I would like to thank the local Chamber of Commerce who made the whole trip possible. As you know, we see the European market as very important for our company. (3) .... , it is central to our future plans. (4) .... , I'm sure that we can look forward to even closer cooperation between our two companies in the future.
(5) .... I think it's better to keep the ceremonies short on occasions like this,
(6) .... , I would just like to take this opportunity to leave you with something to remember our visit, and so I have great pleasure in presenting this book with photographs of Korea to your director, Chris Armstrong. (7) .... , I hope that we may soon have the pleasure of welcoming some of you to our country in the future. Perhaps the next time we meet it will be in Seoul
(8) .... Cardiff! Once again, thank you all very much.'

44 Developing an argument 2

A Personal comment

> *The thing is, the venture capital market is giving these start-ups a lot of money to go out and be a threat to existing companies.*
> **(Asiaweek website)**

● There are many words and short phrases that come at the beginning of a sentence and help us to make a personal comment.

Giving your own ideas	*From my point of view, In my opinion/view, Personally*
Information you have heard	*Apparently, It seems that*
Most people know this	*Clearly, Of course, Obviously*
Good/bad luck	*Luckily, Fortunately, Happily, Sadly, Unfortunately, Unhappily*
You are being honest	*To be honest/frank, Actually, Frankly*

***Fortunately**, there are plenty of signs that Mexico may finally have reached a new level of political and economic maturity.* (Global Business Magazine website)

*'**Frankly**, I didn't know what I was going to do,' says Park about starting up his bank. 'I just wanted to replicate the services of firms in the U.S. I was making pretty good money at Merrill Lynch and I thought I could make more on my own.'* (Asia Inc On-Line website)

● Other words used to make a personal comment include: *admittedly, coincidentally, curiously, incredibly, interestingly, ironically, naturally, paradoxically, predictably, significantly, surprisingly, unbelievably, understandably, unexpectedly.*

● If you want to give your ideas from one particular point of view you can use a phrase like: *Technically (speaking), Scientifically (speaking), From a financial/technical point of view,* etc.

B Other linking words and phrases

● Study this list of common linking words and phrases used in speech.

Giving the most important example or situation	*Especially, In particular, Above all*
Correcting yourself	*I mean, Or rather*
Supporting a previous statement	*After all*
Changing the subject (informal)	*By the way, So, Anyway*
Changing the subject (more formal)	*In relation to, As regards, Moving on to, As far as … is concerned*
Dismissing something/Preparing to finish	*Anyway*

C Structures to focus on important information

● We can focus on important information with the structure *The* + noun + *is*. The second part of the sentence is usually a 'that' clause or a 'wh-' question (*which, what, when, how*, etc).
The thing is (that) the whole idea is just too risky.
The thing is, how much money will all this cost?

Nouns used with this structure include: *answer, fact, point, problem, question, solution, thing, trouble, truth.*
The question is, what are we going to do about it?
The trouble is (that) it's going to be very expensive.

● We can focus on important information using a clause that begins with *what*:
What we need is a few days to think about this in more detail.
What I'm going to do is call our warehouse and see how many we have in stock.
What worries me is the time they're taking to make a decision.

D *At the end, in the end, at last*

● The phrases *at the end, in the end* and *at last* do not have the same meaning:

At the end refers to a point in time

*I spoke for 20 minutes, but there were a lot of questions **at the end**.*

In the end means 'after a lot of time' or 'eventually'

*I waited until ten, and **in the end I left**.*   (+ past tense)

At last makes a comment that we are pleased now because a long wait has ended

***At last I've finished** this report!* (+ present tense eg: present perfect)

*Bear markets are a natural part of stocks, in the same way that fires are a natural force in the forests. Even though it's tough to watch, the market is usually healthier **in the end**.* (Wall Street Journal website)

E *If, unless, otherwise*

● Conditionals with *If* (units 17 and 18) are important for developing an argument.

The linking words *unless* and *otherwise* have the meaning 'if not'. Look at the next three examples which all have the same meaning:

***If** we **don't** pay the invoice now, they'll cut back our credit.*
***Unless** we pay the invoice now, they'll cut back our credit.*
*We should pay the invoice now, **otherwise** they'll cut back our credit.*

*What partners can the London Stock Exchange reach out to? A tie-up with Frankfurt probably won't happen, **unless** a radically different type of proposal can be put together.* (accountancy age website)

F Abbreviations in written English

● Note the following abbreviations which are common in written English:

ie   = that is to say (from the Latin 'id est')

eg   = for example (from the Latin 'exempli gratia')

NB   = note (from the Latin 'nota bene')

*Miami-based global B2B food exchange Foodtrader expects no more than 1% of South and Central America's US$375bn food market be conducted online in 2001. Of that amount, Foodtrader hopes to capture 10%, **ie** some US$375mn.* (business news americas website)

"Oh, by the way, do you have any money? Will you send me any money? Do you know anyone who has any money? Will they send me any money?"

44 Practice

Exercise 1 A B D E F

<u>Underline</u> the correct words.

1   I like all the marketing ideas, but *in particular*/*in particularly* the free samples.

2   *From our point of view*/*In our point of view* that would not be a good solution.

3   *It seems*/*Apparently*, the Board is going to appoint a new CEO.

4   *It seems that*/*Apparently that* the Board is going to appoint a new CEO.

5   *Fortunately*/*With good fortune* she wasn't listening.

6   *Actually*/*Truly*, I've never really trusted him.

7   *Moving on*/*Moving on to* the question of finance, we'll need to raise about $2m.

8   We tried arguing with them, but *at the end*/*in the end* we just gave up.

9   Frankie's managed to get a job *at last*/*in the end*!

10   *Unless*/*Otherwise* we decide within the next few weeks it'll be too late.

11   It'll be too late *unless*/*otherwise* we decide within the next few weeks.

12   We must decide within the next few weeks, *unless*/*otherwise* it'll be too late.

13   Some countries in Europe, *ie*/*eg* Spain and Ireland, are growing strongly.

14   Europe's three biggest economies, *ie*/*eg* Germany, France and the UK, are all growing strongly.

Exercise 2 A B

Complete the replies to the comments below by following the instructions in brackets and using the words and phrases from the list below.

~~personally~~   anyway   of course   by the way   above all   apparently
after all   or rather   unfortunately   to be frank

1   'We should have the prototype ready by June.'
    (give your ideas) .....Personally..... , I think August is more realistic.

2   'The insurance on this system doesn't look too expensive.'
    (most people know this) .... , it needs to be renewed every year.

3   'I've got two spare tickets for the opera tonight. Are you interested?'
    (you would like to go but can't) .... , I've got a previous commitment.

4   'So at the end of the day I think we did quite well.'
    (change the subject) .... , what did Matthew say about Paris?

5   'The joint venture with Optika is running into all sorts of problems.'
    (be honest) .... , we should never have entered into it in the first place.

6   'I think it might be time to set up an office in Estonia.'
    (support the previous statement) .... , we already operate in Finland.

7   'Why didn't Robert get the new sales job?'
    (give information you have heard) .... , his interview was a disaster.

8   'Everything seems very well prepared. There shouldn't be any problems.'
    (prepare to finish) .... , we can talk about it again nearer the time.

9   'Carmen really deserved to get the new sales job.'
    (give the most important reason) .... , because of her experience.

10   'I think we should target our next line of clothes at a younger market.'
    It's a good idea, (correct yourself) .... it could be a good idea if we don't lose our existing customers by doing so.

Exercise 3 A B D unit 43

50   <u>Underline</u> the correct words in this presentation about robotics. This exercise includes some revision of unit 43.

(1) *First of all*/*After all*, I'd like to thank Keiko Ishida for her kind words of introduction, and for inviting me here to speak to you this morning. The title of my talk is 'The Age of the Robot', and I'll be talking today about robotics, and (2) *anyway*/*in particular* their commercial exploitation.

(3) *Especially*/*Clearly* there's huge interest in the subject, as can be seen by the number of people in the audience today, and this is not surprising as we predict that over the next decade robotics is going to be one of the world's fastest growing industries. (4) *To give an example*/*However*, we predict that health-care robots in Japan alone will be a $1 billion market by 2010. They'll be present in hospitals and nursing homes, reminding patients to take medicines, delivering food trays, cleaning, supporting patients who have problems walking, and doing almost everything else (5) *except for*/*instead of* peeling the grapes!

(6) *As far as the general public is concerned*/*Concerning the general public*, Sony Corporation thinks that the best place to launch the robot revolution is home entertainment, because singing and dancing robots don't do anything essential and it's OK if they make a mistake sometimes. (7) *Especially*/*Furthermore*, home entertainment is likely to be the biggest market (8) *eventually*/*at last*, with some households having two or three robots, just like they have PCs today. (9) *As a matter of fact*/*Moving on* all the leading players (10) *such as*/*for example* Matsushita, NEC and Omron are investing tens of millions of dollars in the development of personal robots. (11) *I mean*/*As a result* progress has been rapid, and scientists now understand the technology necessary for complex actions like walking on two feet without falling over.

(12) *On the other hand*/*At the end*, it's clear that the development of 'robo sapiens' with something that approximates human intelligence will take longer, (13) *especially*/*or rather* a lot longer.

(14) *Nevertheless*/*In general* it's clear that in terms of competition between countries Japan leads in robotics at the moment, (15) *although*/*apart from* the Americans are trying hard to catch up. And Japan does urgently need a whole new area of products to sell to the world as profit margins in other areas of consumer electronics gets smaller.

So, (16) *in fact*/*to sum up*, I've tried to show you how I believe we're entering a new age, the age of the robot, and it's an age that's full of business opportunities.

Exercise 4 A B D unit 43

Check the answers to exercise 3 before you do this exercise. Then find words and phrases from the correct answers that are similar to the expressions below.

1	To begin with	......First of all......	9	However	....
2	In fact	....	10	in short	....
3	As regards	....	11	apart from	....
4	For instance	....	12	despite the fact that	....
5	On the whole	....	13	in the end	....
6	Obviously	....	14	I mean	....
7	In addition	....	15	especially	....
8	Because of this	....			

45 Prepositions of place

1 A man with a scarf *around* his neck is *in* a lift. He is leaning *against* the wall of the lift. The lift is coming *up* from the street *below*.
2 In a moment the man will walk *through* the lift doors and *into* the office. He will put his jacket *on* the coat stand which is *by/near* the lift.
3 There is a man waiting for the lift. He has pressed the button to go *down*.
4 *On the other side of* the lift doors is Jane. She is walking *away from* the lift *across* the room, *past* the photocopier *towards* a meeting room.
5 Jack is *beside/next* to the photocopier. *Above* the photocopier is a shelf. He is moving the boxes of paper *off* the shelf *onto* the floor.
6 Sue and Mark are sitting *at* their desks *opposite* each other. Their computers are *in front of* them *on* their desks. *Between* them is a waste-paper bin and the photocopier is *behind* Sue.
7 Mark has put his coat *over* the back of his chair. Sue's bag is *under* her chair.
8 Sue is putting a letter *inside* an envelope and Mark is taking something *out of* his drawer.

A *At* or *in*?

- We use *at* to talk about the position of something, or about the place where something happens. *At* shows a general location.
  Meet me ***at my office****. There's someone* ***at the door****.* (position)
  I'll see you ***at the meeting****.* (where something happens)
- We use *in* with the name of a container, place or area to show that someone or something is inside it.
  There's plenty of paper ***in the photocopier****.*
  She's ***in the third room*** *on the left.*
  Our head office is ***in France/the north/Paris****.*
- Study these examples for public buildings:
  I'll see you ***at*** *the airport.* (the place in general)
  I'll see you ***in*** *the airport terminal.* (inside the building)
  I had a hard day ***at*** *the office.* (perhaps I spent some time out of the building)
  I'll be back ***in*** *the office at three.* (inside the building)

B Expressions with *at, in* and *on*

- Note these fixed expressions with *at*:

at the front/back	*at* the top/bottom	*at* the beginning/end
at the seaside	*at* the station/airport	*at* home/work/school

- Note these fixed expressions with *in*:

in the middle	*in* my hand	*in* a queue/line/row
in the corner	*in* the country	*in* a book/magazine/newspaper
in the mirror	*in* the photo/picture	*in* hospital/prison
in the chair (= in charge of the meeting)		

- Note these fixed expressions with *on*:

on the left/right	*on* television/the radio	*on* the phone/the computer
on the screen	*on* the page/map	*on* the M6 (motorways and roads)
on the first floor	*on* the platform/pavement	*on* the Rhine (rivers)

  on the plane/bus/train (but *in* a car/taxi because you are contained in a smaller space where you can't stand up)

- With addresses, we use *in* for the street name and *at* when we say the street number as well. Americans use *on* for streets.
  *Our offices are **in** Piccadilly.*
  *Our offices are **at** 14 High Street.*
  *I went shopping **on** Fifth Avenue.*

C *Above/below, Over/under*

- *Above/below* mean 'higher/lower than'. They can be used without an object.
  The floor above/below us is occupied by an insurance company.*
  *From the mountain I could see the lake **below**.*

- *Over/under* mean 'directly above/below'. They both need an object.
  *We flew right **over** Windsor Castle on our way into Heathrow.*
  *There's still a lot of oil **under** the sea.*

  Over can also be used for movement. In this case it is like 'across'.
  *We have to **go over/across** to the other side of the street.*

  Over can also mean 'covering'.
  *They've put a plastic sheet **over the hole** in the roof.*

- All four words can be used for positions in a management hierarchy.
  Above me is the Sales Director. **Under me** there are four sales staff.*

D *Opposite, next to/beside, near/by*

- *Opposite* means 'exactly on the other side of' a space.
  *We sat **opposite each other** in the meeting.*

- *Next to* and *beside* mean 'exactly at the side of'. *Beside* can be more formal.
  *John should sit **next to/beside** Irene at the meeting.*

- *Near* means 'close to'. *By* means 'at the side of'.
  *There are one or two good restaurants **near here**.*
  *Can we have a table **by the window**?*
  *We had a holiday **near** the sea.* (close to the sea – a few kilometres away)
  *We had a holiday **by** the sea.* (we stayed on the beach most of the time)

45 Practice

Exercise 1 A B C D

Underline the correct word.

1   Look in the Appendix <u>at</u>/by the end of the report.
2   When I got *in/on* the plane someone was sitting in my seat.
3   What a fantastic view! The sky *above/over* and the sea *below/under*.
4   Next week I'll be *at/in* Hungary for a few days.
5   Turn into Western Avenue and you'll see our offices *on/at* your left.
6   You can't miss it. The restaurant is exactly *by/opposite* the cinema.
7   I often work *in/at* home in the evening.
8   I bought this tie *in/at* Madison Avenue.
9   She'll be here in a few minutes – she's just *at/on* the phone at the moment.
10   The power socket is over there, *by/at* the door.
11   This graph isn't labelled properly. Write the units *by/next to* the X axis.
12   I went to visit my son *in/at* hospital yesterday.
13   Put a sheet *above/over* the machine to stop it getting dusty.
14   Siena is quite *near/by* Florence.
15   I'll see you tomorrow at ten thirty, *in/by* my office.
16   It's a large block. Our offices are *at/on* the fifteenth floor.
17   I saw Simon *at/in* the station while I was waiting for a train.
18   I must have been standing *in/at* the queue for half an hour.
19   You'll see our offices – they're *by/near* a furniture store. (the next block)
20   You'll see our offices – they're *by/near* a furniture store. (the next building)

Exercise 2 A B

Complete the sentences with *in*, *at* or *on*.

1   I live ....in.... Manor Road, ...at.... number 295.
2   You shouldn't really park .... the pavement.
3   I had a lovely meal .... the plane.
4   I'd like to live .... the country when I retire.
5   Go to the end of the road, and you'll see the bank .... the right.
6   I'll be arriving .... your offices .... Barcelona at three.
7   Lisbon is .... the middle of Portugal, ... the coast.
8   I'll meet you .... the front of the building in ten minutes.
9   I wonder what's .... television this evening.
10   The size of the text .... the screen is very small. Couldn't it be bigger?
11   I live .... a small village .... the road to Dover.
12   .... the beginning of my career I worked in marketing.
13   It was a very well-run meeting. Erika was .... the chair.
14   I wasn't looking .... the mirror and I nearly had an accident.
15   She works .... Seville, ... the University.
16   The sales figures? Yes, I have them right here .... my hand.
17   I waited patiently .... the back of the queue.
18   I think I left my briefcase .... the chair .... the restaurant.
19   I'm off sick at the moment, but I should be back .... work next week.
20   The last Finance Minister is still .... prison.

Exercise 3 A B C D

Complete this email by choosing the correct preposition from the list below.

towards   over   past   through   in front of   by   in   ~~to~~   at (x2)   on (x2)

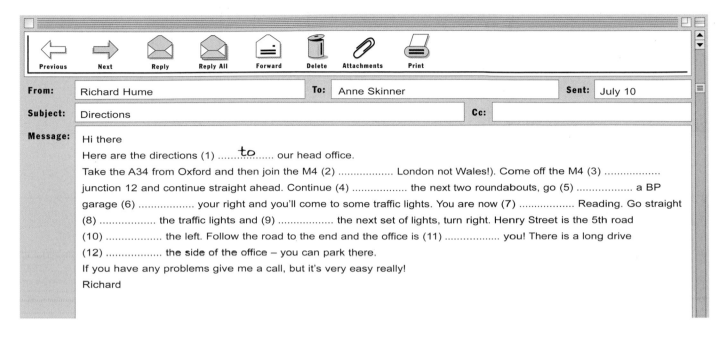

From: Richard Hume   **To:** Anne Skinner   **Sent:** July 10

Subject: Directions   **Cc:**

Message:

Hi there

Here are the directions (1) ....to...... our head office.

Take the A34 from Oxford and then join the M4 (2) .... London not Wales!). Come off the M4 (3) .... junction 12 and continue straight ahead. Continue (4) .... the next two roundabouts, go (5) .... a BP garage (6) .... your right and you'll come to some traffic lights. You are now (7) .... Reading. Go straight (8) .... the traffic lights and (9) .... the next set of lights, turn right. Henry Street is the 5th road (10) .... the left. Follow the road to the end and the office is (11) .... you! There is a long drive (12) .... the side of the office – you can park there.

If you have any problems give me a call, but it's very easy really!

Richard

Exercise 4 A B C D

Complete this email by putting <u>one</u> suitable word in each space. As well as the words in sections A, B, C and D it is also possible to use *to*.

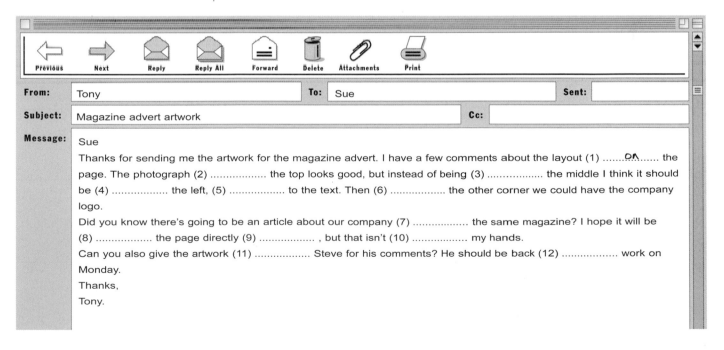

From: Tony   **To:** Sue   **Sent:**

Subject: Magazine advert artwork   **Cc:**

Message:

Sue

Thanks for sending me the artwork for the magazine advert. I have a few comments about the layout (1) ....on...... the page. The photograph (2) .... the top looks good, but instead of being (3) .... the middle I think it should be (4) .... the left, (5) .... to the text. Then (6) .... the other corner we could have the company logo.

Did you know there's going to be an article about our company (7) .... the same magazine? I hope it will be (8) .... the page directly (9) .... , but that isn't (10) .... my hands.

Can you also give the artwork (11) .... Steve for his comments? He should be back (12) .... work on Monday.

Thanks,

Tony.

46 Verb + preposition

A Verb + preposition

● Here is a list of verbs and the prepositions normally used with them:

apply for	*concentrate on*	*insist on*	*refer to*
approve of	*consist of*	*know about*	*rely on*
believe in	*cooperate with*	*lead to*	*specialise in*
belong to	*decide on*	*listen to*	*suffer from*
benefit from	*depend on*	*object to*	*sympathise with*
compete against	*focus on*	*pay for*	*take care of*
comply with	*hope for*	*qualify for*	*wait for*

I've **applied for** a new job.   Can you **take care of** the office while I'm out?

*European stocks may advance, led by phone companies including Nokia and Ericsson that will **benefit from** rising sales of mobile phones that can access the Internet.* (Bloomberg.com website)

*The new economy is **focused on** knowledge and technology.* (The Straights Times Interactive website)

*Regulators seem to understand the need for banks to merge and don't often **object to** these huge deals.* (Business Week website)

● Some of the verbs above can be used without preposition + object.
I hope/know/insist.   It depends.   I've decided.   I'm listening/waiting.

Others must have a preposition + object.
The process consists **of four main stages**.   It belongs **to me**.
I'm relying **on you** for your support.   This will lead **to a lot of problems**.

See unit 16 ● In questions the preposition usually goes at the end.
Who does this belong **to**?   What does it consist **of**?   Who are you waiting **for**?

B Verb + object + preposition

● With some verbs the object comes before the preposition. Here are some common examples:

add something **to**	**explain** something **to**	**share** something **with**
ask someone **about/for**	**inform** someone **about/of**	**spend** something **on**
blame someone **for**	**insure** something **against**	**split** something **into**
borrow something **from**	**invest** something **in**	**supply** someone **with**
compare something **with/to**	**invite** someone **to**	**tell** someone **about**
congratulate someone **on**	**protect** someone **from**	**thank** someone **for**
divide something **into**	**prevent** someone **from**	**translate** something **into**

Can they **insure** us **against** fire risk?   We've **spent** $2m **on** advertising this year.

*Nobody in Russia is prepared to **invest** money **in** production.* (Le Monde Diplomatique website)

*Oracle chairman Larry Ellison has offered a solution to what he sees as Microsoft's monopoly: 'They should **split** the company **into** two and let [Microsoft president] Steve Ballmer run one company and let Bill Gates run the other.'* (Wired magazine website)

● With *remind* there is a difference in meaning between *about* and *of*.
Gillian **reminded** me **about** the appointment. (= she told me not to forget)
Gillian **reminds** me **of** my sister.   (= she is like my sister)

C Verb + different prepositions

● Some verbs can go with several different prepositions.

agree to/with/about
*They agreed **to** give us better terms of payment.*
*OK, I agree **with** you **about** the need for cutting costs.*

apologise to/for
*I must apologise **to** Susan **for** my awful behaviour last night.*

ask for/about
*Shall we ask **for** the bill?*
*Ask the waiter **about** the dish of the day.*

complain to/about
*I'm going to complain **to** the manager **about** the service in here.*

hear about/from/of
*I heard **about** the news **from** a colleague **of** mine.*
*I've never heard **of** that company – they're not very well-known.*

learn about/from
*I learnt a lot **about** insurance **from** my last job.*

look at/for
*Look **at** this!*
*Can you help me – I'm looking **for** meeting room 3.*

result from/in
*This problem results **from** bad planning, and it will result **in** chaos.*

talk to/about
*I need to talk **to** you **about** the new construction project.*

think of/about
*What did you think **of** the meeting?*
*What are you thinking **about**?*

write to/about
*They've written **to** us to complain **about** our poor service.*

D Uses of different prepositions

● Some prepositions are used to introduce particular kinds of information. Knowing this can help you to understand some of the differences in section C.

about often introduces the subject matter
*Do you **know about** EU regulations in this area?*
*We're **thinking about** changing our advertising slogan.*

at often shows direction
*I'm **looking at** your order details on the screen right now.*
*I hate it when my boss **shouts at** me.*

for often shows purpose or reason
*I must **apologise for** being late.*
*I've **asked** the waiter **for** the bill.*

from often shows the origin of something
*I haven't **heard from** them for a long time.*
*This problem **results from** bad planning.*

on often shows confidence or certainty
*Can we **agree on** a discount of 5%?*
*We're **depending on** you to finish the job by Friday.*

to often refers to a person
*Could you **explain** this clause **to** me, please?*
*I don't think he was **listening to** me.*

"I hereby empower you, Ambrose T. Wilkins, to water my plants. And let's hear no more talk about how I never delegate authority."

46 Practice

Exercise 1 A

Complete the sentences with a word from list A and a word from list B.

A: approve depend know lead believe suffer ~~sympathise~~ wait

B: about for from in of on to ~~with~~

1 I really ..*sympathise with*.. your problem, but there's not a lot I can do.
2 Positive thinking is so important. You really have to .... yourself.
3 I'll .... you outside.
4 What you're saying can only .... one possible conclusion.
5 Of course the size of our order will .... the price.
6 Your CV is strong in most areas, but what do you .... marketing?
7 Imports always .... the effects of a strong dollar.
8 I always have to look smart – my boss doesn't .... informal clothes.

Exercise 2 B

Underline the correct word.

1 I think we should ask them *for*/*about*/*with* more information.
2 Can you supply us *for*/*about*/*with* enough parts for 5,000 vehicles?
3 You remind me *about*/*of*/*for* someone I know.
4 If I forget, remind me *about*/*of*/*for* it again at the end of the meeting.
5 The management blamed the union *against*/*from*/*for* causing the strike.
6 I'm writing to inform you *for*/*about*/*on* our new range of products.
7 We might have to split the order *for*/*in*/*into* two separate shipments.
8 Can you thank Mr Mateus *about*/*for*/*with* all his help?
9 I'd like to congratulate Patricia *on*/*for*/*about* winning Employee of the Month.
10 This safety feature prevents the operative *against*/*from*/*with* suffering any injury.
11 This year we'll be investing more than £4m *on*/*in*/*to* plant and new machinery.
12 This year we'll be spending more than £4m *on*/*in*/*to* plant and new machinery.

Exercise 3 C D

Complete these sentences with prepositions. Choose from: *about, at, for, from, in, to, of* or *with*.

1 I'm writing .....*to*..... all our customers ...*about*... offers this month on selected models.
2 Who was George talking .... ? And what exactly was he talking .... ?
3 Have you heard anything .... Head Office? They said they'd decide this week.
4 Who's Giuseppe Saponi? I've never heard .... him.
5 Do you like the new design? What do you think .... it?
6 Do you agree .... me .... this?
7 The improved sales figures result .... all the investments we made last year.
8 The investments we're making now should result .... better sales next year.
9 I must apologise .... not contacting you earlier, but I've been very busy.
10 I'd like to complain .... the manager .... the food.
11 Make sure you look .... the small print before you sign anything.
12 Unless their quality improves, we'll have to look .... a new supplier.

Exercise 4 A B C D

Complete the sentences with one word from list A and one word from list B.

A: agreed apologised apply belong comply explain heard hoping insist listen ~~pay~~
qualify rely remind

B: about on on from with with to to to ~~for~~ for for for for

1 You can ....pay.......... ....for..... the goods in twelve monthly instalments.
2 Excuse me, but does this umbrella .... you?
3 The first thing is to .... the client to find out their needs.
4 I asked my lawyer to .... the contract .... me.
5 Everybody .... the decision. It was unanimous.
6 There's a new job in R&D. I wonder if Chris is going to .... it.
7 Jill is a good team member. You can always .... her in a crisis.
8 They've .... the delay and said that the items are in the post.
9 I'm certain to forget. .... me .... it nearer the time.
10 It's been a disappointing year. We're .... better results soon.
11 Have you .... Jackie recently? She hasn't written for ages.
12 Does this product .... European safety standards?
13 No, no, I .... paying. You're my guest.
14 If we build the factory in that area we'll .... a regional aid grant.

Exercise 5 A B C D

Complete the emails with the correct prepositions. The second number in each bracket shows the number of letters in the word.

From:	Peter Carey	To:	Customer queries	Sent:	11 December ...

Message:

I've just been looking (1-2) ......at...... your website and comparing your on-line banking facilities (2-4) .... your competitors. There's a few things I'd like to ask you (3-5) ....
a) If I want to borrow money (4-4) .... you, how much will I pay (5-3) .... the loan? I assume that your cheaper operating costs will result (6-2) .... a lower interest rate than a normal bank.
b) I see that if I open an account this month I qualify (7-3) .... a credit card with special payment terms. Do you offer insurance (8-7) .... on-line fraud with this card to protect card-holders (9-4) .... hackers who might steal the number)?
I look forward to hearing (10-4) .... you. Thank you.

From:	Customer queries	To:	Peter Carey	Sent:	13 December ...

Message:

Thank you (11-3) .... your recent email and I apologise (12-3) .... taking so long to reply.
Here is the information you requested.
a) You can rely (13-2) .... the fact that our interest rates are very competitive, but I cannot give exact figures as it depends (14-2) .... the amount you want to borrow. I invite you (15-2) ....check the table on our website for this information. I can assure you that we deal with the process very quickly – after applying (16-3) .... the loan you shouldn't have to wait more than a few days before hearing (17-4) .... us.
b) Yes, as soon as you inform us (18-5) .... any possible fraud associated with your card we take care (19-2) .... everything and refund any money that you have lost. In relation to our own customer accounts, we do everything necessary to prevent hackers (20-4) .... entering the system, and have invested heavily (21-2) .... this area over recent years.
I hope this answers your questions. Please do not hesitate to contact us again if you think (22-2) .... anything else.

47 Adjective + preposition

A Adjective + preposition

> Information technology is not important enough on its own to generate a sustained recovery. Rather, sustained growth will be dependent on a recovery in private consumption.
> (FT.com website)

● Some adjectives can have a preposition after them. The preposition may be followed by a noun or noun phrase.
We're all **disappointed with** the poor figures.
I'm **responsible for** a sales team of eight people that covers the south of the country.

When followed by a verb, the -ing form must be used.
We might be **interested in placing** more orders in the future.

● An adjective can also be followed by a to infinitive. If we need to mention a person, we use for between the adjective and the infinitive.
It's **important to follow** the safety procedures.
It's **important for us to move** quickly in these negotiations.

It's **good for children to make** their own choices. Too much well-meaning liberalism means that it's harder for us to set boundaries for them. (Guardian website)

B Feelings

● Many examples of adjective + preposition are connected with feelings.

afraid of	fed up with	proud of
amazed at/by	fond of	satisfied with
bored with	interested in	serious about
disappointed with	keen on	shocked at/by
doubtful about	nervous of	surprised at/by
enthusiastic about	optimistic about	suspicious of
excited about	pessimistic about	tired of
fascinated by	pleased with	worried about

I'm really **excited about** starting my new job.
I'm not very **keen on** fried food, to be honest.

Six banks are **interested in** buying an 86% stake in Peru's Banco Latino. (Business News Americas website)

● For behaviour towards another person we use adjective + to. Examples include good to, kind to, nice to, polite to, rude to.
When my mother was ill my colleagues were all very **kind to** me.
I thought he was rather **rude to** the waitress.

"No, Thursday's out. How about never—is never good for you?"

C Other adjectives

● Here are some other common examples of adjective + preposition.

accustomed to	married to
answerable to	opposed to
attached to	popular with
aware of	prepared for
capable of	ready for
certain about	related to
compatible with	relevant to
covered in	rich in
dependent on	right about
different from/to	safe from
famous for	the same as
fit for	similar to
full of	suitable for
guilty of	sure of
important for	typical of
involved in	used to (= accustomed to)
late for	useful for
lacking in	wrong about

*My opinions are very **different from** yours.*
*Our company is **famous** all over the world **for** the quality of its engineering.*
*She was **full of** enthusiasm when I explained our idea.*
*We're **used to** the delays on the metro. They happen all the time.*

D Adjective + choice of preposition

● Some adjectives can be followed by different prepositions with a small difference in meaning. Often one preposition is used for things and another for people.

*'We are each **responsible for** a particular geographical area.' – Export Services Adviser* (cebd website)

angry about	*I'm very **angry about** the delay.*
angry with	*I'm very **angry with** them for causing this delay.*
annoyed about	*He was **annoyed about** what the journalist wrote.*
annoyed with	*He was **annoyed with** the journalist.*
good/bad at (ability)	*I've never been very **good at** dealing with conflict.*
good/bad for	*A new person at the top would be **good for** the company.*
good/bad with	*She's very **good with** difficult customers.*
happy about/with	*Are you **happy with** my suggestion?*
happy for	*Congratulations! I'm very **happy for** you both.*
responsible for	*I'm **responsible for** all the transport and logistics.*
responsible to	*The Finance Director is directly **responsible to** the CEO.*
sorry about	*I'm **sorry about** all the trouble I've caused.*
sorry for (+ -ing)	*I'm **sorry for** causing so much trouble.*
feel sorry for	*I felt **sorry for** George when he didn't get the promotion.*

47 Practice

Exercise 1 B C D

Complete each sentence 1–10 with an ending a)–j).

1	Are you interested	j	a)	at motivating people.
2	This model is different		b)	with us for sending the wrong goods.
3	Are you aware		c)	for another drink?
4	They were really annoyed		d)	of the difficulties you are creating?
5	He's become very keen		e)	about this, but I don't think it's going to work.
6	Jane is really good		f)	by the number of Internet cafés in this town.
7	I'm so tired. I'm not used		g)	in any other items from the catalogue?
8	Are you ready		h)	from the old one in some important ways.
9	I was quite surprised		i)	to the time difference yet.
10	I could be wrong		j)	on keeping fit recently.

Exercise 2 B C

Complete the sentences with one word from list A and one word from list B.

A: attached   tired   dependent   ~~popular~~   involved   safe   suitable   serious

B: about   for   from   in   of   on   to   ~~with~~

1 This fund is very ...popular... ...with... investors looking for long-term growth.

2 The firewall should make the network .... attack by hackers.

3 For further details, see the copy of the contract .... this letter.

4 Starting salary is .... previous experience.

5 I don't think they're .... this, they haven't been in touch for weeks.

6 We're .... every stage of the process, from design to production.

7 I need a change. I'm .... doing the same thing every day.

8 Hedge funds are very risky. They're not .... the private investor.

Exercise 3 D

<u>Underline</u> the correct word.

1 I'm really angry *about/<u>with</u>* them for not letting us know sooner.

2 I've spoken to Robert and I'm reasonably happy *with/for* all the arrangements.

3 I'm really happy *with/for* Maggie, she deserved to get promoted.

4 I'm a bit annoyed *about/with* all this confusion with the wrong invoices.

5 I'm a bit annoyed *about/with* them for sending the wrong invoices.

6 I'm sorry *about/for* what happened yesterday.

7 I'm sorry *about/for* arriving so late – I got delayed in traffic.

8 I feel very sorry *about/for* Frances. She didn't deserve to be treated like that.

9 Low inflation is good *at/for/with* every sector of the economy.

10 She'd be excellent in Human Resources, she's really good *at/for/with* people.

11 Richard, can you help us with this translation? You're good *at/for/with* French.

12 If you need to refer the decision upwards, who are you responsible *for/to*?

13 As head of department, how many staff are you responsible *for/to*?

14 Who is responsible *for/to* the Scandinavian market?

Exercise 4 B C D

Complete the second sentence so it has a similar meaning to the first sentence.

1 Consumers find the old models a bit boring.
  Consumers are a bit bored .... *with the old models* ....

2 Julia is Adrian's wife.
  Julia is married ....

3 I'm not accustomed to driving on the left.
  I'm not used ....

4 I need to get the room prepared for the meeting.
  I need to get the room ready ....

5 Do you find archaeology interesting?
  Are you .... ?

6 What he said has made me angry.
  I'm angry ....

7 Mathematics was always my best subject.
  I was always very good ....

8 The advertising campaign was a disaster. You said it would be.
  You were right .... It was a disaster.

9 There were lots of people in the conference hall.
  The conference hall was full ....

10 I don't really like her idea.
  I'm not really very keen ....

Exercise 5 B C D

Complete the sequence of emails with a word from the list below.

~~aware~~ attached capable compatible covered dependent involved lacking late opposed
prepared right similar useful

From:	Melena	To:	David	Sent:	
Subject:	Customer Relationship Management			Cc:	

Message:
David

Are you (1) ....*aware*.... of the article about Customer Relationship Management (CRM) in the latest Business Week? I've scanned it and (2) .... it to this email.
Basically, it says that in the past companies were (3) .... on their brand name, but in the future we'll have to be (4) .... for customers changing supplier more often.
To give better service we'll need CRM software (5) .... of integrating customer information across the sales force, call centre and website. That information also becomes (6) .... for marketing – things like understanding buying behaviour. I remember you saying something (7) .... to this in a meeting last year, and as you are (8) .... in IT purchasing decisions I thought you should see the article.
Melena

From:	David	To:	Melena	Sent:	
Subject:	Re: Customer Relationship Management			Cc:	

Message:
Melena

Thanks for the email. You're absolutely (9) .... about the importance of CRM, and if you remember I proposed at that meeting that we invest in new CRM software. Most people were (10) .... to the idea, partly because of the difficulty in finding software (11) .... with our other IT systems. I said at the time that they were a bit (12) .... in vision, but it's not too (13) .... for us to start. I'll put together a short report based on the ideas (14) .... in the article and circulate it. Thanks again.
David

48 Noun + preposition

This represents an enormous market opportunity for delivery companies.
(Connectis website)
Mboweni hinted at strong disagreement with government over inflation targeting.
(Business Day South Africa website)

A Noun + preposition

● Here is a list of nouns and the prepositions normally used with them:

ability in	example of	price of
advantage of	experience of/in	reason for
advice on	hope of	reply to
alternative to	knowledge of	solution to
benefit of/from	lack of	substitute for
cause of	matter with	success at/in
cost of	method of	tax on
difficulty with	opinion of	trouble with

B Noun + preposition (from unit 46)

● Many of the verbs in unit 46 have related nouns with the same preposition. Here are some examples:

agreement with/about	insurance against
approval of	investment in
belief in	invitation to
comparison with	knowledge about
complaint about	objection to
decision about/on	payment for
division into	protection from
focus on	reference to
information about	responsibility for
insistence on	wait for

C Noun + preposition (from unit 47)

● Many of the adjectives in unit 47 have related nouns with the same preposition. Here are some examples:

awareness of	opposition to
certainty about	optimism about
disappointment with	pessimism about
doubt about	preparation for
excitement about	satisfaction with
fear of	similarity to
interest in	suitability for
involvement in	worry about

D *Rise, fall + of/in*

● Words referring to increases and decreases (like *rise, fall*, etc) can be followed by *of* or *in*. *Of* refers to an amount. *In* refers to the thing that has increased or decreased.
*There has been an increase/rise/reduction/fall **in** operating profit **of** 3%.*

E Connection, relationship + *with*/*between*

- *One thing has a **link** with another.*
  *There is a link **between** two things.*
  Words that can be followed by either preposition include: *connection, link, relationship, contrast, difference.*
  *There is a connection/relationship/contrast **with** what happened last year.*
  *There is a connection/relationship/contrast **between** last year and this year.*

F *Need, wish, request + for*

- Nouns meaning 'need' or 'request' have *for* after them. Examples include: *application for, demand for, need for, order for, preference for, request for.*

G Prepositional phrases

- Here is a list of common prepositional phrases (preposition + noun phrase):

  at short notice, **at** cost price, **at** a good price, **at** a profit/loss, **at** first sight

  *I've had to call this meeting **at short notice** because of the urgency of the situation.*
  *It's difficult to sell **at a** reasonable **profit** when labour costs are so high.*

  by accident, **by** car/bus/taxi, **by** chance, **by** credit card, **by** hand, **by** law, **by** mistake, **by** post/courier, **by** return (of post)

  *We met in the street **by chance**. It was quite unexpected.*
  *Please let us know your decision **by return** as further delay will result in higher costs.*

  for a change, **for** lunch, **for** pleasure, **for** sale

  *Would you like to join us **for lunch**?*
  *We always eat pizza. Tonight let's go to a Thai restaurant **for a change**.*

  in advance, **in** bulk, **in** cash, **in** charge of, **in** connection with, **in** debt, **in** the end, **in** favour of, **in** general, **in** a hurry, **in** the market (companies), **in** my opinion, **in** stock, **in** financial terms, **in** the pipeline, **in** touch, **in** trouble, **in** other words, **in** writing

  *We need 25% of the total price **in advance**, with the balance on receipt of the goods.*
  *I'm sorry, we don't have that model **in stock**. We're expecting some more next week.*

  *'Investors just bought whatever stocks were available in the belief that more positive news was **in the pipeline**,' an analyst said. (Shanghai Daily website)*

  on the basis of, **on** business, **on** foot, **on** hand, **on** hold, **on** holiday, **on** the Internet, **on** the other line, **on** loan, **on** the market (products), **on** order, **on** the phone, **on** purpose, **on** sale, **on** strike, **on** television, **on** track, **on** a trip, **on** the whole

  *I think we can move forward **on the basis of** what we've discussed.*
  *We don't have any in stock right now, but there are 20 items **on order**.*

  *Paul Achleitner, an experienced dealmaker from Goldman's German operation, was **on hand** to do the financial engineering. (Business Week website)*

  *The economy was **on track** for recovery, Mr Sakaiya insisted. There would, he said, be growth during the current quarter. (FT.com website)*

  out of date, **out** of order, **out** of business

  *Version 6? Your software is a bit **out of date** isn't it? They're selling version 8 now.*
  *Sorry, the lift is **out of order**. You'll have to use the stairs.*

  up to date, **up** to you

  *I use version 8 of this software – it's the most **up to date**.*
  *I don't mind which restaurant we go to. It's **up to you**.*

48 Practice

Exercise 1 A D E F

Complete the sentences with a preposition from the list below.

between   between   for   for   in   in   of   of   ~~to~~   to   with   with

1   Have you received a reply ....to....... the email you sent yesterday?
2   The demand .... microchips is very cyclical.
3   The results this year are in strong contrast .... those of the year before.
4   There is a strong contrast .... these results and those of the year before.
5   What's the matter .... your PC? Has it crashed?
6   Last year there was a fall .... unemployment .... 0.5%.
7   Is there any difference .... these two boxes? They both look the same.
8   At the moment I can't think of any solution .... the problem.
9   The increase .... profits was disappointing. There was a rise .... only 4%.
10 I'd like to place an order .... forty cases of single malt whisky.

Exercise 2 A B C

Complete the sentences with a word from list A and a word from list B.

A: advantage   focus   involvement   objection   payment   price   suitability   ~~trouble~~
B: of   of   for   for   in   on   to   ~~with~~

1   We're going to change suppliers. We have so much ....trouble.... ..with.. them.
2   The .... oil has gone down by $2 a barrel since January.
3   The .... using a small company is that they're usually cheaper.
4   We're wasting time, we need to .... the main issue.
5   We haven't received .... the last invoice yet.
6   Does anyone have any .... that proposal? OK, it's agreed.
7   There are rumours of their .... illegal arms deals.
8   It's a violent film. I'm not sure about its .... a young audience.

Exercise 3 G

Underline the correct words.
1   *At/In* first sight it looks like a good deal, but we need more details *at/in* a hurry.
2   A: Shall we try using a different supplier *by/for* a change?
    B: It's *up/out* to you.
3   Are you paying *by/in* cash or *by/in* credit card?
4   The house next door is *for/at* sale. It's been *on/in* the market for ages.
5   Very few Board members are *at/in* favour of the merger. *In/On* the whole, they think it will create more
    problems than it solves.
6   We need to keep *in/on* touch with the situation as it develops.
7   Are you here *on/for* business or *on/for* pleasure?
8   A: Did you do it *by/on* purpose?
    B: No, of course not, I did it *by/on* mistake.
9   *By/In* financial terms they're not doing well. They're $10m *in/out of* debt.
10 A: Patrick, it's Paul Brock from Tyco *at/on* the phone.
    B: Can you put him *at/on* hold while I look for his file? OK, I've found it – I'll take it *at/on* the other
    line.

Exercise 4 **G**

Study the underlined prepositional phrases. Write the sentence letter a)–l) containing each phrase next to a similar phrase 1–12 below.

a) I'm sorry, I think we were talking <u>at cross purposes</u>. Let me make myself clear.

b) <u>For the time being</u> I think we should wait. We can make a decision later.

c) It's to our advantage to work together on this. We're all <u>in the same boat</u>.

d) It was fantastic news. And it came completely <u>out of the blue</u>.

e) There's two new products <u>in the pipeline</u>. They'll be launched later this year.

f) You have to be really <u>on the ball</u>. The situation changes all the time.

g) I'm speaking <u>off the record</u> of course, but the company is close to bankruptcy.

h) As you can see it's quite complicated. But, <u>in a nutshell</u>, we must act soon.

i) We're <u>on thin ice</u> here. If they take us to court we'll probably lose.

j) I'm afraid the new CEO is <u>out of his depth</u> with this latest crisis.

k) Sorry, it's <u>out of the question</u>. We could never agree to that.

l) <u>In the long run</u> shares are a better investment than bonds.

1	about different things without realising	*a*	7	unexpectedly
2	quick-thinking and quick-acting		8	being planned and prepared
3	to say it briefly and clearly		9	over a long time period
4	in the same unpleasant situation		10	for a short period of time
5	in a situation that is too difficult for him		11	not possible
6	in a situation that might cause trouble		12	unofficially

Exercise 5 **A** **B** **F** **G**

Complete the sequence of emails with the correct prepositions. The second number in each bracket shows the number of letters in the word.

From:	Pete	To:	Erika	Sent:	
Subject:	IT manager			**Cc:**	

Message:

Erika

The interviews for the post of IT manager are happening next week, and Personnel have just sent me information (1-5) _about_ all the candidates. I thought we should get together to discuss the CVs and the questions we are going to focus on in the interviews.

Here are my thoughts. (2-2) .... my opinion there is a need (3-3) .... someone with a good knowledge (4-2) .... systems integration, because the difficulty (5-4) .... our current IT system is that all the parts work separately – our website, the back-office processing, billing, our supply chain etc. I hope we can find a candidate who has shown success (6-2) .... dealing with all these processes in their previous job, but Personnel have already warned me that there's a lack (7-2) .... really strong candidates.

Also, a lot of our IT infrastructure is quite (8-3) .... of date and we'll have to make a big investment (9-2) .... new hardware soon. We need someone who's (10-2) .... touch with what's (11-3) .... sale (12-2) .... the market and can take responsibility (13-3) .... the whole purchasing process.

What do you think? It's (14-2) .... to you – I'm free for a meeting most mornings next week.

From:	Erika	To:	Pete	Sent:	
Subject:	Re: IT manager			**Cc:**	

Message:

Pete

Yes, we should have a meeting. It will be good to discuss these things (15-2) .... advance (16-3) .... a change. Usually the interviews are (17-2) .... such short notice that we don't get a chance to really look at the CVs together and make decisions (18-5) .... the kind of questions we're going to ask. Next Tuesday morning would be good for me, say 9.30 am.

49 Trends, graphs and figures

A Graphs and figures

For the month of June, industrial output increased 23.1% yr/yr, which was a rise of 2.5% from the previous month. First-half export sales grew 30.9%. Six-month industrial sales volume was up 20.3% yr/yr. (cebd website)

● Here are some common types of graph:

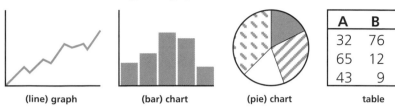

● Numbers can be written as symbols (10) or words (ten). In formal writing use symbols for large amounts and words for everything else (ordinals like *second*, two numbers together, estimates, etc). See exercise 4 on page 205.

● Note the following ways to say numbers:

Currencies:

$6.50 *six dollars fifty*   £6.15 *six pounds fifteen*

Decimals:

Note that a decimal point is written as a 'dot', not a comma like in some languages.
6.5 *six point five*   0.25 *nought/zero point two five* (NOT ~~point twenty-five~~)

Large numbers:

A comma can be used to separate thousands from hundreds. Notice the use of 'and' in British English.
6,200 *six thousand two hundred* (in BrE and AmE)
6,280 *six thousand two hundred **and** eighty* (in BrE, but AmE has no 'and' here)
2m   *two million* (NOT ~~millions~~)
2.5m   *two point five/two and a half million*

B Trends

● Study these verbs that describe different *trends* (= tendencies).

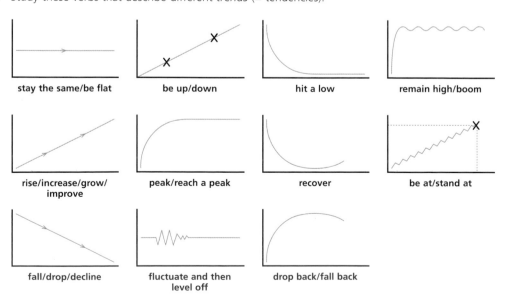

- Note also: *to double, to triple, to halve.*

- Note these irregular verb forms:
go – went – gone	*grow – grew – grown*
rise – rose – risen	*fall – fell – fallen*

- Note these nouns:
  a rise, growth, an improvement, a fall, a drop, a peak, a recovery, a half, a doubling

  *Manufacturing industry orders in January **rose** 11.1% from the same period a year earlier, compared with forecasts of **an** 11.2% **rise**.* (Wall Street Journal website)

See also unit 48
- Note the following prepositions:
*Sales increased **from** $5.4m **to** $5.8m.*	(start and finish figures)
*Sales increased **by** $0.4m.*	(difference between start and finish figures)
*There was an increase in sales **of** $0.4m.*	(after a noun or noun phrase)
*There was a 3% increase **in** sales.*	(before the thing that is changing)

  *The share of U.S. capital spending devoted to information technology **has more than tripled** since 1960, **from** 10% **to** 35%. Fields such as biotechnology are **booming**.* (Business Week website)

C Verbs and objects

See also unit 25
- It is important to use verbs in the right way. Study these three groups.

  Transitive verbs are always followed by an object:
  *We'll **raise/lower/cut/maintain** his salary.* (with an object)
  (BUT NOT ~~His salary will raise/lower/cut/maintain.~~)

  Intransitive verbs are never followed by an object:
  *Inflation will **rise/fall/grow/go up**.* (without an object)
  (BUT NOT ~~The government's policies will rise/fall/grow/go up inflation.~~)

  Transitive/Intransitive verbs can be used with or without an object:
  *We'll **increase/decrease/improve/recover** our market share.* (with an object)
  AND *Our market share will **increase/decrease/improve/recover**.* (without an object)

D Adverbs and adjectives

- We can use adverbs and adjectives to give more details about verbs and nouns.

Speed		Amount	
quickly/quick	rapid change	*significantly/significant*	large change
gradually/gradual	constant, regular change	*sharply/sharp*	sudden change
steadily/steady	slow, step-by-step change	*slightly/slight*	small change

  *Sales **grew steadily**. There was a **steady growth** in sales.*

  *So far, 6.25 billion USD has poured into Romania over the last decade, with last year's figures showing **a slight increase** on 1998, according to latest Trade Registry data.* (Bucharest Business Week website)

E Linking words and phrases

- Linking words are useful for describing trends. They can join parts of a sentence or link across sentences. See units 41–44. Here are just a few examples:
addition	*and, in addition*
contrast	*but, although* (+ subject + verb), *in spite of* (+ noun phrase), *however*
reason	*because* (+ subject + verb), *because of/due to* (+ noun phrase)
result	*so, therefore*

49   Practice

Exercise 1 A

Write in words how you would say the numbers in brackets, in British English. There is an example in section A and another one below to help you.

1 (456,780)   *four hundred and fifty six thousand, seven hundred and eighty*
2 (1,230)   ....
3 (12,300)   ....
4 (12,030)   ....
5 (12,330)   ....
6 (120,300)   ....
7 (123,000)   ....
8 (123,330)   ....
9 (1,230,000)   ....

Exercise 2 B C D

<u>Underline</u> the correct words.

1 There was a *slightly*/<u>*slight*</u> rise in profits last month.
2 We *rose/increased* our profits *slightly/slight* last month.
3 There was a sharp fall *in/of* our sales last quarter.
4 Our sales fell *by/of* 6% last quarter.
5 We *fell/recovered* our market share last quarter.
6 Our share price *hit/beat* a *low/down* last month, but it has since *recuperated/recovered* and now stands *at/in* £3.78.
7 Our share price *reached/met* a *top/peak* in May, but it's fallen back since then.
8 Inflation is increasing *slow/slowly* at the moment, *in/by* about 1% a year.
9 There is a *slow/slowly* increase in the rate of inflation, *of/by* about 1% a year.
10 Operating profits went from £2.5m *to/until* £3.1m.
11 Dividends paid to shareholders *raised/rose* by 6%. Last year they *fell/cut*.
12 This year we *raised/rose* dividends to shareholders. Last year we *fell/cut* them.

Exercise 3 E

Complete the sentences with a word or phrase from the list below. Look carefully at the punctuation to see if the words join parts of sentences or link across sentences.

because   because of   so   although   in spite of   ~~In addition~~   however   therefore

1 Sales are up 5%. ....*In addition*...., market share is up 2%.
2 Sales are up 5%. .... , market share is down 2%.
3 Sales are up 5%, ... market share is down 2%.
4 Sales are up 5%, ... a drop in market share of 2%.
5 Sales are up 5%. .... , we should get a bonus at the end of the year.
6 Sales are up 5%, ... we'll all get a bonus at the end of the year.
7 Sales are up 5% .... the new advertising campaign.
8 Sales are up 5% .... the new advertising campaign has started.

Exercise 4 A

Match the rules for formal writing 1–6 with the examples a)–f).

1 Use symbols for dates and large amounts	☐ c	a) We'll need twenty four-person teams.
2 Use words for ordinals (*first, second*)	☐	b) Twelve people took part in the meeting.
3 Use words for two numbers together	☐	c) $100 will be paid on 28 August.
4 Use words at the beginning of a sentence	☐	d) There are three main recommendations.
5 Use words for estimates	☐	e) We have about two hundred employees.
6 Use words for numbers below ten	☐	f) This is our third annual report.

Exercise 5 A

Write the phrases from the list below on the appropriate lines 1–6.

considerably more than 50%   around 50%   a little over 50%   exactly 50%   almost 50%

a little under 50%   much less than 50%   about 50%   precisely 50%   slightly more than 50%

40%	1		
48%	2a	/	2b ....
48–52%	3a	/	3b ....
50%	4a	/	4b ....
52%	5a	/	5b ....
60%	6		

Exercise 6 A B C D E

 51 Complete the conversation between a financial consultant, Andrew Cutting (AC:), and a sales director, Chris Wood (CW:), by underlining the correct words.

AC: Right. Before we decide on the conditions for the loan, we need to have a careful look at your business. I've got the sales (1) *graph / graphic* for last year right here. Um, can you just go through the figures for me?

CW: Of course. As you can see, sales at the start of the year were quite (2) *flat / level*, (3) *so / although* that's not surprising (4) *because / due to* we always have a quiet period after Christmas.

AC: OK, but there wasn't much of a (5) *recover / recovery* over the spring period, was there? From your graph I see that at the (6) *peak / high* in June you were only (7) *increased / up* (8) *by / with* two (9) *million / millions* (10) *pounds / of pounds* (11) *since / on* the January figure. What happened?

CW: Well, it … it was a difficult trading period for us – our main competitor (12) *cut / fell* their prices (13) *significant / significantly*. (14) *However / In spite of* in the second (15) *half / halve* of the year things started to improve.

AC: Um. How did that happen?

CW: Well, we launched a series of new products onto the market, and you'll see that sales (16) *rised / rose* (17) *sharp / sharply* over the autumn.

AC: Ah. Oh, yes.

CW: In fact the figure went (18) *to / until* a little (19) *under / over* fifteen million by the end of the year. Now, we were very happy with those results. And we expect the increase (20) *of / in* sales to continue this year. Our sales forecasts are looking very good.

AC: Um, well, that does look promising. I think we can …

50 Punctuation

A Capital letters

- Capital letters (also called upper-case letters) are used:

to begin a sentence	*Thank you for your letter of 28 July.*
for names of people	*Jim, Helen, Mr Armstrong, Mrs Jones*
for names of organisations	*European Community, Ministry of Finance*
for titles of books, etc	*As Jim Tucker said in 'Managing Change', ...*
for names of places	*Paris, France, Europe*
for calendar information	*Monday, March, New Year's Day*

- In book and film titles, small words like *and, a/the* and prepositions do not usually have capitals, unless they are at the beginning.
  His latest film is called 'In the Heat of the Night'.

- Some words can be written with capitals, or in lower case. These are:

seasons	*in Spring, in spring*
decades	*the Nineties, the nineties*
jobs	*She is a good sales director* (general use), *Sales Director* (job title)
compass points	*the east of Scotland* (description), *the Far East* (place name)

B Full stop (.)

- Full stops are used at the end of sentences.

- Full stops are sometimes used in abbreviations to show that letters in a word are missing. In modern British English they are not used so often.
  Prof. E. Taylor   M.P.   e.g.   i.e.   etc.

C Comma (,)

- A comma in writing represents a brief pause in speech. When a sentence has several clauses, commas are placed between them to make the sentence easier to read.
  We do a lot of business with Asia, and it's an important market for us.
  We do a lot of business with Asia, which is an important market for us.

  But we use a full stop, not a comma, to separate complete sentences.
  We do a lot of business with Asia. It's an important market for us.
  (NOT ~~We do a lot of business with Asia, it's an important market for us.~~)

- A comma is used in lists, except for the last two items where we use *and*.
  *This product is safe, hygienic, practical **and** cheap.*

  We can use a comma before *and* if the last two items in the list are long.
  *This product is safe, easy to maintain, **and** kind to the environment.*

- Linking words at the beginning of a sentence are followed by a comma.
  In fact, the Portuguese market is growing fast.

  Linking words in the middle of a sentence have commas before and after.
  The Portuguese market, on the other hand, is growing fast.

See Unit 28 - Commas are used with non-defining relative clauses.
  This product, which is the top of our range, retails at £250.

- A comma can introduce direct quotes.
  A Lloyds agent said, 'This will mean some very large claims.'

- When writing direct speech we use a comma before the actual words spoken. In reported speech commas are not used. Compare:
  Your sales director said, 'Yes, that might be possible.'
  Your sales director said it might be possible.

- Study where we put a comma with large numbers:
  260   1,569   18,500   127,000   4,650,000

  Note that in some other languages a dot is used here. A dot in English represents a decimal point.

D Semi-colon (;)

- We can join two sentences with related meanings using a semi-colon.
  We need better technology; better technology costs money.

- A semi-colon is also used to separate long items in a list. Notice the use of commas and semi-colons in this example:
  Institutional investors include Nomura, the Japanese securities house; GEC of the US; and Charterhouse, the UK investment bank.

E Colon (:)

- A colon introduces items in a list.
  The input selector has four positions: CD, DVD, tuner and auxiliary.

- A colon can introduce an explanation of the previous part of the sentence.
  China is booming: output is up, profits are up, confidence is high.

- A colon is also used to introduce examples.
  We're entering a lot of new markets, eg: the Baltic states.

F Speech marks (' ') (" ")

- Speech marks (also called quotation marks) are used when we write the actual words that someone says. Punctuation goes inside. They can be single or double.
  'This share issue will supply the capital we need,' said Alan Jones of MSD.
  Alan Jones of MSD said, 'This share issue will supply the capital we need.'

- Titles of books, reports, films, etc, are sometimes put inside single speech marks, and we put punctuation outside in this case.
  I strongly recommend Jim Tucker's new book 'Managing Change'.

  Book titles, etc, can also be put in italics rather than speech marks.

G Question mark (?) and exclamation mark (!)

- Question marks only occur after the question.
  He asked, 'What are the most important issues facing our company?'

- Exclamation marks are used in informal writing, but are not considered appropriate in formal writing. They show surprise, pleasure, etc.
  Guess what's happened! I've just got engaged!

50 Practice

Exercise 1 A

Rewrite each sentence, putting in any necessary capital letters.

1 we're meeting professor thomas on tuesday evening at eight.
We're meeting Professor Thomas on Tuesday evening at eight.

2 last february i met mary carpenter for the first time.

3 tim works in the north of france, about 50 kilometres from paris.

4 my favourite hitchcock film is 'strangers on a train'.

5 carol works as an office manager in a marketing consultancy.

6 i've just received the report published last may by the world trade organization.

7 on christmas day we'll go to my parents' house near brighton in sussex.

8 i think jean is going to be interviewing the deputy finance minister next week.

Exercise 2 B C D E F G

Tick (✓) the one sentence in each group a)–c) which is punctuated correctly.

1 a) 'What's the best way to control our costs, she asked?' ☐
   b) 'What's the best way to control our costs?' she asked. ✓
   c) 'What's the best way to control our costs,' she asked? ☐

2 a) We all agreed, that protectionism, was not the answer. ☐
   b) We all agreed that protectionism, was not the answer. ☐
   c) We all agreed that protectionism was not the answer. ☐

3 a) Helen who is a very experienced investment analyst, agreed. ☐
   b) Helen, who is a very experienced investment analyst, agreed. ☐
   c) Helen, who is a very experienced investment analyst agreed. ☐

4 a) He told me not to wait and said, 'I'll see you later.' ☐
   b) He told me, not to wait and said 'I'll see you later.' ☐
   c) He told me not to wait and said I'll see you later. ☐

5 a) The problem is simple, there's too little investment, and too much waste. ☐
   b) The problem is simple; there's too little investment; and too much waste. ☐
   c) The problem is simple: there's too little investment and too much waste. ☐

6 a) The figures are: inflation 4%, unemployment 5.4% and interest rates 8%. ☐
   b) The figures are: inflation, 4%, unemployment, 5.4%, interest rates, 8%. ☐
   c) The figures are inflation 4%, unemployment 5.4%, and interest rates 8%. ☐

7 a) Ann explained that nobody had made a decision yet. ☐
   b) Ann explained, that nobody had made a decision yet. ☐
   c) Ann explained that, nobody had made a decision yet. ☐

8 a) Sales last year were $4500000 while profits were just $620000. ☐
   b) Sales last year were $4,500000, while profits were just $620,000. ☐
   c) Sales last year were $4,500,000, while profits were just $620,000. ☐

Exercise 3 B C E F G

Rewrite each group of words so that it contains the punctuation listed in brackets.

1 First of all is there a demand in the market asked Sue (*one full stop, one comma, one question mark, speech marks*)

   'First of all, is there a demand in the market?' asked Sue.

2 I'm sorry Kim he said the goods would arrive on time but they didn't (*one full stop, two commas*)

3 Jack said that we should tear up the plans forget about it and start again (*one full stop, two commas*)

4 When I saw my boss I went up to him and said Can I have Friday off please (*one question mark, three commas, speech marks*)

5 On the other hand we could use a different firm couldn't we said François (*one full stop, two commas, one question mark, speech marks*)

6 Hello Alan said Tina how was the meeting yesterday (*one full stop, three commas, one question mark, two pairs of speech marks, one capital letter*)

7 If I were you I'd ask for some help or perhaps look at the manual again (*one full stop, two commas*)

8 Oil shares did well last week Standard Oil was up 2% Exxon was up 1.8% and the Anglo-Dutch group Shell gained 2.3% (*one full stop, two commas, one colon*)

Exercise 4 A B C G

Rewrite this email, adding any necessary capital letters and punctuation. The exercise also includes using apostrophes for contracted verb forms (*I've, I'm,* etc).

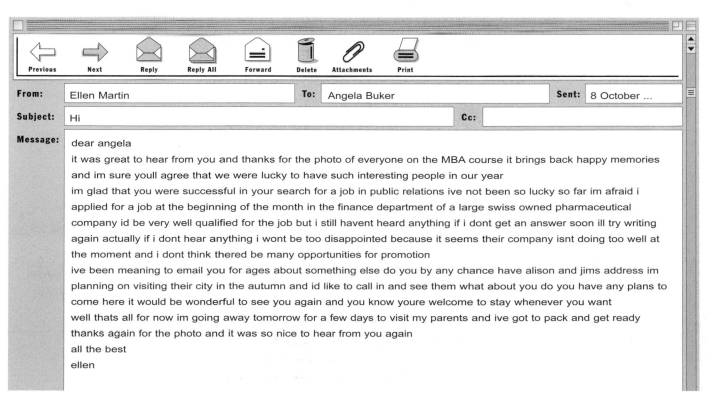

From: Ellen Martin **To:** Angela Buker **Sent:** 8 October ...

Subject: Hi **Cc:**

Message:

dear angela

it was great to hear from you and thanks for the photo of everyone on the MBA course it brings back happy memories and im sure youll agree that we were lucky to have such interesting people in our year

im glad that you were successful in your search for a job in public relations ive not been so lucky so far im afraid i applied for a job at the beginning of the month in the finance department of a large swiss owned pharmaceutical company id be very well qualified for the job but i still havent heard anything if i dont get an answer soon ill try writing again actually if i dont hear anything i wont be too disappointed because it seems their company isnt doing too well at the moment and i dont think thered be many opportunities for promotion

ive been meaning to email you for ages about something else do you by any chance have alison and jims address im planning on visiting their city in the autumn and id like to call in and see them what about you do you have any plans to come here it would be wonderful to see you again and you know youre welcome to stay whenever you want

well thats all for now im going away tomorrow for a few days to visit my parents and ive got to pack and get ready thanks again for the photo and it was so nice to hear from you again

all the best

ellen

Test 1 Verb tenses: present (units 1–2)

Exercise 1

Complete the sentences by putting each verb into the present simple or present continuous. Use contractions (*I'm* instead of *I am, don't* instead of *do not*, etc) where possible.

1 A: What .... do you do .... (you do)?

   B: I'm an engineer.

2 A: What ..... are you doing ...... (you do)?

   B: I'm looking for a file.

3 Can you help me? I .... (not understand) Spanish.

4 Can I call you back? I .... (talk) with a client.

5 This product .... (not sell) as well as we hoped.

6 I'll get in touch with you as soon as I .... (know) the results.

7 I .... (stay) at the Marriott Hotel. I'll be there until Friday.

8 .... (you offer) any special deals over the summer?

9 Our company .... (make) parts for the automobile industry.

10 When .... (you usually arrive) at work in the morning?

11 Jack .... (come) to work with us on the NBC project for a few weeks.

12 Jack .... (come) from Leeds in the north of England.

Exercise 2

Decide if uses a)–h) are usually associated with the present simple (*PS*) or present continuous (*PC*).

a) facts and permanent situations   PS

b) actions and events in progress now ☐

c) arrangements for the future ☐

d) verbs of thinking and feeling ☐

e) habits and routines ☐

f) temporary situations ☐

g) fixed timetables ☐

h) current trends and changes ☐

Match sentences 1–8 below with uses a)–h).

1 She's talking on another line right now, can I ask her to call you back?   b

2 We offer a networking solution that is customised, reliable and secure. ☐

3 We release figures for total sales and net earnings every quarter. ☐

4 I'm arriving in Munich at 10.30. ☐

5 The plane arrives in Munich at 10.30. ☐

6 I'm working in our customer services department this month. ☐

7 Internet fraud and cybercrime is increasing all over the world. ☐

8 OK, I understand what the problem is now. ☐

Exercise 3

Put the time expressions from the list below into two categories: those usually used with the present simple, and those usually used with the present continuous. Write the expression in the correct column.

after, always, as soon as, before, currently, every day, hardly ever, never, at the moment, most of the time, next time, normally, now, nowadays, occasionally, often, rarely, sometimes, these days, twice a year, until, usually, when

Present simple

after

Present continuous

currently

Exercise 4

Put the words into the correct order. The first word is given each time.

1 I at about one o'clock have usually lunch.   I ....
2 Lunch just a sandwich often is.   Lunch ....
3 I from time to time visit in Paris Head Office.   I ....
4 I ever hardly am late in the morning.   I ....
5 I ever hardly take the train to work.   I ....
6 I prepare once a month a sales report.   I ....
7 I miss a Board meeting never.   I ....
8 I am late for a Board meeting never.   I ....

Exercise 5

Some of the following sentences are right and some are wrong. Put a tick (✓) next to the right ones, and correct the wrong ones.

1   I'm supplying you with everything on your last order.   ....✓................
2   ~~I'm agreeing~~ with you completely.   ....I agree............
3   Our chocolates are containing only the finest ingredients.   ....
4   Our chocolates are winning prizes all over the world.   ....
5   We're setting up subsidiaries in Peru and Bolivia.   ....
6   We're owning subsidiaries in Peru and Bolivia.   ....
7   I'm thinking they will make a decision this week.   ....
8   I'm thinking about what they will decide this week.   ....
9   At first sight, it's seeming to be a sensible suggestion.   ....
10 At first sight, he's making a sensible suggestion.   ....
11 We're having a lot of trouble with our suppliers.   ....
12 In these circumstances we're having no alternative.   ....

Exercise 6

Complete the sentences by putting each verb into a form of the present simple or present continuous. In each sentence the verbs may be in the same or different tenses.

1 Every time inflation .... (go up), people .... (demand) higher wages.
2 Inflation .... (fall) quite quickly, which .... (mean) that the government can keep interest rates low.
3 .... (you/wait) for Victoria Chambers? I .... (not/think) she'll be long.
4 What exactly .... (our customers/want)? Nobody around here .... (seem) to know.
5 Carlo doesn't have much experience of this situation. I .... (hope) he .... (know) what he .... (do).
6 What exactly .... (you/mean)? I .... (not/understand).
7 What exactly .... (you/say)? .... (you/want) to renegotiate the whole contract?
8 .... (your chicken/taste) OK? The food here is usually very good, but of course it all .... (depend) on which particular chef .... (work) in the kitchen on that day.

Test 2 Verb tenses: past (units 3–4)

Exercise 1

Write the past simple form of these irregular verbs.

1	become	8	fall	15	meet ....
2	begin	9	find	16	pay ....
3	break	10	forget	17	send ....
4	bring	11	grow	18	shut ....
5	buy	12	keep	19	spend ....
6	choose	13	lead	20	understand ....
7	eat	14	lend		

Exercise 2

Underline the correct words.

1 When I _got_/_was getting_ home, I _heard_/_was hearing_ your phone message.
2 When I was at Norcom I _used to claim_/_was claiming_ all my travel expenses.
3 When the computer _crashed_/_was crashing_ I _printed out_/_was printing out_ last month's figures.
4 While the plane _took off_/_was taking off_, I _started_/_was starting_ to feel unwell.
5 We _wanted_/_were wanting_ a reliable firm, so we _chose_/_were choosing_ Phillips.
6 We _used to have_/_were having_ an office in Latvia and Lithuania, but then we _combined_/_were combining_ all our Baltic operations at our Estonia office.
7 When I _arrived_/_was arriving_ at the office Jan _waited_/_was waiting_ for me.
8 The door was open so I _knocked_/_was knocking_ and _came_/_was coming_ in.
9 They _argued_/_were arguing_ about the merger when he suddenly _lost_/_was losing_ his temper.
10 When I _was_/_used to be_ in London last summer I _visited_/_was visiting_ a different museum every day.

Exercise 3

Complete the second sentence so it has a similar meaning to the first sentence and contains the word in brackets. This exercise practises the past perfect and _used to_.

1 Michael made some notes and started writing. (had)
   After .... _Michael had made_ .... some notes, he started writing.
2 This Internet connection is slower than before. (didn't)
   This Internet connection .... to be so slow.
3 I was sure the disk was in this box! (forgotten)
   I was sure .... the disk!
4 In the past, the factory produced 4,000 units every month. (used)
   The factory .... 4,000 units every month.
5 I thought the article seemed familiar. (had)
   I thought .... the article before.
6 Franz left before my arrival. (already)
   By the time I arrived, Franz ....
7 When I was younger I went skiing a lot. (used)
   I .... a lot when I was younger.
8 The meeting finished late so we went straight back to the hotel. (had)
   We went straight back to the hotel because .... late.

Exercise 4

Complete each sentence with a suitable time expression from the list below.

at   on   in   when   while/when

1   The computer crashed ...**while / when**... I was loading up the new software.
2   .... did you first notice the fault?
3   We sent you the invoice .... the end of last month.
4   Central Europe was changing very rapidly .... the nineties.
5   We sent the goods .... the fifteenth. Haven't you received them yet?
6   .... they raised interest rates the euro recovered against the dollar.
7   .... she was checking the invoices, she noticed a small mistake.
8   The two companies merged .... 1998.
9   We met .... eight for a business breakfast.
10 What were you doing .... I called you this morning?
11 We changed our advertising campaign .... the beginning of the year.
12 I'll check my files and call you .... the morning.

Exercise 5

Complete the sentences by putting one verb in the past simple and one in the past perfect.
1   When the film started I ....**realised**............ (realise) I ....**had seen**............ (see) it before.
2   By the time I .... (get) to the phone it .... (stop) ringing.
3   How .... (you/find out) that you .... (got) the job?
4   Before I .... (join) ABN I ,, (work) as an investment analyst.
5   I .... (send) her an email just to see how things were going. Meanwhile, my boss .... (already/spoke) to her boss.
6   I .... (always/suspect) that the contract .... (not/be) legal.

Exercise 6

Complete the sentences by putting the verb in brackets into either the past perfect or past perfect continuous.
1   By last Christmas I ....**had decided**.......... (decide) it was time to change my job.
2   I ....**had been thinking**.... (think) about changing my job for some time before I finally decided.
3   I .... (wait) for over an hour by the time he arrived.
4   Actually, I .... (already hear) the news before she told me.
5   Their share price .... (rise) steadily before the merger was announced.
6   I couldn't give him a lift because I .... (not finish) work.
7   They get on very well, but they .... (never meet) until this year.
8   My eyes were hurting because I .... (look) at the screen all day.
9   After I .... (see) the new design I realised it was going to be a great success.
10 They closed down the factory because it .... (lose) money for years.

Test 3 Verb tenses: past and present (units 5–6)

Exercise 1

Underline the correct or most appropriate answers.

1 *I'm waiting/I've been waiting* here for ages.
2 The markets *have had/had* a sharp fall last week.
3 The markets *have had/had* a sharp fall this week.
4 Wait a moment, *I've left/I left* the instruction manual in the other room.
5 *I've left/I left* the instruction manual next to the PC when I was using it earlier.
6 How long *are you working/have you been working* here?
7 Hurry up! How long *are you going/have you been going* to be?
8 We can't supply the goods because they *haven't paid/didn't pay* the deposit.
9 We couldn't supply the goods because they *haven't paid/didn't pay* the deposit.
10 I'm waiting for Sue. When *have you last seen/did you last see* her?
11 I'm waiting for Sue. *Have you seen her?/Did you see her?*

Exercise 2

Cross out the mistake in each sentence and write the correction at the end.

1 She ~~is~~ sending emails all week but hasn't placed an order yet. .... has been ....
2 We have started this course three weeks ago. ....
3 A: 'What have you been doing all morning?'
   B: 'I've been written letters.' ....
4 When have you arrived in this city? ....
5 You have ever been to India? ....
6 Paula has been organised a press conference. ....
7 Sales have been rising since three months. ....
8 I live in this city since I was born. ....
9 I wait here a long time. Where have you been? ....
10 I didn't give a presentation before, so I'm a bit nervous. ....
11 I'm waiting for their reply to our letter for three weeks. ....
12 How long do you work in this company? ....

Exercise 3

Complete the sentences with a suitable time expression from the list below.

yet for ~~since~~ often ever never already so far just always

1 I've lived in my city-centre flat ...since... 1998. I love it there.
2 Thanks for the present! I've .... wanted a gold Rolex!
3 I don't think I should drink any more. I've .... had four whiskies.
4 Have you .... been self-employed?
5 I've .... heard that we've won the contract! Congratulations everybody!
6 Hurry up! Haven't you finished .... ?
7 Nina has worked in this company .... over five years now.
8 I've .... been white-water rafting before. It's an interesting experience!
9 I've .... passed this building, but this is the first time I've been inside.
10 We've been very busy on the stand this morning. .... we've given away over 200 brochures.

Exercise 4

Complete the second sentence so it has a similar meaning to the first sentence. You may need a new verb, or a time expression like those in exercise 3. Use contractions where possible.

1 Jane doesn't work at this company now.

Jane .... *has left* .... this company.

2 This is the first time I've been to the United States.

I .... to the United States before.

3 That's strange! My wallet isn't here!

That's strange! .... disappeared.

4 I saw a friend of yours a few moments ago.

I .... a friend of yours.

5 I'm still writing this report.

I .... this report yet.

6 We started working here three years ago.

We've been .... three years.

7 Is this your first visit to Latin America?

Have you .... before?

8 It's a long time since I spoke to Giorgio.

I .... to Giorgio for a long time.

9 Is Anna still out of the office?

Has .... back yet?

10 I'm sorry, but Rachel Dawson isn't here.

I'm sorry but Rachel Dawson has .... out.

11 I last saw David in 1996.

I .... since 1996.

12 I came to live here three months ago.

I've been .... three months.

13 How stupid of me! My laptop is still in the car.

How stupid of me! I .... my laptop in the car.

14 I'm still reading this report.

I .... reading this report yet.

15 Paul left the building a moment ago.

Paul has .... the building.

16 Have you been to Scandinavia at any time?

Have you .... to Scandinavia?

17 I've had English lessons in my company since January.

I've been .... English since January.

18 It's ages since we last had an order from CWP.

We .... an order from CWP for ages.

19 This is the first time I've eaten snails.

I've .... snails before.

20 I started playing tennis about six months ago.

I've been .... about six months.

21 I don't remember Helen's phone number.

I've .... Helen's phone number.

22 She has a different opinion now.

She .... her mind.

23 The last time I saw Margaret was Monday.

I haven't .... Monday.

Test 4 Verb tenses: future (units 7–8)

Exercise 1

<u>Underline</u> the correct answers.

1 Wait for me. *I'll be/I'll have been* ready in a moment.

2 We'd better wait here until the rain *stops/will stop*.

3 That looks very heavy. *Will I/Shall I* help you?

4 We finish the course tomorrow so *we're going out/we go out* for a drink.

5 I've just heard the weather forecast, and *it's/it's going to be* sunny tomorrow.

6 A: 'Do you want me to phone them?'

   B: 'No, it's all right, *I'll do/I'm doing* it.'

7 Please don't leave until I *come back/will come back*.

8 Julie won't be here next week. *She'll work/She'll be working* at our other office.

9 The flight attendant is calling us. I think *we will/we're going to* board the plane.

10 *They'll probably/They probably will* cut back the training budget next year.

Exercise 2

Cross out the mistake in each sentence and write the correction at the end.

1 ~~I go to play~~ tennis on Saturday. Would you like to come? ....*I'm going to play*....

2 The visitors from Japan will here at 9.30. ....

3 Justine will probably to get the sales job. ....

4 Sue is going lend me her copy of the report. ....

5 Bye for now. I see you later this evening. ....

6 Sorry, I'm not see you tomorrow. I have to go to London. ....

7 What you going to discuss at the next meeting? ....

8 The flight probably will be delayed. ....

Exercise 3

Decide if uses a)–h) are usually associated with *will, going to*, the present continuous (*I'm doing*), the future continuous (*I'll be doing*) or the future perfect (*I'll have done*).

a) future facts ....*will*...............

b) fixed future arrangements ....

c) instant decisions ....

d) future plans and intentions ....

e) predictions with present evidence ....

f) general opinions about the future ....

g) looking back from the future ....

h) activities in progress in the future ....

Match sentences 1–8 below with uses a)–h).

1 We're going to launch the new model at the Bologna Show. | d |

2 Sorry about this confusion. I'll look into it right away and I'll call you back. | |

3 I'm meeting my bank manager on Thursday. We're having lunch together. | |

4 I think we'll probably make a small loss this year. | |

5 Next year will be the tenth anniversary of our company. | |

6 During my presentation I'll be describing the key benefits of our new service. | |

7 Judging by these figures, we're going to make a small loss this year. | |

8 It's not a difficult job. We'll have finished by lunchtime. | |

Exercise 4

Complete the second sentence so it has a similar meaning to the first sentence. The answers include these forms: *will*, *won't*, *shall*, present simple, present continuous and future continuous.

1 I promise to phone you when I get back.

When I get back, ...*I'll phone*............. you.

2 Would you like me to close the window?

.... I close the window?

3 After the conference we can travel back together.

When the .... we can travel back together.

4 They refuse to lower their price.

They .... lower their price.

5 What job will you have after the company reorganisation?

What .... doing after the company reorganisation?

6 I'll wait here until it stops raining.

When it stops raining .... leave.

7 How about having a drink after work?

.... we have a drink after work?

8 Are you free tomorrow evening?

Are .... anything tomorrow evening?

Exercise 5

Rewrite each sentence with *will*, *shall* or *going to*, using the verb underlined.

1 Sarah doesn't plan to <u>get</u> involved in any research yet.

....*Sarah isn't going to get*.... involved in any research yet.

2 How about <u>having</u> a game of tennis at the weekend?

.... a game of tennis at the weekend?

3 I've decided to <u>study</u> Arabic in Cairo.

.... Arabic in Cairo.

4 I promise to <u>be</u> back before midday.

.... before midday.

5 I have an appointment to <u>see</u> the doctor, so I can't come.

.... the doctor, so I can't come.

6 I promise not to <u>forget</u>.

....

7 I plan to <u>do</u> my MBA in France.

.... my MBA in France.

8 Would you like me to <u>help</u> you with those bags?

.... with those bags?

9 It's possible for us to <u>come</u> back later if you like.

.... back later if you like.

10 I intend to <u>ask</u> my boss about opportunities for promotion.

.... my boss about opportunities for promotion.

11 I want to <u>have</u> the salmon.

.... the salmon, please.

12 I've decided to <u>have</u> the salmon.

.... the salmon.

Test 5 Passives (units 9–10)

Exercise 1

Cross out the mistake in each sentence and write the correction at the end.

1 Nils ~~has been offer~~ a new job in Brazil.   _has been offered_
2 Your parcel was been posted yesterday.   ....
3 A new industrial site is be developed outside the town.   ....
4 All the food at the reception was ate.   ....
5 Gold is still produce in large quantities in South Africa.   ....
6 Nothing will being decided before next week.   ....
7 The presentation is giving at the Hotel Intercontinental.   ....
8 I've just heard that Carla is been promoted to Marketing Director. ....
9 The introduction to the report was writing by the CEO.   ....
10 Many customers are losing through poor after-sales service.   ....

Exercise 2

Rewrite each sentence with a passive verb, without mentioning who did the action.

1 The authorities have closed the casino.
   .... _The casino has been closed._ ....

2 Someone broke into our house last week.
   ....

3 People all over the world speak English.
   ....

4 The local authorities have finally opened the new motorway.
   ....

5 Someone left this umbrella in reception.
   ....

6 The city council will ban all traffic from the city centre.
   ....

7 First we mix the two liquids, then we leave them for 24 hours.
   ....

8 The organisers are postponing the meeting.
   ....

Exercise 3

Complete the second sentence so it has a similar meaning to the first sentence and contains the word in brackets.

1 They have just serviced all our machines. (had)
   We .... _have just had all our machines serviced._ ....

2 Tomorrow they are repairing my car. (having)
   Tomorrow I ....

3 They printed some business cards with the new logo. (had)
   We ....

4 They are coming to clean the carpet tomorrow. (having)
   We ....

5 They have just refused my request for credit. (had)
   I ....

Exercise 4

 52   Underline the correct words in this article.

A Race Against Time

Governments across Europe are already (1) *starting/being started* to worry. Why? Because low birth rates combined with longer life expectancy (2) *mean/are meant* that the Continent will soon have fewer people working and fewer people paying taxes. As a result, a whole range of measures must (3) *take/be taken* to deal with the problems that this change in demographics (4) *will bring/will be brought*.

At the recent Annual World Economic Forum in Davos, Switzerland, a session called 'Reforming Pension Systems' (5) *took place/was taken place*. The speaker, director of the population division of the United Nations, (6) *highlighted/was highlighted* that this is a global problem, not just a European one. However the facts cannot (7) *ignore/be ignored*: the situation in Europe is particularly serious. Look at the findings of a recent European Commission study: Italy's population (8) *expects/is expected* to drop from 58 million to 48 million by 2050, Spain's (9) *will fall/will be fallen* from 40 million to 35 million, and Germany's from 82 million to 76 million. Sweden is one of the few countries where the population will probably (10) *increase/be increased*.

And as the populations get smaller, they are also getting older. From 2007 onwards an enormous part of Europe's population (11) *will start/will be started* to retire. Solutions will have (12) *to find/to be found* to deal with the problems that this will (13) *create/be created*. Certainly governments must (14) *encourage/be encouraged* private pension plans, and old-fashioned tax and social security models must (15) *look at/be looked at* in a completely new way. ∎

Exercise 5

Complete the second sentence so it has a similar meaning to the first sentence. Do not mention who did the action.

1   Someone checked these figures for me last week.
    I .... *had these figures checked* .... last week.

2   They grow much less coffee in Colombia these days.
    These days ....

3   Someone delivered this package this morning.
    This package ....

4   The city council is redeveloping the old docklands area.
    The old docklands area ....

5   They've put up interest rates again.
    Interest rates ....

6   We'll discuss your idea in the meeting tomorrow.
    Your idea ....

7   The technician installed some new software on my PC yesterday.
    Yesterday I .... on my PC.

8   Tokyo is my place of birth.
    I .... in Tokyo.

9   When is your date of birth?
    When exactly .... born?

10   Someone stole Peter's car last week.
    .... stolen last week.

11   Did anyone tell Alex about the meeting?
    .... about the meeting?

12   Has anyone made a backup copy of this file?
    .... made?

Test 6 Modals (units 11–14)

Exercise 1

<u>Underline</u> the correct word/s.

1 That looks like Carlos over there, but it <u>*can't*</u>/*mustn't* be. He's in Germany.
2 Marie isn't at her office, so she *can*/*must* be on her way here.
3 I think you *need to*/*have necessity to* get some advice from your colleagues.
4 Is your car door damaged? Someone must *tried*/*have tried* to break in.
5 It's getting very late. I think *we'd better*/*we would* pay the bill and leave.
6 I *might*/*can* be able to help you, but I'm not sure.
7 Yes, it's a good idea, we *should*/*must* consult more closely with the unions.
8 It's absolutely necessary, we *should*/*must* consult more closely with the unions.
9 Lucy *can't have*/*must have* heard the bad news. She looks so happy.
10 Sorry, I *must to*/*have to* go now. I don't want to be late.
11 You *might not*/*don't need to* come to the meeting if you're busy.
12 This invoice *can't*/*mustn't* be right. It says £550 to repair the photocopier!

Exercise 2

Complete each sentence with a word or phrase from the list below.

have to   had to   ~~don't have to~~   didn't have to   must   mustn't   must have
might have   should   could

1 We're trying a new dress code. We ..*don't have to*.. wear formal clothes on Fridays.
2 You .... touch that button! The whole production line will stop!
3 I'm not sure, but I think I .... made a mistake.
4 Before we agree, we'll .... study the contract in more detail.
5 Sorry I can't stay any longer. I really .... go now or I'll miss my train.
6 If you needed the goods urgently, we .... speed up the order.
7 Sorry I'm late, but I .... go to the doctor's.
8 It .... been embarrassing for you to forget his name.
9 I think we .... accept their offer. It's the best we'll get.
10 Luckily, I .... attend the meeting yesterday, so I managed to finish all my paperwork.

Exercise 3

Match the uses of *would* a)–g) with the sentences 1–7 below.

a) offering help   b) offering things   c) polite request   d) invitations
e) reporting what someone said   f) imaginary future with 'if'   g) past refusal

1 Would you mind calling back later? | C |
2 What would you do if they refused to negotiate? | |
3 Would you like some milk in your coffee? | |
4 Would you like to join us for dinner tomorrow evening? | |
5 They wouldn't reduce the price under any circumstances. | |
6 Would you like me to open the window? | |
7 He said he would call back later. | |

Exercise 4

Complete the second sentence so that it has a similar meaning as the first sentence. Use a word or phrase from the list below.

can't   might   should   have to   don't have to   ~~ought to~~   can't be   might be
must be   should be

1 It would be a good idea to bring in a firm of consultants.
   We ......*ought to*...... bring in a firm of consultants.
2 It's not necessary for you to leave a deposit.
   You .... leave a deposit.
3 I'm sure that isn't John, because he's in Paris.
   That .... John, because he's in Paris.
4 Ann is almost certainly with a customer.
   Ann .... with a customer.
5 I expect the meeting will be finished by ten.
   The meeting .... finished by ten.
6 It's possible that I'll be late.
   I .... late.
7 We are not allowed to dispose of waste in that way.
   We .... dispose of waste in that way.
8 Perhaps I'll see you on Thursday evening.
   I .... see you on Thursday evening.
9 It's the rule that we check all bank references.
   We .... check all bank references.
10 You'd better speak to her as soon as possible.
   You .... speak to her as soon as possible.

Exercise 5

Complete the second sentence so that it has a similar meaning as the first sentence. Use a phrase from the list below.

~~might have~~   can't have   could have   should have (x2)   must have   shouldn't have   might not have

1 Perhaps David made a mistake.
   David ......*might have*...... made a mistake.
2 I'm sure that she worked very hard on this project.
   She .... worked very hard on this project.
3 I'm sure the warranty hasn't expired already.
   The warranty .... expired already.
4 It would have been a good idea for you to tell me.
   You .... told me.
5 Perhaps you didn't see the line we launched at the Munich Fair.
   You .... seen the line we launched at the Munich Fair.
6 I was expecting them to call by now.
   They .... called by now.
7 It was a bad idea for us to drop our prices so much.
   We .... dropped our prices so much.
8 It was possible for us to see this problem coming.
   We .... seen this problem coming.

Test 7 Questions (units 15–16)

Exercise 1

When we make questions in spoken English, we often leave out the auxiliary verb and the subject pronoun. For example, instead of saying, '*Do you like it?*' we say, '*Like it?*'. Write full questions using the <u>underlined</u> verb.

1 <u>Finished</u> yet? We're all waiting! .... *Have you finished yet?* ....
2 <u>See</u> you tomorrow? Are you busy all day? ....
3 You look relaxed. <u>Have</u> a nice time? ....
4 Paul's a bit difficult. <u>Know</u> what I mean? ....
5 Hi, Tim. <u>Coming</u> out for a drink later? ....
6 <u>Been</u> waiting long? Sorry for the delay. ....
7 Interesting conference, isn't it. <u>Enjoying</u> yourself? ....
8 <u>Heard</u> the latest? Isabel is taking early retirement! ....

Exercise 2

Rewrite each question, beginning as shown.

1 What's the time?
    Could you tell me .... *what the time is?* ....
2 What does this mean?
    Do you know .... ?
3 How much does this cost?
    Could you tell me .... ?
4 What time does the bank open?
    Do you know .... ?
5 Am I in the right seat?
    Could you tell me if .... ?
6 Where's the Opera House?
    Do you know .... ?
7 Is this the way to the Science Museum?
    Could you tell me if .... ?
8 Who is the speaker at the next session?
    Do you know .... ?

Exercise 3

Match the beginnings of the phrases with their endings.

1 Do you mind if I ...   a) closing the window?
2 Would you mind if I ...   b) closed the window?
3 Would you mind ...   c) close the window?

Somebody asks *Would you mind if I closed the window?* You want the window closed. Tick (✔) the answers you could give.

4 Yes, I would.   ☐
5 No, of course not. ☐
6 Go ahead.   ☐
7 Please do.   ☐

Exercise 4

Write short answers for each question, beginning as shown. Use contractions (*don't* instead of *do not*).

1 Do you like Brazil? Yes, ...I do........ . No, ...I don't........ .
2 Does Karen like Brazil? Yes, ... No, ...
3 Have you worked here long? Yes, ... No, ...
4 Are you coming with us tonight? Yes, ... No, ...
5 Is Karen coming with us tonight? Yes, ... No, ...
6 Can you come on Friday? Yes, ... No, ...
7 Will you be here tomorrow? Yes, ... No, ...
8 Did you have to pay a lot? Yes, ... No, ...
9 Is that your coat? Yes, ... No, ...

Exercise 5

Complete each sentence, using the verb in brackets where necessary.

1 A: '.....You have got..... (have got) the file, haven't you?'
   B: 'Yes, of course.'
2 A: 'They'll be back by 4.00, ... ?'
   B: 'I expect so.'
3 A: 'You .... (leave) now, are you?'
   B: 'Sorry, I really have to go.'
4 A: 'They've been here before, ... ?'
   B: 'Yes, I think so.'
5 A: 'You can meet Marjoleine at the station, ... ?'
   B: 'Yes, of course.'
6 A: 'You .... (forget) the samples, did you?'
   B: 'No, of course not.'
7 A: '................................. (be) here yesterday, were you?'
   B: 'No, I wasn't'
8 A: 'You don't happen to know the time, ... ?'
   B: 'Sorry, I don't'
9 A: 'Let's have a break now, ... ?'
   B: 'OK, good idea.'
10 A: 'You had the same thing for lunch yesterday, ...?'
    B: 'Yes.'

Exercise 6

Put the words in the correct order to make questions.

1 take Visa do you? ....Do you take Visa?..........................
2 please I can see the menu? ....
3 excuse me here anyone is sitting? ....
4 from which country do come you? ....
5 to who you were just now talking? ....
6 what mean do you exactly by that? ....
7 a little more specific you could be? ....
8 what time the next train to Brussels is? ....
9 you can tell me what time is the next train to Brussels? ....
10 this briefcase to who does belong? ....
11 could I from here a phone call make? ....
12 do think you I could make from here a phone call? ....

Test 8 Conditionals (units 17–18)

Exercise 1

<u>Underline</u> the correct words.

1 If we sent the goods by sea, the transport costs *will/<u>would</u>* be much lower.
2 If they *promote/promoted* the brand better, they'll gain market share.
3 If you *left/had left* earlier, you might have got there on time.
4 If anyone from Head Office visits, they always *stay/will stay* in a five star hotel.
5 If I were you, *I'd/I'll* call their Technical Support number.
6 If I *have/had* more time, I'd be able to come up with a solution.
7 If it *breaks down/will break down*, it takes days for the service engineer to arrive.
8 If you needed the money urgently, I *could phone/could have phoned* Accounts now to try and speed up your payment.
9 If you enter the date in the wrong format, the computer *doesn't/didn't* recognise the information.
10 If *we'd been/we were* more careful, we wouldn't have lost so much money.
11 If I had bought more shares, I *would become/would have become* rich!
12 If your second interview *goes/will go* well, I'm sure they'll offer you the job.
13 If you *would have backed up/backed up* your files more often, you *wouldn't risk/didn't risk* losing all your work.
14 If you *hadn't/wouldn't* have acted so quickly, *we'd be/we are* in big trouble.
15 I need to contact Head Office. I wish I *have/had* my mobile phone with me.
16 I wish it *is/was* Friday!

Exercise 2

Complete each sentence, using the verb in brackets in one of these forms: *will do, would do, would have done*.

1 If we got a virus on the network, we ....would lose............ (lose) all our data.
2 If my train isn't late, I .... (be) in Paris at six.
3 If your talk had been shorter, I think they .... (ask) more questions.
4 If you tell me what you want, I .... (get) it for you at the airport.
5 We .... (get) more inquiries if we advertised more often.
6 If we hadn't left so early, we .... (miss) the train.
7 If I worked abroad, I .... (not see) my family so often.
8 If you haven't got any change, I .... (leave) the tip.
9 We .... (sort out) the problem much sooner if we had had the manual.
10 If you were in his situation, what .... (you/do)?

Exercise 3

Complete each sentence using *if* or *unless*.

1 Their offices are very near. We'll walk there, ... it's raining.
2 We would probably get the contract .... we dropped our price a little.
3 Come on! .... we hurry, we'll miss the plane.
4 .... you have any questions, please feel free to call.
5 What would you do .... they refused to negotiate?
6 I don't feel able to take a decision .... I have all the figures.

Exercise 4

Complete the sentence for each situation.

1   Emma didn't leave early, and so she missed her flight.

If Emma ......_had left early_...... , she _wouldn't have missed_.. her flight.

2   He didn't make more copies, so we don't have enough for everyone.

If he .... , we .... enough for everyone.

3   I forgot to bring your map, so I went to the wrong building.

If I .... , I .... to the wrong building.

4   They didn't invest in new technology, so they didn't survive the recession.

If they .... , they .... the recession.

5   You didn't wait, so this has happened.

If you ...., this ....

6   I didn't realise you were so busy when I asked you to help me.

If I .... , I .... to help me.

7   The Government didn't collapse, so there wasn't a crisis.

If the Government .... , there .... a crisis.

8   They didn't bring out their new model on time, so they lost market share.

If they .... , they .... market share.

Exercise 5

Choose the correct continuation for each sentence.

1   I wasn't taking notes, and now I can't remember what she said. | b |

a) I wish I took notes. b) I wish I'd taken notes.

2   This is a very unusual situation. | |

a) I wish I'd known what to do. b) I wish I knew what to do.

3   Our offices are in the city centre and the rent is very high. | |

a) I wish we were outside the centre. b) I wish we are outside the centre.

4   They gave the job to an external candidate, but now they regret it. | |

a) They wish they hadn't done it. b) They wish they didn't do it.

5   I can't enter the system because I don't have the password. | |

a) If only I would have the password. b) If only I had the password.

6   There are too many similar models on the market now. | |

a) If only we launched our version earlier. b) If only we had launched our version earlier.

7   I'm worried about the meeting next Friday. We need to reach an agreement. | |

a) I wish we succeed. b) I hope we succeed.

Exercise 6

Complete each sentence using the verb in brackets.

1   We're not the market leader, but I wish we ...._were_.......... (be).

2   He made a mess of all my photocopying. I wish I .... (do) it myself.

3   I pressed the wrong key on the computer. If only I .... (not do) it.

4   I can't understand anything Marie says. I wish I .... (speak) French.

5   You dessert looks good. I wish I .... (order) that too.

6   They're meeting at the moment. I wish I .... (be) a fly on the wall.

7   This information is important. I wish you .... (give) it to me before.

8   Look! There's a sale at Harrods. If only I .... (have) my Visa card with me.

Test 9 Verbs + *-ing* or infinitive (units 19–20)

Exercise 1

<u>Underline</u> the correct words.

1   I really can't afford *to eat*/*eating* in such an expensive restaurant.
2   Do you mind *to come*/*coming* back in half an hour?
3   Do you want *to come*/*coming* back in half an hour?
4   Kate denied *to give*/*giving* the office keys to anyone else.
5   He admitted *to make*/*making* a serious mistake.
6   *Remind*/*Remember* me to call Sylvia this afternoon.
7   We have been trying *to enter*/*entering* the Chinese market for some time.
8   I hope *to be*/*being* at the next meeting, but I'm not sure if I can make it.
9   I expect *to be*/*being* at the next meeting. I think I can make it.
10 If she isn't in the office when you call, keep *to try*/*trying*.
11 I considered every possible option. I even imagined *to resign*/*resigning*.
12 I refuse *to believe*/*believing* that we can't do it. We have to try harder.
13 I admit *to be*/*being* a little careless last time, but I won't do it again.
14 I can't stand people *to interrupt*/*interrupting* all the time. It's so rude.
15 Where do you fancy *to go*/*going* for lunch today?
16 I've arranged *to meet*/*meeting* them at their hotel.
17 We guarantee *to deliver*/*delivering* the goods by the end of June.
18 Imagine *to win*/*winning* the lottery!
19 The manager refused *to see*/*seeing* me.
20 I realised I had forgotten *to pack*/*packing* any spare batteries.
21 If I miss my connection, it means *to arrive*/*arriving* in Bonn after midnight.
22 I tried *to lift*/*lifting* it, but it was too heavy.
23 I enjoy *to get away*/*getting away* to the coast at the weekend.
24 I'd love *to get away*/*getting away* to the coast this weekend.
25 I tried to persuade him, but he refused *to listen*/*listening* to me.
26 I really enjoyed *to visit*/*visiting* your factory. Thank you very much.
27 They decided *to order*/*ordering* 1,000 units.
28 He offered *to meet*/*meeting* me at the airport.

Exercise 2

Complete the sentences with a verb from the list below. Choose either the *-ing* form or *to* + infinitive.

cause   come   compromise   get   get through   give   ~~make~~   rise   unpack   wait

1   He admitted ....**making**........ a mistake on the invoice.
2   Do you fancy .... with us for a drink?
3   Wages tend .... faster than inflation.
4   I can't manage .... when I call. I keep .... an engaged tone.
5   Do you mind .... for a couple of minutes while I write this email?
6   They agreed .... us thirty more days to pay the invoice.
7   The transport company deny .... the damage.
8   Their negotiating position was very rigid. They refused ....
9   I saw him .... the goods, and there was no damage visible.

Test 10 Reported speech (units 21–22)

Exercise 1

Complete each question in direct speech, ending as shown.

1 Jack asked me whether I was going out for lunch.
........'Are you going out for lunch?'............ Jack asked me.

2 Carol asked Ann what she had done the day before.
'.. , Ann?' asked Carol.

3 John asked us if we often went to Germany for meetings.
'.. ?' John asked us.

4 Kate asked me how many interviews I'd done that day.
'.. ?' Kate asked me.

5 George asked Sue if she was going to change jobs.
'.. , Sue?' asked George.

6 Alice asked me who I had talked to at the conference.
'.. ?' Alice asked me.

7 The technician asked me if I would be there the next day.
'.. ?' the technician asked me.

8 Mary asked me where our new offices were.
'.. ?' Mary asked me.

9 He asked me if I'd seen Bill recently.
'.. ?' he asked me.

10   He asked me if I'd be seeing Bill at the conference.
'.. ?' he asked me.

Exercise 2

Rewrite each sentence in reported speech, using a verb from the list below.

advised   apologised for   congratulated on   invited   offered   ~~promised~~
refused   suggested

1 'I'll meet you at the airport, Sue,' said Mike.
Mike ......promised to meet Sue.......... at the airport.

2 'Would you like to come to the product launch, Jean?' asked Chris.
Chris .... the product launch.

3 I wouldn't sign the contract if I were you, Dave,' said Patsy.
Patsy .... the contract.

4 'How about getting an alternative quote?' said Nick.
Nick .... an alternative quote.

5 'I'm terribly sorry for arriving so late,' said Serena.
Serena .... so late.

6 'Shall I give you a lift?' said Mark.
Mark .... me a lift.

7 'Well done, you've won the Employee of the Year award!' he said.
He .... her .... Employee of the Year award.

8 'No, I can't accept any further delays,' said Pat.
Pat .... any further delays.

Test 11 Phrasal verbs (units 23–24)

Exercise 1

Match the beginnings of sentences 1–12 with their endings a)–l).

1 In my job I deal `c`
2 The Government is trying to cut
3 Here's the application form. Can you fill
4 I deal with the retail side of the business, and Kate looks
5 I hope John gets better soon. We can't do
6 Thanks for your call, and I look
7 First I'll talk about the history of our company, then I'll move
8 Before you switch off the PC, make sure you back
9 Some of the smaller companies in the market will probably be taken
10 We need some new office chairs. I'll look
11 These days you need to do a lot of reading to keep
12 It's important to find a candidate who fits

a) after the wholesale side.
b) up with developments in the field.
c) with all the paperwork related to customer accounts.
d) without him on the negotiating team.
e) up all your files.
f) in with the company culture and the other people in the department.
g) down on bureaucracy.
h) on to our product range and markets.
i) over in the next few years.
j) forward to meeting you on the tenth.
k) through the catalogue and see what I can find.
l) in both sides and sign it at the bottom.

Exercise 2

Rewrite each sentence by replacing the underlined words with a phrasal verb from the list below.

come across   deal with   go on   go over   ~~look forward to~~   pick up   put back to
run out of   sort out   take up

1 <u>I think</u> I'm <u>going to enjoy</u> the weekend very much.
   ......<u>I'm looking forward to</u>.... the weekend very much.
2 The machine <u>uses</u> about four square metres of floor space.
   The machine .... about four square metres of floor space.
3 I think we'll have to <u>delay</u> the meeting until next week.
   I think we'll have .... next week.
4 They are not an easy company to <u>do business with</u>.
   They are not an easy company ....
5 Can you <u>collect</u> me from the airport <u>in your car</u>?
   Can you .... from the airport?
6 Sorry, I'm really busy, I have to <u>continue</u> writing these reports.
   Sorry, I'm really busy, I have .... these reports.
7 There's a small problem. We're just trying to <u>put</u> it <u>right</u> now.
   There's a small problem. We're just trying .... now.
8 Before we finish, I'd just like to <u>summarise</u> the main points again.
   Before we finish, I'd just like .... the main points again.
9 I've lost my pen. Let me know if you <u>find</u> it <u>by chance</u>.
   I've lost my pen. Let me know if ....
10 We'll have to continue the meeting tomorrow. We have <u>no more</u> time <u>left</u>.
   We'll have to continue the meeting tomorrow. We have ....

Exercise 3

Complete the sentences with a word from the list below.

> away   back   by   down   into   off   ~~on~~   over   out   through   up

1 Hold ......on...... a moment, that's not exactly what I said.
2 Clare will take .... my job when I change department next month.
3 I hate it when they put you on hold and you can't get ....
4 The total bill for four nights works .... at £380.
5 The factory will close .... next year. They're moving production to China.
6 It's going to be difficult to get .... with such a small budget.
7 Paola grew .... in a little village outside Venice.
8 I'll drop you .... at the station on my way home.
9 I'll look .... the problem and get .... to you tomorrow.
10 No, I don't have it any more. I threw it ....

Exercise 4

Complete the sentences with a phrasal verb from the list below.

> catch up with   cut down on   ~~drop in on~~   face up to   get back to
> get on with   get round to   look forward to   move on to   run out of

1 Will we have time to ...drop in on... Gunter while we're in Berlin?
2 If you've all helped yourself to coffee, I think we should .... the meeting.
3 The report says we can .... a lot of waste in the factory.
4 I've tried everything and I've completely .... new ideas.
5 Sorry it's taken so long to .... answering your email.
6 Are you going out for a drink right now? I have a few things to do here in the office, but I'll .... you later.
7 Please feel free to contact me if you have any further questions. I .... hearing from you soon.
8 It's not going to be easy, but you have to .... your responsibilities.
9 Now I'd like to .... the next slide which shows our sales by region.
10 I need some time to look into this. Can I .... you later?

Exercise 5

Match the beginnings of sentences 1–12 with their endings a)–l).

1 My parents were quite strict and brought me	c	a) it back to Friday?
2 When are you arriving? Would you like me to pick		b) it forward to Wednesday?
3 When are you leaving? Would you like me to drop		c) up in a very traditional way.
4 Peter? Any comments? Would you like to come		d) off the lights when you leave?
5 Would you make sure you turn		e) up smoking.
6 I can't make the meeting on Thursday. Can we bring		f) you off?
7 I can't make the meeting on Thursday. Can we put		g) you up?
8 Yes, it is a strange word. Have you tried looking		h) off when we entered a tunnel.
9 I hope the cost of our raw materials will come		i) in here?
10 I'll try and find her. Can you hold		j) on for a moment?
11 Hello? Are you there? I think we were cut		k) it up in a dictionary?
12 My doctor says I should give		l) down a little now.

Test 12 *Make/do/get/have* (unit 27)

Exercise 1

Match the uses of *get* in sentences 1–8 with their dictionary definitions a)–h).
(sth. = something, sb. = somebody)

1 I didn't get home until eight last night.	☐ d	a) obtain/buy
2 I'm getting a direct flight to Dusseldorf.	☐	b) receive/be given
3 We're only getting a 4% pay rise this year.	☐	c) become
4 My name is Hugh, H-U-G-H. Did you get that?	☐	d) move/arrive
5 It's no good. We'll never get them to agree.	☐	e) bring sth. to a place/fetch
6 I'm getting tired. Shall we continue tomorrow?	☐	f) understand
7 I should get something for my wife at the airport.	☐	g) persuade sb. to do sth.
8 I'll get last year's figures. Just wait a moment.	☐	h) travel by/catch (transport)

Now match these sentences with some of the definitions a)–h) above.

9 I'm sorry, I didn't quite get that last point. ☐

10 Don't worry, you'll soon get used to it. ☐

11 I'm getting a bit of a headache from looking at the screen for too long. ☐

12 Is that your new car? When did you get it? ☐

13 Can I get you a coffee while you're waiting? ☐

14 I got here by taxi. ☐

Exercise 2

Complete the sentences with *make, do* or *have*. You may have to change the form.

1 What are you ....**doing**.... at the weekend?

2 I'm .... serious doubts about the whole thing.

3 OK, shall we .... a start?

4 Could you .... me a favour?

5 Can I .... a suggestion? Why don't we .... a meeting to discuss what to ....

6 I think we need to .... more tests before we .... a final decision.

7 The company .... a lot of money last year, but this year we're not .... so well. We might even have to .... some people redundant.

8 It .... me really mad when people can't .... their jobs properly. I'm .... difficulty in .... any plans when the situation is so confusing.

9 Go on! .... a go! It doesn't matter if you .... a mistake.

10 The help I got from my employer .... it possible for me to .... an MBA.

11 I'm .... my best but I really can't .... sense of these figures. I'm .... a lot of trouble seeing what they all refer to.

12 The menu looks really good. I'm going to .... French onion soup as a starter, and then the steak with béarnaise sauce. But I think I'll .... without dessert. I'm .... a bit of an effort to lose weight.

Test 13 Relative clauses (units 28–29)

Exercise 1

<u>Underline</u> the correct words. In number 10 choose the most common usage.

1 The stationery *who/<u>which</u>* you ordered has arrived.

2 The speaker *which/whose* presentation I heard before lunch was very good.

3 Everyone *which/that* I met in the Milan office asked how you were.

4 The person of *which/whose* newspaper I borrowed has disappeared.

5 The person *who/whom* is responsible for this is Antonio Platini.

6 This product, *which/whose* features are described in the leaflet, sells very well.

7 This product, *which/whose* is our best seller, is available in four colours.

8 The person *whose/that* book this is wants it back.

9 The person *whose/that* lent me this book wants it back.

10 John is someone *with whom I use to work/who I used to work with*.

Exercise 2

Decide if you can miss out the relative pronoun (*who, which, that*). If you can, put a bracket round it. If you can't, <u>underline</u> it.

1 There is an attachment (that) you can use to link to a PC.

2 The attachment, <u>that</u> comes free with the product, is used to link to a PC.

3 The person who I told you about is standing over there.

4 The meal, which was nothing special, cost us more than £50 a head.

5 The meal that we had last night wasn't very good.

6 The first thing that your customers will notice is the price.

7 The information, which is strictly confidential, comes from a very good source.

8 I cannot provide the information that you want.

Exercise 3

Rewrite each pair of sentences as one sentence using the word in brackets.

1 Rani showed me a magazine article. It was really interesting. (which)
   Rani ...*showed me a magazine article which was*.... really interesting.

2 Some Japanese visitors came yesterday. They gave me this gift. (who)
   The Japanese visitors .... this gift.

3 This is a gift. The Japanese visitors who came yesterday gave it to me. (that)
   This is the gift .... gave me.

4 I borrowed a friend's laptop. He wants it back. (whose)
   The friend .... back.

5 A marketing manager works in my department. She's leaving the company tomorrow. (who)
   The marketing manager .... is leaving the company tomorrow.

6 We went to a presentation yesterday. It was very interesting. (that)
   The presentation .... very interesting.

7 I met a woman. Her sister works for ABN. (whose)
   I met .... ABN.

8 A man is waiting in reception. He wants to see you. (who)
   The man .... see you.

Test 14 Nouns, pronouns and articles (units 30–35)

Exercise 1

Cross out the mistake in each line and write the correction at the end.

1 I spent ~~a time~~ talking to Jack, and then I went home. ....*sometime*..............
2 Karl's sister is doctor. ....
3 Is this umbrella your or mine? ....
4 They say that the wine is good for you in small amounts. ....
5 Write down the reference number all the time you sell something. ....
6 Can you give me an advice? ....
7 I'm sorry, we have two lifts but either one is in service. ....
8 I need some informations about accommodation in London. ....
9 We tried to get the machine working again but no one of us could do it. ....
10 Walking will take too long – let's go with the taxi. ....
11 Sorry I'm late, the traffic were very busy. ....
12 Our marketing director is excellent, she has so much good ideas. ....
13 A: How many people visited your stand this afternoon?
   B: No at all. ....
14 Have you ever met the colleague of Jane? ....
15 There's coffee and there's tea. You can have both. ....
16 There is too few information to make a decision. ....
17 We have two payment options – every one has different features. ....
18 Have you seen the inflation predictions in the Ministrys report? ....
19 We haven't got chairs enough for the meeting. ....
20 There are none spare parts in stock at the moment. ....
21 The news are on in a few minutes. ....
22 You'll find all the statistics at the report's end. ....
23 We're a leading player in either the film and music industries. ....
24 There are enough free samples for one every. ....
25 Alison keeps talking about that idea of her's. ....
26 Could you give me an information, please? ....
27 Can you speak up? I can't hear nothing. ....
28 We looked at two sites but either of them were too small. ....
29 At the end of my presentation, there was none single question. ....
30 Please come back tomorrow. There isn't no one to see you today. ....
31 Please put the manual back in it's proper place when you finish. ....
32 He's only got the job because he's the boss son. ....

Exercise 2

Each pair of words contains one countable noun and one uncountable noun. Put the words into the correct column and write a/an or some before the word.

accommodation/flat   desk/furniture   bag/luggage   work/job   travel/trip
trouble/problem   chance/luck   wine/litre   equipment/machine   dollar/money
email/correspondence   fact/information   advice/suggestion   hour/time

Countable nouns	Uncountable nouns
a flat	some accommodation

Exercise 3

Complete the second sentence so that it has a similar meaning to the first sentence and contains the word in brackets.

1   The box isn't empty. (something)

......................*There's something in*...................... the box.

2   Let me tell you what I think you should do. (advice)

Let me give you ....

3   We travelled there on the train. (by)

We travelled there ....

4   I feel worried. (something)

.... me.

5   Every morning I walk to the office. (foot)

Every morning I come to the office ....

6   Martin is a friend of my boss. (one)

Martin is ....

7   Chris advises people about their tax. (adviser)

Chris is ....

8   Manuela knows this business better than anyone. (knows)

.... better than Manuela.

9   I haven't got anything to do. (got)

I've .... do.

10   We are all tea drinkers here. (everybody)

.... tea.

11   People who are unemployed need better training programmes. (the)

.... better training programmes.

12   The prototype needs to be changed a lot. (redesigning)

The prototype needs ....

13   We can't do anything. (nothing)

There .... do.

14   What did that piece of machinery cost? (how)

.... that piece of machinery cost?

15   There is little travel in my job. (much)

There .... travel in my job.

16   Clara does people's accounts for her living. (accountant)

Clara is ....

17   No one was on time yesterday. (late)

.... yesterday.

18   There was nothing I could do about it. (couldn't)

I .... about it.

19   Nobody at all was available to see me. (single)

.... was available to see me.

20   There isn't any reason to worry. (no)

.... reason to worry.

21   The report did not contain the information I wanted. (in)

The information I wanted .... the report.

22   This copy belongs to the customer. (copy)

This is ....

23   There's nothing in the post this morning. (anything)

.... in the post this morning.

Test 15 Adjectives and adverbs (units 36–40)

Exercise 1

Cross out the mistake in each line and write the correction at the end.

1 I'm really ~~interesting~~ in foreign travel. .... interested ....
2 They'll have finished the new shopping centre until the end of the year. ....
3 Peter has been working very hardly recently. ....
4 I bought a blue lovely silk tie. ....
5 We had a great time on holiday. The people were too friendly. ....
6 This magazine article is extremely excellent. ....
7 I thought the meeting went very good. ....
8 Using my PC for a long time makes my eyes feel tiring. ....
9 We give discounts never on these products. ....
10 Are you interesting in extending the guarantee? ....
11 There is too much new equipment that we're still learning how to use it. ....
12 It was so a risky project that we decided to cancel it. ....
13 In my opinion their management team is not enough experienced. ....
14 Their company is larger as ours. ....
15 Their company is just as large than ours. ....
16 It's the better price I can offer. ....
17 I've been working in this company since three months. ....
18 The negotiation was such tense we had to call a short break. ....
19 When I will get back, I'll give you a ring. ....
20 I have to pick up my ticket until the travel agency closes. ....
21 You work much harder as I do. ....
22 The presentation was enough long, and so the audience got bored. ....
23 The meeting wasn't very useful. It was much little useful than last week's. ....
24 Golf isn't as good for your health than swimming. ....
25 I'll wait here by six, so try and be here by then. ....

Exercise 2

Complete each sentence with one of the following words: Choose from *in, on, at, for, since, during, ago, afterwards, after, later*.

1 Shall we all go out for a meal ....on......... my birthday?
2 He started working here four years ....
3 I won't phone him now, I'll phone him ....
4 I haven't heard from them .... three weeks.
5 I haven't heard from them .... last week.
6 This bar closes .... midnight.
7 Luckily I arrived just .... time to catch the train.
8 Let's try to start the meeting .... time.
9 My presentation will finish at mid-day, so we could meet for lunch ....
10 .... my presentation I'll be talking about three main areas.
11 Don't worry. .... your presentation you'll be able to relax.
12 I've been waiting .... more than an hour.
13 Don't wait for me, I have some things to finish here. I'll see you all ....
14 We have three shifts in the factory, including one that works .... night.

Exercise 3

Complete the second sentence so that it has a similar meaning to the first sentence and contains the word/s in brackets.

1 Your speech was really excellent. (spoke)
   You .... *spoke really well* ....

2 We started working on the project in January. (working/since)
   We ....

3 Retail banking isn't as profitable as investment banking. (more)
   Investment banking ....

4 She's a very careful worker. (works)
   She ....

5 I haven't seen worse service than this. (ever)
   This is ....

6 Monica left Paris in July. (stayed)
   Monica .... July.

7 Do you find opera interesting?
   Are ....

8 The meeting had a positive finish. (finished)
   The meeting ....

9 This has been hard work for you. (worked)
   You ....

10 Frank is a good writer. (writes)
    Frank ....

11 Kate is ill. (well)
    Kate ....

12 Could you not talk so fast, please? (slowly)
    Could you ....

13 The Chinese market is bigger than the Indian market. (as)
    The Indian market ....

14 Alan sells the same number of products as Richard. (just)
    Alan sells ....

15 The other members of the team are more experienced than Romy. (least)
    Romy ....

16 I'll see you in a few hours. (later)
    I'll ....

17 I started this job in 1998. (doing/since)
    I ....

18 Diane is on holiday. She's back next week. (away on holiday)
    Diane is .... next week.

19 The train arrived exactly when it was supposed to. (time)
    The train arrived ....

20 His intervention was too late to save the negotiations. (time)
    He didn't intervene ....

21 I won't arrive there later than two. (get/by)
    I ....

22 We tried hard but finally we gave up. (end)
    We tried hard but ....

23 It's twelve and I've been waiting for you since ten. (two)
    I've been waiting for you .... hours.

Test 16 Prepositions (units 45–48)

Exercise 1

Complete each sentence with a preposition of place. Choose from *at, in, on, over, to, under.*

1   My brother works ......*at*...... the airport.
2   Can you call me back? I'm .... the middle of a meeting.
3   The taxi dropped me off .... my hotel .... the city centre.
4   We flew .... the new sports stadium as we were landing.
5   He had a suitcase .... one hand, and his guitar .... the other.
6   Go down the corridor and my office is .... the right.
7   There's a fire escape .... the back of the building.
8   She wasn't feeling well and her doctor sent her .... hospital.
9   We had a lovely holiday .... the country.
10   He had a portrait of himself hanging .... the wall.
11   The author's name is .... the bottom of the page.
12   Before the tunnel was built, you had to drive .... the Alps.
13   I have six junior managers working .... me.
14   I'll be working .... home for most of tomorrow.
15   Hello. This is Ulrike speaking. I'm .... Paris, ... the Hotel Versailles.
16   Susanna's just rung. She's .... the restaurant.
17   Susanna's just rung. She's .... the bus stop.
18   Jim gave me a lift .... the station .... his car.
19   I met Kati .... the bus yesterday.
20   Stratford is .... the river Thames.

Exercise 2

Decide which preposition from the list below goes with each verb.

about (x2)   against   for (x3)   from   in   into   of (x2)   on (x3)   to (x2)   with (x2)

1   I must apologise .....*for*...... being late.
2   I'd just like to add something .... what Jawad just said.
3   Is the factory insured .... fire?
4   The cost? Well, it depends .... what you're looking ....
5   The whole package consists .... the main unit plus all these accessories.
6   I've divided my presentation .... three main parts.
7   We need to diversify to prevent us .... becoming too dependent on one product.
8   Please, let me pay .... this.
9   We can supply you .... a full range of sizes.
10   We specialise .... commercial catering equipment.
11   Do you know anything .... the Portuguese market?
12   He congratulated us .... getting the contract.
13   Lisbon reminds me a bit .... San Francisco.
14   I agree .... you .... that.
15   Does this bag belong .... anyone here?
16   In the next meeting I think we should focus .... the planning schedule.

Exercise 3

<u>Underline</u> the correct word in these adjective + preposition combinations.

1 Are you certain *to/about/from* that?

2 I hope they don't go on strike. We're dependent *of/on/by* them for our supplies.

3 This line is very popular *for/to/with* customers looking for value for money.

4 Our country is lacking *in/of/for* energy resources – we have to import all our oil.

5 Are you aware *to/by/of* just how serious this problem is?

6 Are you interested *in/for/of* long-term growth for your savings?

7 I'm responsible *for/to/by* a team of eight consultants.

8 If anything goes wrong, I'm directly responsible *for/to/by* the CEO.

9 Let me use a calculator. I'm not very good *at/for/by* maths.

10 It would be good *at/for/by* your career if you worked abroad for a few years.

11 I'm annoyed *with/for/about* their lack of flexibility.

12 I'm annoyed *with/for/about* them *with/for/about* being so inflexible.

Exercise 4

Complete the sentences with a noun from list A and a preposition from list B.

> A: advantage advice investment lack matter pessimism ~~price~~ reason reply solution
>   substitute   trouble
>
> B: about for for in ~~of~~ of of on to to with with

1 At the moment the ....*price of*......... oil is about $25 a barrel.

2 Can you tell me the .... the delay? We've been waiting a long time.

3 The main .... proposal B is that it's much cheaper.

4 The .... proposal A is that it's very expensive.

5 What's the .... Jill? She looks rather upset.

6 Have they sent a .... your last email?

7 There's a .... experience at the top of the company.

8 I'm sure we can find a .... this problem, but it may take some time.

9 Clever advertising is no .... good quality at a reasonable price.

10 This year we're making a major .... new technology.

11 Can you give me some .... the best way to invest my savings?

12 Everyone's worried. There's a lot of .... the future of the economy.

Exercise 5

Complete the text with the prepositions of place from the list below.

> across at (x3) down inside near next to off on (x3) opposite to

Liz left early to go to her job interview. She got (1) ....*on*..... the bus, paid her fare and went (2) .... She sat down (3) .... a woman. They started talking and discovered they were both going (4) .... the same stop. 'I've got an interview (5) .... a place called Murcott House,' said Liz. 'Is it (6) .... the bus stop?' 'Yes, it's not far. You walk (7) .... the park, (8) .... Forbes Road, and it's (9) .... the right, (10) .... the end,' the woman replied. 'In fact, I live (11) .... the other side of the road, just (12) .... , so I can show you the way.' When they arrived (13) .... their stop they got (14) .... together.

Appendix 1 Regular verbs: all forms

Present simple (unit 1)

Affirmative: I/you/we/they **work**. She/he/it **works**.

Question: **Do** I/you/we/they **work**? **Does** she/he/it **work**?

Negative: I/you/we/they **don't work**. She/he/it **doesn't work**.

Present continuous (unit1)

Affirmative: I **am helping**. You/we/they **are helping**. She/he/it **is helping**.

Question: **Am** I **helping**? **Are** you/we/they **helping**? **Is** she/he/it **helping**?

Negative: I'm **not helping**. You/we/they **aren't helping**. She/he/it **isn't helping**.

Past simple: regular (unit 3)

Affirmative: I/you/she/he/it/we/they **started**.

Question: **Did** I/you/she/he/it/we/they **start**?

Negative: I/you/she/he/it/we/they **didn't start**.

Past simple: irregular (unit 3)

Affirmative: I/you/she/he/it/we/they **went**.

Question: **Did** I/you/she/he/it/we/they **go**?

Negative: I/you/she/he/it/we/they **didn't go**.

Past continuous (unit 3)

Affirmative: I/she/he/it **was helping**. You/we/they **were helping**.

Question: **Was** I/she/he/it **helping**? **Were** you/we/they **helping**?

Negative: I/she/he/it **wasn't helping**. You/we/they **weren't helping**.

Past perfect (unit 4)

Affirmative: I/you/she/he/it/we/they **had left**.

Question: **Had** I/you/she/he/it/we/they **left**?

Negative: I/you/she/he/it/we/they **hadn't left**.

used to (unit 4)

Affirmative: I/you/she/he/it/we/they **used to work**.

Question: Did I/you/she/he/it/we/they **use to work**?

Negative: I/you/she/he/it/we/they **didn't use to work**.

Present perfect (unit 5)

Affirmative: I/you/we/they have left. She/he/it **has left**.

Question: Have I/you/we/they left? **Has** she/he/it **left**?

Negative: I/you/we/they haven't left. She/he/it **hasn't left**.

Present perfect continuous (unit 6)

Affirmative: I/you/we/they **have been waiting**. She/he/it **has been waiting**.

Question: **Have** I/you/we/they **been waiting**? **Has** she/he/it **been waiting**?

Negative: I/you/we/they **haven't been waiting**. She/he/it **hasn't been waiting**.

APPENDIX 1 REGULAR VERBS   239

will (unit 7)

Affirmative:	I/you/she/he/it/we/they **'ll** (= *will*) + verb.
Question:	**Will** I/you/she/he/it/we/they + verb?
Negative:	I/you/she/he/it/we/they **won't** (= *will not*) + verb.

going to (unit 7)

Affirmative:	I'm/you're/she's/he's/it's/we're/they're **going to help**.
Question:	**Am** I/Are you/Is she/Is he/Is it/Are we/Are they **going to help**?
Negative:	I'm not/You **aren't**/She **isn't**, etc **going to help**.

Future perfect (unit 8)

Affirmative:	I/you/she/he/it/we/they **will have finished**.
Question:	**Will** I/you/she/he/it/we/they **have finished**?
Negative:	I/you/she/he/it/we/they **won't have finished**.

Passive (unit 9)

Active	Passive
She helps.	She **is helped**.
She is helping.	She **is being helped**.
She helped.	She **was helped**.
She was helping.	She **was being helped**.
She had helped.	She **had been helped**.
She has helped.	She **has been helped**.
She will help.	She **will be helped**.
She will have helped.	She **will have been helped**.

Reported speech (unit 21)

Actual words spoken	Report
'I always work there.'	He said (that) he **worked** there.
'I'm working there.'	He said (that) he **was working** there.
'I took it.'	He said (that) he **took** it/**had taken** it.
'I was reading it.'	He said (that) he **had been reading** it.
'I had left by then.'	He said (that) he **had left** by then.
'I've forgotten it.'	He said (that) he **had forgotten** it.
'I've been reading'	He said (that) he **had been reading**.
'I can help.'	He said (that) he **could** help.
'I will help.'	He said (that) he **would** help.
'I may help.'	He said (that) he **might** help.
'I could/would/might go.'	He said (that) he **could/would/might** go.
'I must/should go.'	He said (that) he **must/should** go.

Infinitives

Present:	to like
Present passive:	to be liked
Past:	to have liked
Past passive:	to have been liked

Appendix 2 Irregular verbs

Verb	Past simple	Past participle
arise	arose	arisen
be	was, were	been
bear	bore	born
beat	beat	beaten
become	became	become
begin	began	begun
bend	bent	bent
bet	bet	bet/betted
bind	bound	bound
bite	bit	bitten/bit
bleed	bled	bled
blow	blew	blown
break	broke	broken
breed	bred	bred
bring	brought	brought
broadcast	broadcast	broadcast
build	built	built
burn	burnt/burned	burnt/burned
burst	burst	burst
buy	bought	bought
catch	caught	caught
choose	chose	chosen
come	came	come
cost	cost	cost
creep	crept	crept
cut	cut	cut
deal	dealt	dealt
dig	dug	dug
do	did	done
draw	drew	drawn
dream	dreamt/dreamed	dreamt/dreamed
drink	drank	drunk
drive	drove	driven
eat	ate	eaten
fall	fell	fallen
feed	fed	fed
feel	felt	felt
fight	fought	fought
find	found	found
flee	fled	fled
fly	flew	flown
forbid	forbade	forbidden
forget	forgot	forgotten
forgive	forgave	forgiven
freeze	froze	frozen
get	got	got
give	gave	given
go	went	gone
grind	ground	ground
grow	grew	grown
hang	hung	hung
have	had	had
hear	heard	heard
hide	hid	hidden
hit	hit	hit
hold	held	held
hurt	hurt	hurt
keep	kept	kept
kneel	knelt	knelt
know	knew	known
lay	laid	laid
lead	led	led
lean	leant/leaned	leant/leaned
leap	leapt/leaped	leapt/leaped
learn	learnt/learned	learnt/learned
leave	left	left

Verb	Past simple	Past participle
lend	lent	lent
let	let	let
lie	lay	lain
light	lit/lighted	lit/lighted
lose	lost	lost
make	made	made
mean	meant	meant
meet	met	met
pay	paid	paid
put	put	put
read	read	read
ride	rode	ridden
ring	rang	rung
rise	rose	risen
run	ran	run
say	said	said
see	saw	seen
seek	sought	sought
sell	sold	sold
send	sent	sent
set	set	set
sew	sewed	sewn/sewed
shake	shook	shaken
shine	shone	shone
shoot	shot	shot
show	showed	shown
shrink	shrank	shrunk
shut	shut	shut
sing	sang	sung
sit	sat	sat
sleep	slept	slept
slide	slid	slid
smell	smelt/smelled	smelt/smelled
speak	spoke	spoken
speed	sped/speeded	sped/speeded
spell	spelt/spelled	spelt/spelled
spend	spent	spent
spill	spilt/spilled	spilt/spilled
spin	spun	spun
spit	spat	spat
split	split	split
spoil	spoilt/spoiled	spoilt/spoiled
spread	spread	spread
spring	sprang	sprung
stand	stood	stood
steal	stole	stolen
stick	stuck	stuck
sting	stung	stung
strike	struck	struck
swear	swore	sworn
sweep	swept	swept
swim	swam	swum
swing	swung	swung
take	took	taken
teach	taught	taught
tear	tore	torn
tell	told	told
think	thought	thought
throw	threw	thrown
understand	understood	understood
wake	woke	woken
wear	wore	worn
weave	wove/weaved	woven/weaved
weep	wept	wept
win	won	won
wind	wound	wound

Appendix 3 Spelling

Present simple

In the third person singular, a present simple verb ends in -s. But verbs ending in *o, s, ch, sh, x* add -es.

*He go**es** He miss**es** She watch**es** He wish**es** She relax**es***

When a verb ends consonant + *y*, the *y* changes to -ies. But we do not change the -*y* after a vowel.

*hur**ry** – hurr**ies** co**py** – cop**ies***   BUT *st**ay** – sta**ys** enj**oy** – enjo**ys***

Present continuous (and adding *-ing* generally)

We leave out *e* when we add -*ing* to a verb. But we keep a double *ee*.

*decid**e** – decid**ing** writ**e** – writ**ing***   BUT *s**ee** – se**eing** agr**ee** – agr**eeing***

When a verb ends in -*ie*, we change *ie* to -*ying*. But *y* does not change.

*d**ie** – d**ying** l**ie** – l**ying***   BUT *hur**ry** – hurr**ying***

Sometimes we double a final consonant. This happens when a verb ends in 'consonant-vowel-consonant'.

*p**lan** – plan**ning** s**top** – stop**ping***   BUT *m**ee**t – meeting w**or**k – working*

Most two-syllable verbs are regular. But if the final syllable is stressed we double the last consonant.

market – marketing   BUT *beg**in** – beg**inning** dis**cuss** – dis**cussing***

Past simple (and adding *-ed* generally)

When a verb ends in consonant + **y**, we change **y** to **-ie**.

*tr**y** – tr**ied** den**y** – den**ied** hur**ry** – hurr**ied** co**py** – cop**ied***

Sometimes we double a final consonant. This happens when a verb ends in 'consonant-vowel-consonant'.

*p**lan** – plan**ned** reg**ret** – regret**ted** s**top** – stop**ped***   BUT *m**ee**t – meeting*

Plural nouns

Nouns add *s* to make a plural. But after -*ch, -sh, -ss, -x* we add -es.

*mat**ch** – mat**ches** wi**sh** – wi**shes** gla**ss** – gla**sses** bo**x** – bo**xes***

Most nouns ending in *o* add -*s*. But a few have -es.

*kilo**s** photo**s** piano**s** studio**s***   BUT *hero**es** potato**es** tomato**es***

When a noun ends in consonant + *y*, we change *y* to -ies. But we do not change *y* after a vowel.
*par**ty** – part**ies** sto**ry** – stor**ies***   BUT *da**y** – da**ys** journe**y** – journe**ys***

Adverbs

We form many adverbs from an adjective + *ly*. On a few occasions we leave out *e*.

*saf**e** – saf**ely** strang**e** – strang**ely***   BUT *tru**e** – tru**ly** whol**e** – who**lly***

When an adjective ends in consonant + *y*, we change y to -ily.

*ea**sy** – eas**ily** ang**ry** – angr**ily***

When an adjective ends in consonant + *le*, we change e to -*y*.

*proba**ble** – proba**bly** sensi**ble** – sensi**bly***

When an adjective ends in -*ic*, we add -*ally*. There is one exception.

*automat**ic** – automat**ically** romant**ic** – romant**ically***   BUT *publ**ic** – publ**icly***

The suffix *-ful* has only one *l*. When *-ly* is added for adverbs, a double *l* is formed.

success**ful** – success**fully**

ie or *ei*?

There is a useful rule: *i* before *e*, except after *c* when the sound is /i:/.

f*ie*ld   bel*ie*ve   sc*ie*nce (sound is not /i:/)   rec*ei*ve (sound is /i:/)

Exceptions to this rule are *their, weigh* and *weight*.

q and *u*

The letter *q* is always followed by *u*.

question   re**qu**ire   **qu**ality

Silent letters

Many words contain letters which do not obviously form a sound. These are sometimes called 'silent letters'. The silent letters are underlined.

bt	dou_b_t	ps	_p_sychology _p_sychiatrist
mb	plum_b_er thum_b_	sc	s_c_ience des_c_end
gn	si_g_n forei_g_n	wh	_w_ho _w_hy
kn	_k_now _k_nife	wr	_w_rong _w_rite

Same sound, different spelling

The same sound in English is often spelt using different letters. In each group below, the sound underlined is the same.

Vowels

c_o_mpany   tr_ou_ble   r_u_bbish   bl_oo_d

r_oa_d   m_o_st   h_o_me   th_ou_gh

_ea_rth   f_u_rther   w_o_rd   sh_i_rt

w_ai_t   gr_ea_t   l_a_te   w_ei_ght

n_ow_   l_ou_d   d_ow_n   f_ou_nd

Consonants

rela_ti_on   _sh_are   _s_ure   con_sc_ious   deli_ci_ous

_ch_eap   furni_t_ure   wa_tch_

_ph_one   _f_inish   lau_gh_

Same pronunciation, different spelling and meaning

These words are called 'homophones'. Common examples are:

allowed/aloud   court/caught   fare/fair   find/fined   knew/new   no/know

saw/sore   two/too   wait/weight   warn/worn   waste/waist   write/right

Words with a syllable which is not pronounced

Some words are spoken with fewer syllables than they look. This often leads to spelling problems. Examples are:

library   people   Wednesday   (spoken with 2 syllables, not 3)

temperature   vegetable   interesting   comfortable   (spoken with 3 syllables, not 4)

Nouns and verbs with *c* and *s*

advice   practice (nouns)   advise   practise (verbs)

Appendix 4   Diagram of the English verb system

Notes to the diagram

The diagram is a way of showing the whole English tense system in a simplified form. Using the diagram has three benefits:

• It can help to study the individual tenses if you see at the same time how they are all related.

• It shows that there is a pattern and logic to English verbs.

• Some people like a visual picture to help them to understand and learn.

Read through these notes and refer to the diagram at the same time:

1   The first time line shows the past simple as a completed action/situation, the present simple as referring to actions/situations that go all along the time line (facts, habits, etc), and the *will* future as a future fact or general belief.

2   The second time line shows the three continuous tenses, which all have the meaning of an action in progress (there is also an associated meaning that the action has a limited duration).

3   The third time line shows the three perfect tenses, which all have the meaning of looking back. The past perfect looks back from the past, the present perfect looks back from the present, and the future perfect looks back from the future.

4   The fourth time line shows the three perfect continuous tenses, which all have the meaning of looking back at an action in progress. Note that this is a combination of the meanings of the previous two lines.

5   The fifth time line shows the two ways to use *going to*, which both have a meaning of looking forward.

Units 1–8 of the book have a much fuller explanation of all these verb tenses.

There are some uses of English verbs that a diagram cannot show. Many of these other uses can be explained by one idea: 'the past' in English can refer to *social distance* and *distant probability* as well as its more obvious meaning of *distance in time*. So:

• Knowing that we can use the past to show social distance helps to understand why *Could I ...?* is more formal or polite than *Can I ...?*

• Knowing that we can use the past to show distant probability helps to understand why we use it for imaginary or unlikely situations (*If I **were** the Finance Minister, **I'd** ...*).

	In progress	Looking back	Looking back at an action in progress	Looking forward
Key				

Past

Present

Future

Past Simple

I **started** this job three years ago.

Present simple

I usually **leave** home around 7:30.

will **future**

I'**ll** be forty next year. Inflation **will** probably rise in the long term.

Past continuous

While I **was working** at ABC I moved from Sales to Marketing.

Present continuous

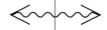

We'**re developing** two new products at the moment.

Future continuous

I'**ll be working** at our Paris office next year.

Past perfect

The merger **had** already **happened** when I joined the company.

Present perfect

I'**ve been** in this job for three years.
I'**ve finished** the report.

Future perfect

By the end of the year sales **will have improved**.

Past perfect continuous

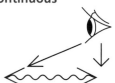

We'd **been selling** the same product for years before we changed the design.

Present perfect continuous

I've **been writing** this report all morning.

Future perfect continuous

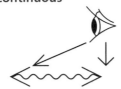

If I retire when I'm sixty I'**ll have been working** here for more than twenty years.

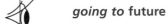

was going to

Sorry, I **was going to call** you, but I completely forgot.

going to **future**

I'm **going to ask** my boss for a pay rise. That's **going to be** difficult.

Appendix 5   British and American English

Most differences between British English and American English are matters of pronunciation, vocabulary and spelling. These are not covered here. In terms of grammar, there are few differences in formal, written English. But in informal, spoken English there are some differences. The following are the most important.

have and *have got*

In BrE *have got* is more common. In AmE *have* is more common. But both countries use both forms.

British English	**American English**
Have you got any children?	***Do you have*** any children?
I've got two children.	***I have*** two children.
I haven't got any children.	***I don't have*** any children.

Present perfect and past simple

In BrE the present perfect is used for the present result of a past action and life experience up to now (unit 5). In AmE the past simple is more common, especially with *just, already, yet, ever* and *never*.

Your taxi **has** just **arrived**.	Your taxi just **arrived**.
I**'ve** already **spoken** to her about it.	I already **spoke** to her about it.
Have you **finished** the report yet?	**Did** you **finish** the report yet?
Have you ever **eaten** sushi?	**Did** you ever **eat** sushi?
It**'s** never **done** that before.	It never **did** that before.

gotten

In AmE *gotten* is usually used as the past participle of the verb *get*.

It's **got** quite late. Maybe we should go.	It's **gotten** quite late. Maybe we should go.
He's **got** a new job.	He's **gotten** a new job.

shall and *should* for suggestions

In AmE *should* is used in suggestions where *shall* is more common in BrE.

Shall we break for lunch now?	**Should** we break for lunch now?

Question tags

Question tags (unit 16) are much less common in AmE.

You can speak French, **can't you**?	You can speak French, **right**?
I'll call a taxi, **shall I**?	I'll call a taxi, **OK**?

Adverbs

In informal AmE the *-ly* ending to adverbs is often left out. Also, in informal AmE an adjective is sometimes used in place of an adverb.

It's working **really slowly** at the moment.	It's working **real slow** at the moment.
It's working **really well** at the moment.	It's working **real good** at the moment.

can't and *mustn't*

In BrE *can't* is used to say that something is logically impossible (see unit 13). In AmE *mustn't* is also used.

I called but there's no answer. They **can't** be at home.	I called but there's no answer. They **can't/mustn't** be home.

Prepositions

Note the following differences in the use of prepositions.

British English	American English
*What did you do **at** the weekend?*	*What did you do **on** the weekend?*
*Pat is **in** the team now.*	*Pat is **on** the team now.*
*It's ten minutes **past** three.*	*It's ten minutes **past/after** three.*
*It's twenty **to** three.*	*It's twenty **to/of** three.*
*We're open from Monday **to/till** Saturday.*	*We're open from Monday **through** Saturday.*
*I looked **out of** the window.*	*I looked **out the** window.*
*I stayed **at** home **on** Saturday.*	*I stayed home Saturday.*
*He wrote **to** me about his visit.*	*He wrote me about his visit.*
I met an old colleague yesterday.	*I met **with** an old colleague yesterday.*
*I looked **round/around** the museum.*	*I looked **around** the museum.*
*She walked **towards/toward** me.*	*She walked **toward** me.*
*I haven't seen him **for** several weeks.*	*I haven't seen him **in** several weeks.*

Go and ...

In AmE the word 'and' is often left out of this structure.

*I'll **go and speak** to Mary.*	*I'll **go speak** to Mary.*

Emphatic *do*

In BrE *do* can be used with an imperative for emphasis. This is rare in AmE.

***Do** have some more coffee.*	***Have** some more coffee.*

somewhere and *someplace*

In informal AmE *someplace*, *anyplace* and *no place* can be used as well as *somewhere*, *anywhere* and *nowhere*.

*Let's find **somewhere** to eat.*	*Let's find **somewhere/someplace** to eat.*

The

Note this difference for the word 'hospital'.

*My mother is **in hospital**.*	*My mother is **in the hospital**.*

Numbers

*two hundred **and** fifty*	*two hundred fifty* OR *two hundred and fifty*

On the telephone

*Hello, is **that** Paul?*	*Hello, is **this** Paul?*

Answer key

Unit 1 Present time 1

Exercise 1

2 don't know   3 do you know   4 doesn't work   5 Yes, I do   6 she works
7 I'm writing   8 They're not replying   9 is happening   10 Are you enjoying
11 She's speaking   12 Yes, she is

Exercise 2

2 c   3 d   4 b   5 a

Exercise 3

2 a   3 b   4 a   5 a   6 b

Exercise 4

2 is   3 knows   4 'm   5 do you do   6 work   7 make   8 don't make   9 involves
10 isn't   11 supplies   12 're   13 do you often come   14 has   15 doesn't take

Exercise 5

2 a is raising / b plants
3 a is getting / b right
4 a beginning / b expectations
5 a is approaching / b market share
6 a is attracting / b attention
7 a is making / b flexible
8 a is modernising / b law

Unit 2 Present time 2

Exercise 1

2 are you doing   3 are you working   4 do you work   5 I come   6 I'm coming
7 I'm dealing with   8 I deal with   9 are you going   10 do you go

Exercise 2

2 look at   3 doesn't work   4 isn't working   5 think   6 'm thinking   7 is staying
8 stays   9 take   10 are taking   11 are   12 are being

Exercise 3

3 I don't believe it   4 ✓   5 ✓   6 I don't understand   7 contains   8 ✓

Exercise 4

2 need   3 Do you know   4 's working   5 think   6 work   7 organise
8 're expecting   9 have   10 gives   11 are your visitors staying   12 don't know
13 's dealing   14 don't work / 'm not working

Exercise 5

2 is moving   3 is looking for   4 provides   5 relies   6 is trying to
7 is investigating   8 wants

Unit 3 Past time 1

Exercise 1

2 did you feel / told   3 tell / I did   4 didn't see / got

Exercise 2

2 Did / have   3 Did / make   4 were   5 made   6 didn't take   7 Didn't / like
8 wasn't   9 sold   10 weren't   11 was   12 did / think   13 didn't have   14 bought

Exercise 3

2 went   3 were promoting / dropped   4 was working   5 called / said
6 mending / was moving

Exercise 4

2 had   3 gave   4 came   5 supplied   6 began   7 built   8 joined   9 took
10 won   11 became   12 ran   13 sold   14 cut   15 meant   16 turned
17 changed   18 made   19 grew   20 bought

Exercise 5

3 happened / called   4 was explaining / interrupted   5 were investigating / resigned
6 finished / gave   7 was waiting / called   8 was cleaning / dropped
9 found / was looking   10 arrived / told

Unit 4 Past time 2

Exercise 1

2 used to / was   3 had bought / started   4 used to have / changed
5 said / hadn't arrived   6 had locked / was   7 used to be / used to walk
8 went back / found / had taken   9 saw / knew / had met
10 was looking / turned / saw / had grown

Exercise 2

2 was sure / had set   3 called / still hadn't finished   4 had spoken / realised
5 had given / felt   6 became / had already worked   7 hadn't seen / put
8 had to / had run out of   9 had stopped / got out of   10 was / had already left

Exercise 3

2 campaigned / had campaigned   3 did the Danes reject   4 was / had been
5 was / had been   6 performed / had performed   7 had fallen   8 were / had been
9 focused / had focused   10 made   11 feared   12 wanted

Exercise 4

2 had been   3 did you get   4 finished (or had finished)   5 went
6 hadn't decided   7 were   8 was looking   9 gave   10 'd already taken
11 completed   12 sent   13 interviewed   14 felt   15 changed   16 went
17 was working   18 was becoming (or had become)   19 didn't have   20 had

Exercise 5

2 used to   3 used to / would   4 used to

Unit 5 Present and past 1

Exercise 1

2 've never seen   3 haven't complained   4 've already spent   5 Have they replied
6 haven't got   7 has gone up   8 's just left   9 have fallen   10 Have you ever taken

Exercise 2

3 a   4 b   5 a   6 b   7 b   8 a   9 b   10 a

Exercise 3

2 just   3 for   4 never   5 yet   6 always   7 since   8 ever

Exercise 4

2 has been   3 has fallen   4 have performed   5 have cut   6 have launched
7 has withdrawn   8 has had   9 has spent   10 has taken

Exercise 5

2 D – been   3 A – for   4 C – just   5 B – already   6 D – yet   7 B – gone
8 A – so far   9 C – ever   10 D – never

Unit 6 Present and past 2

Exercise 1

2 have worked here   3 has just arrived   4 have made   5 I saw   6 went
7 has been   8 was   9 left   10 has left

Exercise 2

2 operate / have set up   3 doesn't look / have come   4 Have you seen / left
5 have just met / Do you know   6 have never spoken / spoke
7 work / have been / Do you know   8 have worked / want / Have you heard

Exercise 3

2 've been phoning / 's gone   3 Have you seen / 've been looking forward
4 have you been producing / 've invested

Exercise 4

2 haven't been   3 've been   4 left   5 could   6 talked   7 's been
8 've never done   9 imagined   10 Have you ever been
11 've often thought (or often think)   12 had   13 've known   14 've had
15 have become   16 've already done   17 put   18 didn't get   19 have you put
20 've just finished

Exercise 5

2 began   3 have crashed   4 announced   5 has peaked   6 fell   7 was
8 dropped   9 released   10 have risen   11 has gained   12 has managed
13 has not hit   14 bought   15 have become

Unit 7 Future 1

Exercise 1

2 c   3 a   4 f   5 b   6 e

Exercise 2

2 We're going to open   3 it'll probably succeed   4 I'll see you then
5 what are you going to do?   6 Are you doing anything

Exercise 3

2 am meeting   3 is going to be   4 will be   5 is going to have
6 will probably replace   7 are going to test/are testing   8 am going   9 won't be

Exercise 4

2 'll tell   3 are going to be   4 're going to restructure   5 is it going to happen
6 will be   7 will probably disappear   8 're going to have (or 're having)   9 'll let
10 're going to offer   11 'll have   12 will be   13 will the new job involve
14 're going to expand   15 'll be   16 'll mean   17 'll need
18 won't be (or 're not going to be)   19 'm going to visit (or 'm visiting)
20 Will you have   21 'll give

Exercise 5

2 'll arrive   3 will be   4 're seeing   5 'll probably take   6 aren't doing   7 'll have
8 're staying   9 'm going   10 'll give

Unit 8 Future 2

Exercise 1

2 will be moving   3 will have moved   4 does your train   5 you leave
6 we've received   7 will have repaid   8 they're   9 was going to write   10 I hope
11 due to arrive   12 I hope I won't   13 I don't think I'll   14 is   15 Shall we
16 I'm just about to have

Exercise 2

2 d   3 a   4 c   5 f   6 h   7 g   8 e

Exercise 3

2 leaves/arrives   3 will be seeing   4 will have finished   5 will be playing   6 hear
7 will have started   8 will you have learnt   9 Will you be using   10 see

Exercise 4

2 B – expect   3 D – will fall   4 B – will probably   5 A – about to   6 C – is due to
7 A – will have begun   8 B – will be fighting   9 D – is planning to
10 C – happens

Exercise 5

2 were going to be   3 will be collecting   4 'll have produced
5 'll be discussing   6 will have agreed   7 happens   8 come   9 gets   10 meet
11 will have finished   12 will be sending   13 have   14 was going to have

Unit 9 Passive 1

Exercise 1

2 is seen   3 will not be finished   4 have been closed   5 are being reviewed
6 cannot be shipped

Exercise 2

3 ✓   4 by a technician   5 ✓   6 by someone

Exercise 3

3 This line was created by one of our best young designers.
4 I'm sorry, that can't be done.
5 ✗
6 This year more than a million dollars is being spent on advertising. / More than a million dollars is being spent on advertising this year.
7 This payment may not be authorised by the Accounts Department.
8 ✗

Exercise 4

2 are put   3 is distributed   4 are sent back   5 is offered   6 is analysed
7 is outsourced

Exercise 5

2 will be needed   3 are being ordered   4 are being printed   5 should be finished
6 might be needed

Unit 10 Passive 2

Exercise 1

2 b   3 a   4 a   5 b

Exercise 2

2 to grow   3 was born   4 cleaned   5 have demanded   6 assembled
7 were you born   8 to be looking

Exercise 3

2 I was given   3 were promised delivery   4 This fabric was made   5 We were sent
6 The flight was booked

Exercise 4

3 has been brought   4 has been encouraged   5 has privatised
6 have also invested   7 has been moved (or has moved)   8 have been solved

Exercise 5

2 is said to be   3 are known to be looking at   4 is believed to be developing
5 is reported to have spent   6 is thought to be/is thought to have been
7 is understood to have negotiated

Exercise 6

2 is being dealt with   3 will be delivered   4 has been included (or is included)
5 can be opened   6 are only guaranteed

Unit 11 Modals and related verbs 1

Exercise 1

2 I can come   3 be able to   4 I couldn't   5 I wasn't able to   6 Will you
7 can we do   8 to be able   9 I must speak   10 I managed to   11 I could
12 I managed to

Exercise 2

2 be able to   3 couldn't   4 could   5 can/be able to   6 can/can't
7 can't/be able to   8 be able to/can't   9 couldn't   10 could

Exercise 3

2 d   3 g   4 c   5 f   6 e   7 a   8 h

Exercise 4

2 I'll put you through   3 can I help you   4 Could you tell me   5 I'll just go
6 Could you hold   7 I'll wait   8 can't see   9 I'll need   10 Can I call you
11 could you speak   12 Can you hear   13 Could you repeat   14 I'll be on
15 I'll get back to you   16 can you send   17 I'll put one

Exercise 5

2 h   3 e   4 c   5 d   6 b   7 a   8 f   9 l   10 m   11 i   12 k   13 j   14 n

Unit 12 Modals and related verbs 2

Exercise 1

2 d 3 b 4 a 5 h 6 f 7 e 8 g 9 l 10 k 11 j 12 i

Exercise 2

1 must 2 have to 3 have to 4 must 5 have to 6 must

Exercise 3

2 D 3 I 4 I 5 S 6 I 7 D 8 I 9 I 10 S 11 I 12 I 13 D 14 I

Exercise 4

2 can 3 have to 4 should 5 can 6 can't 7 should 8 don't have to
9 have to 10 shouldn't 11 should 12 can

Exercise 5

2 had to 3 couldn't 4 had to 5 couldn't 6 should have 7 shouldn't have
8 didn't have to 9 shouldn't have 10 didn't have to

Unit 13 Modals and related verbs 3

Exercise 1

2 can't be 3 must be 4 might be 5 may not be 6 can't be 7 must be
8 should be 9 could be 10 can't 11 could be 12 must be

Exercise 2

2 d 3 b 4 a 5 f 6 g 7 e

Exercise 3

2 might 3 can't 4 must 5 might 6 can 7 can't 8 must

Exercise 4

2 a 3 d 4 c 5 c 6 b 7 a 8 d

Exercise 5

2 will definitely 3 might 4 is almost certain to 5 is unlikely to
6 definitely won't

Exercise 6

2 might have 3 can't have 4 might 5 can't 6 must have

Unit 14 Modals and related verbs 4

Exercise 1

2 Would you 3 Would you like 4 May I 5 talking 6 Shall I 7 Let me
8 Could I 9 you should 10 could you 11 I could 12 open 13 opened
14 Would you sign

Exercise 2

1 b 2 c 3 a

Exercise 3

2 f 3 b 4 a 5 c 6 e 7 h 8 i 9 g 10 l 11 k 12 m 13 j

Exercise 4

2 Would you like 3 I don't mind 4 Do you mind 5 Of course not
6 Would you like me to 7 I'd appreciate that 8 Shall we 9 Would you mind
10 I should 11 Would you like to 12 Of course

Exercise 5

Line 3 Could you spell that for me, please?
Line 5 Would you mind leaving your passport?
Line 6 Do you think you could book me an early morning call?
Line 8 I wonder if you could tell me when breakfast is?
Line 10 Would you mind if I left a message for a colleague?
Line 11 Would you like me to lend you a pen?

Unit 15 Questions 1

Exercise 1

2 say 3 Yes, I do 4 does this machine work 5 set up Microsoft
6 did Microsoft set up 7 telephoned me 8 did you telephone

Exercise 2

2 Do you work from home? 3 Can you understand German?
4 Have you already had lunch? 5 Will you be back in time for lunch?
6 Are you enjoying the conference? 7 Did you agree with her?
8 Have you ever spoken to Pierre?

Exercise 3

2 have you invited 3 are you going 4 did you park 5 are you here
6 will you have

Exercise 4

2 What have you done? 3 Where did you put the report?
4 Why do you stay here? 5 How were you feeling yesterday?
6 Where are you staying? 7 Who do you report to?
8 Whose is this bag/Whose bag is this?

Exercise 5

2 What do you do? 3 How long have you been working there?
4 What did you do before that? 5 Does your job involve much travelling?
6 Is this your first visit to Lyon? 7 When did you arrive?
8 How long are you staying for? 9 Where are you staying? 10 What's it like?

Exercise 6

2 How many 3 how much 4 how far 5 how long 6 What 7 Whose
8 how often 9 Which 10 what 11 which

Unit 16 Questions 2

Exercise 1

2 don't you 3 didn't you 4 have you 5 has he 6 will you 7 is he
8 didn't we 9 aren't I 10 shall we

Exercise 2

2 sent the fax, didn't you 3 isn't Mr Peters, is it 4 is Mr Peters, isn't it
5 have cancelled their order, haven't they 6 haven't cancelled their order, have they

Exercise 3

2 the marketing seminar is 3 we can 4 you left 5 I could

Exercise 4

2 Who did you get the information from? 3 Which funds do you invest in?
4 What was the weather like in Sweden? (or What was the weather in Sweden like?)

Exercise 5

2 shall we 3 won't he 4 shouldn't he 5 wasn't it 6 haven't they
7 wouldn't it 8 isn't it 9 have they 10 doesn't it

Exercise 6

2 b 3 a 4 b 5 a 6 b

Unit 17 Conditionals 1

Exercise 1

2 take/we'll arrive 3 worked/we'd get 4 goes/is 5 don't hurry/we'll be
6 change/give me 7 click/it won't 8 order/send 9 lend/will you return
10 hear/let me

Exercise 2

3 have/'ll deal 4 banned/wouldn't be 5 knew/'d tell 6 leave/'ll catch
7 wait/'ll give 8 had/'d love

Exercise 3

2 b   3 a   4 b

Exercise 4

2 won't   3 don't   4 will   5 is   6 unless   7 is going to be   8 be   9 Unless
10 won't   11 would   12 wouldn't   13 didn't   14 would

Exercise 5

2 do/will give   3 worked/wouldn't be   4 would happen/reoccurred
5 miss/don't seem   6 fancy/give

Unit 18 Conditionals 2

Exercise 1

2 took/might feel   3 had listened/wouldn't have made
4 we'd found/we'd have moved   5 kept/might present
6 I'd known/wouldn't have done   7 had been/could have succeeded
8 wouldn't/were

Exercise 2

2 in case   3 as long as   4 unless   5 as long as   6 in case   7 when   8 unless

Exercise 3

2 had   3 could stay   4 enjoy   5 had taken   6 knew   7 could type
8 didn't interrupt   9 had   10 have   11 could do   12 hadn't bought

Exercise 4

2 can   3 As long as   4 'd have   5 'd   6 wouldn't have   7 'd   8 would/have
9 in case   10 unless   11 'll   12 unless

Exercise 5

2 a   3 d   4 c   5 g   6 h   7 e   8 f

Unit 19 Verb + *-ing* or infinitive 1

Exercise 1

2 going   3 to use   4 spending   5 to close down   6 to deliver   7 calling
8 losing   9 to prepare   10 to be   11 waiting   12 to sign   13 postponing

Exercise 2

2 to recognise   3 advertising   4 to receive   5 writing   6 to speak   7 making
8 thinking   9 to fly   10 to help

Exercise 3

2 persuade him to   3 remind me to   4 help you to   5 expect her to
6 encouraged me to   7 forced us to

Exercise 4

2 losing   3 to crash   4 to do   5 to fix   6 to come   7 calling   8 to wait
9 to do   10 asking   11 to type

Exercise 5

2 talking   3 to pay   4 worrying   5 to be   6 pretending   7 referring   8 to show
9 to take   10 receiving

Unit 20 Verb + *-ing* or infinitive 2

Exercise 1

2 to meet   3 meeting   4 being   5 to make   6 to speak   7 saying   8 to open
9 opening   10 giving   11 to look at   12 to announce   13 quitting   14 selling
15 to describe

Exercise 2

1 a   2 b   3 d   4 c

Exercise 3

2 being   3 to be   4 to be   5 being   6 being

Exercise 4

2 to book   3 to start   4 to come   5 to go   6 missing   7 to give   8 working
9 to have   10 to join   11 working   12 getting (or to get)   13 missing out
14 to have   15 being   16 taking   17 finishing (or to finish)

Exercise 5

2 to take   3 hearing   4 to return   5 to risk   6 buying   7 returning
8 to accept   9 taking   10 to copy   11 being   12 to bring   13 thinking
14 behaving   15 to train   16 to deal

Unit 21 Reported speech 1

Exercise 1

2 He'll be back after lunch   3 She's going to contact the printers
4 I want to make a phone call   5 I'm meeting the bank manager at eleven
6 I found out about the problem a long time ago
7 I have to be back in the office by three thirty   8 I'll let you know

Exercise 2

2 there/me   3 they'd/our/before   4 she/right then

Exercise 3

2 (that) he'd read the report and (that) he didn't understand section   4
3 he finished his presentation he was going to have a drink
4 (that) she was preparing the figures but (that) she wouldn't be long
5 (that) she liked playing tennis but (that) she didn't do it very often
6 (that) she was going to visit their Polish subsidiary but (that) she wasn't sure when

Exercise 4

2 P/TC   3 P/ST   4 P/TC   5 I   6 P/TC   7 P/TC   8 I   9 P/ST   10 P/TC

Exercise 5

2 his   3 he'd sent   4 the day before   5 the   6 they've   7 me   8 there   9 was
10 before   11 had gone   12 was   13 that   14 me

Unit 22 Reported speech 2

Exercise 1

2 say   3 tell   4 said   5 told/said   6 said/said   7 said/told   8 said to/tell

Exercise 2

2 e   3 b   4 a   5 d   6 k   7 i   8 f   9 g   10 l   11 h   12 j

Exercise 3

2 what the letters 'URL' meant
3 if/whether I had prepared the figures
4 when her birthday was
5 if/whether he had remembered (or he remembered) to back up the file
6 why I had turned off the air conditioning
7 if/whether I spoke Italian
8 how much he had paid (or he paid) for his car

Exercise 4

2 suggested   3 proposed   4 agreed   5 decided

Exercise 5

2 told them   3 to listen   4 said   5 it would   6 take   7 setting up   8 not to say
9 to chair   10 should report   11 reminded them that   12 to meet

Unit 23 Phrasal verbs 1

Exercise 1

2 b   3 d   4 a   5 b   6 d

Exercise 2

2 hold (or hang) *on*   3 fill *in*   4 go (or carry) *on*   5 give *up*   6 deal *with*
7 pick *up*   8 go (or come) *back*   9 take *up*   10 look *after*

Exercise 3

2 look up the information/look the information up/look it up
3 keep down our costs/keep our costs down/keep them down
4 do without my mobile phone/do without it
5 turned down the idea/turned the idea down/turned it down
6 sort out the problem/sort the problem out/sort it out

Exercise 4

2 drop off   3 turn up   4 checking in   5 get by   6 sort out   7 draw up
8 looking through   9 call on   10 ring up   11 keep down   12 find out
13 breaking down   14 print out   15 back up

Exercise 5

2 back   3 off   4 down   5 through   6 on   7 out   8 over

Unit 24 Phrasal verbs 2

Exercise 1

2 back to   3 down on   4 out of   5 on to   6 in with   7 up with   8 up to

Exercise 2

2 e   3 a   4 c   5 b

Exercise 3

2 a   3 c   4 a   5 c   6 b

Exercise 4

2 up   3 off   4 behind   5 of   6 back   7 with   8 on   9 on   10 through
11 to   12 out   13 in   14 with

Exercise 5

2 get through   3 call/back   4 hold on   5 go ahead   6 rang/up   7 look into
8 get back to   9 speak up   10 breaking up   11 cut off   12 sort/out   13 go over

Unit 25 Verbs and objects

Exercise 1

2 ✓   3 ✗   4 ✓   5 ✗   6 ✗   7 ✓   8 ✗   9 ✓   10 ✗

Exercise 2

3 ✓   4 ✗   5 ✗   6 ✓   7 ✗   8 ✓   9 ✓   10 ✗   11 ✓   12 ✗   13 ✗   14 ✓

Exercise 3

2 a) I   2b) T / the marketing department
3 a) T / this hotel   3b) I
4 a) T / her job   4b) I
5 a) I   5b) T / my family and friends
6 a) I   6b) T / my laptop
7 a) T / Dr Goschel   7b) I
8 a) I   8b) T / olives

Exercise 4

2 suggest to them   3 promised me   4 explained to them   5 causing us problems
6 the chicken to you   7 the fault to the technician   8 sold them
9 the whole situation to them   10 told me   11 introduce you to Joseph Lee
12 showed the visitors

Exercise 5

2 lent Jackie the article about marketing
3 sent them an email yesterday
4 sent an email to their customer services department yesterday
5 sold him the display model that's been in the window
6 sold the display model to a woman who came in this morning
7 gave her my report this morning
8 gave my report to her secretary this morning

Exercise 6

2 to/for   3 for/to   4 to/for   5 for/to   6 to/for   7 to/for   8 to/for

Unit 26 The *-ing* form

Exercise 1

2 a   3 c   4 b   5 g   6 f   7 e   8 h

Exercise 2

Noun: 3, 5, 6, 8
Adjective: 4, 7

Exercise 3

2 meeting   3 shopping   4 interesting/confusing   5 wearing/lasting
6 welcoming   7 cutting   8 selling

Exercise 4

2 meet   3 take   4 taking   5 working   6 work

Exercise 5

2 of being   3 by taking over   4 Before going   5 instead of using
6 without increasing

Exercise 6

2 ~~who is~~   3 ~~that is~~   4 ~~who are~~

Exercise 7

2 c   3 a   4 e   5 f   6 d

Exercise 8

3 hoping that the market would go up
4 Not being an experienced negotiator
5 Assuming she wouldn't mind
6 not knowing it would create so many problems

Unit 27 *make/do/get/have*

Exercise 1

2 did   3 make   4 do/make   5 do   6 do/make   7 make   8 made/do
9 did/made   10 did/made   11 make/do   12 do

Exercise 2

2 a   3 f   4 b   5 e   6 c   7 h   8 g

Exercise 3

3 ✗   4 ✓   5 ✓   6 ✗

Exercise 4

sentence numbers: 2, 3, 6

Exercise 5

2 holiday   3 lunch   4 chance/look   5 time   6 alternative   7 break
8 appointment   9 the fish   10 doubt   11 difficulty   12 headache/day off
13 word   14 go   15 conversation

Exercise 6

2 get   3 doing   4 make   5 made   6 doing   7 got   8 made   9 done   10 make
11 do   12 got   13 made   14 got   15 made   16 do   17 do   18 got   19 made

Unit 28 Relative clauses 1

Exercise 1

2 ND   3 ND   4 D   5 D   6 ND

Exercise 2

2 that   3 who   4 whose   5 who   6 who   7 whose   8 that   9 who   10 who
11 who   12 whose

Exercise 3

3 (which)   4 ✓   5 (that)   6 ✓   7 ✓   8 (who)   9 ✓   10 (that)

Exercise 4

2 have been waiting for   3 stayed at   4 usually deal with
5 choose the samples from   6 am responsible for

Exercise 5

2 P   3 P   4 I   5 P   6 P   7 I   8 P   9 I   10 P   11 P   12 P

Exercise 6

1 a–T   b–F   c–T   d–F
2 a–T   b–F   c–T   d–F
3 a–T   b–F   c–F   d–F

Unit 29 Relative clauses 2

Exercise 1

2 who could be a useful contact for you
3 whose CV is on your desk
4 who is coming next week
5 that Tom took me to
6 whose presentation I heard
7 that I was telling you about
8 where they're going to build the new factory

Exercise 2

3 ✓   4 it   5 they   6 it   7 ✓   8 it

Exercise 3

2 whose   3 who   4 whom   5 that   6 that   7 What   8 that   9 where   10 that

Exercise 4

3 ✓   4 who   5 what   6 which   7 ✓   8 which   9 ✓   10 What   11 ✓   12 what

Exercise 5

 2 which was the largest luxury goods company in the world
 3 which would decide the future of the industry
 4 who he could trust
 5 who was the chief financial officer
 6 which was meant to be a message for Arnault
 7 which represented 34% of Gucci's total stock
 8 who Gucci had been looking for
 9 who was the head of a non-food retail group called PPR
10 which was a 42% stake in Gucci

Unit 30 Countable and uncountable nouns

Exercise 1

2 Are/many   3 Is/much   4 How much   5 are   6 are   7 equipment   8 machines
9 a piece of equipment   10 a machine   11 some/was   12 much   13 is/some
14 some/any   15 any

Exercise 2

2 some   3 much   4 many   5 an   6 some   7 many   8 much   9 much   10 many
11 some   12 much

Exercise 3

2a) G   2b) S   3a) S   3b) G   4a) S   4b) G

Exercise 4

car: There's a; It's a
food: There's some; There's
clothes: I haven't got many; There are some; They're
work: I haven't got much; There is some; There's
job: I haven't got a; There's a; It's a
money: I haven't got much; There is some; There's
dollars: I haven't got many; There are some; They're
expenses: I haven't got many; There are some; They're
idea: I haven't got much; I haven't got an; There is an; It's an

Exercise 5

2 a   3 d   4 f   5 c   6 e

Exercise 6

2 is   3 some   4 an   5 person   6 a   7 much   8 an   9 some   10 a   11 much
12 progress   13 is   14 a lot of   15 information   16 an

Unit 31 Pronouns

Exercise 1

2 no one   3 anything   4 anyone   5 Something   6 someone   7 everyone
8 anything   9 everything   10 Nothing

Exercise 2

2 nothing   3 anything   4 Someone   5 anywhere   6 something   7 someone
8 anything   9 anything   10 No one

Exercise 3

2 enjoyed ourselves   3 taught himself/is teaching himself   4 hurt yourself
5 express herself   6 help yourselves   7 prepare yourself   8 introduce myself
9 blame yourself   10 make yourselves

Exercise 4

2 felt/relaxed   3 anytime, anywhere   4 remember/worry   5 every one
6 has/their   7 anywhere   8 somewhere   9 themselves   10 each other

Exercise 5

2 somewhere   3 anywhere   4 someone   5 Everyone   6 Anyone   7 something
8 everything   9 anything

Exercise 6

3 help yourself   4 met   5 introduce yourself   6 change   7 ask myself   8 relax

Unit 32 Determiners

Exercise 1

2 a few of them   3 some of them   4 many of them   5 most of them
6 all of them

Exercise 2

2 each   3 Not one   4 Some of   5 Some   6 either   7 Our customers each
8 both days   9 All of   10 any   11 Everything   12 a mobile phone each
13 Every option has been   14 everything

Exercise 3

2 no/either   3 neither   4 All   5 every/all   6 each   7 every   8 none   9 any
10 both   11 either   12 each

Exercise 4

2 Every participant   3 Not a single person   4 Neither idea/Neither of the ideas
5 Some of the audience didn't   6 None of my colleagues   7 All we want is
8 weren't any documents   9 Neither hotel was/Neither of the hotels were
10 Both the proposals are/Both of the proposals are
11 None of these items are   12 none at all

Exercise 5

2 A – each one   3 C – Neither company   4 A – all its   5 C – They are both
6 C – every   7 B – most of   8 C – everything

Unit 33 Possessives and compound nouns

Exercise 1

2 your   3 yours   4 yours   5 our own   6 ourselves   7 mine   8 My   9 her   10 its

Exercise 2

2 Alice's friend's name's Bill. He's one of Merrill Lynch's top analysts.
3 Toyota's deal on its company cars is better than ours.
4 I went to my doctor's and he's computerised all the patients' records.
5 It's important to recognise that every company has its own particular culture, however ...
6 My boss's PA reads all the customers' letters.
7 Look at those two Mercedes. One's our director's and the other's a visitor's.

Exercise 3

 2 staff meeting/sales forecast   3 credit card/department store
 4 Internet access/summer sale   5 inflation figures/price range
 6 market survey/rush hour   7 information technology/car keys
 8 shop assistant/power failure   9 shopfloor worker/working lunch
10 insurance contract/bank loan   11 product features/production costs
12 market leader/marketing budget

Exercise 4

2 lack of   3 error of   4 range of   5 level of   6 piece of   7 stroke of   8 flood of
9 method of   10 pace of

Exercise 5

2 my pen   3 mine   4 James's documents   5 colleague of hers   6 is your boss's
7 an expert in company   8 shows the sales figures   9 customer of ours
10 a management training

Exercise 6

2 ~~check~~   3 ~~offer~~   4 ~~process~~   5 ~~output~~   6 ~~share~~   7 line   8 ~~market~~   9 ~~trend~~
10 ~~decision~~

Unit 34 Articles 1

Exercise 1

2 an/the   3 a/The   4 a   5 the/the   6 The/a   7 a   8 a   9 a   10 an/the
11 an/the other   12 the/the   13 the   14 The Portuguese

Exercise 2

2 a   3 an/–   4 –/–   5 a/–   6 –   7 a/a   8 –/a   9 an/–   10 a/a

Exercise 3

2 –/a   3 a/–/the   4 –/the   5 –/the/a   6 –   7 a/the   8 the/a/the   9 –/–
10 A/an/a   11 a/the   12 –

Exercise 4

2 the   3 –   4 –   5 a   6 a   7 The   8 –   9 the   10 the   11 –   12 –   13 The
14 the   15 an   16 the   17 the   18 –   19 a   20 the   21 –

Exercise 5

4 a   5 –   6 –   7 –   8 the   9 a   10 –   11 –   12 an   13 the   14 –   15 –
16 the   17 –   18 a   19 the   20 –   21 a   22 a   23 the   24 the   25 –

Unit 35 Articles 2

Exercise 1

2 Crete   3 hospital/school   4 Heathrow/underground
5 Helmut Kohl/the Chancellor/Germany
6 the Alps/Mont Blanc   7 the near future   8 home
9 New York/the United States   10 lunch
11 Deutsche Bank/the City of London/the start   12 university
13 Lake Windermere/the Lake District/the north-west/England   14 Bond Street
15 the poor   16 the UK/the south-east/Canterbury Cathedral   17 court
18 John/work/the moment   19 Italy/car   20 The Danube/Central Europe

Exercise 2

2a) The   2b) –   3a) –   3b) The   4a) –   4b) the   5a) The   5b) –
6a) –   6b) The   7a) –   7b) The

Exercise 3

2 at   3 the end of the   4 in the   5 at   6 the station on   7 at   8 at

Exercise 4

2 the   3 the   4 The   5 the   6 –   7 –   8 –   9 The   10 –   11 –   12 –   13 –
14 –   15 the   16 the   17 the   18 –   19 the   20 the   21 – (or the)   22 the
23 the   24 the   25 – (or the)   26 the   27 the   28 the   29 –   30 –   31 the
32 the   33 the   34 the   35 the   36 the   37 –   38 the   39 the   40 –

Unit 36 Adjectives and adverbs

Exercise 1

2 improved dramatically   3 has dropped significantly   4 pause briefly   5 have
improved steadily   6 recovered slowly   7 has risen gradually
8 has grown considerably

Exercise 2

2 bored   3 boring   4 exciting   5 worried   6 large   7 enormous   8 bad
9 freezing

Exercise 3

2 heavily promoted   3 badly designed   4 extremely helpful
5 easily recognisable   6 unexpectedly delayed   7 completely illegal
8 quite late

Exercise 4

2 two square wooden cartons
3 an amazing new software package
4 a difficult three-month transition period
5 high-quality Taiwanese computer chips
6 a well-planned investment strategy
7 cheap high-speed Internet access
8 a revolutionary new handheld computer
9 a wonderful new washing powder
10 awful cheap plastic souvenirs

Exercise 5

2 late – adv.   3 late – adj.   4 well – adv.   5 hardly – adv.   6 good – adj.
7 hard – adj.   8 hard – adv.   9 fast – adv.   10 fast – adj.

Exercise 6

2 conventional   3 rapidly   4 properly   5 good   6 good   7 well   8 badly   9 easy
10 slow   11 directly   12 easy   13 cheap   14 quickly   15 right   16 huge

Unit 37 Comparing 1

Exercise 1

2 the most profitable   3 recent   4 than   5 worse   6 best   7 as long as   8 worse
9 longer than   10 further

Exercise 2

2 smaller than   3 less interesting than/not as interesting as   4 the hottest
5 better than   6 as good as   7 more difficult   8 as large as   9 worse than
10 the worst

Exercise 3

2 as/as   3 than/does   4 least   5 best   6 most   7 than/had   8 as/as   9 just/as
10 not/as

Exercise 4

2 best investment analyst
3 more sections of the report than me
4 as long as I expected/as long as I'd expected
5 bigger than ours
6 most important presentation I have ever given
7 as interesting as
8 eat as much as
9 the best communication skills
10 the most interesting people I have ever met

Exercise 5

2 lower   3 better   4 more attractive   5 riskiest   6 greater   7 worst
8 more sensible   9 easier   10 most aggressive   11 higher   12 best
13 larger   14 nearer

Unit 38 Comparing 2

Exercise 1

2 as   3 the better   4 more and more   5 the second largest   6 slightly   7 fastest
8 more and more expensive   9 more quickly   10 much better   11 the same as
12 the best

Exercise 2

a little/a bit   far/much   more or less/roughly   just/exactly
2 nearly/virtually   3 just/exactly   4 a little/a bit   5 far/much

Exercise 3

2 the fastest growing   3 the most cleverly designed   4 best selling
5 the least known   6 the most rapidly changing

Exercise 4

2 roughly the same   3 slightly less   4 almost as many   5 almost as much
6 considerably less   7 more than twice   8 by far   9 not nearly   10 a lot

Exercise 5

2 roughly the same   3 considerably more   4 similar   5 different   6 a lot
7 by far   8 twice as many   9 twice as much   10 a little

Unit 39 Adverbs of degree

Exercise 1

2 c   3 d   4 a   5 g   6 f   7 h   8 e

Exercise 2

2 so few   3 too much   4 such   5 so   6 too much   7 so much   8 so many
9 so little   10 too short   11 tall enough   12 enough money

Exercise 3

2 so much   3 so many   4 so few   5 so little   6 too   7 such   8 enough   9 so
10 too   11 so   12 such

Exercise 4

2a) so successful that   2b) such a success that
3a) so well that   3b) such a good order processing system that
4a) such large bank debts that   4b) so large that
5a) so fast that   5b) such a fast Internet connection that

Exercise 5

2 was such a difficult problem   3 were too few copies   4 too little space
5 presentation was so good   6 didn't sell enough units   7 is so busy
8 so many brochures that   9 too little time

Unit 40 Time adverbs

Exercise 1

2 at   3 at   4 on   5 in   6 at   7 on   8 in   9 in   10 on   11 on   12 in   13 at
14 at   15 on   16 at

Exercise 2

2 a   3 k   4 m   5 f   6 j   7 e   8 i   9 b   10 l   11 n   12 h   13 d   14 c

Exercise 3

2 next week   3 the day after tomorrow   4 at night   5 on time   6 in time   7 for
8 during   9 two years ago   10 before   11 During   12 While   13 while
14 during   15 by   16 until   17 then   18 afterwards   19 After   20 later

Exercise 4

2 Q: How long have you had a subsidiary in Portugal? A: Since 1998.
3 Q: How long has Peter Middelhoff been CEO? A: Since the start of the year.
4 Q: How long has your company had the same logo? A: For twenty years.
5 Q: How long have you owned your Telekom shares? A: Since privatisation.
6 Q: How long have you known Alex Scott? A: For a long time.
7 Q: How long have you lived in this town? A: Since I was born.

Exercise 5

2 ago   3 for   4 during   5 after   6 before   7 for   8 since   9 for   10 while
11 since   12 ago   13 Before   14 while   15 afterwards   16 after

Unit 41 Linking words 1

Exercise 1

2 Although   3 despite   4 while   5 Whereas   6 though   7 but   8 whereas
9 anyway   10 In spite of   11 although   12 Although

Exercise 2

1b) Paula visited the Madrid office as well as the Barcelona office.
2a) We can handle the transport arrangements and also the insurance.
2b) We can handle both the transport arrangements and the insurance.
3a) I want the sales figures for October and November as well.
3b) I want the sales figures for October as well as November.
4a) We're setting up offices in Peru and also (in) Ecuador.
4b) We're setting up offices in Peru and (in) Ecuador too.

Exercise 3

2 but   3 still   4 though   5 In spite of   6 whereas   7 anyway

Exercise 4

2a) In spite of my headache I still went to the meeting./In spite of having a
headache I still went to the meeting.
2b) I had a headache, but I still went to the meeting.
3a) Some analysts think that stocks will fall in value, whereas others disagree.
3b) Although some analysts think that stocks will fall in value, others disagree.
4a) Despite the difficulties in the negotiations, we won the contract.
4b) Even though there were difficulties in the negotiations, we won the contract.
5a) Whereas oil prices rose slightly last year, this year they have gone down.
5b) Oil prices rose slightly last year, although this year they have gone down.
6a) I've written twice, yet I still haven't received a reply.
6b) Despite writing twice, I still haven't received a reply. (or Despite having written
twice, I still haven't received a reply.)
7a) Although he didn't use any notes, he gave an excellent presentation.
7b) He didn't use any notes. He gave an excellent presentation, though.

Exercise 5

2 also   3 despite   4 although   5 as well   6 Both   7 whereas   8 as well as
9 yet   10 although   11 despite   12 Although

Unit 42 Linking words 2

Exercise 1

2 so I sent her a copy of the minutes.
3 because I had a lot of paperwork to finish.
4 so I have to go now.
5 he doesn't know, I'll ask someone else.

Exercise 2

2 so   3 so that   4 in order to   5 for   6 can   7 could   8 wouldn't   9 won't
10 to see

Exercise 3

3 a   4 b   5 b   6 a   7 a   8 b   9 b   10 a   11 a   12 b   13 a   14 b

Exercise 4

2 I   3 P   4 I   5 P   6 I   7 P   8 P   9 I   10 P

Exercise 5

2 as/like   3 like   4 as/like   5 like   6 as   7 like   8 as/like

Exercise 6

2 to   3 like   4 because   5 so that   6 so   7 as if   8 for   9 like   10 to
11 so as not to worry   12 as   13 like   14 so that   15 to   16 like

Unit 43 Developing an argument 1

Exercise 1

2 hand   3 As a rule   4 except   5 either   6 As a matter of fact   7 On the whole
8 On the other hand   9 Besides   10 such as   11 for example   12 instead of

Exercise 2

2 except   3 therefore   4 instead   5 In general   6 such as   7 Either
8 As well as this   9 Nevertheless   10 So

Exercise 3

In general, taking an MBA is a good idea for an ambitious young professional,
however you do have to make some sacrifices. You miss out on two years'
valuable work experience, for example, and it can be very expensive.

Exercise 4

2 B – First of all   3 A – as well as   4 D – Secondly   5 C – as a result
6 A – However   7 B – In addition   8 D – for example   9 A – such as
10 B – in conclusion

Exercise 5

2 In addition 3 In fact 4 Therefore 5 As a rule 6 however 7 In conclusion
8 instead of

Unit 44 Developing an argument 2

Exercise 1

2 From our point of view 3 Apparently 4 It seems that 5 Fortunately 6 Actually
7 Moving on to 8 in the end 9 at last 10 Unless 11 unless 12 otherwise
13 eg 14 ie

Exercise 2

2 Of course 3 Unfortunately 4 By the way 5 To be frank 6 After all
7 Apparently 8 Anyway 9 Above all 10 or rather

Exercise 3

2 in particular 3 Clearly 4 To give an example 5 except for
6 As far as the general public is concerned 7 Furthermore 8 eventually
9 As a matter of fact 10 such as 11 As a result 12 On the other hand
13 or rather 14 In general 15 although 16 to sum up

Exercise 4

2 As a matter of fact 3 As far as ... is concerned 4 To give an example
5 In general 6 Clearly 7 Furthermore 8 As a result 9 On the other hand
10 to sum up 11 except for 12 although 13 eventually 14 or rather
15 in particular

Unit 45 Prepositions of place

Exercise 1

2 on 3 above/below 4 in 5 on 6 opposite 7 at 8 in 9 on 10 by
11 next to 12 in 13 over 14 near 15 in 16 on 17 at 18 in 19 near
20 by

Exercise 2

2 on 3 on 4 in 5 on 6 at/in 7 in/on 8 at 9 on 10 on 11 in/on 12 At
13 in 14 in 15 in/at 16 in 17 at 18 on/in 19 at 20 In

Exercise 3

2 towards 3 at 4 over 5 past 6 on 7 In 8 through 9 at 10 on
11 in front of 12 by

Exercise 4

2 at 3 in 4 on 5 next 6 in 7 in 8 on 9 opposite 10 in 11 to 12 at

Unit 46 Verb + preposition

Exercise 1

2 believe in 3 wait for 4 lead to 5 depend on 6 know about 7 suffer from
8 approve of

Exercise 2

2 with 3 of 4 about 5 for 6 about 7 into 8 for 9 on 10 from 11 in
12 on

Exercise 3

2 to/about 3 from 4 of 5 of 6 with/about 7 from 8 in 9 for
10 to/about 11 at 12 for

Exercise 4

2 belong to 3 listen to 4 explain/to 5 agreed with 6 apply for 7 rely on
8 apologised for 9 Remind/about 10 hoping for 11 heard from
12 comply with 13 insist on 14 qualify for

Exercise 5

2 with 3 about 4 from 5 for 6 in 7 for 8 against 9 from 10 from
11 for 12 for 13 on 14 on 15 to 16 for 17 from 18 about 19 of
20 from 21 in 22 of

Unit 47 Adjective + preposition

Exercise 1

2 h 3 d 4 b 5 j 6 a 7 i 8 c 9 f 10 e

Exercise 2

2 safe from 3 attached to 4 dependent on 5 serious about 6 involved in
7 tired of 8 suitable for

Exercise 3

2 with 3 for 4 about 5 with 6 about 7 for 8 for 9 for 10 with 11 at
12 to 13 for 14 for

Exercise 4

2 to Adrian 3 to driving on the left 4 for the meeting
5 interested in archaeology 6 about what he said 7 at mathematics
8 about the advertising campaign 9 of people 10 on her idea

Exercise 5

2 attached 3 dependent 4 prepared 5 capable 6 useful 7 similar
8 involved 9 right 10 opposed 11 compatible 12 lacking 13 late
14 covered

Unit 48 Noun + preposition

Exercise 1

2 for 3 with 4 between 5 with 6 in/of 7 between 8 to 9 in/of 10 for

Exercise 2

2 price of 3 advantage of 4 focus on 5 payment for 6 objection to
7 involvement in 8 suitability for

Exercise 3

2 for/up 3 in/by 4 for/on 5 in/On 6 In 7 on/for 8 on/by 9 In/in
10 on/on/on

Exercise 4

2 f 3 h 4 c 5 j 6 i 7 d 8 e 9 l 10 b 11 k 12 g

Exercise 5

2 In 3 for 4 of 5 with 6 in 7 of 8 out 9 in 10 In 11 for 12 in 13 for
14 up 15 in 16 for 17 at 18 about

Unit 49 Trends, graphs and figures

Exercise 1

2 one thousand, two hundred and thirty
3 twelve thousand, three hundred
4 twelve thousand and thirty
5 twelve thousand, three hundred and thirty
6 one hundred and twenty thousand, three hundred
7 one hundred and twenty three thousand
8 one hundred and twenty three thousand, three hundred and thirty
9 one million, two hundred and thirty thousand

Exercise 2

2 increased/slightly 3 in 4 by 5 recovered 6 hit/low/recovered/at
7 reached/peak 8 slowly/by 9 slow/of 10 to 11 rose/fell 12 raised/cut

Exercise 3

2 However 3 although 4 in spite of 5 Therefore 6 so 7 because of
8 because

Exercise 4

2 f 3 a 4 b 5 e 6 d

Exercise 5

1 much less than 50%
2a almost 50%   2b a little under 50%
3a around 50%   3b about 50%
4a exactly 50%   4b precisely 50%
5a a little over 50%   5b slightly more than 50%
6 considerably more than 50%

Exercise 6

2 flat   3 although   4 because   5 recovery   6 peak   7 up   8 by   9 million
10 pounds   11 on   12 cut   13 significantly   14 However   15 half   16 rose
17 sharply   18 to   19 over   20 in

Unit 50 Punctuation

Exercise 1

2 Last February I met Mary Carpenter for the first time.
3 Tim works in the north of France, about 50 kilometres from Paris.
4 My favourite Hitchcock film is 'Strangers on a Train'.
5 Carol works as an office manager in a marketing consultancy.
6 I've just received the report published last May by the World Trade Organization.
7 On Christmas Day we'll go to my parents' house near Brighton in Sussex.
8 I think Jean is going to be interviewing the Deputy Finance Minister next week.

Exercise 2

2 c   3 b   4 a   5 c   6 a   7 a   8 c

Exercise 3

2 I'm sorry Kim, he said the goods would arrive on time, but they didn't.
3 Jack said that we should tear up the plans, forget about it, and start again.
4 When I saw my boss, I went up to him, and said, 'Can I have Friday off, please?'
5 'On the other hand, we could use a different firm, couldn't we?' said François.
6 'Hello, Alan,' said Tina, 'How was the meeting yesterday?'
7 If I were you, I'd ask for some help, or perhaps look at the manual again.
8 Oil shares did well last week: Standard Oil was up 2%, Exxon was up 1.8%, and the Anglo-Dutch group Shell gained 2.3%.

Exercise 4

Dear Angela, (optional comma)

It was great to hear from you, and thanks for the photo of everyone on the MBA course. It brings back happy memories, and I'm sure you'll agree that we were lucky to have such interesting people in our year.

I'm glad that you were successful in your search for a job in public relations. I've not been so lucky so far, I'm afraid. I applied for a job at the beginning of the month in the finance department of a large Swiss-owned pharmaceutical company. I'd be very well qualified for the job, but I still haven't heard anything. If I don't get an answer soon, I'll try writing again. Actually, if I don't hear anything, I won't be too disappointed because it seems their company isn't doing too well at the moment, and I don't think there'd be many opportunities for promotion.

I've been meaning to email you for ages about something else. Do you by any chance have Alison and Jim's address? I'm planning on visiting their city in the autumn and I'd like to call in and see them. What about you? Do you have any plans to come here? It would be wonderful to see you again, and you know you're welcome to stay whenever you want.

Well, that's all for now. I'm going away tomorrow for a few days to visit my parents, and I've got to pack and get ready. Thanks again for the photo, and it was so nice to hear from you again.

All the best, (optional comma)

Ellen

Test 1

Exercise 1

3 don't understand   4 'm talking   5 isn't selling   6 know   7 'm staying
8 Are you offering/Do you offer   9 makes   10 do you usually arrive
11 's coming   12 comes

Exercise 2

b) PC   c) PC   d) PS   e) PS   f) PC   g) PS   h) PC
2 a   3 e   4 c   5 g   6 f   7 h   8 d

Exercise 3

Present simple: always, as soon as, before, every day, hardly ever, never, most of the time, next time, normally, occasionally, often, rarely, sometimes, twice a year, until, usually, when
Present continuous: at the moment, now, nowadays, these days

Exercise 4

1 I usually have lunch at about one o'clock.   2 Lunch is often just a sandwich.
3 I visit Paris Head Office from time to time.
4 I am hardly ever late in the morning.   5 I hardly ever take the train to work.
6 I prepare a sales report once a month.   7 I never miss a Board meeting.
8 I am never late for a Board meeting.

Exercise 5

3 contain   4 ✓   5 ✓   6 We own   7 I think   8 ✓   9 it seems   10 ✓   11 ✓
12 we have

Exercise 6

1 goes up/demand   2 is falling/means   3 Are you waiting/don't think
4 do our customers want/seems   5 hope/knows/is doing
6 do you mean/don't understand   7 are you saying/Do you want
8 Does your chicken taste/depends/is working

Test 2

Exercise 1

1 became   2 began   3 broke   4 brought   5 bought   6 chose   7 ate   8 fell
9 found   10 forgot   11 grew   12 kept   13 led   14 lent   15 met   16 paid
17 sent   18 shut   19 spent   20 understood

Exercise 2

2 used to claim   3 crashed/was printing out   4 was taking off/started
5 wanted/chose   6 used to have/combined   7 arrived/was waiting
8 knocked/came   9 were arguing/lost   10 was/visited

Exercise 3

2 didn't use   3 I hadn't forgotten   4 used to produce   5 I'd read (or seen)
6 had already left   7 used to go skiing/used to ski   8 the meeting had finished

Exercise 4

2 When   3 at   4 in   5 on   6 When   7 While/When   8 in   9 at   10 when
11 at   12 in

Exercise 5

2 got/had stopped   3 did you find out/had got   4 joined/had worked
5 sent/had already spoken   6 had always suspected/wasn't

Exercise 6

3 had been waiting   4 had already heard   5 had been rising   6 hadn't finished
7 had never met   8 had been looking   9 had seen   10 had been losing

Test 3

Exercise 1

2 had   3 have had   4 I've left   5 I left   6 have you been working
7 are you going   8 haven't paid   9 didn't pay   10 did you last see
11 Have you seen her?

ANSWER KEY 259

Exercise 2

2 started 3 been writing 4 did you arrive 5 Have you
6 has been organising/has organised 7 for three months
8 have lived/have been living 9 I've been waiting here 10 I haven't given
11 I've been waiting 12 have you worked/have you been working

Exercise 3

2 always 3 already 4 ever 5 just 6 yet 7 for 8 never 9 often 10 So far

Exercise 4

2 've never been 3 My wallet has 4 've just seen 5 haven't finished (or writing)
6 working here for 7 ever been to Latin America (or ever visited Latin America)
8 haven't spoken 9 Anna come 10 gone 11 haven't seen David
12 living here for 13 've left 14 haven't finished 15 just left 16 ever been
17 learning (or studying) 18 haven't had 19 never eaten 20 playing tennis for
21 forgotten 22 's changed 23 seen Margaret since

Test 4

Exercise 1

2 stops 3 Shall I 4 we're going out 5 it's going to be 6 I'll do 7 come back
8 She'll be working 9 we're going to 10 They'll probably

Exercise 2

2 will be here 3 will probably get 4 is going to lend 5 I'll see you
6 I won't (or can't) see 7 What are you going 8 will probably

Exercise 3

b) present continuous c) will d) going to e) going to f) will g) future perfect
h) future continuous
2 c 3 b 4 f 5 a 6 h 7 e 8 g

Exercise 4

2 Shall 3 conference ends (or finishes or is over) 4 won't 5 will you be
6 I'll 7 Shall 8 you doing

Exercise 5

2 Shall we have 3 I'm going to study 4 I'll be back 5 I'm seeing
6 I won't forget 7 I'm going to do 8 Shall I help you 9 We'll come
10 I'm going to ask 11 I'll have 12 I'm going to have

Test 5

Exercise 1

2 was posted 3 is being developed (or is to be developed) 4 was eaten
5 is still produced 6 will be decided 7 is being given 8 has been promoted
9 was written 10 are lost (or are being lost)

Exercise 2

2 Our house was broken into last week.
3 English is spoken all over the world.
4 The new motorway has finally opened. (or been opened).
5 This umbrella was left in reception.
6 All traffic will be banned from the city centre.
7 First the two liquids are mixed, then they are left for 24 hours.
8 The meeting is being postponed.

Exercise 3

2 am having my car repaired
3 had some business cards printed with the new logo
4 are having the carpet cleaned tomorrow
5 have just had my request for credit refused

Exercise 4

2 mean 3 be taken 4 will bring 5 took place 6 highlighted 7 be ignored
8 is expected 9 will fall 10 increase 11 will start 12 to be found 13 create
14 encourage 15 be looked at

Exercise 5

2 much less coffee is grown in Colombia 3 was delivered this morning
4 is being redeveloped 5 have been put up again
6 will be discussed in the meeting tomorrow 7 had some new software installed
8 was born 9 were you 10 Peter's car was 11 Was Alex told
12 Has a backup copy of this file been

Test 6

Exercise 1

2 must 3 need to 4 have tried 5 we'd better 6 might 7 should 8 must
9 can't have 10 have to 11 don't need to 12 can't

Exercise 2

2 mustn't 3 might have 4 have to 5 must 6 could 7 had to 8 must have
9 should 10 didn't have to

Exercise 3

2 f 3 b 4 d 5 g 6 a 7 e

Exercise 4

2 don't have to 3 can't be 4 must be 5 should be 6 might be 7 can't
8 might 9 have to 10 should

Exercise 5

2 must have 3 can't have 4 should have 5 might not have 6 should have
7 shouldn't have 8 could have

Test 7

Exercise 1

2 Will I see you tomorrow? 3 Did you have a nice time?
4 Do you know what I mean? 5 Are you coming out for a drink later?
6 Have you been waiting long? 7 Are you enjoying yourself?
8 Have you heard the latest?

Exercise 2

2 what this means 3 how much this costs 4 what time the bank opens
5 I'm in the right seat 6 where the Opera House is
7 this is the way to the Science Museum
8 who the speaker is at the next session (or who the speaker at the next session is)

Exercise 3

1 c 2 b 3 a 4 – 5 ✓ 6 ✓ 7 ✓

Exercise 4

2 she does/she doesn't 3 I have/I haven't 4 I am/I'm not 5 she is/she isn't
6 I can/I can't 7 I will/I won't 8 I did/I didn't 9 it is/it isn't

Exercise 5

2 won't they 3 aren't leaving 4 haven't they 5 can't you 6 didn't forget
7 You weren't 8 do you 9 shall we 10 didn't you

Exercise 6

2 Can I see the menu, please?
3 Excuse me, is anyone sitting here?
4 Which country do you come from?
5 Who were you talking to just now?
6 What exactly do you mean by that?
7 Could you be a little more specific?
8 What time is the next train to Brussels?
9 Can you tell me what time the next train to Brussels is?
10 Who does this briefcase belong to?
11 Could I make a phone call from here?
12 Do you think I could make a phone call from here?

Test 8

Exercise 1

2 promote   3 had left   4 stay   5 I'd   6 had   7 breaks down   8 could phone
9 doesn't   10 we'd been   11 would have become   12 goes
13 backed up/wouldn't risk   14 hadn't/we'd be   15 had   16 was

Exercise 2

2 will be   3 would have asked   4 will get   5 would get   6 would have missed
7 wouldn't see   8 will leave   9 would have sorted out   10 would you do

Exercise 3

1 unless   2 if   3 Unless   4 If   5 if   6 unless

Exercise 4

2 had made more copies/would have had
3 had brought your map/wouldn't have gone
4 had invested in new technology/would have survived
5 had waited/wouldn't have happened
6 had realised you were so busy/wouldn't have asked you
7 had collapsed/would have been
8 had brought out their new model on time/wouldn't have lost

Exercise 5

2 b   3 a   4 a   5 b   6 b   7 b

Exercise 6

2 had done   3 hadn't done   4 spoke (or could speak)   5 had ordered
6 was (or were)   7 had given   8 had

Test 9

Exercise 1

2 coming   3 to come   4 giving   5 making   6 Remind   7 to enter   8 to be
9 to be   10 trying   11 resigning   12 to believe   13 being   14 interrupting
15 going   16 to meet   17 to deliver   18 winning   19 to see   20 to pack
21 arriving   22 to lift   23 getting away   24 to get away   25 to listen   26 visiting
27 to order   28 to meet

Exercise 2

2 coming   3 to rise   4 to get through/getting   5 waiting   6 to give   7 causing
8 to compromise   9 unpacking

Test 10

Exercise 1

2 What did you do yesterday (or 'the day before')
3 Do you often go to Germany for meetings
4 How many interview have you done today
5 Are you going to change jobs
6 Who did you talk to at the conference
7 Will you be here (or there) tomorrow
8 Where are your new offices
9 Have you seen Bill recently
10 Will you be seeing Bill at the conference

Exercise 2

2 invited Jean to come to   3 advised Dave not to sign   4 suggested getting
5 apologised for arriving   6 offered (to give)   7 congratulated/on winning
8 refused to accept

Test 11

Exercise 1

2 g   3 l   4 a   5 d   6 j   7 h   8 e   9 i   10 k   11 b   12 f

Exercise 2

2 takes up   3 to put back the meeting to/to put the meeting back to
4 to deal with   5 pick me up   6 to go on writing   7 to sort it out   8 to go over
9 you come across it   10 run out of time

Exercise 3

2 over   3 through   4 out   5 down   6 by   7 up   8 off   9 into/back   10 away

Exercise 4

2 get on with   3 cut down on   4 run out of   5 get round to   6 catch up with
7 look forward to   8 face up to   9 move on to   10 get back to

Exercise 5

2 g   3 f   4 i   5 d   6 b   7 a   8 k   9 l   10 j   11 h   12 e

Test 12

Exercise 1

2 h   3 b   4 f   5 g   6 c   7 a   8 e   9 f   10 c   11 b   12 a   13 e (or a)   14 d

Exercise 2

2 having   3 make   4 do   5 make/have/do   6 do/make   7 made/doing/make
8 makes/do/having/making   9 Have/make   10 made/do
11 doing/make/having   12 have/do/making

Test 13

Exercise 1

2 whose   3 that   4 whose   5 who   6 whose   7 which   8 whose   9 that
10 who I used to work with

Exercise 2

3 (who)   4 which   5 (that)   6 (that)   7 which   8 (that)

Exercise 3

2 who came yesterday gave me
3 that the Japanese visitors who came yesterday
4 whose laptop I borrowed wants it
5 who works in my department
6 that we went to yesterday was
7 a woman whose sister works for
8 who is waiting in reception wants to

Test 14

Exercise 1

2 is a doctor   3 yours (or your umbrella)   4 that wine   5 every time
6 some advice   7 neither one   8 some information   9 none of us   10 by taxi
11 the traffic was   12 so many good ideas   13 None at all   14 Jane's colleague
15 either   16 too little information   17 each one   18 Ministry's
19 enough chairs   20 no spare parts   21 The news is   22 the end of the report
23 both   24 everyone   25 hers   26 some information   27 can't hear anything
28 both of them   29 there wasn't a single question   30 isn't anyone   31 its
32 the boss's son

Exercise 2

Countable nouns: a desk, a bag, a job, a trip, a problem, a chance, a litre,
a machine, a dollar, an email, a fact, a suggestion, an hour
Uncountable nouns: some furniture, some luggage, some work, some travel, some
trouble, some luck, some wine, some equipment, some money, some
correspondence, some information, some advice, some time

Exercise 3

2 some advice   3 by train   4 Something is worrying   5 on foot

6 one of my boss's friends   7 a tax adviser

8 Nobody (or No one) knows this business   9 got nothing to

10 Everybody (or Everyone) here drinks   11 The unemployed   12 redesigning

13 is nothing we can   14 How much did   15 isn't much   16 an accountant

17 Everybody (or Everyone) was late   18 couldn't do anything

19 Not a single person   20 There's no   21 wasn't in   22 the customer's copy

23 There isn't anything

Test 15

Exercise 1

2 by the end   3 very hard   4 lovely blue   5 so friendly (or very friendly)

6 extremely good (or absolutely excellent)   7 very well   8 feel tired

9 We never give   10 interested in   11 so much   12 such a risky project

13 not experienced enough   14 larger than   15 as large as   16 the best price

17 for three months   18 so tense   19 When I get back   20 before   21 than I do

22 too long   23 much less useful (or not as useful as)   24 as swimming

25 until six

Exercise 2

2 ago   3 later   4 for   5 since   6 at   7 in   8 on   9 afterwards   10 During

11 After   12 for   13 later   14 at

Exercise 3

2 've been working on this project since January.

3 is more profitable than retail banking.

4 works very carefully.   5 the worst service I've ever seen.   6 stayed in Paris until

7 you interested in opera?   8 finished positively.   9 have worked hard.

10 writes well.   11 isn't well (or is unwell)   12 speak more slowly, please.

13 is not as big as the Chinese market.   14 just as many products as Richard.

15 is the least experienced member of the team.   16 see you later.

17 've been doing this job since 1998.   18 away on holiday until   19 on time.

20 in time to save the negotiations.   21 'll get there by two.

22 in the end we gave up (or gave up in the end)

23 for two hours

Test 16

Exercise 1

2 in   3 at/in   4 over   5 in/in   6 on   7 at   8 to   9 in   10 on   11 at   12 over

13 under   14 at   15 in/at   16 in   17 at   18 to/in   19 on   20 on

Exercise 2

2 to   3 against   4 on/for   5 of   6 into   7 from   8 for   9 with   10 in

11 about   12 on   13 of   14 with/about   15 to   16 on

Exercise 3

2 on   3 with   4 in   5 of   6 in   7 for   8 to   9 at   10 for   11 about

12 with/for

Exercise 4

2 reason for   3 advantage of   4 trouble with   5 matter with   6 reply to

7 lack of   8 solution to   9 substitute for   10 investment in   11 advice on

12 pessimism about

Exercise 5

2 inside   3 next to   4 to   5 at   6 near   7 across   8 down   9 on   10 at

11 on   12 opposite   13 at   14 off

Index

A

a u34

    a or **an**? p142C

    determiner u32

    indefinite article u34

    with singular countable nouns p127D, 142B

abbreviations p183F

about

    be about to (referring to future) p39F

    preposition p191C, D

above p187C

absolutely

    before non-gradable adjectives p151C

active u9, u10

    person or organisation who does action p42

actually p178C

adjectives u36, u37, u47

    + preposition u47

    + **to** + infinitive p194A

    adjectives and adverbs p150A, p203D; AmE and BrE

    differences Appendix 5 p246

    adjectives and adverbs with same form p150B

    comparatives u37

    ending in **-ed** p110B, p151E

    ending in **-ing** p110B, p151E

    gradable and non-gradable p151C

    irregular adjectives p154B

    order of adjectives p151D

    possessive adjectives p138A

    superlatives u37

adverb phrases

    with present simple p10C

adverbs u36, u39, u40

    + verb p150A

    adverb endings (**-ally**, **-ily**, **-y**) p150B, Appendix 3 p242

    adverbs and adjectives p150A, p203D

    adverbs of degree u39

    comparatives u38

    frequency adverbs p10C, p150A

    comparing adverbs p159D

    order of adverbs p150A

    other adverbs p150A

    time adverbs u40

after

    after and **past** (AmE/BrE difference) Appendix 5 246

    after that (showing a sequence) p43C, p167F

    in time expressions p167F

    with past simple or past perfect p22B

    with present simple or present perfect p38A

afterwards p167F

ago p166C

agree

    + **about** p191C

    + **(that)** p107C

    + **with** p191C

    in passive as reporting verb p95C

all p134B, C

    be allowed to/not allowed to

    permission/prohibition p54B, C

already

    with past perfect p22C

    with past simple in AmE Appendix 5 p246

    with present perfect p26C

also p170B

although p170C

    and **whereas** p171F

always

    with present continuous p14C

    with present perfect p27C

    with present simple p10C

and

    as linking word p170A, B

    in comparisons p158B, 159D

    words and phrases meaning **and** p178A

any

    any or **some**? p127D, p130B

    in affirmative sentences p127D

    in negatives and questions p127D, p130B

    in offers and requests p127D

    not … any (in negative sentences) p135D

anybody/anyone p130A, B

anything p130A, B

anytime p130A, B

anywhere p130A, B

    or **anyplace** (AmE) Appendix 5 p247

apart from p179G

apostrophe s (**'s**) p138B, p139C

articles (**a**, **the**, etc) u34, u35

    in relative clauses p122A

    no article when talking generally p143E, p147E

    no article with names of countries, companies etc p143E, p146A

    special uses of no article p147D

as

    as … as (in comparisons) p155D, p158A

    linking word p174A, p175E

    with past continuous p19F

as if p175E

as long as

    with conditionals p78C

as soon as

    with present perfect p38A

    with present simple p38A

as well p170B

    as well as p170B

at

    as preposition p191C, D

    in noun phrases p199G

    in time expressions p18C, p166A

    position/location p186A, p187B

at last p183D

auxiliary verbs/phrases

    be with present continuous p11D

    had with past perfect p22A

    had been with past perfect continuous p23D

    have with present perfect p26A

    in comparisons p155E